Governing Water

Global Environmental Accord: Strategies for Sustainability and
Institutional Innovation
Nazli Choucri, series editor

A complete list of books published in the Global Environmental
Accord series appears at the back of this book.

Governing Water

Contentious Transnational Politics and Global Institution Building

Ken Conca

The MIT Press
Cambridge, Massachusetts
London, England

MIT Press books may be purchased at special quantity discounts for business or sales promotional use. For information, please email special_sales@mitpress.mit .edu or write to Special Sales Department, The MIT Press, 55 Hayward Street, Cambridge, MA 02142.

This book was set in Sabon on 3B2 by Asco Typesetters, Hong Kong.
Printed and bound in the United States of America.

Library of Congress Cataloging-in-Publication Data

Conca, Ken.
Governing water : contentious transnational politics and global institution building / Ken Conca.
   p.   cm.
Includes bibliographical references and index.
ISBN 0-262-03339-9 (alk. paper) — ISBN 0-262-53273-5 (pbk. : alk. paper)
1. Water-supply—Management—International cooperation. 2. Water-supply—Political aspects. 3. International rivers. 4. Environmental policy—International cooperation. I. Title.
TD345C6563   2005
333.91—dc22   2005041659

Printed on recycled paper.

10 9 8 7 6 5 4 3 2 1

In memory of John Steinhart—an educator for change

Contents

Series Foreword

A new recognition of profound interconnections between social and natural systems is challenging conventional constructs and the policy predispositions informed by them. Our current intellectual challenge is to develop the analytical and theoretical underpinnings of an understanding of the relationship between the social and the natural systems. Our policy challenge is to identify and implement effective decision-making approaches to managing the global environment.

The series Global Environmental Accord: Strategies for Sustainability and Institutional Innovation adopts an integrated perspective on national, international, cross-border, and cross-jurisdictional problems, priorities, and purposes. It examines the sources and the consequences of social transactions as these relate to environmental conditions and concerns. Our goal is to make a contribution to both intellectual and policy endeavors.

Nazli Choucri

Preface

During the summer of 1999, as I found myself struggling with the ideas that would shape this book, a newspaper article on the last solar eclipse of the millennium caught my attention. An eclipse provides a useful metaphor for how we think about international relations and global ecology early in the twenty-first century. Like those fearful of looking directly at the sun, we avert our gaze from the heart of the problem of global environmental governance. Instead of seeing the problem in truly global terms, we cobble together the intellectual equivalent of a child's cardboard-and-pinhole apparatus. This allows us to see the reflected shape of the problem, projected onto the comfortable viewing surface of sovereign diplomacy. We pretend that the limited instruments at hand, including interstate diplomacy, treaty instruments, and intergovernmental organizations, are up to the task. We allow pollution and environmental degradation to appear on the menu of international problems only when they cross our socially constructed borders or impinge on a euphemistic "commons" such as our climate, which we envision as somehow lying outside those borders.

We avert our gaze because staring directly at the problem would do serious harm to the lenses through which we see the international system on a daily basis. These intellectual lenses encourage us to see a world characterized by the legitimacy of states, the ultimate rationality of governments, and the thin institutionalization of a world system based on a gradually maturing anarchy. To gaze directly at the real world—with states that are often authoritarian in instinct, incompetent in practice, and lacking in collective rationality; and with a world-scale politics that is deeply institutionalized through the structures of capitalism and the modern project—would be to damage those lenses beyond repair. So, instead, we gaze at an image of interstate environmental diplomacy that we see reflected through the pinhole. Careful scholarship on a few important but limited successes somehow ended up being hammered into a stylized narrative that, for much of the 1990s, created the illusion of progress, while the heart of the problem remained largely unaddressed and out of focus. Useful dissections of the processes of bargaining that produce particular kinds of compliance monitoring systems or technical advisory groups have provided important insights at the microlevel of institutional design. However, we have failed to ask the larger question, and the international environmental community seems to return again and again to the same flawed and ineffective institutional forms.

As I was thinking through the meaning of this astronomical metaphor, I had cause to reread some material that I wrote as a graduate student at Berkeley in the late 1980s. The following passage appeared in a chapter that I contributed to *The State and Social Power in Global Environmental Politics*:

The patterns of explicit environmental politics reflect a marked tendency toward *re-structuring* (in the sense of reproducing) rather than *restructuring* (in the sense of fundamentally altering) the modern, sovereign, capitalist features of the current world order. International regimes legitimize new regulatory capacities and tasks for states, extending state sovereignty in important new directions. Collective responses consistent with the premises of freely flowing goods and capital are, to say the least, advantaged. And the technocratic, modernist elements within the environmental movement are empowered by their preferential access to the bargaining table. (The *State and Social Power in Global Environmental Politics*, New York: Columbia University Press, 1993, pp. 310–311)

Reconsidering this passage a decade later, it occurred to me that I was now trying to take such reasoning to the next step: documenting newly emerging institutional forms and contrasting them with the prevailing ones that have dominated our attention.

Using water—dynamic, flowing, difficult to contain—to illustrate these ideas reminds me of a book that my children and I have often enjoyed reading together, *The Jade Stone* by Carolyn Yacowitz. The book recounts what is said to be a "traditional Chinese folktale" and begins this way:

Long ago in China there lived a stone carver named Chan Lo. Chan Lo spent his days carving birds and deer and water buffalo from the colored stones he found near the river. "How do you know what to carve?" his young apprentice asked. "I always listen to the stone," replied Chan Lo. "The stone tells me what it wants to be." (*The Jade Stone*, Holiday House, 1992, p. 3)

I would never claim to be a wise and patient artisan of the sort found so often in children's tales. But I have tried, nonetheless, to listen to the stones I found near the world's rivers.

Acknowledgments

I am grateful to the many people who commented on various parts of the manuscript or discussed with me the ideas behind it, including Rebecca Abers, Sulan Chen, Ken Cousins, Geoffrey Dabelko, Elizabeth De-Sombre, Dan Deudney, Navroz Dubash, Sara Glasgow, Peter Gleick, Virginia Haufler, Wanda Haxton, Margaret Keck, Tim Kessler, Richard Matthew, Ron Mitchell, Jacob Park, Jesse Ribot, Frances Seymour, Paul Steinberg, Larry Swatuk, Johannes Stripple, Karen Travis, Anthony Turton, Jan Frederick Valentin, Ivani Vassoler, Paul Wapner, Aaron Wolf, Fengshi Wu, and Oran Young.

I am thankful for the intellectual collaboration of Fengshi Wu and Joanne Neukirchen on a project that provided the bulk of the data and analysis presented in chapter 4. Over the course of preparing the manuscript I benefited from the help of several able research assistants, including Stephen Boyenger, Stephen Grimes, Nick Gurdian, Tina Liu, Serap Rada, Cassie Staley, Kady Waterhouse, and Eleanor Wilson. Support from the Harrison Program on the Future Global Agenda and the Graduate Research Board of the University of Maryland proved invaluable to the writing of this book. Thanks to Clay Morgan and Katherine Almeida of The MIT Press for guiding the manuscript through the process of review and production.

Finally, I am grateful to the many "water people" who were willing to discuss water issues with me along the way, including individuals connected with the Global Water Partnership, the International Rivers Network, the World Commission on Dams, the World Bank and the many water experts, activists, and practitioners with whom I spoke at one time or another in Brazil and South Africa. I did not conduct these conversations as questionnaire-guided or otherwise formally structured interviews, and although I allude to those conversations occasionally, I have not quoted by name or otherwise cited any of the individuals involved. I think of the various documents, statistics, and scholarly works in the pages that follow as the supportive skeleton and tissue of the argument presented here, and of these conversations as its soul.

Several of the ideas presented here have appeared in preliminary form in other publications. The call for a broader paradigmatic understanding of global environmental governance draws upon ideas I presented as part of an Earth Summit retrospective panel at the 2002 annual meeting of the International Studies Association, later published as "Beyond the Earth Summit Framework" in *Politics and the Life Sciences* (vol. 21 no. 2 September 2002: 53–55). Chapter 4 builds upon data, analysis, and interpretation presented in Ken Conca, Fengshi Wu, and Joanne Neukirchen, "Is There a Global Rivers Regime? Trends in the Principled Content of International River Agreements" (Harrison Program Research Report, College Park: University of Maryland, 2003). An earlier version of chapter 5 appeared as "Growth and Fragmentation in Expert Networks: The Elusive Quest for Integrated Water Resources Management," in Peter Dauvergne, editor, *International Handbook of Environmental Politics* (Cheltenham, UK: Edward Elgar, 2005). I first developed my thinking about the hybridization of authority in an essay entitled "Old States in New Bottles? The Hybridization of Authority in Global Environmental Governance," which became a chapter in John Barry and Robyn Eckersley, eds., *The State and the Global Ecological Crisis* (Cambridge, Mass.: MIT Press, 2005). Some of my ideas about the World Commission on Dams appeared previously in "The World Commission on Dams and Trends in Global Environmental Governance" in *Politics and the Life Sciences* (vol. 21 no. 1 March 2002: 67–70). No doubt a careful reader comparing those texts with this one will find that my thinking has evolved on some points, as it continues to do.

Governing Water

1

Managing the Global Environment or Protecting the Planet's Places? Institutional Forms of Global Environmental Governance

To expose the fundamental norms of a society, often so fundamental as to re-main hidden and inarticulated, it was useful to investigate the fate of those who openly violated the norms.
—From the introduction to *The Oxford History of the Prison*

In March 2000, water experts from around the world gathered in The Hague for the Second World Water Forum. The meeting was the brainchild of the World Water Council (WWC), an elite international body established by the World Bank, the UN Development Programme (UNDP), and several international groups representing industry, profes-sional associations, and water policy experts.[1] Held within walking dis-tance of the International Court of Justice, the forum was organized around two reports meant to provide an authoritative frame for address-ing global water problems and solutions. The first report, the *World Water Vision*, framed the global water challenge as a case of inadequate supply in the face of greatly increasing demand.[2] Without dramatic tech-nological innovations, institutional change, and substantial new invest-ment, the world in 2025 was projected to face an even more sizable "water gap" than that of today, when an estimated 1.3 billion people lack access to safe drinking water and 2.6 billion lack access to adequate sanitation.

The second report, *World Water Security: A Framework for Action*, presented a blueprint for achieving that vision. The *Framework* called for dramatically expanded investment in water-supply infrastructure, primarily by mobilizing the private sector through incentives such as privatization and full-cost pricing of water. The *Framework* also called for more effective water governance based on a paradigm of integrated water resources management (IWRM).[3]

Taken together, the *World Water Vision* and the *Framework for Action* offered a model for a global water regime. They put forward a set of norms—prescriptive rules and standards of appropriate behavior meant to govern water-related actions on a global scale.[4] Water management should be based on a holistic approach that links socioeconomic development with environmental protection; water should be valued as a scarce economic resource; an adequate water supply should be seen as a basic human need; transparency and public participation should be the hallmarks of water sector decision making; shared river basins should be governed cooperatively through international agreements. The hope was that as these norms became institutionalized, sovereign governments would improve their domestic practices and strengthen their international partnerships, resulting ultimately in better governance of water. This strategy of articulation, dissemination, and legitimization of norms and incremental institutionalization was not much different from efforts (with highly variable levels of success) to establish something resembling global governance of environmental problems ranging from climate to toxics to protection of the ozone layer.

However, a funny thing happened on the way to the World Water Forum. During the opening plenary session, as World Water Council President Mahmoud Abu-Zeid prepared to address the conferees, hecklers began jeering from the audience. A naked man and woman leaped onto the stage, shouting "Stop the Itoiz Dam." A protestor hung from the balcony with a large banner; another began scaling the wall of the conference hall. Chaos reigned for several minutes, with Abu-Zeid effectively blocked from speaking as security forces struggled to remove the protesters. The crown prince of the Netherlands, honorary chairman of the forum, took the stage and politely rebuked those causing the disruption, accusing them of lacking civility. The specific focus of the protest was a controversial dam project in the Basque region of Spain. More generally, the demonstrators were challenging what they saw as the forum's underlying bias toward capital-intensive, supply-side measures and technocratic, nonparticipatory decision making.

Calm was eventually restored, and the forum proceeded more or less as planned over the next several days. Panels were held on water economics, pollution control, national water law reform, dam projects, and a host of other issues. Representatives of so-called major groups, including nongovernmental organizations (NGOs), women, youth, scientists, and industry, met to ratify mostly prewritten comments on the *World Water Vision* and the *Framework for Action*. A simultaneous ministerial conference endorsed both documents. Forum participants left The Hague with baseball caps bearing the forum's logo and website address. The official report on the forum and ministerial conference made no mention of the disruptive incident or other expressions of dissent throughout the meeting.

One motive for writing this book is to examine the stark disconnect between the forum's blueprint for forging a global water regime and the contentious politics surrounding water all around the world. As the protestors showed, and as much of the discussion at the forum underscored, the model presented in the forum's glossy documents has little hope of forging consensus or even containing the controversies that swirl around water issues. The *Vision* asserted that governments, as sovereign and legitimate decision-making bodies, are the key actors, thereby ignoring the central reality that authority is fundamentally contested in the domain of water. Whose water is it? Who should have the legitimate power to decide? What does it mean to describe governments as sovereign and legitimate while also calling for virtually all of the new investment in global water supply to come from the private sector?[5] What is the relationship between authority in a watershed, authority in a boardroom, and authority in a nation-state? Generalizations about the need to involve stakeholders barely hint at the contested character of authority relations surrounding water. Yet without confronting these contestations, what hope is there for a cooperative and broadly legitimate approach to governance of water?

Similarly, both the *Vision* and the *Framework* glossed over the central reality of radically different constructions of knowledge—of the facts, causal mechanisms, and larger truths about the world's water problems, their sources, and their solutions. As pointed out by the Indian publication *Hindu*,

If the organizers of the meet, which has brought together over 3,500 people from 158 countries, had hoped for orderly discussions on a range of issues revolving around water use and management, they had clearly underestimated the strength of sentiments on this issue in many parts of the world.... While the doomsdayers, who included a group that has raised an alarm about the availability of water and the water gap, want to stress issues like water management, the nongovernmental groups are more concerned about issues such as privatization of water, and the systems of water management, like large dams, which have adverse impacts on people and the environment. The International Rivers Network states in its critique that the real crisis is one of over-consumption, waste, pollution, watershed degradation, rampant dam-building, poorly-conceived and operated infrastructure projects, corruption and inequality.[6]

That this observation appeared in *Hindu* is fitting, because nothing illustrated the contrasting constructions of the problem more sharply than the way in which India's water issues were injected into the global discussion. The Indian government, worried about international criticism of its dam-building enterprises, sent a large official delegation to launch a counteroffensive, framing the problem as one of building water infrastructure in order to combat poverty. Others from India carried a dramatically different message: anti-dam activists, environmentalists, and grassroots development groups also came to The Hague in force, decrying the human and ecological toll of the government's understanding of the problem. Powerful multinational industrial groups formed a third pole in this complex struggle to define the problem; they were supportive of the Indian government's capital-intensive, supply-oriented vision, but wary of its statist instincts in the water sector. Rather than acknowledge these radically different understandings and views, the *Framework for Action* offered only a depoliticized notion of integrated water resources management, which it described as holistic, comprehensive, and knowledge-based—and thus, by implication, unobjectionable.

We seem, therefore, to be at an impasse. Attempts to create a broadly cooperative international approach to managing water—to govern water globally, so to speak—seem doomed to founder on more fundamentally contested questions. Should it be the privatized, supply-oriented vision of the forum? Or the grassroots, watershed-scale vision of the forum's most ardent critics? Or an updated version of the state-led model of infrastructure expansion and water as a public good that so many governments have historically favored?

This impasse is not unlike the fate of the effort to forge a regime for world forests. The forest talks collapsed at the 1992 Rio de Janeiro Earth Summit, and an array of ineffective commissions and draft agreements in the ensuing decade did nothing to revive them. As with many other festering socioenvironmental problems, it has not been possible to hold either water or forest issues within the standard institutional vessel of sovereign, authoritative governments, fixed and meaningful borders, and unambiguous knowledge-based truths.

However, the failure to build a global water regime is only half of the story. The world's water is indeed subject to deeply and increasingly transnational forms of governance. We have been witnessing the development, proliferation, and growing embeddedness of rules, roles, and practices that shape water-related policy decisions and political struggles all over the world. The World Water Council is but one reflection of this process of institution building; so too are the many commissions, international lobby groups, and intergovernmental organizations that came together to create the council. Other manifestations include entities as diverse as the Global Water Partnership (GWP), a coordinating group for donors providing water sector development assistance; the World Commission on Dams, a mixed-membership international panel representing various stakeholder interests and seeking common ground on the controversies surrounding large dams; and International Rivers Network (IRN), a transnational nongovernmental activist network that coordinates and supports the struggles of local groups affected by large dams and other projects that tamper with the natural flow of the world's rivers. The net effect of this panoply of increasingly embedded roles and rules is not a neat, uncontested set of water norms of the sort proffered by the *World Water Vision*, but the result, nevertheless, is a form of global governance. Water-related struggles are being bounded, channeled, regularized, and normalized, with tangible consequences for the behavior of national governments and other actors. If global governance consists of governing acts that have a broadly international reach, and if those acts include such things as the framing of policy, the setting of standards, and the mobilization and allocation of resources, then water is indeed subject to governance that is increasingly, though certainly not exclusively, global.[7]

This book is about struggles to establish rules of global environmental governance under the highly conflictual circumstances that surround water. The goal is not to deepen our understanding of the handful of global-scale environmental problems that have attracted most of the attention and most of the international institution-building energy: climate change, damage to the ozone layer, pollution of the world's oceans, or international trafficking in hazardous waste or endangered species. Rather, my concern is to understand the politics of global institution building around local ecological systems that are found all around the planet—forests, soils, grasslands, wetlands, tundras, deserts, rivers, lakes, and coastlines. These systems share a triple meaning: they are critical ecosystems with both local and global significance; they are important sources of community livelihoods and cultural meaning for millions of people; and, in an increasingly global world economy, they are marketable international commodities, either as natural resource goods or eco-tourist services. They also share a common problem. According to a mounting body of evidence, the global response to the cumulative ecological toll on these local systems has been woefully inadequate. I will argue that the threats to these systems are indeed "global" problems demanding "global" governance—even if their global character lies hidden behind the façade of sovereignty or our ignorance of the global consequences of millions of local insults.

A major reason for the inadequacy of the global response is that it has, for the most part, insisted on reproducing a particular institutional form: the negotiated international agreements among sovereign states that are commonly known as international regimes. Such agreements are meant to draw sovereign governments into cooperative action by creating a consensual understanding of a particular environmental problem and by fostering new norms of behavior that will correct the problem. Regimes typically involve stages of cooperative multilateral bargaining, framework agreements that are given greater depth of meaning and specificity over time, and international secretariats to encourage implementation and compliance. Regimes have been developed, with varying degrees of success, around a growing number of transboundary pollution problems such as acid rain or cross-border river pollution; they have also been created in response to problems of the global commons, such as depletion of the ozone layer, ocean pollution, or global climate change.

However, the regime approach has made little headway on more local environmental problems that take a cumulative toll on the health of the planet and its people. Grounded as they are in international law, modern science, and bureaucratic administration, regime-building efforts tend to ignore, paper over, or further polarize the deeply rooted conflicts about authority, territory, and knowledge that characterize this class of environmental problems. The result, too often, is an agreement fated to die on the negotiating table, prove ineffective, or make the problem worse. Sometimes the failure is spectacular, as in the aborted attempt to negotiate a regime for world forests at the 1992 Earth Summit. In other cases, as with the world's freshwater resources, it is the less noted but more fundamental failure to get a serious regime-building effort launched in the first place.

Against this pessimistic view I will balance a growing conviction based on several years spent studying the politics of local but globally cumulative environmental problems. Beyond the familiar blueprint of the international environmental regime lies a plethora of institutional forms that do in fact constitute the global governance of these problems. Unlike most conventional international environmental regimes, these emerging institutions have found a way to incorporate more pluralistic understandings of authority, more flexible conceptions of territorial sovereignty, and more heterogeneous ways of knowing about problems and solutions. Certainly we can imagine such institutional forms, however difficult the political struggle to bring them into being might be. To help with the process of imagining, chapter 2 presents a framework for imagining institutional forms that lie beyond conventional regimes, by treating key institutional orientations related to authority, territoriality, and knowledge as variables rather than constants. The argument is more ambitious than merely showing the imaginability of alternative institutional forms that lie beyond regimes. I will suggest that we can already see new institutional forms emerging and shaping water-related behavior on a broad and expanding scale. Although they are largely informal, the emerging sets of rules and norms described in this book are becoming increasingly embedded in the political fabric of water struggles all around the planet. Seeing them, however, requires us to step outside the box of the regime paradigm, with its specific formulations about governmental authority, sovereign territory, and universal scientific knowledge.

Stepping outside that box requires two shifts of focus. The first is to look away from those environmental problems that fit the regime box most neatly. Problems relatively amenable to the regime approach, I will argue, include global commons issues such as climate, the oceans, and the ozone layer, as well as transboundary flow problems such as hazardous waste shipments or regional airsheds. Rather, the focus here is on the more hidden, creeping, incremental, and cumulative dimensions of the assault on the global environment. This distinction among types of environmental challenges will be described in terms of conflicting paradigms, one of governing pollution beyond borders, the other of protecting the planet's places. Conventional regimes may or may not respond effectively to the problem of pollution beyond borders, but they have been largely powerless in protecting the planet's places.

To illustrate both the limits of the regime approach and the emergence of other institutional forms of environmental governance, I will focus centrally on water, rivers, and watersheds. Water is emblematic of the triple meaning of critical ecosystem, local livelihood and culture, and market commodity. It is also a prototypical example of the resulting social controversies and political contentiousness that surround this category of issues. Governance of water involves enduring, chronic, and sometimes raging controversies about local practices of resource management, conservation, and environmental protection in an increasingly transnational context. As such, water is illustrative of a whole array of socioecological controversies that we can think of under the rubric of contentious transnational environmental politics (figure 1.1).

The second necessary shift is to move the focus away from the substantive content of environmental cooperation and toward the procedural aspects of socioenvironmental conflict. The challenge in protecting the planet's places is not simply to find institutionalized rules about what constitutes proper treatment of the environment, but also to find rules that contain or channel deeply divisive, contentious debates when a broad consensus on substance may be unattainable. Therefore my analy-

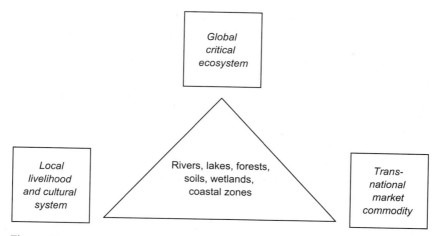

Figure 1.1
Contentious transnational environmental politics.

sis does not center on a conventionally framed environmental issue such
acid rain or ocean pollution. In these cases, a relatively stable construction of the problem hints that some degree of closure has been achieved
(through bargaining, consensus, or imposition of rules) on the deeper
questions of authority, territoriality, and knowledge that are my central
concern. Again, water provides a powerful example. As discussed in subsequent chapters, water has not been an area of extensive or effective
governance through the conventional institutional form of one or more
international regimes. When it comes to water, persuasive formulations
or plausible fictions about competent state authority; fixed and bordered
territory; and unambiguous, universal knowledge cannot be sustained.
The question is whether other institutional forms, responsive to the increasingly transnational challenges of environmental governance, can
emerge where regimes have failed to take root.

Regimes as the Grand Strategy of Global Environmental Governance

The past few decades have seen an unprecedented flurry of international
activity on global environmental problems. Treaties have been negotiated
and ratified on a host of environmental ills. Principles of sustainability

have been articulated and debated. The World Bank and other multi-lateral organizations have come under intense pressure to take environmental considerations seriously. Transnational environmental advocacy networks, linking countless citizens' organizations and protest groups, have emerged as a force with which governments and corporations must reckon. These diverse activities have been highly variable in effectiveness, have faced strong opposition and, often, have been poorly coordinated. Nevertheless, they have woven at least the beginnings of a fabric of global environmental governance.

Much of this activity has been based on a straightforward premise: Global environmental problems result from the poor fit between national borders and a planetary ecology that ignores those borders. Ecosystems straddle borders, and natural cycles are constantly producing transboundary flows of water, energy, nutrients, and pollutants. As a result, the global environment is often described as Garrett Hardin's tragedy of the commons writ large, in the sense that even the best efforts by individual countries to protect the environment can be overwhelmed by the failings of others, upstream or upwind, to do so. In the words of the Brundtland Commission, "The Earth is one but the world is not."[8] By this logic, if environmental protection is to be effective, it must be international, indeed global, in its conception, scope, and implementation.[9]

Given all the well-known barriers to international cooperation, how is this daunting challenge of international collective action to be accomplished? The standard prescription is for governments to sit down at the bargaining table and negotiate multilateral agreements on specific problems such as global warming, damage to the stratospheric ozone layer, ocean dumping, trafficking in hazardous waste, or destruction of the world's forests. Typically, the goal of these negotiations is to create a formal agreement to be signed and then ratified by individual states, such as the Framework Convention on Climate Change, the Montreal Protocol on Substances that Deplete the Ozone Layer, the International Tropical Timber Agreement, or the Convention on Biological Diversity. Some of the "rules" that these agreements create take the form of general principles: that the polluter should pay, that uncertainty demands caution, or that sovereign rights entail environmental responsibilities. Other rules are much more specific: defining what may or may not be shipped, burned, extracted, dumped, harvested, or manufactured; identifying what governments must monitor, enforce, fund, or report; or establishing how specific grievances or disputes are to be addressed.[10]

Skeptics note that such international rules are rarely enforceable in a strictly legal sense. The standard response to this concern is that what matters is not the legal instrument per se but rather the institutionalization around that legal instrument of a bundle of common understandings, shared expectations, and cooperative norms. These, it is hoped, will shape behavior through subtler channels than formal, legalistic enforcement procedures. In other words, the strategy is to create not just an international treaty but rather an international regime, a set of agreed-upon "rules of the game" that will yield convergent expectations, normative prescriptions, information flows, and institutionalized relationships that move governments toward compliance with the agreement's major aims.[11] Regimes are thus instruments of governance without government; they promote rule-conforming behavior in an international system marked by the absence of centralized governmental authority.

Scholars have identified and documented several ways that regimes may affect behavior.[12] Governments may recalculate national interests in the light of new knowledge that is created in the process of developing the regime's rules. Behavior may change once governments have different expectations about what others will do or when actions become more transparent through monitoring and reporting requirements. Managerial and administrative capacity may be enhanced through international exchange. Bureaucracies and interest groups that favor the regime's aims may be strengthened in their domestic political struggles once authoritative international principles have been articulated. Advocates inside and outside the state can pressure governments to honor the rhetorical commitments they have made through an international agreement. Governments or other actors may be socialized by transnationally diffused norms. As compliance with rules becomes the norm, reputations may be tarnished by noncompliance.

A wide array of liberal internationalists in government, academia, international organizations, environmental groups, and the media have embraced this particular logic of global environmental governance. Spurred on by these advocates, the regime-building approach has become the centerpiece of responses to problems as diverse as trafficking in endangered species, desertification, the loss of biodiversity, and degradation of the fragile Antarctic environment. The dominance of the regime approach becomes apparent when new environmental problems are identified. Advocates now move quickly and seamlessly from sounding the warning to launching the effort to build a new interstate regulatory regime, as seen in areas ranging from persistent organic pollutants (POPs) to invasions of alien plant and animal species. Even unprecedentedly complex, multifaceted global problems such as climate change and loss of biodiversity are assumed to be suitable for the creation of international regimes. Three decades after the seminal 1972 UN Conference on the Human Environment, it is no exaggeration to say that regime building has become the grand strategy of global environmental protection.

Is the regime approach working? Undoubtedly, several important international agreements have been concluded, such as the Montreal Protocol on Substances that Deplete the Ozone Layer, the Convention on International Trade in Endangered Species (CITES), and various regional agreements to protect enclosed seas, combat acid rain, or preserve the Antarctic environment. Although few environmental advocates would describe any of these agreements as perfect, even fewer would care to imagine the scope of the problem in their absence. Nevertheless, the failings of the regime approach are at least as noteworthy as the handful of alleged successes. In many cases it has proven impossible to push governments to make the necessary commitment or even to start the bargaining process. There are no significant regime-building initiatives to speak of on such pressing problems as the destabilization of critical global nutrient cycles, the global decline of plant pollinators, the protection of freshwater ecosystems, or the manufacture of hazardous materials.

Also, proponents and skeptics alike acknowledge that many existing environmental accords have had little or no demonstrable impact on environmental quality.[13] Although formal international agreements are central to most regime-building strategies, the mere act of reaching such an agreement does not guarantee the dynamic process of institutionalized cooperation, convergent behavior, and shared expectations envisioned by regime builders. The Ramsar accord on "wetlands of international importance," for example, has had little measurable impact in slowing the global assault on wetlands; nor can it be said to be the catalyst for a broader process of rule making, convergence of norms, and behavioral change. Desertification provides another example of regime failure. Despite more than two decades of effort to galvanize international action on the spread of deserts and related problems of land conversion, governments have made only a weak, vague set of commitments that can scarcely be called a regime. The 1994 United Nations Convention to Combat Desertification called for more attention to the problem, unspecified national action plans, more international aid, and better aid coordination—all themes that were on the table at the UN Conference on Desertification almost two decades earlier.[14] The biodiversity convention signed with such fanfare at the 1992 Earth Summit has also faltered, a victim of its own vagueness on the conservation obligations of states and the choice of its framers to dodge the tensions between genetic material as an economic resource and biodiversity as community-based common property.[15] Often, the hope of regime builders is that vague, nonbinding, or otherwise weak agreements can set in motion a gradual process of deepening cooperation and strengthening of rules. However, the failure of this model in the wetlands, desertification, and biodiversity accords reminds us that the slope of international environmental cooperation is not always slippery.

The absence of regimes for many pressing problems and the inability of many formal agreements to produce meaningful regimes does not invalidate the regime approach; the task may simply be incomplete. Yet even if it can be ultimately effective, the regime approach suffers from an inherent limitation: the narrowly skewed subset of environmental problems around which regimes are most likely to form. Most of the problems that have attracted serious, sustained regime-building efforts involve environmental harm that flows directly across borders. Regimes are commonly formed around specific cross-border flows from point A to point B, such as acid rain, water pollution in shared river basins, or cross-border shipments of hazardous waste. Formation of a regime has also been a common remedy for problems associated with an international commons that exists outside the territory of states, such as a regional sea, the world's oceans, or the global atmosphere. What these two clusters of problems share is that they involve a direct physical, chemical, or biological effect that extends beyond borders.

What happens when we turn our attention from the problem of pollution across borders to the ecological health of the millions of particular locales that lie within those borders? What if the heart of our global environmental problem is the failure to respond to the system-wide pressures and cumulative effects on the world's myriad forests, deserts, grasslands, meadows, soils, wetlands, lakes, rivers, and watersheds? Here, the regime approach has alternated between silence and failure. These physically local systems tend to be "governed" by international regimes only when they are tied to a particularly obvious, immediate, and physically tangible transnational effect, as might occur when they happen to straddle a border.

This narrow, border-reinforcing view of our planetary predicament dominated the 1992 Earth Summit, which was probably the high-water mark for interstate environmental cooperation. High-profile problems surrounding the global commons of climate and biodiversity were subjected to intense, sustained efforts to form regimes, resulting in a treaty on biological diversity and a framework convention on climate change. However, when it came to the equally daunting array of local, incremental, cumulative environmental challenges, regime formation either stalled in the face of political controversy or was not even attempted. Talks on a forest regime collapsed in acrimony, and most of the planet's local, accumulating ecological problems were not subject to regime-building efforts at all. Instead, they were relegated to a set of loose, nonbinding, and largely rhetorical commitments clustered under the rubric of Agenda 21. They were to be dealt with later, voluntarily, and by individual states, if they were to be dealt with at all.

The failure of the regime approach to grapple with the local, cumulative dimensions of the planet's ecological health is deeply troubling when one considers some facts about these "local" environmental problems:

Forests According to the Food and Agriculture Organization (FAO) of the United Nations, the world suffered a net loss of roughly 180 million hectares of forest between 1980 and 1995, an area roughly the size of Mexico.[16] Forest degradation is proceeding even more rapidly than the loss of forest cover, as forest plantations and intensively logged landscapes make up an increasing share of the world's so-called forests.

Soils The World Resources Institute (WRI) reports that by 1990, poor agricultural practices had led directly to the degradation of 562 million hectares of cropland, or about 38 percent of the world's total cropland. It is estimated that losses as a result of severe soil degradation are occurring at the rate of an additional 5 to 6 million hectares annually—an area larger than Serbia, Bosnia, or Croatia.[17] It has been estimated that soil degradation has resulted in a 13 percent loss in productivity for the world's croplands over the past 50 years.[18]

Freshwater ecosystems Of the more than one-third of the world's species of fish that are endangered, most live in freshwater ecosystems. The assault on freshwater ecosystems comes from a variety of sources, including water diversion, industrial discharge, agricultural and urban runoff, overfishing, siltation, and bioinvasions. Damming and other water-diversion schemes have taken an enormous toll. Estimates suggest that there may be as many as 800,000 dams on the world's rivers, including about 40,000 of what are generally referred to as "large dams" and more than 300 giants such as Hoover, Itaipu, Aswan, and Three Gorges. During the twentieth century, the number of large dams increased roughly eightfold while the number of waterways altered for navigation increased from fewer than 9,000 to almost 500,000.[19]

Drylands According to the United Nations Environment Programme (UNEP), 70 percent of the world's drylands are degraded, meaning that they have suffered a loss of economic or biological productivity and complexity. More than 250 million people are directly affected by desertification and an additional 1 billion or more are at risk.[20]

Coral reefs A 1998 assessment by the World Resources Institute concluded that 58 percent of the world's coral reefs were at risk from human activity, with 27 percent at high or very high risk. Overfishing and coastal development were identified as the largest threats. Although comprehensive data on reef degradation do not exist, one reef ecologist estimated that by the early 1990s, 10 percent of the world's reefs were already severely degraded and that the figure would jump to 30 percent within two decades.[21]

Similarly depressing sketches could be drawn for the world's grasslands, coastlines, fisheries, or wetlands. In large part because of these
globally accumulating "local" problems, the UN Environment Programme's *Global Environmental Outlook* report observed on the tenth
anniversary of the Earth Summit in 2002 that

> The environment is still at the periphery of socio-economic development. Poverty
> and excessive consumption ... continue to put enormous pressure on the envi-
> ronment. The unfortunate result is that sustainable development remains largely
> theoretical for the majority of the world's population of more than 6000 million
> people. The level of awareness and action has not been commensurate with the
> state of the global environment today; it continues to deteriorate.[22]

It may be tempting to think of the destruction of wetlands, the erosion
of soils, the abuse of watersheds, and the ravaging of coastlines as local
environmental problems. They typically manifest themselves over spatially limited areas, and only occasionally will those manifestations occur
just upwind or downstream of a nation's border. In narrowly physical
terms, these problems are global only in the cumulative sense that they
are happening all over the planet.[23]

However, if we think of the natural world not only as a spatial distribution of locales but also as a set of life-supporting natural cycles and
ecosystem services, the genuinely global dimension of local ecosystem
health becomes apparent. An extreme version of this view is the so-called
Gaia hypothesis, which posits the Earth as an integrated, lifelike system
making self-correcting adjustments to stresses in its component systems.[24] One need not leap all the way to Gaia to see the globally linked
dimensions of local ecosystems; such links are apparent in the way that
local interventions add up to global-scale perturbations of nutrient cycles.
For carbon, nitrogen, phosphorus, and other key nutrients, the amount
introduced or displaced by human activity now approaches or even
exceeds some of the critical natural flows in the global cycle. For example, fertilizer use, fossil fuel combustion, and land clearing have grown to
the point that the amount of human-generated nitrogen available for
plant uptake (some 210 million tons annually) exceeds the background
natural supply (an estimated 140 million metric tons per year).[25]

Another important global dimension to local environmental degradation comes from the growing social interconnectedness of the world sys-

tem. Our physically and biologically integrated world is fragmented by political division into sovereign states, but it is also constantly being reassembled by massive, rapid flows of people, goods, money, ideas, images, and technology across increasingly porous borders. These flows produce a dense, socially constructed web that can transmit the causes and effects of seemingly local environmental problems from one place to another just as surely as a river or a rainstorm might carry them.[26] These transnational linkages are at times more subtle than cross-border flows of acid rain, toxic waste, or animal pelts, making their global interconnectedness less readily apparent than that of the oceans, atmosphere, or ozone layer, but no less real.

Consider the problem of soil degradation (a catchall concept that includes erosion, salinization, compaction, nutrient depletion, and other negative impacts on soils). In globally cumulative terms, the problem is immense, encompassing more than a third of the world's croplands. This constitutes an enormous global squandering of natural capital. One effort to value ecosystem services placed the economic value of soil formation processes at $53 billion annually, a figure roughly equal to the annual world total of foreign aid.[27] Yet in purely physical terms, soil degradation manifests itself on the local scale of specific watersheds and landscapes. The primary culprits are the use and abuse of agricultural practices such as irrigation, mechanical tilling, intensive cropping, and modern agrochemicals. From the vantage point of sovereign international cooperation, the problem is a local one unless a specific site of intense erosion happens to straddle a specific border. There may be a perceived role for international aid or outside expertise in addressing such problems. However, only rarely does this sort of construction of the problem lead to a broader regime-building process, replete with convergent norms, the articulation of sovereign responsibilities, the legal codification of cooperative means and ends, and international standard setting.

The tendency to view this problem as a local one ignores the powerful transnational economic, political, and social forces that contribute directly to soil degradation.[28] Damaging practices are often the result of cash-crop production, driven by the lure of international markets, pressures to boost exports, the need to service external debt, or the preferences of international development agencies. As with the causes, the social effects of soil degradation also transcend the local. According to one estimate, between 1945 and 1990 soil degradation reduced potential world food production by roughly 17 percent, putting upward pressure on world food prices and exacerbating national- and regional-scale food insecurity.[29] Threatened livelihoods and undermined communities can also generate border-crossing environmental refugees. These effects are felt far from the point of soil degradation, and they can be transmitted much farther and faster than any direct physical consequences. Without a broadly international response, efforts to deal with the transnational drivers of the problem are overwhelmed by pressures for global economic competitiveness or negated by international trading rules that challenge local environmental laws as restraints on trade. Efforts to treat the transnationally disseminated consequences suffer a similar fate.

Rivers, and the freshwater ecosystems that they anchor, provide a particularly important and compelling example of the tight social connections of the global environment. Once again, both the drivers and the cumulative consequences of damming, draining, diverting, and dumping in the world's river basins move through deeply embedded transnational channels. The financing and technical expertise to "push rivers around" has long been transnational. While the environmental consequences are felt most directly and immediately on the more local scale of an individual watershed, they also accumulate to produce genuinely global effects: rapid declines in freshwater biodiversity, destruction of critical wetlands and floodplain ecosystems, and an extraordinary degree of human intervention in the global water cycle (tapping more than half of the accessible global runoff).

The genuinely global ramifications of growing socioecological interconnectedness are potentially enormous. One not-so-subtle hint is provided in an effort by a group of leading ecological economists to estimate the value of global ecosystem services (table 1.1). There are, of course, large uncertainties involved in generating such estimates. Indeed, one may quarrel with the idea of assigning economic value in the absence of price-setting markets for these services. What remains indisputable is the vast social utility of these critical natural regulatory processes and cycles, and thus the potentially enormous economic dislocations resulting

Table 1.1
Estimated value of the world's ecosystem services and natural capital (billion 1994 US$ per year)

By Type of Service		By Biome Type	
Gas regulation	1,341	Open ocean	8,381
Climate regulation	684	Coastal marine	12,568
Disturbance regulation	1,779	Tropical forest	3,813
Water regulation	1,115	Temperate and boreal	894
Water supply	1,692	forest	
Erosion control	576	Grass and rangelands	906
Soil formation	53	Wetlands	4,879
Nutrient cycling	17,075	Lakes and rivers	1,700
Waste treatment	2,277	Desert	n.a.
Pollination	117	Tundra	n.a.
Biological control	417	Ice and rock	n.a.
Habitat or refugia	124	Cropland	128
Food production	1,386	Urban	—
Raw materials	721		
Genetic resources	79		
Recreation	815		
Cultural	3,015		
Total global value	33,268	Total global value	33,268

Notes: n.a. = not available; — = negligible. Columns may not add, owing to rounding.
Source: Costanza et al. 1997.

from their disruption. Yet these services depend integrally on the health of local ecosystems, which are themselves suffering under the cumulative toll of millions of insults. The critical ecosystems of wetlands, tropical forests, and coastal marine environments—among the most besieged of the planet's places—accounted for almost two-thirds of the estimated service value of ecosystems cited in table 1.1.

In other words, local environmental problems have profoundly global implications through their cumulative impact on key global systems and cycles and their increasingly far-flung reverberations across a densely interconnected social world. This means that the challenge of global environmental governance is not simply one of managing the spaces outside state boundaries or limiting the spillover of pollutants across those boundaries. Rather, as Wendell Berry explains it, "The question that *must* be addressed ... is not how to care for the planet, but how to care for each of the planet's millions of human and natural neighborhoods."[30] The challenge is to deal with the accumulating impact on local ecosystems in a world where political, economic, cultural, and informational borders have been obliterated more quickly than strictly ecological ones.

The failure to account for the socially transnational character of the planet's places may help to explain why the regime approach has faltered in an era of globalization. It has not fared well in the context of globalization, even for those conventional international issues where regime formation has been possible. The Basel Convention, which first sought to control and then to ban outright the shipment of hazardous wastes to developing countries, has been weakened by the threat of a challenge through the World Trade Organization (WTO).[31] A similar threat confronts the stratospheric ozone regime; its restrictions on trade with non-parties, a key element of the regime, are of questionable validity in the view of the General Agreement on Tariffs and Trade (GATT) and the WTO.[32] It is difficult to imagine the conclusion today of an agreement such as the 1973 Convention on International Trade in Endangered Species, which deliberately delegitimizes a lucrative form of international trade. Indeed, in the current global economic climate, rules on trade, investment, foreign aid, or intellectual property have become much more fundamental institutions of global governance than any international environmental regime. The idea of weaving the fabric of global governance one regime strand at a time is confronted with the harsh reality that deeply institutionalized practices of trade liberalization, development assistance, and capital mobility already constitute a preexisting and tightly woven fabric in the world political economy.[33]

Regimes as Extremes

Why is the regime approach so often silent or ineffective in addressing this broad class of environmental threats? I will argue that it is because most environmental regimes and the regime concept in general are founded on highly stylized notions about territory, authority, and knowledge. Not all of the social struggles that swirl around environmental problems can be resolved by cramming the problem into the institutional mold offered by the regime approach. Many physically local but globally cumulative problems have been particularly poor fits.

One of the strong, indeed extreme, presumptions of the regime approach can be seen in the need to argue that "local" environmental problems are appropriate subjects in a discussion of "global" environmental governance. The regime approach internalizes a narrowly territorial notion of what constitutes an "international" problem. It stresses the transnational character of certain physical systems, but not the transnational character of economic, social, and political institutions. This means that creeping, incremental, local manifestations of the planetary predicament are relegated to the domestic sphere. This problem is not limited to the environmental realm, of course; it also plagues efforts to manage the increasingly global macroeconomy, to respond to problems of violent intergroup conflict within nominally sovereign nations, or to prevent the spread of disease. In each case, the fiction of neatly separable "domestic" and "international" realms produces limited responses to problems with causes and consequences that flow through increasingly porous borders.

The problem runs deeper than just the territorial underpinnings of the regime concept. A second limit of the regime approach involves its position toward questions of authority, legitimacy, and role definitions in the process of governance. Simply put, regimes are the vehicles of states. Because a codified international agreement lies at the heart of most processes of regime building, regimes internalize strong presumptions about state authority, the legitimacy of state actions, and the essential difference between governments and other collective agents. As a result, the regime approach embodies strong and rigid presumptions about who governs whom. Many regimes do allow roles for nonstate actors; a few even give (selected) nonstate actors substantial standing and voice. However, rarely do these roles challenge the core presumption of state authority. Consider *Our Common Future*, the highly influential report of the World Commission on Environment and Development and the inspiration for the 1992 Earth Summit. An appendix to the report recommends twenty-three principles for environmental protection and sustainable development. After an initial principle defining the individual's right to a sound environment, the remaining twenty-two principles each begin with the same phrase: "States shall ...".[34]

This presumption of state authority comes at a high cost. Problems over which states lack the uncontested, legitimate authority to govern are not likely to yield effective regimes. It is telling that struggles over authority and challenges to state legitimacy are often the essence of the politics that surrounds the local, cumulative dimensions of global environmental change. The conflicts that arise in the effort to control people and nature in these cases make it impossible to create institutions based on authoritative states whose governing acts are clothed in broadly based legitimacy. In other words, these problems lie beyond the regime approach not only because they are spatially "domestic," but also because they involve hotly and explicitly contested struggles over authority. As discussed in chapter 2, increasingly common invocations of "stakeholder participation" barely hint at the scope of the question of authority.

Along with territory and authority, the third key pillar of the regime approach is its stance toward knowledge. The regime approach gravitates toward issue areas constructed by an authoritative understanding of both problem and solution. One of the biggest challenges facing regime builders is to create a foundation of officially sanctioned knowledge. Simply put, regimes demand a definitive outcome to the struggles over knowledge that are inherent to environmental politics. A resolution may be attained by consensual negotiation or hegemonic imposition, but without it, regime formation becomes problematic. Despite the desire of environmentalists to elevate the "precautionary principle" to the status of an international norm, regimes tend not to form when the understandings of a problem and its solution remain highly contested for an indefinite period. As I will argue in chapter 2, for a wide array of the planet's local, cumulative environmental problems there is no neat closure on knowledge and probably it is not possible, making regime-based governance problematic.

Combining these presumptions about territoriality, authority, and knowledge, regimes can be understood as high-modern expressions of the same bordered, statist, functional-rational worldview that yielded the institutional monoculture of the Westphalian international interstate system. These presumptions have allowed a modicum of progress on certain important environmental problems that involve pollution beyond borders. Even those gains now face growing tensions between their regime-based institutional foundation and the precepts of economic globalization. When confronted with the more fundamental problem of protecting the planet's places, replete with its struggles over bordered enclosure, governing authority, and the validity of knowledge, the regime approach leaves us with unpalatable choices: to deny the existence of those struggles, to seek to impose neat resolutions upon them, or to founder in the face of their depth and complexity.

Institutionalizing the Nonstate?

What happens, then, when international regimes are infeasible, undesirable, or unimaginable? Are there other institutional forms, either existing or conceivable, on which to build responses to the pressures on the planet's places? If the limitation of the regime approach is a tightly circumscribed attitude toward territorially delineated sovereignty, state authority, and official knowledge, then one obvious place to turn for alternatives are entities that are not states—the rich array of networks, coalitions, grassroots activism, and transnational campaigns created by a global panoply of citizens' organizations, activist groups, and social movements. Might these agents and processes be creating alternative mechanisms of global environmental governance that can circumvent the limits of the regime approach?

The answer is difficult to gauge, in part because scholars have taken many different approaches to understanding the diverse array of actors, campaigns, and ideas that constitute the nonstate. Some conceptualize transnational nonstate processes in terms of networks of well-positioned individuals or small groups wielding forms of knowledge power. Haas, for example, identifies networks of technical experts functioning as "epistemic communities" that use the power of technical expertise to move governments toward cooperation.[35] Litfin examines the role of the "knowledge entrepreneurs" who frame understandings of international environmental problems in ways that either hinder or facilitate cooperation.[36] Although these approaches differ in their view of what constitutes knowledge and of who has the power to legitimize it, they share an emphasis on the nonstate dimensions of power in the form of the political construction and use of technical expertise.

Another way to capture the nonstate emphasizes the power of its explicit values; Keck and Sikkink identify "transnational advocacy networks" made up of value-driven activists both inside and outside the state, linked by "shared values, a common discourse, and dense exchanges of information and services."[37] These networks exploit information, symbols, and powerful discursive frames of injustice to hold governments accountable transnationally. Yet another approach stresses the organizational foundation of the nonstate. Wapner, for example, identifies transnational environmental organizations such as Greenpeace, Friends of the Earth, and the Worldwide Fund for Nature as the pillars of an emergent global civil society, disseminating new ideas, practices, values, sensibilities, and techniques on a global scale.[38] Still others stress the role of less bureaucratic forms of social organization, finding the transnational effects of the nonstate in social movements, protest campaigns, and coalition-building activities.[39]

These forays into the politics of the nonstate reveal a wide array of approaches to governance, many of which transcend the territorial, statist, and functional-rational limits of the regime approach to grapple directly with the problem of protecting the planet's places. They offer reconceptualizations of sovereign territoriality; they challenge monocultures of governance and authority; they validate pluralistic, local forms of knowledge and alternative ways of knowing.

One striking aspect of research on the nonstate is how little its chroniclers have had to say about institutionalization. The emphasis is on movements, actors, networks, and relationships, but not on embedded, enduring sets of roles and rules that give shape and form to a whole array of struggles over time. Perhaps this is not surprising; the first intellectual task has been simply to persuade a world equating governance with "the state" that the nonstate exists and matters.[40] Too, the newness of these activities may make it premature to look for evidence of their entrenchment and regularization as an alternative to interstate institutions. After all, they depend fundamentally on such recent trends as the communications revolution, the partial opening of institutional settings such as the United Nations and global conferences, and the expansion of democratic political space in previously closed societies. It may simply be too early to look for recurring patterns, embeddedness, routinization, or permanence.

Nevertheless, the lack of scholarly attention to the institutionalization of the nonstate is troubling if one's goal is to find institutional foundations for protecting the planet's places. In the realm of global environmental activism, every struggle seems to be a new one. Highly general concepts about sustainability and democratic accountability may survive as organizing principles across individual episodes and campaigns, as do some specific network relationships among individuals or organizations. When reading this literature, however, one is left with the distinct impression that the process must be rebuilt each time, essentially from scratch. Again, perhaps this is no surprise. Networks built around the politics of expertise or the value orientations of well-placed activists are by definition difficult to institutionalize or to translate across particular issue areas. Campaigns spearheaded or linked by transnational organizations depend on the survival and continuity of those organizations, which cannot be taken for granted. Social movements, too, are notoriously impermanent. The lack of staying power of environmental social movements in Eastern Europe in the 1990s is a cautionary tale for global governance strategies rooted in citizen activism and "global civil society."[41] And in transnational expression, they are also prone to the same internal cleavages of power and voice that plague interstate relations.[42]

To be sure, research on the nonstate teaches us a great deal about transnational techniques to protect the planet's places. It offers a rich set of alternatives to the high-modern position toward territory, authority, and knowledge that permeates the regime approach. Thus far, however, it has told us surprisingly little about the stability of the institutional forms meant to convey those techniques.

Toward a Political Sociology of International Institutions

In chapter 2 I develop more fully the argument suggested here—that the bordered, statist, and functional-rational features of the regime form prevent it from confronting the problem of protecting the planet's places. If so, can we find institutional forms with different configurations for these key institutional properties? Or is the struggle to protect the planet's places caught between the rock of interstate regimes and the hard place of global civil society? Are we left with a Hobson's choice between unhelpful practices that can be institutionalized and helpful ones that cannot?

Answering these questions means asking why regimes systematically display the tendencies I have described. If these features of regimes are merely poor design choices, then other choices can be made. If they are the preferences of powerful actors, then political struggles can be joined. If, on the other hand, they reflect deeply embedded systemic tendencies and powerful, overarching metanorms of world politics—as some sociologists of the international system have argued—then the challenge is structural and of a different order of magnitude entirely.

As suggested in chapter 2, mainstream scholarly research in international relations provides little insight into this question. Regimes are taken as the product of bargaining in the context of anarchy; a regime is understood to have the form it does because this is what the dominant coalition in favor of regime formation wanted as an outcome, subject to the requisites of building that coalition. In contrast, a more sociological orientation toward the institutionalization of global governance calls attention to the prior foundation of global norms within which regime bargaining takes place. This work provides a potentially powerful tool for identifying alternatives to the regime approach. It suggests that regimes are a peculiar, specific form of institution that fixes certain key properties as constants. The reason for this is that regimes are built within the context of an overarching structure of values, such as those legitimizing scientific rationality and bureaucratic administration.

Drawing on these insights from the sociology of international institutionalism, I will argue that international regimes—both conceptually and in practice—tend to reproduce these powerful value orientations of the international system, thereby holding constant certain key institutional features that we could otherwise imagine as variables. As already suggested, I will argue that these critical variables include the institution's position toward sovereignty, borders, and territoriality; its premises about the legitimacy of state authority and the subjects and objects of governance; and its view of rationalist constructions of problems that rest on officially sanctioned knowledge. To differentiate these deeper value orientations and to emphasize that they give shape to more specific institutions, I will refer to them as metanorms of authority, territoriality, and knowledge.

Once these strong presumptions of the regime approach are exposed, regimes can be seen as one specific form among the range of institutions we can imagine. By allowing these metanormative orientations to vary, we can at least visualize a much wider range of different institutional forms, some of which may be better suited to the controversies that surround the local dimensions of our planetary predicament.

Where I disagree with the sociological-institutional view of the international system is with its relatively pessimistic implications: that the structure of metanorms within which regimes form is so powerfully constructed and embedded as to be essentially inevitable. Because the goal of that research has been to show the link between an underlying normative structure and resulting patterns of international cooperation or formal organization, the strong implication is that these norms are fully determinate both of the issues around which cooperation will occur and the form that cooperation will take.[43] In contrast, I will argue that metanorms of scientific rationality, fixed territoriality, or statist bureaucratic administration are powerful but not entirely hard-wired determinants of the resulting institutional form. Instead, I interpret the building of environmental institutions as a site of struggle among conflicting metanormative orientations, some of which are more powerful than others, but none of which are inevitable or universally determinate. In this view, international regimes are not synonymous with international institutions, as many international relations theorists presume; nor are they the inevitable expression of hegemonic metanorms, as the world-polity sociologists strongly imply. Rather, they are the institutional expression of a normative struggle that has had a particular type of outcome. Regimes are what results when territorialism, statism, and functional-rationalism prevail in this struggle. Those triumphs are frequent but not inevitable and are even less so when we recognize institution building as the site of struggle over these framing properties.

Rivers and Watersheds as the Planet's Places

In the chapters that follow, water—particularly as it relates to the world's rivers, watersheds, and freshwater ecosystems—will provide the substantive focus used to explore and illustrate the dynamics of institution building. Global water politics provides an opportunity to contrast a wide range of such dynamics. On the one hand, there has been a sustained and concerted effort to build a conventional global regime for international rivers. More than three decades of effort to articulate global legal principles for shared watercourses culminated in a 1997 United Nations framework convention, passed by a large margin in the General Assembly (but not ratified subsequently by a sufficient number of states to enter into force). There have also been many efforts at regime formation around specific international rivers. There are now more than 150 basin-specific treaties that set out the rights and responsibilities of states sharing a particular waterway. In both global and basin-specific expressions, regime-building efforts have been based on a traditional transboundary construction of a problem: the cooperative governance of border-crossing rivers.

During the past few decades, less formal but increasingly embedded processes of institution building have also emerged. One such process has emanated from the controversies surrounding the traditional instrument of aggressive river modification, the large dam. A pro-dam alliance that links the World Bank, international firms, bilateral aid agencies, and governments bent on developing water resources has collided with an increasingly transnational network of dam opponents grounded in movements for human rights, the environment, indigenous peoples, grassroots development, and democratic reform. The result has been white-hot political conflict, social protest, even violence, but also a surprising degree of institution building, in the sense of increasingly routinized, embedded, normalized, rule-based and role-assuming behavior by the key participants.

These two institution-building processes involve strikingly different constructions of the problem and its political dynamics. In one view, the objects of governance are the world's physically international rivers; in the other, they are physically local watersheds that are being socioeconomically transnationalized. One stresses interstate relations, the other, transnational state–society relations. One is rooted in a cooperative dynamic of bargaining to overcome barriers to collective action; the other is rooted in bitterly contentious social conflict. One elevates an ideal of managing natural resources for optimal use; the other envisions democratic governance of watersheds for ecological prudence and cultural integrity.

Perhaps most important, these institution-building processes differ dramatically in their metanormative positions toward knowledge, territoriality, and authority—the themes that lie at the heart of the framework developed in chapter 2. The process of building a global regime for international rivers bears all the marks of the traditional regime approach: a territorially bounded construction of the problem; a strong presumption of state authority; and an optimistic, universalizing, rationalist understanding of knowledge. The processes of institution building that emerge from the large-dams controversy involve, to varying degrees, the deterritorialization of localities, disparate conceptions of authority, and radically conflicting ways of knowing.

Global water politics is further complicated by a third process of institution building that emanates from the linked set of processes often referred to as global neoliberalism. When applied to water, structural-adjustment conditionality and neoliberal policy reform have produced pressures for what I will refer to as the marketization of water. The result is a set of strong pronouncements as to how water should be managed, emphasizing its character as a natural resource good with economic value. As with the effort to construct dams, the effort to treat water as a marketable commodity has met with opposition, contestation, conflict, and sometimes even violence. Viewed in regime terms, one might argue that governments marketizing water and suppressing dissent are "leaders" while those declining or failing to do so are "laggards." A closer look at the controversy, however, reveals that what is being institutionalized is not simply marketization or its discontents, but rather a dynamic tension between these opposing forces, rooted in metanorms of territoriality, authority, and knowledge that differ, sometimes markedly, from both the international-rivers and anti-dam cases.

A fourth process of institutionalization around water centers on an increasingly concentrated and extensive international network of water experts, including managers, technologists, economists, analysts, and policy professionals. As discussed in chapter 5, this networking has been plagued by a central tension between planning and marketization. On the one hand there is a universalizing planning paradigm that demands tight connections among social, economic, technical, and cultural choices; on the other there is an underlying emphasis on market values and profit as the basis for water-related behavior. A consequence of this tension has been an ambivalent attitude toward the most fundamentally contested and politicized questions in the water sphere. Nonetheless, water-expert networking processes and the institutions they have generated have produced an important conceptual vocabulary—that of integrated water resources management—within which discussions and struggles over water increasingly take place.

These parallel, sometimes competing, and often conflicting efforts to "normalize" the governance of water—be they grounded in international law, social movement activism, neoliberal marketization, or expert networking—share one important feature: None is a comprehensive watershed governance regime per se. None is sufficiently comprehensive in either scale or scope to be thought of in those terms. Thus the significance of these institution-building processes is not that any one of them constitutes *the* global watershed regime, but rather that each of them articulates what I will refer to as a distinct set of protonorms. I will use this term to refer to norms that have become sufficiently recognizable and well established to become available for application to watershed governance in basins and watersheds that lie beyond their direct reach, but which may or may not become inscribed around those local systems. This raises one of the central questions that this book seeks to address: whether, how, and how much any of these institution-building processes is reaching upstream, so to speak, to shape watershed governance practices in specific locales.

The Stream Ahead

Chapter 2 examines in greater detail the underlying metanormative presumptions about territoriality, authority, and knowledge on which the regime approach is founded. By framing these regime constants as institutional variables, it becomes possible to envision more fluid understandings of borders and territory, more heterogeneous definitions of authoritative roles, and less positivist epistemologies of knowledge.

After a background sketch of the causes and consequences of transformation of the world's rivers, lakes, floodplains, estuaries, and wetlands (chapter 3), chapters 4 through 7 turn to the politics of specific processes by which four distinct sets of protonorms about water have been assembled. I look first at the extent of formal international regime formation around shared rivers (chapter 4). The focus then turns to alternative institutional arrangements that, like regimes, seek to "govern" water, but with normative and metanormative orientations that differ substantially, sometimes radically, from the regime form. Specifically, the focus here will be on elite international water policy networks seeking to promote global water governance according to largely functional-rational norms of integrated water resources management (chapter 5), the transnational political struggle over the practice of building large dams (chapter 6), and transnational water marketization initiatives and controversies (chapter 7). In each of these four chapters, the goal is to map a process of institution building: to identify the specific content of a particular normative framework explicating how water should be governed; to draw a map of the various nodes, sites, networks, and platforms within the international system and world politics where such norms have begun to gain some traction; and to examine how such norms embed metanormative stances toward authority, territoriality, and knowledge. Although the chapters do not ignore the role of specific states as actors and arenas in this process, the emphasis is on the process of institution building in nondomestic political spaces.

Another important question is where institutionalization occurs. Chapters 4 through 7 show that the state is hardly the only relevant political site of normative development. Yet clearly it remains one such site.[44] Both regime-theoretic scholarship and those perspectives focused on nonstate agency via advocacy networks and social movements have taken the answer to this question to be, for the most part, the state. The former approach has viewed interstate institutions as significant primarily because they shape state behavior; the latter has focused primarily on the state as the object of the normative force of advocates. Taking the admonition seriously that we should not understate the state, the next pair of chapters (8 and 9) examines the reach of these transnational institution-building processes into domestic law, policy, and practice in two countries, Brazil and South Africa.

Each country-level case study consists of four steps: (1) a historical overview of water politics and law; (2) a discussion of the mix of domestic and transnational forces prompting nonincremental change in water law, policy, and practice; (3) a step-by-step examination of the half-dozen or so major sites of institutional struggle (e.g., federal agencies, the legal system, infrastructure building, local governments, and social movements); and (4) an assessment of the comparative influence of each of the four sets of transnational protonorms sketched in chapters 4 through 7 (international law, water-expert networks, the anti-dams struggle, and water marketization controversies).

The country case studies show how extensively the state mediates transnational normative influences on water-related practices. Yet the cases also illustrate the dangers of overstating the state. In both countries, there are at least a half-dozen prime sites of contestation over water-related law, policy, and practice. Some of these represent what most international relations scholars seem to mean when they invoke "the state"—the centralized administrative apparatus that is to be mobilized as the agent of global environmental governance via some combination of revealed interest, tutelage, moral suasion, or knowledge-based seduction. Yet those administrative systems are shown in both cases to be strikingly varied and uneven normative terrain. The picture is further complicated when one begins to introduce the multiple levels (e.g., provincial and local) and logics (e.g., legislation versus adjudication versus coercion) of the state. As the cases will show, few of the sites of political life where water is governed lie fully within the grasp of the administrative apparatus of the state, and some stretch well beyond its reach.

Brazil and South Africa have been chosen as case studies for two reasons. First, each is central to the global debate surrounding water and rivers, in both the regime and nonregime domains of institution building. Both countries have important transboundary watercourses, tying them to the evolution of international water law and making them central players in interstate water politics. Both have strong and active social movements protesting large dams and/or privatization of water. Both have strong ties to international professional water policy networks. Both are deeply enmeshed in processes of neoliberal structural adjustment, including those in the water sector. If the question were simply one of detecting international influences, these would be the most likely cases and therefore weak tests in terms of generalizability. They are, however, useful test cases of what happens when national policy frameworks are subjected simultaneously to pressures coming from many different directions and with many different normative orientations. In other words, having illustrated in chapters 5, 6, and 7 that interstate regimes are not the only institutional possibility for governing water, the country-level studies can then shed light on the relative depth and reach of competing ways of institutionalizing the governance of water.

A second justification for choosing these cases is that in both countries the legal, political, and policy-making processes surrounding water have been pried open by turbulent change in recent years. South Africa's transition from apartheid has had profound implications for water politics, given water's importance as an element of social control during the apartheid era. Brazil's postmilitary struggle for democratization has had similar ramifications for questions related to water, rivers, and development policy more generally. These dramatic changes have created more than the usual room for nonincremental shifts in policy. For very different reasons, new ideas about how to govern watersheds have been on the table to an unusual extent in each country. The fact that water governance practices were "up for grabs" to a greater than usual extent is a useful feature of these cases, in that it makes it possible to test more substantially the manner, extent, and channels by which various transnational institutional forms may interact with domestic law, policy, and practice.

Drawing upon the findings and lessons in the four global-level and two country-level cases, chapter 10 then seeks to find a broader message in the specific story of transnational water politics.

Social conflicts around water are pervasive, endemic, and accelerating, on scales ranging from local landscapes to the entire planet. In the face of these conflicts, formal processes of bargaining to achieve cooperation have made little headway. Yet contentious transnational water politics has followed a discernible pattern in which conflicts have become bounded, routinized, embedded, and normalized. To the extent that transnational norms offering some hope of protecting the planet's water places are taking root, they are doing so primarily as a result of contentious environmental politics.

Can global environmental governance mean protecting the planet's places, rather than merely managing pollution across borders? Can it be more than just a technocratic exercise in planetary systems management that is doomed to failure, ripe for capture, or crowded into a tiny corner of global life by the "real" international institutions of transnational capitalism, state sovereignty, and the modern project? If the answer is to be "yes," we must find ways to nurture alternative institutional forms where territorial, state-authorized, and knowledge-stabilized governing frameworks are not possible. Socioecological controversies of the sort that swirl around water will be at the heart of that process.

2
Toward a Social Theory of International Institutions

The Regime Prototype: Montreal and Basel

Perhaps the most famous campaign in the quest for global environmental governance is the Montreal Protocol on Substances that Deplete the Ozone Layer. Reached in September 1987 and entering into force just sixteen months later, the Montreal Protocol was the critical step in consolidation of the stratospheric ozone protection regime. It replaced vague commitments with specific goals and timetables for cutting back on production and use of ozone-damaging chemicals. Montreal also prepared the ground for subsequent agreements that would bring key countries of the global South into the regime, phase out the use of chlorofluorocarbons (CFCs), and tighten restrictions on other culprit chemicals.[1]

The process of building the ozone regime has been recounted as a detective story of science and diplomacy.[2] Scientists raced to prove that the problem was caused by human-induced changes in atmospheric chemistry and to document its full scope and extent. Diplomats searched for a cooperative formula that would balance the interests of North and South and the different concerns of producing and consuming nations. One of the participants in the negotiations, U.S. diplomat Richard Benedick, summarizes the powerful appeal of the Montreal narrative:

It may not be fanciful to imagine that in future eras the story of the protection of the ozone layer might acquire almost a mythic character. Certainly there has been nothing like it before or since. The elements of mythology were there: a mysterious and remote phenomenon that threatened life on Earth; the sheer good luck that led pioneering scientists to follow their curiosity, bringing at first derision and, two decades later, for three of them, the Nobel Prize; an ideal chemical, finding ever more uses, that turned out to be a subtle menace to life; a diplomatic struggle that ended in unprecedented international cooperation and helped to inspire the launching of a new system of global environmental governance.[3]

An equally compelling story in the lexicon of environmental regimes is the Basel Convention on the Control of Transboundary Movements of Hazardous Wastes and their Disposal. After years of polemics on the problem of international trafficking in hazardous wastes, governments meeting in Basel, Switzerland, in 1989 agreed to a plan for "prior informed consent" on international shipments of waste. This initial accord was a weak, loophole-ridden compromise with little tangible effect. Prior informed consent merely meant that approval should be obtained from the relevant authority in the receiving country; it fell far short of the outright ban on the waste trade sought by environmental activists and many waste-receiving states. They argued that developing countries were not in a position to effectively control their own borders on this issue, making prior informed consent meaningless. Also, the emphasis on wastes shipped for "final disposal" left a gaping loophole through which hazardous materials could still be shipped for "recycling" without even the minimal control of prior informed consent, greatly undermining the effectiveness of the regime.

Yet to the surprise of nearly everyone associated with it, the Basel agreement evolved in just five years into an outright ban on the shipment of hazardous wastes to developing countries. Adopted at a 1994 conference of the parties to the original Basel accord, the "Basel ban" amendment embraced an immediate prohibition on the shipment of hazardous wastes for final disposal from countries belonging to the Organization for Economic Cooperation and Development (OECD) to non-OECD countries, as well as a phaseout of waste shipments for "recycling" by 1998. The ban amendment will not enter into force until it is ratified by sixty-two parties to the Basel agreement, and the threat of a challenge through the World Trade Organization has hung over the ratification process. Nevertheless, progress toward eventual ratification has already transformed the global trade in hazardous waste.[4]

If Montreal is a detective story, Basel is a morality play. The idea that waste shipments from North to South constituted "toxic colonialism" became a formidable weapon in the hands of those seeking aggressive regulatory action.[5] Among the catalysts for the ban were investigative journalists who turned vagabond garbage scows and stories about illicit dumping in the Third World into a powerful narrative of international injustice that governments could not ignore. The key diplomatic agent was a coalition of African states, which brought a solid regional front to the global negotiations and built creative partnerships with environmentalists working for the ban.[6] The transnational environmental organization Greenpeace also played an influential role, dramatizing the abuse of loopholes in the original Basel agreement, creating an authoritative source of independent data on transnational shipments of hazardous waste, and coordinating tactics with like-minded diplomats from states pushing for stronger action.[7]

Framed as triumphant breakthroughs in international environmental cooperation, Montreal and Basel became influential models of global environmental governance. The longtime head of the UN Environment Programme, Mostafa Tolba, described Montreal as the beginning of a new era of environmental statesmanship.[8] Whether or not it becomes the stuff of legend as suggested by Ambassador Benedick, Montreal has had a deep impact on choices of institutional design for global environmental protection. Certainly the would-be architects of global climate protection put much hope and energy into creating an equally slippery slope in the negotiations on global warming. In this model, the highly general 1992 Framework Convention on Climate Change was analogous to the general framework on ozone established in the 1985 Vienna Convention, and the subsequent 1997 Kyoto Protocol on climate was to be analogous to the ozone regime's breakthrough Montreal Protocol.[9]

Though less widely feted than Montreal, Basel too emerged as a model. Even critics acknowledge its powerful influence in the broader arena of international regulation of toxic chemicals.[10] Inspired by the Basel ban, activists (including many actors from the Basel drama) turned to the task of building a global regime on persistent organic pollutants.[11] The impetus for an international regime came in the mid-1990s when some environmental scientists began to argue that POPs and other chemicals in widespread use might be "endocrine disruptors," interfering with hormones that control reproduction and fetal development in humans and animals.[12] In short order, the UNEP Governing Council authorized an intergovernmental negotiating committee to prepare an international legally binding instrument for implementing international action on twelve key POPs.[13] As with Basel, the goal was to move from a weak and problematic "prior informed consent" regime—in this case, the nonbinding system of export controls administered by UNEP and the UN Food and Agriculture Organization—to stronger regulatory action.[14]

Montreal and Basel differ in important ways. The problems differ. Montreal involves damage to a global commons, while Basel addresses cross-border pollution flows to specific locations. The path to regime formation also differed. Montreal was driven by scientific discoveries and the political framing of technical knowledge, whereas Basel was driven by shocking revelations of corruption, exploitation, and governmental incapacity. Montreal established goals and timetables that have been tightened incrementally over time; Basel lurched from prior informed consent to an outright ban. Montreal's rapid entry into force contrasts with the slow process of obtaining enough ratifications for the Basel ban to take effect. The two regimes also differ in important aspects of design. Montreal embraces global restrictions; Basel focuses exclusively on the North–South dimension of the problem. Montreal has a formal (although largely unenforceable) procedure for dealing with noncompliance, whereas Basel relies on the responsibility of individual states for implementation and compliance. Unlike Montreal, Basel is working to develop mechanisms for liability and compensation; unlike Basel, Montreal has placed cleaner production and the transition to alternatives at the heart of the regime.

Despite these differences, both Montreal and Basel are prototypical international environmental regimes. Regimes have been defined as "rules of the game agreed upon by actors in the international arena (usually nation states) and delimiting, for these actors, the range of legitimate or admissible behavior in a specified context of activity."[15] Montreal and Basel contain every major element of this definition. Both establish rules of the game; governments should restrict the manufacture and use of CFCs (Montreal) and prohibit the shipment of hazardous wastes from industrialized to developing countries (Basel). Both have been agreed upon by states. Each regime has at its core an international treaty with the status of international law once it is ratified by the requisite number of signatory states. Both delimit the range of legitimate or admissible behavior. Under Montreal, controlled substances may be traded with other parties to the agreement, but trade with nonparties to the agreement is prohibited. Basel draws clear distinctions between legitimate and illegitimate destinations and substances. Finally, both center on a specified context of activity. Montreal focuses on a specific set of chemical compounds with particular effects on atmospheric chemistry; Basel treats the hazardous waste trade as an issue separable from larger questions and controversies in the toxics arena, such as the manufacture and use of hazardous chemicals or the location of toxic facilities.

Montreal and Basel also share more deeply embedded characteristics of institutional form. As rules of the game for interstate affairs, they also reflect several embedded metanorms of the modern international system within which that game plays out. First, in keeping with conventional norms of sovereignty, both regimes draw a sharply territorial distinction between the international and domestic realms. Montreal does not concern itself with local aspects of air pollution or domestic effects of the ozone-destroying chemicals targeted by the regime. Basel has defined "domestic" questions of the location, manufacture, use, or disposal of toxics as beyond its scope. The international realm constructed by these agreements is the physical space outside a state's borders. The raison d'etre of both regimes is the transboundary character of the problem, thereby reaffirming the territorial boundaries on which the construction of the problem is based.

Closely linked to this fixed territorialization of nature and parsing of environmental problems according to borders is a set of underlying presumptions about authority. Both regimes stubbornly cling to the idea that the domestic sphere is the zone of competent state authority, where the legal, technical, and administrative apparatus of the state is to be brought to bear on obligations agreed to voluntarily upon joining the international regime. One of the most powerful arguments for the Basel ban was the supposed inability of weak states to control the flow of toxic waste across their borders. Yet the Basel regime relies upon national interpretations of what constitutes both "hazard" and "waste," national judgments as to whether environmentally sound management practices are being used, and national bureaucracies as the competent legal authorities for the regime's notification and consent mechanisms. The ozone regime has been hailed as breaking new ground in its procedures for review of implementation and noncompliance.[16] However, these systems rely upon national reporting mechanisms. Nominally independent technical working groups (themselves sprinkled liberally with state administrators and regulators) are limited to secondary functions, such as identifying alternatives and advising on appeals for essential-use exemptions from restrictions in the regime. The capacity of states as parties to meet the requirements and expectations varies widely in both cases. What does not vary is the fact that central authoritative roles—the power, standing, and legitimate authority to govern—are reserved for the state.[17]

No less important than these underlying positions toward territoriality and authority is the way that Montreal and Basel deal with knowledge. Both regimes cloak themselves in the mantle of objective, functional rationality grounded in the methods of modern science. They validate their actions by creating technical working groups of authoritative scientific experts whose task is to provide an objective, rational foundation for charting the regime's course and measuring its progress. Along with the always-present debates about fairness and responsibility, questions about the regime's adherence to scientific knowledge become a key measure of its legitimacy.

Unpacking Regimes as an Institutional Form

These shared features of Montreal and Basel suggest an underlying similarity to environmental regimes as an institutional form. Extending the popular metaphor of regimes as rules of the game, Basel and Montreal share strong presumptions about the territorial boundaries of play, about standing and hierarchy among states and lesser players, and about the path to victory through science and bureaucracy. These positions are not always in pure harmony, of course. The possible tensions between statist presumptions of authority and scientific mechanisms of legitimization, for example, are apparent.[18] Yet, contradictory or not, these underlying presumptions pervade most interstate environmental regimes. When the specific content of their rules is contrasted, regimes appear to afford a plethora of approaches and philosophies. Contrasted at this deeper level, they begin to look much more like an institutional monoculture.

One way to see these underlying similarities is to break down a conventional definition of regimes such as Rittberger's (quoted on p. 38) into its components. Drawing out the implicit position of most environmental regimes toward authority relations, territoriality, and the construction of knowledge suggests the following reformulation. Rather than seeing regimes as "agreed upon by actors," we should see them as agreed upon by actors *whose roles as the authoritative agents of governance go largely unquestioned.* Rather than seeing regimes as developing "in the international arena," we should see them as developing in an international arena *defined by a fixed, territorial conception that divides nature into separate domestic and international realms.* And rather than seeing regimes as delimiting behavior "in a specified context of activity," we should see them as doing so in a context *defined by a process of knowledge stabilization around a functional-rational framing of the problem.* In other words, regimes tend to be institutions in which rules may be contested, but roles are not; in which nature is territorialized; and in which legitimacy demands that knowledge be stabilized. I consider each of these underlying features in turn.

Rules May Be Contested, but Roles Are Not

In theory, regimes define not only rules but also roles. Regimes are institutions, which Oran Young defines as "systems of rules, decision-making procedures, and programs that give rise to social practices, *assign roles to the participants in these practices*, and guide interactions among the occupants of the relevant roles."[19] This process of role definition is one of the important pathways by which regimes, and institutions more generally, affect behavior.[20] The nuclear family is a good example of an institution that establishes not only the rules of the game but also the roles of the players, with widespread consequences for behavior and outcomes both inside and outside of families. The parameters of these roles are sometimes flexible or subject to multiple interpretations. However, their renegotiation is often difficult, and they give a powerful shape to social relations through processes of identity formation and the generation of expectations. Another example is the practice by which governments

accord sovereign standing to one another through recognition and diplomatic exchanges. Sovereignty is a set of behavioral rules *and* a construction of roles, in that states' rights and responsibilities are sharply
differentiated from those of other actors in world affairs.

Although many environmental regimes have developed complex sets
of rules, most have done so in a context where roles are taken as relatively fixed. For most states in most regimes, role differentiation exists
in only a limited way and along only a few key parameters: donors versus recipients, members versus nonmembers, leaders versus laggards,
sources versus sinks. To be sure, these distinctions can be important;
they may reify aspects of hierarchy and domination in world affairs, or
they may exempt certain groups of states from burdens facing others.
Both Montreal and Basel, for example, draw a sharp distinction between
"developed" and "developing" countries.[21] Clearly, not all states are created equal within these institutions.

Nevertheless, as institutions go, this handful of dualisms constitutes
a highly limited, indeed primitive, form of role differentiation. Moreover, available roles are not only sharply limited, they are also defined,
framed, and understood functionally rather than constitutively. By this I
mean that regimes may specify various functional roles for governments,
but also assume their constitutive roles as governments. The rules may
deal with tasks, opportunities, capabilities, and obligations, but view
questions of standing, authority, and legitimacy as fixed and given. As a
result, the state is both the subject and the object of most environmental
regimes. National governments are taken as the authoritative subjects of
regimes. Their bargaining, agreement, and ratification determine whether
a legitimate regime exists, and they assume responsibility, and thus
authority, for compliance. States are also taken as the primary objects
of regimes; governmental compliance is the presumed key to effectiveness
of the regime and governmental implementation is the regime's primary
task as a means to that end.[22] This explains the emphasis on regimes as
mechanisms for the dissemination of knowledge and the building of
"state capacity."

Viewing states as both the subjects and objects of regimes yields an
emphasis on how rules legitimize or delegitimize state behavior. However, it also crowds out the crucial question of how authoritative roles

are constructed and allocated. Instead, the flip side of the presumption of state authority is simply to presume the absence of nonstate authority. Here it is important to draw a distinction between nonstate influence, which many regimes recognize explicitly or implicitly, and nonstate authority, which most do not recognize. Nonstate influence is widely acknowledged; research on environmental regimes has been at the forefront of scholarly inquiry into the role of nongovernmental organizations, advocacy networks, scientists' groups, professional associations, corporations, and other nonstate actors. As this body of research illustrates, there are multiple foundations for the expanding influence of nonstate actors. One important source of influence is the ability to wield technical expertise; another is the capacity to press claims grounded in emerging standards of legitimacy based on performance, such as those based on notions of environmental justice or intergenerational equity.[23] As Chayes and Chayes explain it, "A treaty regime in operation is a hugely complex interactive process that engages not only states and their official representatives but also, increasingly, international organizations and their staffs, nongovernmental organizations, scientists, business managers, academics, and other nonstate actors."[24] Acknowledging this complexity, many regimes make explicit provision for nonstate actors. Montreal and Basel both make extensive use of either ad hoc or formal working groups that incorporate nonstate sources of technical, legal, or administrative expertise, and both regimes make provisions for the participation of nonstate actors in conferences of the parties.

We must be careful, however, not to overstate the nonstate in these institutions. Elite individuals who participate in working groups owe their positions to credentialing procedures that are determined by state members. The most reliable path to influence at a global issue summit or conference of the parties is, unquestionably, to gain access to a state delegation. The activism of NGOs at high-profile events is not matched at the more mundane meetings where much of the business of governance is actually transacted. The nineteenth meeting of the Open-Ended Working Group of the Parties to the Montreal Protocol (Geneva, June 1999) included 107 governments that are parties to the agreement, 3 that are not parties to the agreement, observers from 8 UN entities, and representatives from 37 "other organizations." The latter group consisted overwhelmingly of industry associations and business groups, joined by a handful of environmental organizations and networks.[25] Similarly, the third meeting of the Open-Ended Ad Hoc Committee for the Implementation of the Basel Convention (Geneva, June 1997) was attended by 69 states that are parties to the Basel Convention, 2 nonparty states, 5 UN bodies, and 6 nongovernmental organizations, that is, 5 industry groups and Greenpeace.

More fundamentally, there is a critical difference between the creation of political space for influence and the conferring of authority. Within Basel, Montreal, and most other environmental regimes, nonstate actors have some capacity to affect the institutions of governance through political pressure, the wielding of knowledge, the pressing of moral claims, or various other means. However, they do not themselves "govern" in the sense of acquiring the legitimate authority to establish, operationalize, apply, enforce, interpret, or vitiate the regime's behavioral rules. In other words, the regime approach typically casts nonstate actors as influences on authority rather than as potentially or actually authoritative agents. More generally, sovereignty carries with it the presumption of a complex bundle of rights: equality among states, nonintervention, exclusive territorial jurisdiction, the presumption of state competence, restrictions on binding adjudication without consent, exclusive rights to use violence, and the embeddedness of international law in the free will of states.[26] Gaining ground along one or a few of these dimensions, such as standing or competence, does not in itself elevate the nonstate to an equivalent position of authority.

The problem with this fixed, inflexible construction of authoritative roles becomes apparent when we shift from the comfortable regime terrain of transboundary flows of pollutants or an international commons to the realm of local, cumulative environmental problems. Simply put, the presumption of state authority misreads what is often a very different distribution of authority in a particular local context. Frequently, "the state" lacks the uncontested authority to control local access to nature or its uses, and efforts to exert such control become part of larger struggles for legitimate authority or material power. Historically, the ability to control rules of access to the environment and natural resources—to define who may alter, and to what extent, which specific natural materials, systems, and processes—has been a central component of state authority.[27] Conversely, where that power is lacking, authority is not fully consolidated. Consider the following testimony of a veteran field researcher in the Brazilian Amazon:

Wherever one looks in the Amazonian economy, the state is in retreat: unable to finance tax breaks or build highways without the aid of multilateral banks, unable to include more than one percent of the rural population in official colonization schemes, unable to control land titling or land conflicts, unable to register or tax the greater part of the Amazonian economy, unable to enforce federal law on more than a sporadic basis.[28]

The contrast between this state of affairs and the way in which the Brazilian state is constituted in environmental regimes—as the central delivery mechanism for "sustainable development"—could not be more striking.[29]

At the same time, there are also many circumstances under which nonstate actors have at least some power to establish such controls. The growing rhetoric in established national and international institutions about incorporating stakeholders is partly a concession to the ability of local actors to gum up the works of business as usual, but it is also an acknowledgment of the fact that, on the ground, local societal organizations are often better positioned than the state to mediate the process by which people gain access to nature. So-called joint forest management initiatives in India provide an example. Questions remain about the meaning of participation and the particular responsibilities that devolve to societal organizations under these arrangements.[30] Yet the very existence of such endeavors is a concession by the state to the local reality that village-level organizations are at least as authoritative as the centralized bureaucracies of the administrative state. In Canada's western province of British Columbia, the relative weakness of the state vis-à-vis various societal actors in implementing and administering land-use planning had by the early 1990s produced what Mason describes as a "legitimation deficit" for public policy.[31] In Colombia, independently organized cooperatives for recycling urban waste have flourished while state recycling initiatives founder.[32]

Examples such as these, which involve more fluid definitions of roles and complex distributions of authority, often do not yield international regimes in either a formal or a practical sense. Governments may lack the power even to join formal international agreements on those issues. Or they may view doing so as a potential threat to their tenuous hold on authority. Or their joining may be a hollow gesture, given their lack of authority on the ground. It is difficult to imagine an environmental regime having the capacity-building provisions to overcome these obstacles, which are not merely administrative, technical, or financial, but profoundly political. Under these circumstances, the institutionalization of transnational governance will have to take a form that embeds much more complex relationships than the regime approach of states as governors and nonstates as supplicants. The presumption that states, and only states, are the authoritative agents of governance holds constant, at one extreme end of the spectrum, a key group of variables related to the constitution, distribution, and legitimization of authority. We can conceive of institutions that construct more complex, heterogeneous, or fluid spaces for the exercise of authority, but such institutions would not be regimes as typically designed by diplomats, understood by participants, or interpreted by scholars.

Nature Is Territorialized

Along with defining the agents of authority, a central question for all institutions is the domain in which that authority is legitimately exercised. Authoritative agents become sovereign only when authority is given a place as well as a face. Thus, modern norms of state sovereignty in the international system are more than just a presumption of the state's authority. Sovereignty links that presumption to a spatially contiguous, mappable understanding of authority's domain, namely, territory.

Rooted as they are in intersovereign diplomacy, most international environmental regimes territorialize nature. They answer the question of the domain of authority by embracing the founding fiction of the modern state system: that there is a stark, essential difference between domestic and international spheres. The essence of this difference is governability. That which is to be subjected to authority, be it nature or people, must sit still for governance within the domain of authority's reach. In the case of people, this means a population that is anchored both symbolically (through systems of citizenship and construction of a national identity) and in a more literal, physical sense (through border controls and other limitations on entry and exit).

Of course, nature refuses to sit still for the state in important and obvious ways. Wind and water surge across borders; fish, birds, and animals migrate or wander beyond national territory; vast expanses such as the oceans and atmosphere are inherently extraterritorial. The most common solution to this problem is what might be termed the "Principle 21" approach, first articulated at the 1972 Stockholm Conference and reiterated two decades later at the Rio Earth Summit. According to Principle 21 of the Stockholm Declaration,

States have, in accordance with the Charter of the United Nations and the principles of international law, the sovereign right to exploit their own resources pursuant to their own environmental policies, and the responsibility to ensure that activities within their jurisdiction of control do not cause damage to the environment of other States or of areas beyond the limits of national jurisdiction.[33]

This principle has been interpreted variously as an important new acknowledgment of ecological responsibilities, an entrenched defense of sovereign rights, and a "triumph of aspiration" that remains to be put into practice.[34] However, what is not in dispute is that the principle draws a stark contrast between rights within the state's territorial domain and responsibilities outside of it. By asserting a seamless property right within the state's territory, it affirms an essential difference between the two spheres—a difference grounded not just in the presence of state authority but also in the boundability and governability of the domain itself. Domestic nature is the bounded, fixed realm that can be governed by the state as "natural resources"; international nature consists of those expressions of the natural world that lie outside of or link otherwise separate territories, thereby demanding shared governance. In other words, the regime approach flows from a premise that much of nature can in fact be domesticated as territory, relegating to the realm of international cooperation only those exceptional aspects of nature that most obviously resist territorialization.

If most of nature will in fact sit still for governing, then the essence of global environmental governance becomes the much more limited problem of controlling pollution beyond borders. The mapping of statist authority onto a territorialized nature leads to two broad classes of issues where regimes may comfortably be formed: transboundary problems, which involve the pollution of another state's territory, and commons problems, which involve the pollution of extrasovereign realms such as the atmosphere, the world's oceans, or Antarctica. Basel fits the former category and Montreal the latter. The accumulation of hundreds of international environmental regimes around these kinds of problems is an acknowledgment of the most obvious limits to the territorialization of nature.[35] In its limited, qualified character, however, this acknowledgment is also an affirmation of the more fundamental territorial conception from which most regimes, as sovereign legal instruments, emerge. Most of nature is left to be domesticated as territory.

The territorialization and domestication of nature can be seen in the increasingly skewed pattern of regime formation over time. Since the Stockholm Conference, there has been a shift away from regimes stressing the conservation of domestic natural resources and toward pollution control for shared international commons. Haas and Sundgren examined 132 multilateral regimes signed through 1989, classifying them according to the type of problem they address and the type of rights and responsibilities they affirm.[36] Using the 1972 Stockholm Conference as a watershed, they found several differences between the pre- and post-Stockholm eras. First, the formation of regimes accelerated; more multilateral environmental agreements were concluded in the first fifteen years after Stockholm (sixty-seven) than in the entire pre-Stockholm era (sixty-five). A second notable trend was the increasing willingness of governments to adopt restrictions on internal activities; the proportion of treaties involving internal controls increased from 57 percent pre-Stockholm to 84 percent post-Stockholm.

Yet along with this willingness, the data also reveal a strong post-Stockholm shift toward a sovereignty-affirming construct of pollution beyond borders. Whereas 27 percent of pre-Stockholm accords involved some role for a supraterritorial authority to provide information, research, or enforcement, only 10 percent did so post-Stockholm. Most of the post-Stockholm instances were limited to information; none involved enforcement. The authors also found a clear shift in the focus of treaty making. Treaties dealing with the conservation of domestic natural resources constituted half of the sixty-five environmental treaties signed through 1973, but only a third of the sixty-seven treaties signed in the post-Stockholm period of 1974–1989.[37] In other words, agreements in the more recent time period were far more likely to restrict specific polluting acts spilling outside a nation's territory than to create standards for the conservation of natural systems, cycles, and services lying within a nation's territory. Indeed, virtually all of the growth in the share of treaties requiring internal controls was accounted for by agreements on international commons.

The pattern in these data is clear. As the environmental regime-formation process has become more routine, governments have increasingly reaffirmed state authority and the territorialization of nature by forming regimes primarily around problems of pollution beyond borders. Their regime commitments show a much greater willingness to impose collective rules on domestic acts affecting international nature than on domestic nature. The dominant understanding pervading the regime-building enterprise is that most of nature will, in fact, sit still as territory.

As discussed in chapter 1, one problem with this conception of nature is that it overlooks the ways in which nature will not remain still socially in a tightly connected world system. To reiterate the point, the pollution-beyond-borders paradigm stresses the transnational character of certain physical systems but not the transnational character of economic, social, and political institutions. Governing nature through territorial constructs is problematic, not only because of the physically transnational character of environmental problems, but also because of their socially transnational character.

A second problem is that a territorialized view of nature is excessively reductionist. The emphasis is on a set of decontextualized flows instead of integrated systems and cycles. As a result, issue areas are constructed around transboundary flows that are only a subset of the important linkages in perturbed cycles or disrupted systems. Thus, regimes gravitate toward internationally shared river basins, but not toward watershed management practices. They form around transboundary flows of acid rain, but not around the acceleration and distortion of the global nitrogen and sulfur cycles, of which acid rain is but one manifestation. This piecemeal approach is sometimes justified because it provides less complicated constructions of problems in the tricky realm of interstate bargaining. What makes such a construction simpler, as opposed to merely distorted or incomplete? It is the assumption that the shedded portions of the problem can be, or already have been, domesticated.

Finally, the territorialization of nature may also facilitate its commodification. The stripping of state power is sometimes seen, with some justification, as a key to accelerated plunder of resources and its attendant environmental ills. For example, the effort to negotiate a free-logging agreement under the auspices of the World Trade Organization threatens national legislation in several countries that ban round-log exports so as to limit incentives to clear-cut forests.[38] However, whether sovereignty constitutes a defense of nature or its plunder depends very much on the historical character of the state and the types of societal relations on which state power rests.[39] It is no accident that Principle 21 of the Stockholm Conference, quoted earlier, invokes the right of states to exploit their own resources. The stark delineation between the domestic and international spheres creates a monoculture of alienable state property rights that is consistent with accelerated exploitation and plunder of resources. As Thom Kuehls points out, environmental problems create challenges not simply to sovereign borders but also to the prevailing modalities and instrumentalities of government, creating a crisis not simply of sovereignty but also of "governmentality." As Kuehls suggests,

Our attempts today to establish "opulent and completely happy" states still require not only the cultural, and often physical, extinction of many peoples; they continue to require the extinction of thousands upon thousands of nonhuman life forms as well. The transformations that have been carried out in the name of happy states have carried with them massive environmental degradation.... The problem of providing for the welfare of the population has brought the state directly into contact with its territory; and the state's attempts at creating territories capable of providing for its population within the particular standards of this governmentality have greatly contributed to the ecocrises we now face.[40]

What would it mean to institutionalize an understanding of nature that is not territorial? If territory is a spatial expression of the domain of responsibility and authority, then deterritorialization means reconstructing those domains. One such reconfiguration would be a fuller extension of responsibility beyond the state's territorial domain than that encompassed in the pollution-beyond-borders paradigm. The regime approach typically takes the state's territory as the domain from which emanate those polluting acts for which the state is responsible. By this reasoning, Brazil and China are responsible for sizable contributions to global warming via Amazonian deforestation and domestic use of coal, respectively. A deterritorialized approach to responsibility would instead re-link patterns of global production and consumption that move across national borders and through multiple jurisdictions, taking account of the "shadow ecologies" of the world's leading economies and centers of (over)consumption. Efforts to estimate the extent of the shadow ecologies, or to determine the size of a society's ecological "footprint," challenge territorialized understandings and provide an alternative base for roles and rules.[41] So do cradle-to-grave conceptions of liability, proposals for international taxes to internalize pollution externalities, and various ecolabeling schemes that close informational gaps.[42] The common effect of these approaches is to deterritorialize responsibility by refocusing on the social and ecological links that are obscured by drawing sharp borders between the domestic and international spheres.

Another approach would be to reconstitute not responsibility but authority. Studies of sustainable resource management invariably point to the importance of complex, nested property rights systems that separate, differentiate, or otherwise complicate rights of ownership, access, and use.[43] Such schemes stand in marked contrast to the seamless, monolithic property rights attached to the state in most international regimes. As discussed in the case study chapters, the reconstitution of authority need not be limited to simple devolution or aggregation, that is, to changes that retain territorial constructs while shifting the scale of territory. The emergence of hybrid systems of watershed governance, for example, presents a more complex, diversified approach to governing access to nature (see chapters 8 and 9).

Legitimacy Demands That Knowledge Be Stabilized

Environmental regimes are often described as institutional responses to inherently uncertain threats and problems. As Levy et al. describe it, "The only reliable knowledge is that current understandings of the problem will be obsolete in ten or twenty years."[44] It is for this reason that so many environmentalists endorse the so-called precautionary principle: the idea that environmental protection is a form of insurance against uncertain but potentially disastrous consequences, about which we will be certain only when it is too late to stop them if they turn out to be real. There are, however, important ways in which environmental regimes embrace and promote, not a precautionary approach, but a position that can be termed knowledge stabilization.[45] To create an environmental regime is to settle on an authoritative statement of a problem, to begin to establish a body of official knowledge, to adopt an optimistic view toward the reducibility of uncertainty, and to embrace universal, scientific knowledge as the most important way of knowing about environmental problems, their effects, and their potential solutions.

This relatively optimistic, reductionist stance toward environmental problems permeates most environmental regimes. This is because the legitimacy of those regimes derives from their ability to pose as functional-rational institutions. By this I mean that regimes are typically justified and legitimized as a rational means to a functional end, as a way to solve a specified problem by linking cause-and-effect analyses of that problem to an optimized array of solutions. These aspirations to functional-rational legitimacy do not mean, of course, that regimes are depoliticized, technical institutions, or that the formation and development of regimes are model functional-rational processes. Knowledge is not the only currency of power or shaper of purpose within regimes. They remain thoroughly political institutions in which interests are at stake, including interests that have little to do with a regime's nominal function of environmental protection. Moreover, even the more narrowly technical dimensions of regimes are themselves an entry point for politics, given the socially constructed means by which knowledge acquires authoritative standing.[46]

The point is not that regimes are not permeated with politics (they are), but rather that a functional-rational standard of legitimacy is an important element—sometimes the definitive element—within those political struggles. This in turn favors a particular attitude toward science, knowledge, and uncertainty, without which it becomes impossible to legitimize the regime as the rational means to a functional end.

One way to see knowledge stabilization at work is to contrast the different stages of regime formation. As Oran Young has pointed out, the formation of a regime typically involves distinct stages of agenda formation, negotiation, and operationalization.[47] The politics of agenda formation are fluid; this stage typically involves intensive struggles over knowledge that are marked by competing claims about the scope, significance, and causality of problems. The negotiating stage, in contrast, is marked by the construction of an operational consensus that underpins the resulting regime. As Young describes it,

Unlike bargaining in most legislative settings ... the institutional bargaining characteristic of the negotiation stage of regime formation aims at building consensus among as many participants as possible rather than putting together winning coalitions. Put another way, the preferred coalition among those negotiating the terms of a constitutive contract is the coalition of the whole.[48]

Making the transition from pitched knowledge struggle to negotiated operational consensus does not mean that a regime will ever reach full closure on knowledge. Uncertainty may remain pervasive, and knowledge hegemony is rarely so fully consolidated as to obviate all challenges. The means and ends of a regime may be moved in dramatically new directions as newly authoritative "truths" emerge, as seen in the Basel Convention's abrupt swing from prior informed consent to an outright ban on the waste trade. Nevertheless, important aspects of closure do occur. A dominant construction of a problem becomes embedded; an officially sanctioned body of universal, technical knowledge begins to emerge; the boundary between official truths and acknowledged uncertainties is defined; a quest to reduce uncertainty, in particular ways and specific directions, crystallizes. An implicit commitment is made to use the implements of science as key weapons in the struggle to shape the regime from inside. In other words, much more than just a set of rules is being institutionalized; so too are the currencies of knowledge as power in the continuing struggle to shape those rules and the standards of legitimacy against which those rules and struggles will be judged.[49]

The idea that regimes stabilize knowledge contrasts with the attention much of the literature on environmental regimes gives to the flexibility of knowledge. Many scholars have pointed to what Levy et al. call "open-ended knowledge creation" as a key to regime effectiveness, in part because static, fixed rules can be quickly overtaken by new information in the highly uncertain terrain of environmental science.[50] My point is not to dispute the presence of flexibility in the translation of substantive knowledge into governance procedures but rather to emphasize that a regime is a particular type of institution in which such flexibility of knowledge has inherent limits. As Sheila Jasanoff suggests,

Contingency ... is only half the story.... Equally important is the conclusion that, in spite of all indeterminacy and uncertainty, knowledge and social order are not perceived by human societies to be fluid at all points. Both can be made to hold still through institutions, material technologies, and shared norms and practices. The stabilizations brought about by international technical standards and transnational epistemic communities are particularly significant for environmental regimes.[51]

The ultimate source of those limits, through which regimes make important aspects of knowledge "hold still" institutionally, is the functional-rational legitimization process ingrained in the normative structure of most, if not all, international environmental regimes.

Both Montreal and Basel reflect these aspects of the stabilization of knowledge. First, both regimes emerged from struggles over knowledge that yielded to an authoritative statement of a problem, anchoring the regime's purpose in specific and easily comprehensible functional terms. The ozone regime is often described in popular accounts as a series of reactions to frequent, jarring scientific surprises about the rate, mechanics, and geographic scope of depletion of the ozone layer. Karen Litfin has traced the regime's development, however, as the institutionalization of a dominant framing of the problem (chemical alteration of the atmosphere by humans) and, within that frame, a dominant causal mechanism (chlorine loading). She shows that these elements of the dominant frame became so deeply entrenched that control of chlorine loading evolved from being one means to achieving the goal of protecting the ozone layer to become an end in itself.[52] Basel, too, produced a dominant frame that stressed a master function: the need to control international flows of hazardous waste from North to South. This was only one among many competing frames prior to the original Basel Convention of 1989, yet it emerged as the dominant problem and solution by the Basel ban in 1994. Crowded out as a result of this master function were other constructions of the problem and its solution. Many environmentalists preferred a more holistic construct, with the toxification of modern commerce as the problem and source reduction; cradle-to-grave controls; and bans on the manufacture, use, and trade of toxic substances as the solutions. Some governments and many business interests also preferred a different construct: a statement of the problem that emphasized the occasional abuse of a financially important, economically efficient, and ecologically sound international practice, with a less intrusive regime based on information flows and national controls as the solution.

A second way that these regimes stabilize knowledge is by generating an authorized body of facts. This process is part of the emergence of a dominant frame for a problem. Authorized facts allow definitive statements of a problem, which in turn steer the direction of inquiry and generate demand for facts in order to operationalize the regime. The ozone regime, for example, has evolved a fairly sophisticated system of national reporting, which includes holding states publicly accountable for their failure to meet reporting requirements. There is no mechanism for independently scrutinizing the data thus reported, however, or for adjusting them in the face of the large illicit trade in ozone-depleting chemicals. Instead, the unscrutinized aggregation of nationally reported figures creates its own reality, becoming the authoritative benchmark for measuring the scope of the problem and the regime's effectiveness.[53]

Greenpeace played an important knowledge-stabilizing role in the waste-trade regime. Some critics of the Basel regime have stressed the "moralizing" tone of Greenpeace's activism as its main impact on the Basel Convention and the subsequent Basel ban.[54] However, an important component of that organization's influence was its compilation of a detailed and extensive record of waste shipments that came to be the frame of reference for much of the discussion. As a result, Greenpeace built up what was perceived as "an expertise unmatched by most states, NGOs, and possibly UNEP."[55] Although Greenpeace lacked the standing to inject these "facts" into discussions closed to NGOs, it was able to forge an alliance with several African states through which its knowledge base formed a crucial platform for interstate bargaining. Greenpeace research also "proved" that most waste exports to developing countries took place under the guise of recycling. Although Greenpeace's facts have always been disputed by its opponents, they became insinuated into the fabric of the regime as a way to legitimize the regime's existence and rules.

A third dimension of the knowledge-stabilization process involves the position toward uncertainty and its reduction. Authorizations of factual knowledge can produce new controversies, such as the pressure Greenpeace generated to revisit Basel's recycling loophole when it "proved" that the loophole was being abused. However, authorization of knowledge also closes off certain channels of dispute because it shifts emphasis away from ends and toward means. It also positions a regime to take an optimistic attitude toward the reduction of uncertainty, affording some promise of progress and eventual closure in our understanding of the problem and its effects. The rhetorical stance may be precautionary, and fear of the unknown may be a powerful stimulus to action. Nevertheless, the underlying norm is one of attacking and reducing uncertainty through the steady, incremental production of universally applicable knowledge.

A fourth aspect of knowledge stabilization at work in both Montreal and Basel is the elevation of universalist, rationalist discourse. In the process of constructing a problem, authorizing knowledge, and reducing uncertainty, universalized scientific ways of knowing dominate the discussion, analysis, and framing of a problem. Despite the fact that both of Basel's key concepts—"hazard" and "waste"—are ambiguous social constructs, the legitimization of the political decision to treat a particular substance as hazardous waste turns on laboratory tests, epidemiological inference, and other universal validating techniques of modern science.[56] Similarly, in the ozone case, epidemiological models of skin cancers from ultraviolet radiation become the metric for assessing the threat posed by damage to the ozone layer.

If formation of a regime is viewed as a knowledge-stabilization process, it is no surprise that environmental regimes are formed less frequently around the local, cumulative dimensions of global environmental degradation. It is often difficult or impossible to fit these problems into a stabilized framework of knowledge, for several reasons. For many local, cumulative environmental problems, mechanisms for the control of nature are intimately entwined with mechanisms for the control of people; reconfiguring access to soils, forests, watersheds, or wetlands means tampering, in a direct and immediate way, with important aspects of livelihoods, community, and identity for people who live close to nature. Under these circumstances, it is difficult at best to work radically divergent political, economic, and ecological "functions" into an authoritative statement of the problem that specifies a dominant function for the regime. To be sure, this difficulty can appear even in cases of successful formation of a regime around transboundary pollution or global commons issues; the ozone regime nearly failed because of the suspicion that its hidden function was to create competitive advantages for certain firms and nations. However, the particularly tight connection between control of nature and control of people in local, cumulative environmental problems makes the task of constructing an authoritative function substantially more difficult.

Constructing a body of authorized knowledge and adopting an optimistic view toward the reduction of uncertainty are also problematic in the context of many local, cumulative environmental problems. Data on these problems tend to be spotty, inconsistent, discontinuous, and noncomparable. For example, despite three decades of wrangling about threats to the world's forests, globally aggregated, comparable data on local deforestation rates do not exist. As with data, so with causal models. Universal models of cause-and-effect relations or key ecosystem processes are often beyond the current state of the art of environmental science, given the tremendous heterogeneity of local ecosystems, the impossibility of precisely specifying their boundaries, the complexity of feedback linkages, and the often nonlinear character of change.

Finally, a universalist, scientific stance toward knowing is often jarringly different from the diverse, contingent, culturally bound forms of knowledge that surround local environmental problems. This may make it harder to give universal, rational science currency within the regime. Even when the authority of science can be established, it may undermine the capacity of states to administer and implement a regime.

As discussed in chapter 6, the controversies surrounding the impact of dams and water diversion schemes on the world's rivers provide one example of accumulating environmental effects that defy stabilization of knowledge. At one critical juncture in the struggle between pro- and anti-dam forces, the World Bank published a working paper on the most important "environmental" impacts of river development projects. The analysis included a hodge-podge categorization of effects ranging from sedimentation, downstream hydrology, and water quality to involuntary resettlement and impacts on regional economic integration.[57] The effect is similar to the wry observations of the Argentine writer Jorge Luis Borges about an animal classification scheme allegedly found in an unnamed "Chinese encyclopedia," which classifies animals as (a) belonging to the emperor, (b) embalmed, (c) tame, (d) sucking pigs, (e) sirens, (f) fabulous, (g) stray dogs, (h) included in the present classification, (i) innumerable, (k) drawn with a fine camel hair brush, (l) et cetera, (m) having just broken the water pitcher, (n) that from a long way off look like flies. The conceptualization may make perfect sense to the categorizer, but fails to provide the requisite foundation for a broadly based closure on knowledge.[58] Michel Foucault cited this example in asserting the contingent character of all knowledge systems and, as a result, their effect of limiting imagination. However, the politically significant point is that some constructs are more obviously contingent than others. The stabilized knowledge that could mask this contingent character is particularly hard to come by in this and many other cases of local, cumulative effects on complex ecosystems.

What happens when knowledge cannot be stabilized sufficiently to institutionalize an international regime? Can we conceive of institutions in which a dominant functional frame for a problem is lacking? In which a clearly defined and delimited body of official knowledge does not materialize? In which more humble, cautionary attitudes toward uncertainty are embraced? In which pluralistic ways of knowing are fostered and incorporated? In the literature on regimes, such cases are generally assumed to lie beyond the realm of institution building. Much attention has been given to how various definitions of a problem compete and how particular constructions of both problem and solution attain consensus or hegemony in international bargaining.[59] Nevertheless, in the end, states are assumed to be rational problem solvers, or at least to adopt that position in the way that regimes are legitimized. If so, one would not expect serious efforts of collective governance to become institutionalized unless a politically sufficient group came to perceive a collective problem and accepted a shared set of core facts and a plausible path to resolving the problem. Little or no attention has been given to patterns of institutionalization around problems for which these minimal functional-rational conditions of regimes cannot be attained.

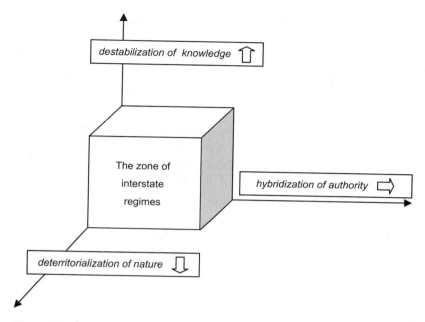

Figure 2.1
Interstate regimes as a subset of institutional forms.

Beyond Regimes: Toward a Social Theory of Institution Building

Figure 2.1 provides a visual sketch of the argument thus far. The figure supposes, merely for the sake of illustration, that the metanormative stance of a particular institution could be understood as a set of three continuous variables. Thus, at one end of the territoriality continuum would be a conception of nature as part of and bounded by state territory; as one moves away from the origin, one would find increasingly fluid and deterritorialized constructions of both nature and sovereignty. Similarly, authority relations at the origin consist of strong presumptions of sole state authority; moving outward, one finds increasingly weaker presumptions about the privileged standing of states. Knowledge orientations near the origin consist of stabilized, legitimized knowledge grounded in universalist modern science; moving outward, there are more heterogeneous forms of knowledge and ways of knowing, in the direction of Paul Feyerabend's arguments that science is a particularistic epistemology that should enjoy no specially privileged standing in a truly free society.[60]

If one were to plot various institutional forms of global environmental governance within this three-dimensional space, the cube-shaped zone in the center of figure 2.1 would be the domain of international regimes. This does not mean that all environmental regimes would plot precisely at the origin. Basel may incorporate functional-rational knowledge stabilization less overtly and extensively than Montreal; the international regime on desertification may allow a bit more semiauthoritative space for NGOs through its accreditation and participation procedures than, say, the International Tropical Timber Agreement. However, compared with the full array of institutional configurations that we can imagine along these three dimensions, most formally codified international environmental regimes cluster near the origin. Moving away from the origin, authority relations become hybridized, nature becomes deterritorialized, knowledge becomes destabilized, and regimelike institutional arrangements become increasingly problematic.

Obviously, there is no particular reason to think of these three institutional properties as continuous variables. Nor should we think of each of them as playing out along a one-dimensional spectrum. Alternative ways of knowing that are grounded in religious absolutism and postmodern relativism may differ from each other as much as they do from high-modern science. More generally, it may be a mistake to think of these as coherent variables. The orientation toward knowledge actually involves a cluster of features, including the properties of how a problem is constructed, the attitude toward uncertainty, and the type of standards that generate legitimacy. The point of figure 2.1 is merely to suggest that these institutional properties are not constants; they need not be limited to the narrow range of configurations they tend to display within international environmental regimes.

Two obvious questions emerge from figure 2.1. First, why do interstate environmental negotiations, when they succeed, consistently produce institutions with properties that cause them to cluster near the origin of these metanormative axes? Second, what possible institutional arrangements lie beyond this regime space of statist authority, nature as territory, and stabilized knowledge?

The regime branch of international relations theory provides no detailed answers to these questions. Because regimes are seen as the intentional result of intergovernmental negotiations, their "form" consists of whatever bargains governments are willing and able to strike. In this view, the cause of the characteristic, recurring attitude toward territory, authority, or knowledge can only be inferred, in terms of task effectiveness or political attractiveness. Yet the checkered performance of so many regimes should leave us skeptical of claims about this form's functional efficiency. The fact that regime formation typically involves battles against entrenched interests would seem to suggest that political expediency or gain is not the only force at work. A choice-based, bargaining explanation seems inadequate.

Nor has mainstream international relations theory addressed the second question of what institutional forms might lie beyond the cubic regime space depicted in figure 2.1. One reason for this is the triumph of a particularly narrow conception of regimes in much of the literature on international cooperation. The idea that regimes were important institutional features of world politics emerged in the 1970s as part of a growing recognition of interdependence and an increasing dissatisfaction with simplistic notions of "anarchy" as a model or metaphor for interstate relations. By emphasizing the institutionalization of rules, the regime concept offered a theoretical explanation for the growth and endurance of patterned, convergent behavior across a wide range of issues, from security matters to commerce to environmental affairs. The regime concept explained this pattern in terms of the convergence of actors' expectations around norms. A popular early definition offered by Stephen Krasner described regimes as "sets of implicit or explicit principles, norms, rules and decision-making procedures around which actors' expectations converge in a given area of international relations."[61] This and other early definitions remained noncommittal on the specificity of rules, the formality of their expression, and the intentionality of their creation.[62] An early collection of essays appearing as a special edition of the theoretically influential journal, *International Organization*, included a wide variety of institutional forms among its case studies. There were formal multilateral accords such as balance-of-payments financing or the General Agreement on Tariffs and Trade, but also much more diffuse, informal rule sets such as those surrounding global food practices, monetary relations after the collapse of the Bretton Woods regime, the Concert of Europe, or colonialism in the period between the partitioning of Africa and World War I.[63]

Thus, early scholars of regimes debated whether it was more useful to view the process of normative convergence as pervasive in international life or to conceive of regimes as a narrower set of explicit, intentional exercises in rule making. The broader conception saw a "regime" in any emergent, patterned behavior in international relations that seemed to express shared norms, whereas the narrower conception saw regimes only when states actively and consciously directed their behavior toward a collective purpose.[64] According to the broader understanding, regimes could be formally codified or informally understood. They could be either state based or involve a diverse array of actors. And they might or might not be conducive to interstate cooperation.

In contrast, the narrow conception rejected this idea of regimes as the revealed normative fabric of the world system. It stressed instead the codified character of regimes (although it recognized that codification per se was not what caused regimes to shape state behavior), the state-based character of regimes (although it allowed for the influence of non-state actors in regime formation and performance), and the intentionality of states in creating regimes (although it recognized the contentious character of distributional issues and the highly political nature of bargaining).

Over time, the narrower conception of regimes prevailed. Most scholars using the concept were doing so to study state cooperation under anarchy. This meant observing not only the independent influence of institutions on state behavior, but also the intentions of states toward those institutions. The narrower conception of regimes, as rules of interstate cooperation, was more useful for this agenda because it kept the focus on the willingness of states to cooperate under various conditions and on a range of different issues. Later, as a body of theory and evidence about regime origins and changes came into being, scholarly interest began to shift from the causes of regimes to their consequences (that is, from regimes as dependent variables to regimes as independent variables). This further deepened the commitment to the narrower conception because it is easier (although certainly not easy) to trace the effects of codified, state-based institutions operating on the basis of an authoritative body of knowledge.

Working with this narrower conception, scholars studying environmental regimes have focused on a smaller question—"Which features of regimes matter?"—and largely overlooked a larger one—"Why regimes as opposed to some other institutional form?" The primary focus has become the search for "effective" regimes, within a narrowly fixed range of institutional forms that treat territoriality, authority, and knowledge in comfortably recognizable ways. A handful of high-profile international commons or transboundary pollution problems dominate the literature, with much of the intellectual effort dedicated to teasing out the implications of subtle, microlevel differences in design across these regimes, such as the specific character of their performance monitoring systems or the way they adjust standards to incorporate new scientific knowledge. In contrast, almost no sustained intellectual effort has been mounted to contrast these regimes and their shared underlying properties with other institutional forms that might be developed, nurtured, or at least imagined. Regime scholars have asked whether environmental regimes inscribe new sovereign rights and responsibilities, but the fixed territorialization of nature that frames the specification of those rights and responsibilities has gone largely unexplored. Much attention has been paid to the central problem of boosting state capacity to implement, enforce, and administer regime commitments, but the underlying presumption of state authority or its crucial corollary of nonstate nonauthority is rarely subjected to critical examination. Many scholars have explored the conflicts over knowledge that typically accompany regime formation, but few have asked whether ways of knowing that differ from the universal, functional, rational modes of modern science can be incorporated into institutions of global environmental governance, or whether institutionalization can proceed in the absence of a sturdy (or at least patchable) foundation of stabilized, legitimized knowledge.

Thus, although scholarship on environmental regimes reveals much about the possibilities and limits of a particular institutional form, it provides little guidance for a wide range of problems where regimes have failed to thrive. Moreover, the narrowness of this research agenda surely must contribute to the lack of imagination we see in global environmental governance. Bargaining to build a standard interstate regime is the now-routine response when new problems find their way onto the international agenda, and only problems fitting the regime form remain consistently on that agenda.

International Regimes as Myth and Ceremony

Although regime scholarship has converged on a narrow conception of formal, voluntary, negotiated institutions, scholars taking a more sociological approach to the world system have kept alive the effort to understand the metanormative fabric in which institutions such as regimes are embedded. For these scholars, Montreal, Basel, and other regimes (environmental or otherwise) reflect not only the results of bargaining among sovereign states but also the more fundamental normative structure of the world system in which that bargaining occurs. This work interprets the international system as a domain with a deep, dense, and increasingly global normative structure. Formal institutions in this domain, such as intergovernmental organizations, codified regimes, or even the sovereign state system itself, are not the creators of that underlying structure as much as they are the reflections of it.

The point of departure for capturing the metanormative fabric of the international system is a fundamentally different understanding of the relationship between norms and the building of formal structures. In a landmark 1977 article, sociologists John Meyer and Brian Rowan suggested that in modern society, formal structures such as large organizations derive their form, not from functional efficiency, but rather from external sources of legitimization.[65] In contrast to then-prevailing theories of modern organization, which assumed the functional superiority of modern, rational, bureaucratic organizational forms, the authors suggested that an organization's formal structure originated from myths embedded in the institutional environment. Such myths were said to have two key properties:

First, they are rationalized and impersonal prescriptions that identify various social purposes as technical ones and specify in a rulelike way the appropriate means to pursue these technical purposes rationally. Second, they are highly institutionalized and thus in some measure beyond the discretion of any individual participant or organization. They must, therefore, be taken for granted as legitimate, apart from evaluations of their impact on work outcomes.[66]

This perspective rejects the starting assumption of most political scientists: that formal structures are built through the intentional application of power to serve particular interests. Instead, the argument here is that choices defining rules and roles in formal aspects of social organization do not occur in a vacuum, but in a context of previously legitimized norms about those choices. For Meyer and Rowan, this process of external legitimization proves to be a self-propagating process in the growth and spread of formal organizations:

The growth of rationalized institutional structures in society makes formal organizations more common and more elaborate. Such institutions are myths which make formal organizations both easier to create and more necessary. After all, the building blocks for organizations come to be littered around the societal landscape; it takes only a little entrepreneurial energy to assemble them into a structure. And because these building blocks are considered proper, adequate, rational, and necessary, organizations must incorporate them to avoid illegitimacy.[67]

Although Meyer and Rowan were seeking to explain the nature of large bureaucratic organizations in the specific context of postindustrial Western society, their interpretation can readily be adapted to the formal structures of a global-scale world system, including intergovernmental organizations, the governing mechanisms that spring up around codified international agreements, organized nongovernmental networks, or the institutions and practices of the sovereign state itself.[68] For example, Meyer and colleagues have interpreted systems of mass public education—the primary state mechanism for the production and reproduction of national culture and citizenry—not simply as a product of national needs and political processes, but rather as emanating from "great and standardized worldwide visions of social and educational progress."[69] Specific aspects of the formal structure of the state (in this case, the educational system and its curriculum) derive from a normative context that is increasingly global in scope. In support of this interpretation they provide evidence of substantial global homogeneity in curricular outlines and the allocation of classroom time. The point is not to deny aspects of local variance but to identify powerful global forces of institutional convergence.

The significance of the world sociological perspective is not simply that it connects institutional development to legitimization by a preexisting set of embedded norms but also that it says something specific about the content of those norms. As Martha Finnemore points out, sociologists working in this tradition "do more than simply argue that social structure matters; they tell us what the social structure *is*."[70] Essentially, their model is based on the global expansion of aspects of Western culture, with particular attention to values of rationalism, progress-oriented developmentalism, and individualism. These underlying norms legitimize formal structures that incorporate "rational" instrumentalities such as bureaucracy and markets.[71]

Meyer and colleagues have also applied this interpretation specifically to the emergence of formal international structures around environmental problems, or what they refer to as "the structuring of a world environmental regime" (acknowledging that their use of the term *regime* is far broader than the conventional usage by international relations scholars). They argue that the post–World War II proliferation of interstate accords, intergovernmental organizations, and nongovernmental associations in the environmental sphere cannot be explained in purely functional, problem-solving terms; earlier periods of great stress on the planet's natural systems, such as the vast expansion of world cropland during the colonial era, did not yield similar institutional developments. Rather, the key to the growth of formal structures in the international environmental domain has been the prior globalization of norms and institutions facilitating such development. Specifically, they point to two key enabling factors, rooted in universalist science and Weberian bureaucracy: "The long-term expansion of rationalized and authoritative scientific interpretation, which structures perceptions of common environmental problems, and the rise of world associational arenas—principally the United Nations (UN) system—with agendas open to broad concerns such as the environment."[72] "Highly organized and interested action by nation states," such as the establishment of environmental bureaucracies or the codification of environmental agreements, came only later.[73]

Applying this perspective specifically to international environmental regimes, the relevant formal structure would consist of the codified interstate agreements lying at the heart of most environmental regimes and the governance apparatus springing up around those agreements (secretariats, advisory bodies, technical commissions, dispute-resolution panels, conferences of the parties, and the like). Rather than viewing this assembled apparatus of governance as a result of free-standing bargaining among states, a sociology of international institutions urges us to interpret the regime's stance, character, and tools as the result of a logically prior normative structure of the world system, grounded in science, bureaucracy, and the state as servants of progress. Seen in this light, it is no surprise that the Westphalian international order has produced regimes embracing and fostering territorial constructions of problems, statist authority relations, and technical-rational standards of knowledge. The regimes are themselves the product of an environment that validates these positions. The understandings of territory and authority, grounded as they are in the sovereign administrative state, can be traced to the globalization of a bureaucratic-administrative logic in which territorialized state authority is the modern conduit of bureaucracy. Similarly, the quest for an authoritative body of knowledge and the reduction of uncertainty through expansion of knowledge is rooted in an underlying norm of scientific rationalism and its particular notions of progress.

Institution Building as Normative Struggle

Thus, the world sociological perspective is consistent with the predominant pattern of institutional development in global environmental governance. The stance of regimes toward territory, authority, and knowledge derives from underlying, and increasingly global, norms of progress as well as particular understandings of universal science, the state, and interstate cooperation as the means to those ends. This perspective also offers an explanation for a second pattern suggested previously: the strong formal institution building around international commons and transboundary environmental problems versus the weak formal institution building around local, cumulative problems. Seen in this light, formation of a regime is less likely when the problems and politics at hand cannot be reconciled with underlying norms and favored forms of rationalism, individualism, and progress, or the scientific and bureaucratic means to those ends. The regime approach has had little success in institutionalizing the global governance of local, cumulative environmental damage because the struggles over authority, the deterritorial character of nature, and the multiple ways of knowing that surround such environmental problems are a poor foundation for building scientifically rational, territorially conceived, and bureaucratically administered regimes.

This raises a parallel question: What happens, institutionally, in those areas where the normative underpinnings needed to build regimes are weak or absent? Here the world sociological model is less instructive. Where a universalized, rationalist frame has taken hold, institutions bearing those characteristics (such as regimes) are assumed to flourish. Where such a frame has not taken hold, the model predicts little world-scale institutional development or none.[74] Yet this view seems overly deterministic. It suggests that there are no tensions to be reconciled among the various components of this globalized Western culture of progress, science, the bureaucratic-administrative state, and the free individual. Can statist presumptions of authority always be reconciled with scientific mechanisms of legitimization? What happens when they clash? What template of external legitimization guides institutional development when bureaucratic administration and free markets come into conflict as mechanisms of collective choice? As Finnemore suggests, "If the world culture they specify is so powerful and congruent, the institutionalists have no grounds for explaining value conflicts or normative contestation—in other words, politics."[75] It is one thing to suggest that broadly prevailing norms shape the perceived legitimacy of prevailing institutional forms, but quite another to assume that such norms are never subject to internal tensions or contradictions. It is exactly those tensions that may create the space for the political struggles that give birth to alternative institutional forms.[76] Under such circumstances, statist-administrative or scientifically rationalist institutions may be normatively privileged, but they are not inevitable.

Moreover, continuing changes in the international system may be creating more space for dispute around those clashing norms. Historically, foreign affairs has been among the least participatory spheres of public policy, even in democratic societies. Thus, the key insight of the sociological perspective—that socialization processes of norm inculcation produce the external legitimization of institutions—presumably operates not at the level of society as a whole but rather among a narrower, internationally focused elite. However, the analogy between bureaucratic organizations in modern society and global governance institutions in the international system breaks down if, in the latter sphere, formal structures are decidedly not *everyone's* myth and ceremony. A changing international system that has created space for a somewhat broader array of voices may be introducing a genuinely antisocial, or at least non-socialized, element into the process by which formal structures are legitimized. For some of these increasingly vocal stakeholders, the underlying norms may not be binding, taken for granted, or even suggestive; they may well be seen instead as irrelevant, misguided, dissonant, or nakedly ideological. Such actors may be weak in a material sense of power, but they are not necessarily weak in their capacity to challenge the legitimization process.[77] Moreover, to the extent that they rely upon the manipulation of symbols, communicative strategies, and related myth-puncturing tactics, their ability to challenge may be enhanced by the information and communications revolution and the emergence of at least semidemocratic spaces on both the national and global levels.[78]

In other words, rather than a deterministic process of norm reproduction, we need to see institution building as a site of struggle with no predetermined outcome. If the normative order of international relations is powerful without being fully determinate—authoritative but not hegemonic—then specific struggles to craft the rules, norms, and institutions of global environmental governance could yield institutional forms other than the statist, territorialized, functional-rational institutional form. Studying these struggles may shed light on whether a richer array of institutional forms that we can imagine can exist in practice. At the very least, studying resistance to closure on the form of a regime should shed light on the relative power of the theorized normative fabric of the world system, and of the possibilities and constraints of working within it. Finally, studying struggles that inhibit closure on a regime while producing alternative institutional forms may provide insight into the relative merits or drawbacks of such alternatives—their ecological effectiveness, democratic accountability, or socioeconomic fairness.

The Search for Alternative Institutional Forms

In other words, the best place to find alternative forms of global environmental governance is in those areas where normative contestation is well established. Following the modified world sociological approach sketched here, it stands to reason that alternative forms are most likely to emerge, not because they are better suited to a task in some functional sense, but in the wake of a normative struggle that inhibits closure on the form of a regime and makes different institutional designs possible.

What would be the properties of a domain conducive to inhibiting closure on a regime form, and thus to the emergence and development of something different? Although this conceptualization breaks the link between institutional form and an internal dynamic of functional efficiency, it nevertheless remains the case that some domains are likely to be more conducive than others. First, rather than focusing on accords among state actors whose roles as the agents of governance are largely unquestioned, good prospects would be those cases in which the authority of states to govern is highly contested, in which role definitions are more complex than simply state or nonstate, and in which nonstate actors have some capacity to take on more authoritative roles than simply pushing states to the bargaining table or pressing for particular state actions. Second, rather than focusing on an international commons or transborder flows of pollutants—problems that tend to fit the standard, territorial distinction between the international and domestic spheres—good candidates would involve environmental problems in which the local environmental governance of a state's own space, terrain, or resources is the central international issue, thereby making the construction of nature as territory problematic. Third, rather than focusing on a case where a knowledge-stabilized construction of a problem has gained hegemonic or consensual status, fertile ground would more likely be found in cases that involve multiple, shifting, and ambiguous ecological goals, so that actors can readily struggle for, or smuggle in, competing constructions of the issue and alternative ways of knowing. As suggested in chapter 1 and developed more fully in the chapters that follow, the political dynamics surrounding water make it just such a case and thus a promising place to look for the emergence of alternative institutional forms of transnational, international, or even global-scale institution building.

The preceding discussion yields a set of specific propositions to be explored in both the global-scale and country-level chapters that follow. First, water, watersheds, and rivers—as sources of local livelihood and culture, as critical global ecosystems, and as transnational market commodities—generate socioecological controversies that are difficult to contain in a metanormative box of statist authority, stabilized knowledge, and territorialized nature. As such, they are likely to impose severe limits on conventional regimelike institution building. This proposition is explored by examining the patterns of institution building around the central tools of interstate regimes: law (chapter 4) and science (chapter 5).

Second, to the extent that conventional institution building cannot bound, contain, and regularize these controversies, we are likely to see institution building that moves outside the state-knowledge-territory box. This proposition is explored by examining the controversies surrounding large dams (chapter 6) and water marketization (chapter 7).

Third, the result of these processes of conventional and unconventional institution building is a proliferation of global protonorms for governing water that are imbued with very different metanormative understandings of territory, authority, and knowledge. These frameworks provide often incongruous and sometimes contradictory approaches to governing water. This suggests that in complex systems such as a country—which consists of multiple sites at which rules may be negotiated and norms may become embedded—the terrain of water-related institutionalization is likely to be highly uneven, much as it is in international political space. This proposition is explored in the country-level cases, which examine how newly built systems of water law and policy in Brazil and South Africa have situated themselves within the pushing and pulling of different normative forces. The cases unpack the state by focusing on multiple nodes of institution building (including administrative structures, legal systems, project enterprises, policy networks, and social movements). As such, they replace the regime literature's metaphor of states as "leaders" and "laggards" in implementing "international" norms with the metaphor of an uneven landscape of multiple normative orientations and institutional developments.

Who wins the normative struggles that define this landscape? The answer will depend, as always, on power, tactics, strategy, and compelling visions of the future. The point is less to predict patterns of institutional development by guessing at the winners than to identify spaces where alternative institutional forms may be found, studied, understood, and nurtured.

3

Pushing Rivers Around: The Cumulative Toll on the World's Watersheds and Freshwater Ecosystems

A river is more than an amenity, it is a treasure.
—Justice Oliver Wendell Holmes, in *New Jersey v. New York* [283 U.S.336 (1931)]

Rivers as the Planet's Places

Freshwater ecosystems—lakes, rivers, wetlands, floodplains, estuaries, and deltas—provide human societies with several critical natural resource goods and ecosystem-based services. The goods include drinking and irrigation water, fish, hydroelectricity, and genetic resources; services include buffering of the timing and volume of water flow, dilution and removal of wastes, cycling of nutrients and movement of sediments, maintenance of biological diversity, and provision of aquatic habitat.[1] Freshwater systems also provide a few notable "bads," or at least great social challenges, such as floods and the harboring of disease-bearing pests (primarily in wetlands).

Ecologically, rivers are central constituents of freshwater ecosystems. Rivers are a critical means of cycling water and nutrients. They catalyze dynamic interactions between aquatic and terrestrial ecosystems through processes of erosion, channeling, flooding, sediment transport, and deposition. Rivers also provide a home for a diverse array of aquatic and terrestrial species and supply crucial services to a broader array of species living in associated areas, such as lakes, wetlands, and floodplains.[2]

The world's rivers are also important anchors of culture and community. Historically, rivers have been critical arteries of transportation, fostering widespread networks of trade and cultural interaction.

Researchers in the Amazon Basin have determined that indigenous peoples used the waterways to carry out trading relations on the scale of hundreds and even thousands of kilometers, well before the arrival of the first Europeans.[3] The centrality of rivers such as the Nile, Mississippi, Ganges, Danube, Zambesi, and Yangtze to community life is embedded in the history and folklore of their respective regions. Mathato Khit'sane, an activist with the Highlands Church Action Group of Lesotho, summarizes the centrality of a river to Besotho life as follows:

A river plays a very big role in our culture. It has a lot to do. If somebody passes away or maybe was killed by the lightning, usually he would be buried next to the river. It is a place where our traditional doctors go to get qualified. Some people say they talk with their ancestors right in the river. If a girl is about to start her first period, a traditional way to guide her is to take her to the river. Apart from that, if someone in the family dreams about a river, it will mean that someone in the family is pregnant; and if I am a mother, I should know that something is wrong with one of my daughters.[4]

As Larry Swatuk has pointed out, before the colonial powers used southern Africa's rivers to define borders for colonial territories, the region's waterways were better understood as life-giving, culture-sustaining arteries.[5]

Rivers are "international" in both senses of the term discussed in the preceding chapters. Because many rivers flow across national borders, they are international in the more narrowly physical and juridical sense favored by the sovereign-state frame. An estimated 263 major rivers, including nearly all the world's largest, either form or cross borders between states (see chapter 4). The ecological harm done to these rivers through damming, draining, diverting, and dumping constitutes a leading class of transboundary environmental problems. In many of these basins, upstream and downstream asymmetries create difficult bargaining situations and substantial potential for conflict. Thus, even within the more limited "pollution-across-borders" framework discussed in chapter 1, international rivers emerge as a central challenge of interstate environmental diplomacy.

Rivers also epitomize the alternative understanding set out in chapter 1, of global environmental governance as protecting the planet's places. Although the proximate causes and immediate consequences of transforming rivers are seen most directly and immediately on the scale of individual watersheds and basins, both the underlying causes and the accumulating consequences reverberate along transnational social links of economics, politics, culture, and group identity. In terms of causes, the technical and financial resources that drive damming, draining, and diverting have long been transnationalized; more recently, so too has been the opposition to those activities (see chapter 6). Many of the consequences of manipulating rivers—including human intervention in the water cycle, effects on freshwater biodiversity, altered land-use patterns, and transformation of critical ecosystems—accumulate in ways that have genuinely global ramifications.

This chapter provides an overview of the sources of ecological stress on the world's rivers and watersheds and sketches what is known of the resulting consequences. The discussion of stresses includes a short history of river manipulation as part of a broader twentieth-century paradigm of developing water resources. Here, particular attention is paid to the socially transnationalized dimensions of damming, draining, and diverting water. In describing the consequences, particular emphasis is given to those effects that resonate beyond the scale of individual rivers and basins.

Stresses on the World's Rivers

The world's freshwater ecosystems have been subjected to a number of stresses from a number of sources. One major set of pressures has come from land-use changes and the transformation of surrounding landscapes through deforestation and agricultural conversion. Carmen Revenga and colleagues estimate that almost a third of the world's watersheds have lost more than 75 percent of their original forest cover and that seventeen of these—including the Indus, Niger, Nile, Seine, Tigris and Euphrates, and Volta—have lost more than 90 percent.[6] Deforestation alters local water, nutrient, and energy cycles in many ways, because forests play a major role in shaping local processes of runoff, soil stabilization, soil moisture, evapotranspiration, and microclimatic energy flows.

Water pollution constitutes another major source of stress. Leading problems include the discharge of heavy metals, persistent organic pollutants, and other chemical contaminants; the dumping of untreated or inadequately treated sewage into rivers and lakes; and excessive loading of the nutrients phosphorus and nitrogen (which leads to accelerated growth of algae, declining oxygen content, and enhanced eutrophication of freshwater bodies). Data on water quality in the world's rivers are sketchy and incomplete. In general, information on nutrients and microbiology is better and more substantial than data on toxic contamination.[7] As the UN Commission on Sustainable Development has pointed out, specific problems of water quality vary by world region and economic structure. The commission's 1997 *Comprehensive Assessment of the Freshwater Resources of the World* identified leading sources of regional water pollution, including the discharge of raw sewage and industrial waste in Latin America and West Africa, irrigation-induced salinity in western Asia, high sediment loading in the Asia-Pacific region, and acid deposition in North America and Europe.[8]

A third, related source of stress has been the growth of human settlements in and around freshwater ecosystems. Approximately 1.6 billion people live in the world's ten most populous watersheds (table 3.1).[9] Population densities in the world's most densely populated watersheds approach or exceed 300 people per square kilometer, which is comparable to the population density of Denmark or Poland (table 3.2).

The transformation of land, pollutants, and population pressures notwithstanding, the largest source of stress on rivers, lakes, and freshwater ecosystems has been large-scale manipulation of the water itself, through damming, draining, and diverting. According to the World Resources Institute:

Freshwater systems have been altered since historical times; however, the pace of change accelerated markedly in the early 20th century. Rivers and lakes have been modified by altering waterways, draining wetlands, constructing dams and irrigation channels, and establishing connections between water basins, such as canals and pipelines, to transfer water. Although these changes have brought increased farm output, flood control, and hydropower, they have also radically changed the natural hydrological cycle in most of the world's water basins.[10]

Damming

Estimates suggest that there may be as many as 800,000 dams on the world's rivers. Ecologically speaking, the most consequential of these are the more than 40,000 so-called large dams (15 m or more in height).

Table 3.1
Approximate population sizes for the world's most populous watersheds

Watershed	Location	Area (km²)	Population Density (people per km²)	Approximate Population (millions)	Number of States with Territory in Watershed
Yangtze	China	1,722,155	224	386	1
Ganges	South Asia	1,016,104	375	381	5
Hwang He	China	945,065	162	153	1
Indus	South Asia	1,081,733	145	157	5
Nile	Africa	3,254,555	44	143	11
Brahmaputra	South Asia	651,334	174	113	6
Xi Jiang	Southern China	409,458	210	86	2
Danube	Central Europe	795,686	103	82	17
Niger	West Africa	2,261,763	31	70	13
Amur	Northeast Asia	1,929,981	35	68	3
Mississippi	North America	3,202,230	21	67	2
Mekong	Southeast Asia	805,627	78	63	6
Godavari	India	319,808	195	62	1
Rhine-Meuse	Central Europe	198,731	304	60	7
Paraná	South America	2,582,672	23	59	5
Volga	Eastern Europe	1,410,994	42	59	5
St. Lawrence	North America	1,049,621	54	57	2
Krishna	India	226,026	248	56	2
Congo	Central Africa	3,730,474	15	55	1
Tigris and Euphrates	Middle East	765,831	58	44	6

Note: Figures for estimated population are calculated from data on area and population density.
Source: Compiled from Revenga et al. 1998.

Table 3.2
Population densities in the world's most densely populated watersheds

Watershed	Location	Population Density (people per km^2)	Number of States with Territory in Watershed
Ganges	South Asia	375	4
Rhine-Meuse	Central Europe	304	7
Krishna	India	248	1
Tapti	India	233	1
Yangtze	China	224	1
Po	S. Europe	215	3
Xi Jiang	China/Vietnam	210	2
Seine	France	201	1
Weser	Germany	198	1
Godavari	India	195	1

Source: Compiled from data in Revenga et al. 1998.

This category includes more than 300 giants typically referred to as major dams, such as Aswan on the Nile, Hoover and Glen Canyon on the Colorado, and Itaipu on the Paraná.[11] These dams have been built for a range of purposes, including hydropower, irrigation, and flood control. As discussed in chapter 6, the extent to which large dams fulfill their nominal purposes has been a subject of intense controversy, with critics charging that they too often serve only to enrich their builders while impoverishing local communities.

The damming of rivers fragments riverine ecosystems by inhibiting the movement of water, sediment, nutrients, and living organisms. The World Resources Institute's Pilot Analysis of Global Ecosystems (PAGE) examined the world's 227 largest rivers (with size defined in terms of average annual flow volume). The PAGE assessment concluded that 60 percent of these rivers, accounting for almost 90 percent of the total volume of water flowing in these basins, are "strongly" or "moderately" affected by fragmentation and altered flows.[12] The assessment also determined that "The only remaining large free-flowing rivers in the world are found in the tundra regions of North America and Russia, and in smaller basins in Africa and Latin America."[13]

Damming imposes upstream and downstream differentiation on river-ine ecosystems, with dramatic alterations in both domains. Upstream, river valleys are transformed into reservoirs by flooding often-vast expanses of land. The water trapped behind the world's dams has inundated almost 500,000 km^2 of land, an area roughly the size of France, Kenya, or Ukraine. Collectively, the volume of trapped water has been sufficient to produce a small but measurable change in the Earth's orbital pattern around the sun.[14] Downstream, in addition to the obvious effect of dramatically changing the volume and rates of water flow, dams also alter morphology by reducing sediment loads and changing erosion rates, reducing the input of nutrients to downstream and delta ecosystems. Finally, dams can have major impacts on the physical and chemical properties of river water, altering its temperature, turbidity, dissolved oxygen levels, and mineral and nutrient concentrations.

Diverting

In its impact on freshwater ecosystems, irrigation is a close companion of dam construction. According to the World Commission on Dams, "Half the world's large dams were built exclusively or primarily for irrigation, and some 30–40% of the 271 million hectares irrigated worldwide rely on dams."[15] Irrigated agriculture currently accounts for about 70 percent of global water withdrawals (including the use of groundwater as well as surface water supplies).[16] It accounts for only about 17 percent of world cropland but generates an estimated 40 percent of world food output.[17] Virtually all projections of future water use assume that irrigated agriculture will be increasingly important in expanding the world food supply, although the potential water efficiency of irrigation remains unclear. Estimates of the current global efficiency of water use in irrigation place the figure at around 40 percent.[18]

Draining

Another major form of manipulation of freshwater ecosystems is the draining and conversion of wetlands. Estimates of the global value of various ecosystem services typically identify wetlands as among the ecosystem types with the very highest "value-added" for human well-being. According to the World Resources Institute,

Wetlands provide a wide array of goods and services, including flood control, nutrient cycling and retention, carbon storage, water filtering, water storage and aquifer recharge, shoreline protection and erosion control, and a range of food and material products, such as fish, shellfish, timber, and fiber. Wetlands also provide habitat for a large number of species, from waterfowl and fish to invertebrates and plants.[19]

The driving forces behind the draining of wetlands include conversion to agriculture, destruction in the wake of large-scale water projects, the expansion of urban settlements and, in some cases, efforts to combat malaria and other diseases. Comprehensive data on the global extent of wetlands are not available, making it impossible to estimate global rates of loss with any precision. The World Resources Institute's PAGE reports a global estimate of 160,600 km^2 of wetlands drained by 1985, an area approximately the size of Iraq.[20] An investigation conducted in 1992 on 344 wetlands sites listed under the Ramsar Convention, the international treaty on wetlands, found that 84 percent were either "threatened" or "experiencing ecological changes."[21]

"Pushing Rivers Around": The Modern Paradigm of Water Resource Development

The manipulation of rivers and the alteration of watersheds have a long history. There are examples of dam construction in Egypt and Mesopotamia from more than 5,000 years ago. The world's oldest known large dam, the 20-m high Sadd-el-Kafra Dam in Egypt, was built before 2800 BC.[22] There are many other ancient examples in China, South Asia, Europe, and North America.[23]

Exploring the history of the social technology of dam building, irrigation, and large-scale water diversions, one finds deep and thick transnational roots. Nicholas Schnitter's *A History of Dams* follows the spread of dams and dam-building technology through the ebb and flow of empire.[24] The Romans learned dam building as a result of their Greek, Etruscan, and Near Eastern conquests, and in turn spread extensive dam-building enterprises throughout the Iberian Peninsula, North Africa, and along the Silk Road through present-day Turkey and Syria. The Muslim empire built scores of dams in North Africa, Iberia, and southwest Asia. Genghis Khan's conquest of Iran introduced a series of dam-construction projects, including a 60-m arch structure near Tabas that was built about 1350 (a height that would remain a world record until the early twentieth century). The Portuguese began advising the Hindu state of Vijayanagara on dam construction in the early 1500s. Britain used colonial India as a vast experimental setting for advancing the dam-builder's art. British India in turn provided an important learning ground for American dam builders as they launched the water-based colonization of the American West.[25]

Struggles to define rivers, to whom they belong, and how they are to be used also have a long history. Gleick's reconstructed account of water-related conflict in the legends, myths, and history of the ancient Middle East contains numerous examples of the use of water as a goal, tool, or target of war.[26] Schnitter describes the "bellicose abuse of dams" in China during the "warring states" period (317–589), with some twenty episodes of building or breaching dams and dikes to flood enemy positions.[27] Nor are cooperative institutions to manage watersheds and water resources a new phenomenon. Research on the communal management of common-property resources has produced a large set of cases of long-standing community governance mechanisms for waterways, irrigation systems, shared aquifers, and community water supplies.[28]

Beginning in the twentieth century, as the technological, administrative, and financial capacity to alter the flow of rivers reached new heights, river alteration commenced on a vastly larger and more aggressive scale. The majority of the world's 40,000 large dams were built in the second half of the twentieth century. Massive damming and water diversion projects became central to twentieth-century paradigms of progress and development—in both capitalist and socialist systems, and in both the industrialized world and the global South. As an American water manager told *Time* magazine in 1951, "We enjoy pushing rivers around."[29] The statement succinctly captures the main characteristics of this vision, including its technocratic orientation, its emphasis on water as a resource good, its link to larger notions of progress, and its implicit denial, or at least ignorance, of any relevant ecosystemic context. It reflects an era (1930–1980) in which the United States built a thousand large dams and ten thousand small ones.[30] Even the Colorado—a river the untamed wildness of which is woven deeply into the folklore of the American West—succumbed to this vision. Today the Colorado ends in a trickle several miles short of its former outlet in the Gulf of California, conquered by a vision of rivers as readily manipulable water resources to be pointed in the proper direction and modulated for the proper flow.[31]

However, the modern practice of pushing rivers around was by no means uniquely American. The comment by the 1950s American water manager could just as easily have been uttered in Russian. Stalin reportedly observed that "Water which is allowed to enter the sea is wasted."[32] The Soviets built the world's first major dam, Dneprostroi, inaugurating it in 1932. The Russian variant of pushing rivers around culminated in the Aral Sea disaster in Soviet central Asia. Once the world's fourth-largest lake, the Aral Sea has lost half its area, three-fourths of its water volume, and 85 percent of its surrounding wetlands. This ecological and social catastrophe is the result of massive diversions of water from its feeder rivers, the Amu Darya and Syr Darya, in order to satisfy the thirsts of Soviet cotton production in central Asia.[33]

Pushing rivers around also became popular in less-industrialized countries as diverse as China, India, and Brazil. Enormous dams built in the 1950s—Aswan in Egypt and Akosombo in Ghana—marked the beginning of the shift in dam construction from North to South. Nehru dubbed large dams the temples of modern India, and India paid a hefty price for this particular devotion, with dams, water projects, and associated facilities absorbing an estimated 15 percent of national government expenditures between 1947 and 1980.[34] In three decades under Mao, China built more than 600 dams each year.[35] Brazil, under military rule from 1964 to 1985, launched a campaign to conquer that country's vast hydropower resources. The military regime poured the foundation for a hydroelectric capacity that is exceeded today only by the United States, Canada, and China. A conservative estimate of the population displaced by nineteen large dams built across Brazil in this era puts the figure at more than 300,000 people.[36]

Obviously, the mix of political, institutional, and financial drivers behind water diversion schemes has varied across different social, economic, and political systems. Nevertheless, there have been some important constants across space and time in giving form to the paradigm of pushing rivers around. One of these has been the central role of the state in concentrating resources and configuring property rights so as to make massive water projects feasible. As Donald Worster has pointed out in the case of the American West, only the state had the capacity to concentrate resources on the requisite scale.[37] This pattern is obvious in socialist regimes, but also in America's experiment with the Tennessee Valley Authority as well as the water-based conquest of the American West, in Canada's development of hydroelectric resources in Quebec, and in Brazil under right-wing military rule.

With the emergence of the World Bank and other development-financing mechanisms after World War II, the model of water diversion projects being fueled by state power and public finance went global. The World Bank reported in 1993 that it had provided $40 billion (in nominal terms) in water sector lending since its inception: $19 billion for irrigation and drainage, $12 billion for water supply and sewerage, and $9 billion for hydro. Of these funds, $28 billion was lent in support of 604 dam projects in 93 countries.[38] A 1996 Bank internal review document reported that its dam-related lending had assisted "directly or indirectly" in the construction of only 3 percent of existing dams in the developing world.[39] Yet this figure dramatically understated the catalytic role of the Bank, other multilateral development organs, and bilateral aid agencies from those donor countries with large dam-building industries. They have played that role in several ways: financing some of the largest projects, advancing the state of the art of water infrastructure planning, and validating the notion of large-scale water diversion as developmental progress.

A second key ingredient in globalizing the model was the emergence of a transnational network of technical expertise in the construction of dams, channels, large-scale irrigation systems, and other aspects of water infrastructure. The International Commission on Large Dams (ICOLD) describes itself as an international NGO that "provides a forum for the exchange of knowledge and experience in dam engineering."[40] ICOLD was founded in 1928 with a mandate to "encourage advances in the planning, design, construction, operation, and maintenance of large dams and their associated civil works, by collecting and disseminating relevant information and by studying related technical questions."[41]

Today ICOLD has approximately 6,000 members, mostly with technical backgrounds, organized into national committees from eighty countries. It has broadened its focus over time to include analysis and advocacy on controversies related to dam safety, environmental impacts, and the financial dimensions of large dam construction. ICOLD operates through technical committees, which disseminate information and techniques through symposia, workshops, technical papers, lectures, and periodic international congresses. Table 3.3 lists ICOLD congresses and tracks the growth of country membership over time.

Another important transnational organization emerging in this era is the International Commission on Irrigation and Drainage (ICID), which

Table 3.3
ICOLD congresses and membership growth, 1933–2003

Congress	Year	Location	Member Countries
First	1933	Stockholm	21
Second	1936	Washington	26
Third	1948	Stockholm	25
Fourth	1951	New Delhi	29
Fifth	1955	Paris	38
Sixth	1958	New York	43
Seventh	1961	Rome	47
Eighth	1964	Edinburgh	52
Ninth	1967	Istanbul	61
Tenth	1970	Montreal	66
Eleventh	1973	Madrid	69
Twelfth	1976	Mexico	74
Thirteenth	1979	New Delhi	71
Fourteenth	1982	Rio de Janeiro	71
Fifteenth	1985	Lausanne	77
Sixteenth	1988	San Francisco	78
Seventeenth	1991	Vienna	78
Eighteenth	1994	Durban	80
Nineteenth	1997	Florence	80
Twentieth	2000	Beijing	80
Twenty-First	2003	Montreal	82

Source: Comité Brasileiro de Barragems (Brazilian Committee on Dams), "Historical Review." http://www.cbdb.org.br/ingles/histe.htm (accessed July 22, 2003).

has been to irrigation what ICOLD has been to dam construction. Beginning in 1950 with eleven founding member countries, ICID today has a membership of eighty-eight national committees. Its self-described mission is "to stimulate and promote the development and application of the arts, sciences and techniques of engineering, agriculture, economics, ecological and social sciences in managing water and land resources for irrigation, drainage, flood management and river training applications, including research and development and capacity building for achieving sustainable irrigated agriculture."[42] Historically, this translated in practice into an emphasis on expanding the supply of water for large-scale irrigated agriculture. Like ICOLD, ICID operates through technical work bodies, with both functional and regional themes, as well as triennial world congresses. Another long-standing organization from this era is the International Association for Hydraulic Engineering and Research (IAHR), established in 1935 with support from the Dutch government.

A third key to the globalization of river manipulation was the emergence of multinational firms engaged in the design and construction of large water-diversion infrastructure and the manufacture of related equipment. McCully estimated that by the late 1990s the dam-building industry had an annual volume of some $20 billion, with most of that money flowing to "a relatively small number of multinational engineering consultants, equipment manufacturers, and construction firms."[43] He identifies forty-one corporations from a dozen industrialized countries, each involved in at least a half dozen prominent dam projects worldwide. As one might expect in a capital-intensive industry driven by international public finance, concentration is high; McCully identifies fifteen engineering or environmental consulting firms, a dozen equipment suppliers, eight construction firms, and a half dozen firms or consortia active at more than one of these stages. As dam construction began to slow in their home countries, these firms increasingly looked overseas for business, usually working in close coordination with the bilateral donor agencies of their home governments. Typically, a donor country would have only one or two major firms actively involved in a particular stage of the business, such as construction or equipment supply, thereby facilitating coordination between firms and national aid or export-credit agencies.[44]

Table 3.4
Alteration of freshwater systems worldwide

	Pre-1900	1900	1950–1960	1985	1996–1998
Waterways altered for navigation (km)	3,125	8,750	n.a.	>500,000	n.a.
Canals (km)	8,750	21,250	n.a.	63,125	n.a.
Large reservoirs[a]:					
number	41	581	1,105	2,768	2,836
volume (km^3)	14	533	1,686	5,879	6,385
Large dams (<15 m high)	n.a.	n.a.	5,749	n.a.	41,413
Installed hydro capacity (MW)	n.a.	n.a.	<290,000	542,000	~660,000
Hydro capacity under construction (MW)	n.a.	n.a.	n.a.	n.a.	~126,000
Water withdrawals (km^3/yr)	n.a.	578	1,984	~3,200	~3,800
Wetlands drainage (km^2)[b]	n.a.	n.a.	n.a.	160,600	n.a.

Notes:
[a] Large reservoirs are those with a total volume of 0.1 km^3 or more. This is only a subset of the world's reservoirs.
[b] Includes available information on drainage of natural bogs and low-lying grasslands as well as disposal of excess water from irrigated fields. There are no comprehensive data for wetland loss for the world.
n.a. = data not available.
Source: Revenga et al. 2000, 16.

Cumulative Effects of River Manipulation

Table 3.4 provides some indicators of the physical alteration of rivers in the twentieth century. The data suggest both the massive scale of river manipulation and the growing extent of such manipulations over time. Not surprisingly, the consequences of these alterations are observed most readily on the scale of an individual river basin or watershed. One example of a heavily altered basin is that of the Rhine. The Rhine-Meuse watershed straddles the borders of seven countries in central Europe. The watershed covers an area approximately equal to the size of France and is home to roughly 60 million people. Virtually all of the land cover within 5 km of the watershed's major rivers is either developed or cropland. Seventy-one percent of the original forest cover has been lost in the watershed. A century of development and channelization along the Rhine and its tributaries, including construction of a half-dozen large dams, has cut the river off from 90 percent of its original floodplain.[45]

The cumulative, global impact of such local insults has also been substantial. One effect of all this damming, draining, and diverting is human intervention in the global water cycle on an enormous scale. The twentieth century saw a more than sixfold increase in freshwater withdrawals, far outstripping the threefold increase in world population or even the fivefold increase in the amount of agricultural land under irrigation.[46] Human societies now appropriate an estimated 16–17 percent of total global runoff, but an astonishing 54 percent of the "accessible" runoff (a category that excludes runoff in remote rivers and unmanageable flood waters).[47]

A second toll is the impact on freshwater biodiversity. Freshwater ecosystems are home to most of the world's endangered species of fish. The global rate for extinction of freshwater fish species is five times that of saltwater species, with dams, channelization, and other forms of river manipulation the chief culprit in their precarious status.[48] Damming the Nile at Aswan has produced a two-thirds decline in the number of fish species commercially harvested from the river; in the United States, myriad damming and diverting schemes have rendered all native fish species in the lower Colorado River either endangered or extinct.[49] Effects on biodiversity are particularly troubling because of the relative richness of freshwater ecosystems. Although they cover only 1 percent of the Earth's surface, freshwater habitats are home to more than 40 percent of known fish species and 12 percent of known animal species.[50]

A third cumulative effect of river alterations has been the impact on the floodplains and wetlands that surround, incorporate, and interact with freshwater riverine ecosystems. As Gleick points out, "River floodplains are among the world's most diverse ecological systems, balancing aquatic and terrestrial habitat, species, and dynamics."[51] The land lost to dam reservoirs is not only vast, it is also, ecologically speaking, among the world's prime real estate. Although global data on the extent of wetlands are insufficient to allow authoritative assessments of the rate of loss, Myers estimates that half of the world's wetlands were lost in the twentieth century.[52]

Finally, modifications of river flows have had a huge impact on human settlements and global land-use patterns. Water diversion schemes have often been central to the colonization of fragile ecosystems ill-suited to dense populations, such as the desert Southwest of the United States. Also, although dams and channelization can be important tools for flood control, they can also provide a false and enormously costly sense of security for human settlements in floodplains. At the same time that they may encourage large numbers of people to settle in certain areas, large water projects have also been responsible for the displacement and outmigration of enormous numbers of settled peoples, often without consent or compensation. The World Commission on Dams (WCD) (chapter 6) estimated that the construction of large dams has displaced 40–80 million people.[53]

The most comprehensive effort to date to aggregate these myriad, cumulative effects is the WRI's PAGE initiative. Recognizing the severe limitations of comprehensive, comparable global data and the difficulty of drawing firm conclusions given the rapid and unevenly dispersed rates of change taking place, the PAGE assessment nevertheless draws an alarming picture of the health of the world's freshwater ecosystems (table 3.5). The assessment used two aggregate indicators, condition and capacity. Current condition refers to the output and quality of vital resource goods and services. A second indicator is the changing capacity of the ecosystem to provide these goods and services into the future. The PAGE assessment examined the current condition and changing capacity of freshwater ecosystems with regard to four critical clusters of goods or services: food and fiber production, water quality, water quantity, and biological diversity.

Regarding food production, the picture is mixed. On the one hand, degradation of habitat and overharvesting have undercut the ability of freshwater ecosystems to support wild fish stocks. On the other hand, freshwater aquaculture has grown rapidly, and is now thought to exceed the annual freshwater catch from wild stocks.[54] With regard to water

Table 3.5
Ecosystem scorecard for the world's freshwater systems

Good or Service Being Assessed	Current Condition	Changing Capacity
Food and fiber production	Good	Mixed
Water quality	Poor	Decreasing
Water quantity	Fair	Decreasing
Biodiversity	Bad	Decreasing

Notes: Current condition "reflects how the ecosystem's ability to yield goods and services has changed over time by comparing the current output and quality of these goods and services with output and quality 20–30 years ago." Changing capacity "reflects the trend in an ecosystem's biological capacity—its ability to continue to provide a good or service in the future."
Source: World Resources Institute et al. 2000, 104–105.

quality, water quantity, and biodiversity, however, the assessment's picture is uniformly one of decreasing capacity on the part of freshwater systems to provide these vital goods and services. The assessment concluded that other than in the United States and Western Europe, water quality appears to be degraded in almost all regions as a by-product of agricultural intensification, urbanization, chemical contamination, and the loss of wetlands' filtering and purification services. On water quantity, the assessment projected that if current consumption patterns continue, roughly half of the world's population will live in conditions of high water stress by 2025.[55] On biodiversity, the assessment concluded that "Of all the ecosystems examined in this report, freshwater systems are by far in the worst condition from the standpoint of their ability to support biological diversity—on a global level."[56]

Water and the Sea of Unmet Human Needs

Despite the tremendous toll of river manipulation—and for some people because of it—water-related human insecurities remain immense. The UN Commission on Sustainable Development estimates that 20 percent of the world's people lack access to a safe supply of clean water and 50 percent lack access to adequate sanitation.[57] The World Health Organization (WHO) estimates that more than 5 million people die each year from diseases caused by unsafe drinking water and inadequate sanitation.[58] According to the WRI's PAGE assessment, 2.3 billion people, or more than 40 percent of the world's 1995 population, lived under conditions of "water stress" (defined as water availability of less than 1700 m^3 per person per year), with 1.7 billion living in "highly stressed" river basins (water availability of less than 1,000 m^3 per person per year). The PAGE assessment projects the share of the world's population living under water stress to increase to almost 50 percent by 2025, or 3.5 billion people, with 2.4 billion under high-stress conditions.[59]

Projections of growth in water demand across competing sectoral uses also suggest difficult future challenges. As the UN Commission on Sustainable Development has pointed out, scenarios for world industry, world agriculture, and global urban demand in the coming decades each typically assume strong growth in water use, in isolation from growth projections for other water-using sectors. Thus, for example, the UN Industrial Organization projects that current trends will lead to a more than doubling of 1995 industrial water use (and a more than fourfold increase in industrial pollutant loading) by 2025, while projections of the amount of water required to provide a healthy diet for the world's growing population typically envision a 50- to 100-percent increase in agricultural water use over the same time frame.[60]

Nature and People Pushing Back

In short, the world faces several water challenges simultaneously: addressing the sea of unmet water needs among the world's poor, accounting for critical ecosystem services and in-stream uses of water, adjusting to growing water stress in many regions of the world, and reconciling conflicting sectoral demands for growth in water use. In light of these enormous and converging challenges, there is no consensus as to what ought to replace the traditional pattern of damming, draining, and diverting the world's rivers. Nor is there anything close to consensus as to how the world's rivers and watersheds should be governed. Instead, rivers and watersheds are being pushed and pulled by several different institution-building processes at once: emerging norms of international water law, basin-specific accords for shared "international rivers," the privatization and marketization of existing or planned water resources and services as part of broader processes of neoliberal economic adjustment, and the transnationalization of struggles over water development projects and water privatization controversies. As discussed in chapters 4 through 7, some of these rule-making, norm-embedding activities have followed the classic design principles of international regimes, while others have taken a decidedly different institutional form.

4

Swimming Upstream: In Search of a Global Regime for International Rivers

(with Fengshi Wu and Joanne Neukirchen)

One entry point for institution building in defense of the world's water-sheds is that nearly all of the world's largest rivers cross national borders. A recent survey of international river basins revealed three striking facts about the extensive internationalization of the world's water.[1] First, the number of international waterways (lakes and rivers) is larger than previously thought: 263, compared with a 1978 UN estimate of 214.[2] Second, the basins through which these watercourses flow cover almost half of the Earth's land surface area (table 4.1). Third, among the world's nonisland states, all but a handful (including Denmark, Singapore, and a few states on the Arabian peninsula) have some portion of their territory in an international basin. Among states occupying international basins, almost two thirds (ninety-two) have at least half of their territory in an international basin; for more than one third (fifty), the figure is 80 percent or more of national territory.

These geographic facts, combined with mounting stresses on water supply and water quality almost everywhere, have led to sometimes dire predictions of "water wars" between upstream and downstream states. In 1995 the World Bank's vice president for environmentally sustainable development, Ismail Serageldin, stated that "The wars of the next century will be over water."[3] In 1999 Libya's Moammar Gaddafi predicted that the next Middle East war would be over water.[4] The influential British publication *The Economist* warned that water shortages would constitute "the stuff of future wars ... conditions are ripe for a century of water conflicts."[5] Researchers looking at the prospects for "environmentally induced" violent conflict have pointed to shared water resources as the single most likely route by which environmental change might trigger interstate hostilities.[6] This fear of international water conflict is not new.

Table 4.1
The world's international rivers

Region	Number of International Rivers	Percentage of Land Area in International River Basins	Number of States with Territory in One or More International Basins
Africa	59	62	47
Asia	57	39	34
Europe	69	54	42
North America	40	35	12
South America	38	60	13
World total	263	45	145

Notes: North America includes Central America and the Caribbean; Asia includes the Middle East. The total number of states does not add because some states straddle continental boundaries.
Sources: Wolf et al. 1999 and Transboundary Freshwater Dispute Database n.d. b.

An inscription dated 1369 on the Anantharaja Dam in South India, listing the conditions for good dam construction, specifies that a dam should not be placed on a site at the boundary of two kingdoms.[7]

Yet the shared character of rivers also creates pressures for international cooperation as a way to allocate water resources and manage interstate disputes. Jesse Hamner and Aaron Wolf identified 145 international treaties since 1814 that deal with some non-navigational aspect of international water issues in a particular river or lake basin.[8] Many of these agreements are sufficiently robust, norm disseminating, and behavior modifying to be reasonably called international regimes. There has also been a long-standing effort, through the International Law Commission (ILC) of the United Nations, to create a broad framework of international legal principles for shared river basins that culminated in the UN Convention on the Law of the Non-Navigational Uses of International Watercourses adopted by the General Assembly in 1997.

Seen through the lens of interstate regimes, one might interpret the seeming absence of water wars, the proliferation of basin accords, and the UN framework convention as grounds for cautious optimism about international river governance. Governments long ago learned to cooperate on questions of river navigation. More recently, some have learned how to cooperate to allocate shared water supplies. Perhaps they are slowly learning to cooperate on issues of water quality, pollution control, ecosystem protection, and watershed management as well.

What would constitute evidence of an emerging global regime on international rivers? Regime theory suggests the process of crafting a global framework convention as one place to start, viewing its existence as indicating either a foundation of shared norms or, at the very least, a set of overlapping interests upon which shared norms might be constructed. On the other hand, it may be that building a global rivers regime is not a top-down process of negotiating a global framework to be applied to individual rivers but a bottom-up process of norm diffusion and normative convergence over time across separate regimes at the basin level. Thus, an increase in the number of basin-specific legal instruments for the world's 263 international rivers would suggest, at the very least, normalization of the idea of shared governance of shared rivers. Stronger evidence of bottom-up regime building would be convergence in the content of those basin-level agreements, suggesting that the same norms were taking root—or at least were in play—across different basin settings.

Of course, most of the world's rivers do not cross international borders, and many threatened watersheds are not located in international basins. A regime bringing the world's border-crossing rivers under effective norms of environmental governance would be only a partial step toward protecting the planet's watersheds more generally. Nonetheless, it would be an important step in that direction, given the large number of countries with international rivers and the vast amounts of national territory encompassed in international basins. These facts suggest that at least in principle, norms that take hold around the governance of international rivers might be able to "swim upstream" in the sense of having broader domestic reverberations.

International Watercourse Law: The 1997 UN Convention

If we look for a global rivers regime to emerge around a codified legal instrument, the closest approximation is clearly the 1997 UN Convention

Table 4.2
National territory within international basins

Percentage	Number of Countries
90–100	39
80–90	11
70–80	14
60–70	11
50–60	17
40–50	10
30–40	10
20–30	13
10–20	9
Less than 10%	11
Total	145

Source: Wolf et al. 1999.

on the Law of the Non-Navigational Uses of International Watercourses (hereafter, the Watercourses Convention).[9] The Watercourses Convention marked the culmination of nearly three decades of effort to develop a framework of globally applicable legal principles for the governance of international rivers. It is meant to be a template for the negotiation and strengthening of accords governing specific international river basins.[10] It articulates several principles, including the right of every state in a river or lake basin to be party to any agreements governing the entire basin; the "equitable and reasonable use" of a watercourse as it passes through a state's territories; an obligation not to cause significant harm to other watercourse states; regular consultation and exchanges of information; peaceful means of dispute resolution; and explicit principles for environmental protection; ecosystem preservation; and the prevention, reduction, and control of pollution.

The effort to create a global framework of legal principles for shared river basins has several decades of history behind it. In 1991, after two decades of often-contentious debate, the International Law Commission approved a set of draft articles on the Law of the Non-Navigational Uses of International Watercourses.[11] These articles formed the basis for negotiations within the Sixth (Legal) Committee of the UN General Assembly over a framework treaty on international watercourses that was meant to set out the general principles that should guide development of basin-specific agreements. The result, again marked by contentious bargaining and delicate compromise among contradictory aims, was a draft version of the Watercourses Convention, a modified version of which the General Assembly approved in 1997.

The convention articulates principles that should shape basin-specific accords, the process by which such accords should be negotiated, and the standing to be accorded to states within a shared basin. Among the central provisions of the convention are the following:

• Article 4 stipulates that every watercourse state is entitled to participate in negotiations that cover an entire watercourse, and to consult on any lesser agreements affecting that state.

• Article 5 calls for states to exercise "equitable and reasonable use" of international watercourses within their territories.

• Article 7 obligates states not to cause "significant harm" to other watercourse states.

• Article 8 obligates states to cooperate, on the basis of "sovereign equality, territorial integrity, mutual benefit and good faith."

• Article 9 calls for regular exchanges of information and data.

• Article 11 requires information exchange and consultation with the other parties on the effects of any "planned measures."

• Article 12 requires prior notification for any planned measures "which may have a significant adverse effect" on other watercourse states.

• Articles 20–23 deal with environmental concerns, establishing general obligations to protect and preserve ecosystems; prevent, reduce, and control pollution; prevent the introduction of alien or new species; and protect and preserve the marine environment.

• Article 33 sets out dispute resolution procedures, including an obligation to resolve disputes peacefully, an endorsement of arbitration and mediation, and procedures for the creation and workings of fact-finding commissions.

In terms of the key institutional features related to territoriality, authority, and knowledge emphasized in chapter 2, the Watercourses Convention employs a standard design template for an interstate regime. In terms of territoriality, the convention defines a watercourse as "a system of surface waters and groundwaters constituting by virtue of their physical relationship a unitary whole and normally flowing into a common terminus" (Article 2). Stephen McCaffrey and Mpazi Sinjela suggest that this definition "not only accords with hydrologic reality, but also calls the attention of states to the interrelationships among all parts of the system of surface and underground waters that makes up an international watercourse."[12] In that sense it could be read as a softening of traditional conceptions of territorialized nature. Yet the emphasis remains on watercourses, as opposed to a more holistic watershed or drainage basin concept. And the emphasis on international watercourses draws the traditionally sharp, territorial line between the domestic and international spheres. The problem is framed as one of cooperatively managing a resource that flows across borders, rather than integrating crucial land-based and ecosystemic considerations that ignore borders. State responsibilities for "domestic" watercourses are largely beyond the scope of the regime, despite the "significant harm" inherent in the globally cumulative problems of loss of freshwater biodiversity, damage to critical ecosystems, and the depletion of natural capital. Even where domestic responsibilities are invoked, the sharply territorial distinction between the domestic and international spheres is reproduced. Thus, states are charged with preserving ecosystems and controlling pollution "individually and, *where appropriate*, jointly" and tasked with protecting marine environments tied to watercourses (e.g., estuaries) "individually and, *where appropriate*, in cooperation with other States."[13]

Authority within the Watercourses Convention also adheres closely to the statist emphasis of conventional international regimes. The convention contains an explicit and detailed conception of "equitable utilization and participation" among states. No state may be excluded from participating in agreements that affect an entire watercourse, and any watercourse state may consult on lesser agreements covering a portion of the watercourse. Along with this standing comes the general presumption of state competence. States as parties are the source of all relevant knowledge, data, and information. States as parties are also the sole bearers of responsibilities to avoid significant harm, to notify other parties about planned measures, or to implement the various obligations of environmental protection.

In contrast, entry points for nonstate actors are quite narrowly circumscribed. Other than "watercourse States," only "regional economic integration" organizations "constituted by sovereign States" are recognized as having standing to enter into an international watercourse agreement (Article 3). Members of dispute resolution commissions are to be appointed by the states involved. There are no provisions for independent sources of knowledge, data, or information. The place where the convention comes closest to challenging traditionally statist presumptions of authority—its nondiscrimination clause—is the exception that proves the rule. Article 32 calls for states not to discriminate on the basis of nationality or residence when granting standing to those persons "who have suffered or are under a serious threat of suffering significant transboundary harm as a result of activities related to an international watercourse." This provision, in principle, creates an opportunity for nonstate actors to press claims across territorial borders and jurisdictional boundaries. However, it also authorizes national judicial systems as the definitive arbiter of those claims and includes an escape clause that allows states to create other arrangements to protect potentially injured parties. It is telling that even this limited standing for citizens across borders met strong resistance from several states. As McCaffrey and Sinjela describe it, "Evidently, not all states are yet comfortable with the idea of granting private persons from other (usually neighboring) countries nondiscriminatory access to their judicial and administrative procedures relating to transboundary harm or the threat of such harm."[14]

The convention also takes a typically optimistic, rationalist position toward knowledge stabilization. Provisions are made (Article 9) for the regular exchange of data and information, and the central dispute resolution mechanism is the creation of an impartial fact-finding commission. The conceptions of equity and harm reveal a similar stance toward knowledge. The entire concept of avoiding significant harm represents a substantially optimistic perspective regarding the capacity to identify and measure harm. This is far from a precautionary approach grounded in a healthy respect for uncertainty. On the contrary, the convention's assumption, or at least its hope, is that a stabilized body of factual knowledge can provide the foundation for bargained compromise as to what constitutes significant harm or equitable use.

With the problem framed as managing cross-border effects, the central entry point for environmental considerations is the downstream effects of upstream water uses. The convention does contain explicit, although highly general, statements of a state's environmental responsibilities (Articles 20–23). States must protect and preserve ecosystems, reduce and control pollution, prevent the introduction of alien species, and protect and preserve affiliated marine environments such as estuaries. The convention creates no specific, action-oriented environmental obligations or duties other than giving all watercourse states the right to consultations on joint management for pollution control and environmental protection. Despite the efforts of several states to strengthen the environmental provisions, only minor changes were made to the ILC's draft articles.[15] As a result, the main entry point for meaningful environmental considerations is not the convention's environmental provisions, but rather the concept that upstream states have the responsibility not to cause significant harm (environmental or otherwise) to downstream states through their water-related actions. In other words, far from fostering a paradigm of integrated watershed management, the convention defines the problem quite narrowly as one of cross-border pollution or disruption of downstream flow.

Balancing upstream and downstream rights and responsibilities was the most contentious aspect of bargaining over the Watercourses Convention. As several analysts have pointed out, and as the negotiating parties clearly understood, there are potentially profound tensions between the principle of equitable and reasonable use (Article 5) and the principle of no significant harm to other watercourse states (Article 7). The principle of no significant harm is generally seen to favor downstream states, in that upstream development of water resources may deny water to human and natural uses downstream, thereby causing potentially significant harm. The principle of equitable use, in contrast, is generally seen to favor upstream states seeking to develop water resources, in the sense that it gives them a legal basis for claiming and using their fair share of the water.[16]

Rather than specify the relationship between these potentially conflicting principles, the Watercourses Convention is ambiguous as to how they are to be reconciled. Yet, seen in historical context, even ambiguity constitutes something of a victory for the principle of no significant harm, and thus for downstream states. The equitable-use concept favored by upstream states had a much stronger foundation in international law than no significant harm. Indeed, Stephen McCaffrey, writing in the early 1990s, concluded that "Attempts by groups of experts to derive general rules from treaties and other forms of state practice have concluded that equitable utilization is a—and perhaps *the*—fundamental rule in the field."[17] The principle of equitable use was emphasized in resolutions issued by two long-standing, influential groups of legal experts in the 1960s. In 1961, the Institute of International Law issued the Salzburg Resolution on the Use of International Non-Maritime Waters, which stated that the rights of a state to make use of shared waters are limited "by the right of use by the other States concerned with the same river or watershed." The resolution also stated that disputes "shall be settled on the basis of equity, taking into consideration the respective needs of the States, as well as any other circumstances relevant to any particular case."[18]

In 1966 the International Law Association (ILA) took an even stronger stand in support of equitable use in the Helsinki Rules on the Uses of the Waters of International Rivers. The rules emphasized that states are entitled to "a reasonable and equitable share in the beneficial uses of the waters of an international drainage basin."[19] In contrast, the principle of no significant harm finds much less support in the Helsinki Rules, which suggest that harm to existing uses is only one factor to be considered in determining what constitutes equitable use. As McCaffrey points out, the ILA's commentary on the Helsinki Rules explicitly states that downstream states could be expected to modify existing uses (e.g., irrigation practices) that were being harmed by new upstream uses if those existing uses were particularly inefficient, based on antiquated technology, or could be met from alternative sources.[20]

Twenty-five years later, the 1991 International Law Commission draft articles that formed the basis for negotiating the Watercourses Convention took a much stronger stand in favor of no significant harm. According to the ILC commentary accompanying the draft articles,

A watercourse State's right to utilize an international watercourse in an equitable and reasonable manner has its limit in the duty of that State not to cause appreciable harm to other watercourse States. In other words—prima facie, at least—utilization of an international watercourse is not equitable if it causes other watercourse States appreciable harm.[21]

As the ILC's draft articles were renegotiated in the General Assembly, however, several qualifications were introduced that obscured the emphasis on no significant harm.[22] The ambiguous final document stops far short of overthrowing the primacy of equitable use in international water law. Nevertheless, it marks a shift in emphasis toward prevention of significant harm. Again, this shift is important because it provides the primary basis for meaningful environmental considerations, albeit in the limited sphere of transboundary flows.

Is the Watercourses Convention the core of an emerging regime? It passed the General Assembly on a vote of 103–3 with 27 abstentions, but the convention lacked support among several key states in global river politics. Two of the three opposing votes came from influential states that are upstream in major river basins marked by interstate controversy —Turkey (the Tigris and Euphrates) and China (the Mekong). Also, environmentalists and human rights activists have criticized both states for controversial domestic water development schemes (Turkey's eastern Anatolia project and China's Three Gorges project).[23] Among the 27 abstentions were several states important in international river politics, including Egypt, Ethiopia, France, India, and Pakistan.

The requirement for entry into force—that thirty-five signatories deposit instruments of ratification with the Secretary General—is relatively modest compared with some recent global environmental treaties.[24] However, the convention failed to collect a sufficient number of ratifying states to enter into force by the specified date of May 20, 2000. Only six states had ratified (seven more had signed the convention but not yet ratified it through domestic legislative processes).[25] It would be a boldly optimistic interpretation to view an unratified framework convention, marked by fundamental ambiguity on the central normative question of equitable use versus significant harm, as a nascent regime.

International Watercourse Law: Basin-Specific Accords

A very different indicator of an emerging global rivers regime would be the inscription of a set of core principles in a growing number of basin-specific international agreements. Basin-specific water accords constitute a large and growing body of international law. The Transboundary Freshwater Dispute Database (TFDD) project of Oregon State University identified 150 accords involving 52 river or lake basins for the period since 1874. The database of the Food and Agricultural Organization (which includes not only basin-specific treaties but also regional accords, less formalized agreements such as memoranda of understanding, and nonbasin-specific agreements) lists 111 water-related agreements for the period since 1980 alone.[26] One river, the Danube, has been the subject of at least 22 bilateral and multilateral accords. Not all of the world's international river basins are covered by an agreement, and the extent, depth, and scope of shared governance varies widely across individual basin accords. However, at least some of these accords can be said to meet the definition of an international regime as rules of the game that delimit "the range of legitimate or admissible behavior in a specified context of activity."[27]

Beyond constituting individual regimes for specific basins, it could be that these agreements are effectively building a global rivers regime from the ground up. If it is increasingly "normal" for states to adopt agreements for shared river basins, and if the content of those agreements is converging on a shared set of governance principles, then that could be interpreted as an emerging global regime, albeit not one organized around a framework of a centralized, explicitly codified accord.

This raises the complex question of the relationship, if any, between the global process of constructing legal principles for shared rivers and a growing set of basin-specific agreements. The question is complex because the two processes have been unfolding side by side. Although the Watercourses Convention was not approved until 1997, its central principles became apparent much earlier, during the ILC deliberations; many of these principles trace their origins to developments in the 1960s. Convergence on these norms across individual basin-specific treaties, which involve highly heterogeneous political, economic, and ecological situations, could be read as significant evidence of a global normative pull. On the other hand, the causal relationship could be the opposite, in the sense that the global framework simply reflects accumulated practice in the basin-specific treaties. According to McCaffrey and Sinjela, "Most of the important elements of the [1997 Watercourses] Convention—equitable utilization, 'no harm,' prior notification—are, in large measure, codifications of existing norms."[28] In other words, it may be that building a global regime for international rivers is a bottom-up process of aggregation and lateral diffusion of norms rather than a top-down process of norm dissemination. Finally, it may be that there is no link between these two levels of institution building; basin-specific accords may reflect a rival set of norms, or they may turn out to be a heterogeneous collection of agreements with no consistent collective normative structure.

Analysts have differed on the question of possible links between the global and basin-specific levels. McCaffrey and Sinjela assert that important principles of the Watercourses Convention are reflected in a few relatively recent accords, just as the Watercourses Convention itself reflects the accumulated principles of prior developments in water law.[29] Wolf, however, concludes that the principles of the Watercourses Convention and its myriad precursor documents over three decades of negotiations "have been explicitly invoked in no more than a handful of water negotiations or treaties."[30] Hamner and Wolf present evidence of a substantial gap between the content of existing basin-specific accords and some of the limited notions of shared watershed management enshrined in the Watercourses Convention. Using the Transboundary Freshwater Disputes Database, they analyzed the content of 145 basin treaties for the period since 1874.[31] Among their findings were the following:

Participation   Eighty-six percent of the agreements are bilateral agreements, although many of the basins covered by those agreements are multilateral. According to Wolf, "Multilateral basins are, almost without exception, governed by bilateral treaties, precluding the integrated basin management long advocated by water managers."[32]

Substantive focus   The main focus of the agreement is usually hydropower (39 percent) or water supply (37 percent). In contrast, only 4 percent (6 of 145 treaties) were seen by the authors to focus primarily on issues of pollution. The authors concluded that none of the treaties in their database could be characterized as being organized around the concept of integrated watershed management.

Links to other issues   Most agreements were seen as being narrowly focused on water issues. Less than half (43 percent) were found to include links with "nonwater" issues and in two-thirds of these, the "nonwater" issue is financial. Only 4 percent were identified as being linked with land issues.

Monitoring, enforcement, and dispute resolution   Almost two-thirds of the treaties were identified as containing provisions on information sharing, and slightly more than half (54 percent) were identified as containing monitoring provisions. Eighty percent of the treaties studied were found to contain no enforcement mechanisms, and more than half (54 percent) were found to contain no mechanism for conflict resolution.

These data caution against viewing the mere existence of a growing body of water accords as evidence of a de facto set of global norms for shared governance of rivers. It appears that few incorporate all riparian states within the basin to which they apply. Few make even rudimentary links to other issues, much less the comprehensive linkages required for integrated watershed management. Most appear to lack significant enforcement mechanisms, or even the "back-door" binding power that many regime theorists posit through processes of monitoring, information exchange, and actively shared governance.

It is also noteworthy that the pace of codification of basin-specific treaties has slowed in recent decades. The TFDD database on river treaties compiled by Wolf and colleagues includes 38 international basin accords for 1957–1966, the decade prior to the ILA's 1966 Helsinki Rules; 19 for the period 1967–1976, the decade immediately following the Helsinki Rules; and only 7 each for the next two ten-year intervals. Nor can this decline in treaty activity be dismissed as the happy result of a shrinking supply of basins lacking accords. Of the world's 263 international river basins, the TFDD identifies only 46, or less than one out of five, covered by one or more international agreement at any time since 1874. Eleven watercourses account for more than half of all agreements in the data (83 out of 150, or 55 percent). These include 22 bilateral and multilateral agreements among various subsets of the Danube's 17 basin states and 11 for the Nile (which has 10 basin states).[33] In other words, much of basin-specific formal cooperation consists of stitching together a

patchwork of accords—which may or may not constitute a "regime"—
in basins with large numbers of states. Finally, the recent decline in treaty
writing cannot be attributed to the end of a prior spurt of treaty making
among newly decolonized states. Several of the earlier agreements in the
TFDD may have been influenced by the redrawing of the map of Europe
after the world wars. However, decolonization in the post-World War II
period had minimal effects; newly independent states were involved in
only 3 of 38 international water treaties in the database for the period
1957–1966 and only 3 of 19 for 1967–1976.[34]

The Normative Structure of International River Agreements

This pattern of sporadic, fragmentary, and sometimes ambiguous cooperation on international rivers casts doubt on the emergence of a global
regime via either a global-framework or basin-cumulative path. What
these observations do not tell us, however, is anything about the principled content of the substantial number of existing basin-level accords.
Even if most of the world's shared basins remain uncovered by international accords, those for which accords are in place could be converging
on a set of norms for shared governance. Moreover, the data sketched
here are limited to formal treaties; they do not include less formal agreements such as memoranda of understanding or joint declarations, which
may also be important instances of the articulation of shared norms.

In order to test whether basin-level agreements reflect a normative
convergence, the University of Maryland's Harrison Program on the Future Global Agenda conducted a detailed study of the principled content
of international river agreements. We assembled a dataset containing all
known international agreements pertaining to international river or lake
basins for the period 1980–2000. We began by pooling the list of agreements in two data sources: the Transboundary Freshwater Dispute Database and the FAOLEX legal database of the UN Food and Agriculture
Organization. The TFDD list was compiled by researchers and included
only formal agreements; the FAOLEX list consisted of items reported by
governments and included "softer" agreements such as memoranda of
understanding and minutes of joint meetings, as well as signed but unratified treaties.[35] We thought it was appropriate to include these instru-

ments because our focus was on governments' willingness to articulate principles when they were engaging in any type of shared watercourse management and governance, not only when they were ratifying treaties. Some of the most important aspects of shared watercourse management, such as the joint construction and operation of hydroelectric facilities or the implementation of flood-control measures, are commonly articulated and codified in these less formal, nontreaty instruments or in legal instruments that are signed by the parties but are not subsequently subject to ratification processes.

From this set we subtracted agreements not relevant to the study, leaving a final set of sixty-two agreements.[36] We then coded several aspects of the content of these agreements, with particular attention to the core principles of the 1997 UN Convention: universal participation among basin states, equitable use, avoidance of significant harm, sovereign equality, information exchange, consultation, prior notification, environmental protection, and dispute resolution.[37] What follows is a brief summary of the project's findings, with particular attention to the question of whether we are seeing convergence on a core set of governing norms.[38]

Distribution of Agreements in Time and Space

One clear pattern in the data is the limited number of basins covered by international agreements. The sixty-two agreements covered a total of thirty-six basins, or roughly one-seventh of the world's international basins. Only about one-fourth of these (sixteen) are the first agreements for the particular basin. For the remaining forty-six agreements, we were able to identify a prior agreement in the same basin (either earlier in the study period or prior to it). In other words, at least three-fourths of the agreements during this period took place in basins with a previously established history of cooperation. The basic idea of creating an instrument of shared governance does not appear to be diffusing rapidly to new, previously uncovered basins.

Nor does the temporal distribution of agreements suggest rapid diffusion. As can be seen in figure 4.1, the temporal pattern is marked by three features: relative consistency, at the rate of a few agreements per year, until the 1992 UN Conference on Environment and Development

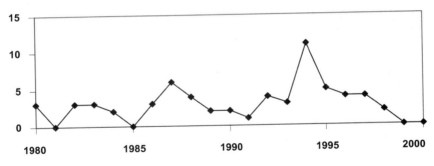

Figure 4.1
Number of international river agreements (source: Conca et al. 2003).

(UNCED); a spike in agreements in the period immediately following UNCED; and a noticeable dropoff in agreements at the end of the study period. In all, there were twenty-nine agreements during the twelve years prior to UNCED (1980–1991) and thirty-three in the post-UNCED period of 1992–2000, including eighteen in the immediate post-UNCED period of 1992–1994.

The notable dropoff at the end of the study period is not a lag in the reporting of concluded agreements; a subsequent search revealed only three new accords for the period 2001–2003. It could be a UNCED acceleration effect, in which accords that otherwise would have been negotiated during this period were speeded up by the effects of the Earth Summit. It may also be the case, however, that the growing articulation and establishment of the principles stated in the 1997 Watercourses Convention has had a chilling effect on the willingness of some states to enter into cooperation, or at least to codify it publicly.

Number of Parties and Trend in Participation
Of the sixty-two agreements in the dataset, forty-six are bilateral (two parties) and sixteen are multilateral (three or more parties). It is important to differentiate between bilateral and multilateral agreements, referring to the number of parties, and bilateral and multilateral basins, referring to the number of states located within the basin. The distinction is important because, as indicated in table 4.3, nearly two-thirds of the bilateral agreements are in multilateral basins. These figures are striking

Table 4.3
Bilateral and multilateral agreements

Type of Basin	Type of Agreement	Number of Agreements, 1980–2000
Bilateral (two basin states)	Bilateral (two parties)	13
Multilateral (three or more basin states)	Bilateral (two parties)	33
	Multilateral (three or more parties)	16

Source: Conca et al. 2003.

on two counts. First, multilateral agreements are dramatically overrepresented in the dataset. Two-thirds of the world's international river basins are bilateral (176 of 263 basins, or 67 percent), yet more than three-quarters of the agreements written during the study period were in multilateral basins (forty-nine of sixty-two, or 79 percent). Second, within those multilateral basins, the most common type of agreement, by a ratio of two to one, is a bilateral agreement, that is, an agreement that excludes one or more of the states located in the basin. In other words, the historical pattern of fragmented cooperation that was identified by Wolf in his study of basin treaties for the period 1874–1995 continues to be the case during our study period of 1980–2000, and holds up when one adds less formal agreements to the dataset.

This fragmented character of cooperation is a major limitation of basin-specific agreements as instruments of integrated watershed management. For this reason, the Watercourses Convention stressed the principle of universal participation by riparian states in agreements affecting an entire basin and universal consultation in agreements or major activities affecting any portion of the basin. To test whether this principle is on the rise over time, we calculated a "participation ratio" for each of the forty-nine multilateral-basin agreements in the dataset. We define the participation ratio as the ratio of agreeing parties to states located in the basin (the participation ratio in a bilateral basin is 1 by definition; there will be no international agreement unless both parties participate). Figure 4.2 shows a slight upward trend in the participation ratio for multilateral basins during the study period. Fitting a line to the data yields a marginally positive and statistically insignificant slope. In other words,

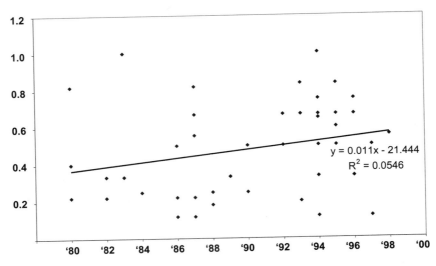

Figure 4.2
Ratio of signatories to basin states for multilateral basins, 1980–2000 (source: Conca et al. 2003).

shared governance of multilateral basins remains fragmentary, although there may be a modest tendency toward more comprehensive participation over the past two decades.

Principles Contained in the Accords

Table 4.4 summarizes the results of coding the agreements for the principles they contained. Among the general principles articulated in the Watercourses Convention, those of regular consultation, environmental protection, peaceful resolution of disputes, and exchange of information were most frequently invoked. Other principles appear less frequently, including prior notification, equitable water use, and avoiding significant harm to other parties. Explicit reservations of sovereign or territorial rights were also relatively uncommon (although they strongly increased in the post-UNCED period, as discussed later).

Evaluating normative change also requires some measure of the depth, breadth, or specificity of the principles invoked in these agreements. The goal is to determine whether we can see a pattern of "deepening" of particular principles over time, in the sense of moving from the more general

Table 4.4
Aggregate results for principles in Watercourses Convention

Principle	Coded Item	Agreements Coding Positively ($n = 62$)	
		Number	%
Equitable use	Generally stated principle of equity	22	36
	Specific water allocation mechanism	16	26
	Specific water use rights reserved	14	23
Avoiding significant harm to other watercourse states	Obligation to avoid significant harm	17	27
	Specific definition or description of significant harm	7	11
Sovereign equality and territorial integrity	Explicit reference to or reservation of sovereign rights	17	27
	Agreement includes exemption of domestic waters	5	8
Information exchange	Provision for regular meetings	31	50
	Obligation to exchange information	38	61
Consultation	Some provision for regular consultation	51	82
	Permanent basin commission or similar body	45	73
Prior notification	Obligation of prior notification	24	39
Environmental protection	Environmental protection as agreement objective	44	71
	Agreement has primarily environmental focus	19	31
	Specific environmental protection clause(s)	42	68
Peaceful resolution of disputes	Obligation for peaceful resolution	39	63
	Specific procedure for dispute resolution	34	55

Source: Conca et al. 2003.

to the more specific, becoming more intrusive on states, or broadening in reach. We developed one or more indicators of deepening for seven of the core ILC principles: equitable use, significant harm, sovereign rights, information exchange, consultation, environmental protection, and peaceful resolution of disputes.[39] For example, we coded the agreements not only for whether they contained a general goal or purpose of environmental protection, but also whether they contained one or more specific clauses on environmental protection. Similarly, we looked not only for a commitment to peaceful resolution of disputes but also for a specified procedure by which disputes are to be resolved. In this way we hoped to gauge the broadening or deepening of principles over time.

Here we see two very different patterns among the most commonly articulated principles. Some principles are invoked in ways that lack depth and specificity for the entire study period. It is not uncommon for agreements to invoke the idea of avoiding significant harm, but only a handful provide a clear or specific indication of what constitutes significant harm or its sources. Sovereign rights are often reserved in the abstract, but few agreements link such reservations explicitly to water rights. In contrast, the principles of environmental protection and peaceful resolution of disputes seem to have acquired a more specific character. Most agreements articulating goals of environmental protection do contain specific environmental clauses, and most creating an obligation of peaceful resolution of disputes also create a permanent basin commission or other standing body as a specific mechanism.

Temporal Pattern of Principles

Given the proximity of two salient events in this arena, the 1992 Earth Summit and the 1991 ILC draft articles, we divided the dataset into two time periods (1980–1991 and 1992–2000) to examine patterns of temporal variation. As table 4.5 indicates, there is a statistically significant increase in the likelihood that a post-UNCED agreement will articulate environmental objectives. Notably, post-UNCED agreements were also significantly more likely to contain an explicit affirmation of the sovereign rights of the parties.[40]

One way to interpret this pattern is that the two trends are in fact linked, in the sense that greater emphasis on transnational environmental

Table 4.5
Variation in content across the two time periods for core principles in Watercourses Convention

Principled Content	1980–1991 ($n = 29$)	1992–2000 ($n = 33$)	Pearson chi square (significance)	Cramer's V
Statistically significant difference between time periods				
Explicit affirmation of sovereign rights	2	15	11.531 (0.001)	0.431
Environmental protection as one objective	17	27	4.031 (0.045)	0.255
Borderline significant difference between time periods				
Obligation to avoid significant harm	5	12	2.836 (0.092)	0.214
Statistically insignificant difference between time periods				
Environmental protection as the agreement's main purpose	6	13	2.541 (0.111)	0.202
Provision for regular consultation	22	29	1.527 (0.217)	0.157
Obligation for peaceful resolution of disputes	16	23	1.395 (0.237)	0.150
Obligation to exchange information	16	22	0.860 (0.354)	0.118
Generally stated principle of equity	9	13	0.471 (0.492)	0.087
Obligation of prior notification	10	14	0.410 (0.522)	0.081

Source: Conca et al. 2003.

responsibilities brings with it greater emphasis on states' rights. Of the thirteen post-UNCED agreements that explicitly affirmed sovereign rights and reservations, almost all (eleven) also had environmental goals among the agreement's objectives. Another possibility is a regional effect. The practice of explicitly reserving sovereign rights was much more common in Africa, Asia, and Europe than in the Americas, and the former regions were the sites of most of the post-UNCED agreements.

Beyond increasing or decreasing prevalence, another question is whether we can see a pattern of deepening of particular principles over time. For most of the principles where we could develop a workable measure, we did not see a notable deepening effect during the study period (table 4.6). In some cases, this is because the principle is relatively well established, at the "deepest" level we measured, for the entire study period. Almost all agreements establishing a general obligation of peaceful resolution of disputes also establish a specific mechanism for resolving them. Most agreements that state a general objective of environmental protection contain one or more environmentally specific articles (with both the general and the specific expression of the principle increasing significantly between time periods, as noted earlier). The general principle of equitable use correlates significantly with its more specific expression, a water allocation mechanism.

In other cases, the absence of a deepening trend is due to the opposite effect: consistent shallowness. Although more than one-fourth of the agreements in the sample create an obligation not to cause significant harm, fewer than half of these provide a specific definition of what constitutes such harm, and agreements in the later time period are not significantly more likely to do so. Similarly, although there is clearly a growing tendency in the 1990s to explicitly reserve the state's sovereign rights in a general sense, there is only a nominal increase in the more specific practice of explicitly exempting domestic waters from the agreement.

Setting aside environmental protection, for which the increase in the deepening measure tracks closely with the increase in frequency of the general principle, consultation is the only principle showing evidence of deepening. There is a notable increase in the likelihood of forming a permanent basin commission as the mechanism for regular consultation,

Table 4.6
Variation in content across the two time periods for measures of normative deepening of principles

Principled Content	1980–1991 (n = 29)	1992–2000 (n = 33)	Pearson chi square (significance)	Cramer's V
Statistically significant difference between time periods				
Environmental protection: Specific environmental protection clause(s)	16	26	3.939 (0.047)	0.252
Borderline significant difference between time periods				
Consultation: Creation of a basin commission or analogous body	16	27	3.025 (0.082)	0.221
Statistically insignificant difference between time periods				
Sovereign rights: Agreement includes exemptions for domestic waters	1	4	1.566 (0.211)[a]	0.159
Equitable use: Specific water use rights reserved	8	6	0.781 (0.377)	0.112
Information exchange: Provision for regular meetings	13	18	0.583 (0.445)	0.097
Dispute resolution: Specific dispute resolution procedure	15	19	0.213 (0.644)	0.059
Equitable use: Specific water allocation mechanism	7	9	0.079 (0.778)	0.036
Significant harm: Specific definition of significant harm	3	4	0.049 (0.825)[a]	0.028

Notes:
[a] Expected cell counts less than 5; Fisher's exact test indicates no significant difference between time periods.
Source: Conca et al. 2003.

from slightly more than half of the agreements in the first time period to more than 80 percent in the second (a change that is of borderline statistical significance for the sample size).

The opposite of deepening is also conceivable, of course. It is interesting that there is at least a hint of this in the data on both equitable use and no significant harm. The relative frequency of these two principles is greater in the post-UNCED time period than in the pre-UNCED period. Yet the more specific practices associated with these principles—identifying specific water-use rights and providing a specific definition of significant harm—become less frequent in the second time period. The small number of agreements involved does not allow us to view these changes as statistically significant and demands a cautious interpretation, but the direction in which the data lean is clearly away from deepening rather than toward it.

Correlation Among Individual Principles

Another important question is that of the interrelationships among individual principles. A pairwise test for correlations among the individual principles (table 4.7) revealed three important findings. First, we noted the absence of a correlation between the principles of equitable use and no significant harm. This suggests that rather than the delicate balance found in the 1997 Watercourses Convention, many basin-level agreements have resisted trying to have it both ways.

Second, we found some evidence of two different clusters of principles. On the one hand, there are some noteworthy correlations among principles related to openness and transparency (information exchange, prior notification, and peaceful resolution of disputes) and environmental protection. None of these principles, however, correlates with the central principles reinforcing the state's right to water: equitable use and sovereign rights. We also found that equitable use correlated with a few more specific content indicators related to the state's rights to water; namely, whether the agreement contained a specific water allocation formula and whether it contained clauses exempting domestic waters from the agreement's provisions. In other words, it seems that one subset of the agreements is anchored by principles of openness and sustainability and another by the principle of the state's rights to water.

Table 4.7
Correlations among the Watercourses Convention principles

Principle	Significantly Correlated Principles[a]
Equitable use	None
Avoiding significant harm	Sovereign rights
	Information exchange
	Prior notification
	Peaceful resolution of disputes
Sovereign rights	Avoiding significant harm
Information exchange	Avoiding significant harm
	Regular consultation
	Prior notification
	Environmental protection (as one objective)
	Environmental protection (as main objective)
Consultation	Information exchange
	Prior notification
	Environmental protection (as one objective)
Prior notification	Avoiding significant harm
	Information exchange
	Regular consultation
	Peaceful resolution of disputes
Environmental protection (as one objective)	Information exchange
	Regular consultation
	Environmental protection (as main objective)
Peaceful resolution of disputes	Avoiding significant harm
	Prior notification

Notes:
[a] Significance at 0.05 level; Fisher's exact test used in instances with expected cell counts < 5.
Source: Conca et al. 2003.

Third, the recently emergent principle of no significant harm relates in an ambiguous fashion to these two distinct normative foundations. On the one hand, it correlates with the "water rights" principle of affirming the state's sovereign rights. On the other hand, it also correlates with several principles from the "openness and sustainability" cluster, including information exchange, prior notification, and peaceful dispute resolution. Perhaps most strikingly, it is not significantly correlated with any of the environmental variables, casting doubt on the idea that its ascendance relative to the equitable-use principle has created significant entry points for environmental protection.

Interpreting the Findings

Several aspects of the data cast doubt on the idea of viewing the aggregation of basin-level developments as a de facto global regime. A relatively small proportion of international basins have been the subject of any kind of agreement in the past twenty years. There is a strong tendency for cooperation to be concentrated in basins with a prior history of water-related cooperation, as opposed to moving into new basins. Setting aside a temporary post-UNCED spike, the rate at which international agreements are being concluded is not increasing.

Nor does the analysis of content reveal dynamic and far-reaching diffusion of norms. Some core principles related to developments in international water law, such as consultation, information exchange, and peaceful dispute resolution, are reasonably well represented in the data. Others are not, including equitable use and no significant harm—the foundational concepts of global-level developments in international water law. Moreover, of the principles we examined, most appeared to be about as well established at the beginning of the study period as they were toward the end. One important exception is environmental protection, which has received much greater emphasis in basin agreements since the 1992 Earth Summit, most likely because of the general upsurge in environmental concerns rather than normative developments specific to water, watersheds, and river basins. Also, a modest increase can be seen in the 1990s in the principle of avoiding significant harm and the practice of creating a permanent basin commission (although not to a level that can be deemed statistically significant for this sample size).

These trends can be read as modest evidence of diffusion of norms. A third exception, and one of the most interesting patterns in the data, is the dramatically greater likelihood that recent agreements will affirm the state's sovereign rights. Moreover, affirming sovereign rights correlates with affirming a responsibility not to impose significant harm. This suggests that it may be a reaction to the emergence of "trans-sovereign" norms stressing the responsibilities as well as rights of states in shared basins.

Another test of norm diffusion is whether we see a pattern of temporal deepening. Of the seven core principles for which we were able to develop a workable test, only one shows signs of deepening. There is a notable increase (although of only borderline statistical significance for this sample size) in the likelihood of forming a permanent basin commission as the mechanism for regular consultation. The other principles for which we tested deepening remained at about the same level of relative specificity or intrusiveness on states across the two time periods examined. Socialization and practice may be deepening the content of these principles, but it does not appear to be happening through the specific mechanism of reaching an international agreement.

Turning from a bottom-up to a top-down perspective, it is clear that the 1997 Watercourses Convention goes well beyond merely codifying existing principles at the basin level. Some of the convention's central principles, including universal participation, equitable use, and avoiding significant harm, appear only sporadically in basin-level agreements. Here, the ILC and the Watercourses Convention have broken new ground relative to the basin-level status quo. However, to break ground is not to build a foundation. We find little evidence that the process of framing global legal norms for international rivers has exerted a notable, systematic effect on the principles contained in basin agreements.

The Watercourses Convention dates only to 1997, of course, but its core principles crystallized much earlier within the ILC, and some important principles that it embraces trace their roots as international legal concepts for water to the 1960s. Were the process of generating global norms exerting a significant top-down pull on content at the basin level, we would expect to see both a diffusion and a deepening of these principles—diffusion in the sense of becoming more widespread over time within the dataset, and deepening in the sense of greater specificity, broader scope, or greater intrusiveness in the responsibilities or obligations created for states.

A caveat is in order; none of this should be read to suggest that the results show no pattern at all of institutional development or normative dynamism. Some principles have spread and deepened, showing signs of progressive development, even if most have not done so. Trends in single principles cannot be divorced from the larger set of developments: environmental and harm-avoidance principles seem to have generated a backlash over sovereignty, and two identifiable groups of linked principles can be seen in the data centered on openness and sustainability and the state's rights to water. Periods of momentum and dropoff can be seen in the temporal distribution. It would be a mistake to dismiss these normative dynamics, just as it would be a mistake to interpret them as evidence of a robust, unidirectional, deepening process of formation of a global regime for international rivers.

Conclusion

Efforts to craft a global legal framework for international rivers have been under way for more than four decades. These efforts have embraced a conventional understanding of authority, territoriality, and knowledge as they relate to international rivers. The culmination of these efforts, the 1997 UN Watercourses Convention, makes a stark, polarized distinction between a domestic sphere that will remain in place for the state's governance and an international sphere that demands intersovereign cooperation. The convention also expresses a strongly statist understanding of authority in both of these realms and an optimistic epistemology of progress through knowledge stabilization.

To be sure, several of the convention's core principles are essential to the protection of international rivers and the watersheds that encompass them. It is hard to imagine sustainable governance of border-spanning rivers and watersheds without the participation of all basin states, without an exchange of information, or in the absence of some institutional means of resolving disputes. However, a fatal by-product of the convention's position toward territory, authority, and knowledge is the failure to address central, contentious issues and linkages. Rivers and watersheds are reduced to "watercourses," thereby ignoring critical links among water quality, land use, and regional development patterns, both within and across state borders. They are further divided into either "domestic" or "transboundary" watercourses, creating an even more narrowly circumscribed notion of environmental protection that limits some vaguely defined "significant harm" to downstream states. States are the sole arbiters of the equity of use and the significance of harm. This reduces the question of which practices in and around watersheds are legitimate to a matter of simply allocating water rights among competing uses. And all of this takes place in a world where an expanding frontier of abstract, stabilized knowledge excludes any possibility of surprise, any need for precaution, or any hint of different ways of knowing.

As a result, the convention's would-be norms have much more to say about striking mutually acceptable interstate water deals than about protecting the planet's watersheds, drainage basins, and freshwater ecosystems. These norms produced a politically acceptable accord within the General Assembly that lasted only until member states had to ratify it back home. They also provide little guidance on the most contentious questions that plague watershed politics and thus offer little hope of effective socioecological governance of watersheds.

Internationally shared rivers have not generated the type of violent conflict sometimes predicted to follow water across borders. To that limited extent, it can perhaps be said that cooperative norms have come to be established (although it seems more likely that fears of violent conflict have been exaggerated, as several skeptics of the idea of environmentally induced conflict have pointed out).[41] Even so, there is little evidence of a common normative structure in the form that interstate cooperation has taken across the world's shared river basins, and there is no compelling evidence that international legal principles are taking on greater depth of meaning or even moving in an identifiable direction.

Meanwhile, left to their own devices or aided by foreign donors, most governments have repeatedly proved themselves to be eager dammers, diverters, and drainers, with little regard for the ecological, social, or even economic costs of those schemes. As the 1997 Stockholm Water Symposium concluded, "The overriding issue—how to reconcile upstream socio-economic development with downstream protection of ecological services—remains unsolved."[42]

5

Expert Networks: The Elusive Quest for Integrated Water Resources Management

Water is affected by everything, and water affects everything and everyone.
—World Commission on Water for the 21st Century, *A Water Secure World*

As discussed in chapter 4, some of the pressure on governments and other actors to change their watershed practices emerges from intergovernmental relations. Central norms emanating from the legal-diplomatic sphere—sovereign cooperation, equitable use of resources, information sharing, avoidance of significant harm, and peaceful resolution of disputes—fit comfortably within the standard regime framework. In most international basins, however, these pressures have fallen short of generating instruments of shared governance. Nor is there a clear pattern of normative convergence across the subset of basins where such instruments have been created.

A deeper problem is that this emerging "international rivers" frame merely hints at the scope of the challenge of global watershed governance. If the problem were simply one of expanding national water supplies in ways that do not spill across borders, and of managing that spillover cooperatively when it does occur, then diplomatic initiatives and basin-scale accords might be sufficient. As suggested in chapter 3, however, rivers are more than just border-spanning pipes provided by nature. They are part of the watersheds through which they flow. They are essential constituents of local and regional ecosystems; central elements of vital ecosystem functions such as ensuring freshwater biodiversity, recharging of aquifers, enrichment of floodplains, and preservation of ecosystem integrity; and are critical components of the global hydrologic cycle. Rivers are also important sociocultural instruments; they are sources of livelihood, anchors of culture and community, and key components of national economic development strategies. Under these circumstances, rivers must be understood, not in isolation, but as elements of broader and more complex socioecological systems. They generate ecological and socioeconomic challenges that spill far beyond the confines of shared basins and sovereign diplomacy, encompassing not only the world's "international" rivers but any waterways being "pushed around" by the conflicting demands of human needs, agro-industrial growth, and in-stream ecosystem uses.

This holistic perspective is closely related to a broader view of water resources management. Water expert Peter Gleick describes what he sees as an ongoing paradigm shift on water use and water resource development:

The twentieth-century water-development paradigm, driven by an ethic of growth, has now stalled as social values and political and economic conditions have changed. More people now place a high value on maintaining the integrity of water resources and the flora, fauna, and human societies that have developed around them. There are growing calls for the costs and benefits of water management and development to be distributed in a more fair and prudent manner and for unmet basic human needs to be addressed. And more and more, efforts are being made to understand and meet the diverse interests and needs of all affected stakeholders.[1]

A central element in the new thinking to which Gleick alludes is integrated water resources management. As a conceptual approach to water problems, planning, and practice, IWRM typically stresses three interrelated themes: recognition of the full range of social, economic, and ecological uses of water; "cross-sectoral" water management, in the sense of integrating planning and practices related to agricultural, industrial, municipal, and ecosystemic or in-stream demands for water; and water management at multiple scales and levels, in the sense of coordinating local, regional, national, and transnational practices and institutions.[2]

These themes are captured in the World Water Council's *World Water Vision*, launched at the second World Water Forum in 2000, which states that

To ensure the sustainability of water, we must view it holistically, balancing competing demands on it—domestic, agricultural, industrial (including energy), and environmental. Sustainable management of water resources requires systemic, integrated decisionmaking that recognizes the interdependence of three areas. First, decisions on land use also affect water, and decisions on water also affect the environment and land use. Second, decisions on our economic and social future, currently sectoral and fragmented, affect hydrology and the ecosystems in which we live. Third, decisions at the international, national, and local level are interrelated.[3]

Similarly, according to the Global Water Partnership, "IWRM is a process which promotes the coordinated development and management of water, land and related resources in order to maximize the resultant economic and social welfare in an equitable manner without compromising the sustainability of vital ecosystems."[4]

IWRM is significant not only as a more complex construction of the problem than pushing rivers around but also as a political force. More than two decades of transnational networking among water policy elites—beginning with the 1977 United Nations Water Conference in Mar del Plata, Argentina, and continuing through a series of global water summits, international water congresses, and task forces—shifted the international conceptual framework for water. A set of transnationally disseminated water management norms that began with a narrow emphasis on expanding the supply of clean water for human needs would change by the late 1990s to bear the unmistakable stamp of IWRM. In the process, IWRM evolved from an expression of frustration on the part of water planners and managers to become the dominant language in which the challenge of global water governance is framed.

The process by which IWRM acquired this mounting "normative force" is suggestive of various cognitive, knowledge-centered models of international institution building.[5] Expert networks have often been an important lubricant for international environmental cooperation. They move information, frame problems and responses, and pressure governments in ways that can promote the creation of institutions for supranational environmental governance, including but not limited to treaty-based interstate regimes. Most studies of the political effects of such networks have focused on their role in promoting interstate collective action on problems of regional or global commons such as climate change, stratospheric ozone depletion, or ocean pollution. Conceptual models of how this process works politically have stressed several different factors: the state-herding influence exerted by "epistemic communities" of technical experts, the problem-framing role of politically savvy "knowledge brokers," and the knowledge-disseminating role of transnational "social learning" networks.[6]

These models differ in how they characterize expert networks and the sources of influence they ascribe to them. However, they share an assumption that actors with shared knowledge foundations and value orientations can be an important—even authoritative—source of norms in world politics. In other words, the combination of the ideas constituting IWRM, the network of water policy elites advocating it, and the growing embeddedness of the settings and channels in which these actors wield these ideas constitute another source of would-be global norms for the governance of rivers, watersheds, and freshwater ecosystems.

As with the interstate international rivers frame, the link between IWRM and rivers is once-removed; the central focus is on water resources, not watersheds per se. Nevertheless, the ramifications of IWRM for watershed governance are enormous. Once water resource development is understood to have important consequences for other fundamental water values and uses—be it ecosystem maintenance, the more efficient use of economic resources, the integrity of local communities, or improved stakeholder participation—then questions about the sustainable management of rivers and watersheds follow in short order.

This chapter examines the pattern of international institution building linked to the idea of IWRM. In tracing that history, I give particular emphasis to three aspects: the ideational content of the concept; the stance of that content toward underlying metanorms of knowledge, authority, and territoriality; and the key events, organizations, programs, publications, and other strands along which transnational networking and institution building have taken place. In other words, IWRM is interpreted in two related but distinct ways: as an increasingly clearly specified conceptual blueprint and as an increasingly embedded, institutionalized set of transnational relationships.

Some noteworthy patterns emerge from this history. IWRM has become *the* discursive framework of international water policy—the reference point to which all other arguments end up appealing. Much like the thoroughly picked-over concept of sustainability, IWRM combines intuitive reasonableness, an appeal to technical authority, and an all-encompassing character of such great flexibility that it approaches vagueness. This feature is well captured in the statement of the World Water Commission given in the epigraph.[7] Vague or not, actors in each of the other institution-building venues analyzed in this book routinely appeal to IWRM arguments, concepts, and rhetoric to bolster their respective positions.

Second, the network of water policy elites engaged in dissemination of IWRM norms and institution building is largely separate from the interstate legal-diplomatic efforts sketched in chapter 4. Some points of overlap exist. International legal instruments make frequent reference to IWRM concepts, and IWRM's multilevel framework pays homage to intergovernmental cooperation. Important points of overlap will also be identified in the country-level case studies (see chapters 8 and 9), in that key individuals and institutions at the domestic level may intersect with both of these international institution-building processes. Nevertheless, the central forum of IWRM in global water politics is the global expert conference, not the diplomatic arena; its currency is the task force report, not the treaty. IWRM networking and river diplomacy are best understood as parallel, occasionally interacting institution-building processes rather than tightly coupled phenomena.

A third pattern is that although they take a broader approach than that of the international rivers frame, IWRM and its networks do not part company entirely with the metanormative framework of interstate regimes. Rather, a careful reading of IWRM—as both conceptual blueprint and institutionalized norms—reveals an ambiguous, complex, and at times contradictory stance toward territoriality, authority, and knowledge. This stance has created a somewhat more fluid political space than is typically found in regimelike institutional forms. In important ways, therefore, IWRM moves outside of the regime space located at the center of figure 2.1, for all three of the metanormative variables defining that space.

Yet, far from generating more workable, consensual norms, this broadened political space has instead become embroiled in chronic conflict and controversy. As we move from the ideas and the networks that sustain them to the various nodes and spaces of international life where they might become embedded as norms, we find a much more mixed pattern. For some, IWRM represents the death of the idea of rivers as resources and substitutes an imperative for comprehensive planning to balance economic, ecological, and social considerations. For others, it constitutes an effort to perfect rather than abandon the rivers-as-resources idea—to shift river development projects and water itself from a state-supplied public good to a private economic good, subject to the disciplining rule and valuation techniques of the market. As a result, the IWRM arena has been marked by struggles over public versus private authority, conflict over market versus nonmarket bases for resource valuation and allocation, and tensions between the territorially fixed character of the state and the transnationally fluid character of contemporary global capitalism.[8]

Transnational water policy networks, even as they have grown in influence, have become fragmented by these central and increasingly bitter controversies engulfing global water politics. If the international rivers framework illustrates the limits of a global rivers regime that is grounded in interstate political bargaining, the IWRM framework, despite its growing embeddedness, shows the limits of an institutionalization that is grounded in authoritative expert knowledge and transnational professional networking.

From Mar del Plata to Dublin: Constructing Water as a Global Problem

Although water was a central concern at the UN Conference on the Human Environment, held in Stockholm in 1972, the emphasis was primarily on various local problems of water pollution that had become hot-button political issues in 1960s Europe and North America.[9] The first attempt to take a more comprehensive look at water problems came five years later with the 1977 UN Water Conference in Mar del Plata, Argentina. The conference brought together representatives of 116 governments, the major multilateral development banks and specialized UN agencies, several regional intergovernmental organizations, eight international river commissions, and observers from sixty-three nongovernmental organizations.[10]

The secretary-general of the conference asserted "For the first time the range and complexity of the problems of water development confronting mankind were being taken up in their totality by a world forum in a systematic and comprehensive manner."[11] In reality, the resulting framing of global water problems was substantially narrower. The principal conference themes were safe drinking water, sanitation, and, to a lesser extent, water for agriculture. The final declaration stressed that "all peoples, whatever their stage of development and their social and economic conditions, have the right to have access to drinking water in quantities and of a quality equal to their basic needs."[12] The action plan emanating from Mar del Plata called for governments to emphasize universal access to safe drinking water supplies and sanitation services. In the wake of the meeting, the UN General Assembly marked the 1980s as the International Drinking Water Supply and Sanitation Decade, with the goal of universal access to safe and adequate water supplies and basic sanitation services by 1990.

This framework for meeting basic human needs for water produced a fairly conventional, regimelike position toward questions of territoriality, authority, and knowledge. Territorially, the recommendations and resolutions in the Mar del Plata action plan drew a sharp distinction between the "domestic" and "international" manifestations of rivers and watersheds. In terms of authority, they strongly reaffirmed state authority in the domestic sphere and broached the idea of sovereign interstate cooperation in the international sphere. The knowledge framework was one of universal expertise to be disseminated to governments by technically competent intergovernmental organizations.

On the domestic side of this comfortably regimelike construction of the problem, watersheds were discussed primarily in the context of specific aspects of river development, including hydropower, navigation, and the need for systematic planning for interbasin water transfers. A few associated problems were also highlighted, specifically the potential of dams to spread disease and problems associated with the destruction of wetlands.[13] However, these considerations were subsumed under the larger concern for development of water supply.

Rivers came into sharper focus on the international side of the problem, with recommended actions following the basic outlines of the international rivers frame described in chapter 4. Efforts to inject the concept of interstate cooperation in shared river basins produced substantial

political controversy. A proposed paragraph on the cooperative responsibilities of states sharing international rivers proved to be one of the
most contentious topics at the conference. A general statement urging cooperation, explicit agreements, and information exchange was adopted
by a roll-call vote of 29 to 13 but with 48 abstentions; resistance focused
on the implications for sovereignty over natural resources. Reflecting the
high level of contentiousness, the resolution drew less support and more
abstentions than a resolution on the polarizing issue of the occupied territories in the Israel–Palestine dispute.[14]

The Rise of the Water Experts' Network

In the ensuing decade, several forces converged to generate a more
complex, comprehensive construction of problems surrounding water in
general and rivers and watersheds in particular. Ecologically oriented
knowledge about water—whether it concerned human impacts on the
global water cycle, the value of ecosystem services, the effects of deforestation and land conversion on watersheds, or the ecological importance
of in-stream uses—was in its infancy at Mar del Plata. As recognition of
these linkages grew, many water analysts, scientists, managers, and
advocates began to seek a more comprehensive conceptual framework
that could incorporate this understanding.[15]

A second driver in the search for a more comprehensive approach was
the increasingly apparent failure of Mar del Plata to produce action on
the conference's declared goal of universal access to basic water services.
According to the World Health Organization, by the end of the International Drinking Water Supply and Sanitation Decade in 1990, an estimated 1.3 billion people worldwide lacked access to safe drinking water
and 2.6 billion lacked adequate sanitation services.[16] Ten years later, a
report to the eighth session of the UN Commission on Sustainable Development stressed the entrenched character of the problem, estimating that
in the year 2000 some 1.1 billion people remained without clean drinking water and almost 2.5 billion without sanitation.[17] In other words,
the rate of expanding access to safe drinking water and sanitation barely
kept pace with population growth during the 1990s.

In 1990, 600 delegates from 115 countries met in New Delhi for the
Global Consultation on Safe Water and Sanitation for the 1990s, spon-

sored by the United Nations Development Programme and hosted by the government of India. The conference's New Delhi statement reiterated the goal of the UN water decade, presenting "an appeal to all nations for concerted action to enable people to obtain two of the most basic human needs—safe drinking water and environmental sanitation."[18] Delhi also offered a new and broader approach to the problem. According to UNDP, "The term 'enable' can be considered a significant new direction, in that the New Delhi statement recognized that international donors and national governments could not achieve the goals of universal coverage without (1) participation of and partnerships with NGOs, (2) human resources development at all levels—from community members to political leaders, (3) education, and (4) community management and ownership of water supply systems."[19]

Reflecting this broader construction of the problem, the New Delhi meeting also embraced four guiding principles:

• protection of the environment and safeguarding of health through the integrated management of water resources and liquid and solid wastes;

• institutional reforms promoting an integrated approach and including changes in procedures, attitudes, and behavior, and the full participation of women at all levels in sector institutions;

• community management of services, backed by measures to strengthen local institutions in implementing and sustaining water and sanitation programs; and

• sound financial practices, achieved through better management of existing assets, and widespread use of appropriate technologies.[20]

These were themes that received only passing mention at Mar del Plata thirteen years earlier.

Both the heightened emphasis on ecological concerns and the push for a more comprehensive approach to water emerged as central themes of IWRM. The growth of IWRM in the 1980s and 1990s was fueled by a process common to many aspects of environmental science and policy more generally: the proliferation of professional membership organizations, specialized publications, professional journals, international congresses, technical meetings, and issue-oriented global summits.

Table 5.1 gives the chronology of important network-building events related to the emergence, growth, and consolidation of IWRM. Networks can be highly fluid in their spatial composition—indeed, they are by definition relational rather than positional—and it is a mistake to define a particular network solely in terms of organizational nodes. Nevertheless, such nodes play an important role in catalyzing networking activities. One such node has been the International Water Resources Association (IWRA). Founded in 1972 as a membership organization for water professionals, today the IWRA has more than 1,400 members in 110 countries. Whereas older professional groups established in the earlier era of pushing rivers around had a narrower focus on irrigation, dam construction, or hydraulic engineering (see chapter 3), the IWRA took a far broader orientation from the start, seeking explicitly to span the boundaries of academic disciplines and geographic settings. According to its mission statement, the IWRA "seeks to continually improve water resource decisions by improving our collective understanding of the physical, ecological, chemical, institutional, social, and economic aspects of water."[21]

As a professional association, the IWRA has facilitated networking among water professionals in several ways. It publishes a membership newsletter and a peer-reviewed journal; holds a triennial World Water Congress; sponsors international meeting, workshops, and symposia; maintains an on-line directory of international water experts; and forms ad hoc committees on topics such as international collaboration. The IWRA also played an instrumental role in the formation of the World Water Council (discussed later).

A second important institutionalizing development has been the routinization of global water conferences, world congresses, and international meetings of experts (table 5.1). The IWRA has held eleven world water congresses since the early 1970s. The Stockholm Water Symposium, held annually since 1991, has emerged as an important networking event between these congresses. Ministerial meetings and expert working-group events accelerated dramatically in the post-Earth Summit 1990s. Early on, such events created important opportunities for frame shifting, as in Mar del Plata's emphasis on human water needs or New Delhi's emphasis on participation and community-scale management.

As these events became far more common in the second half of the 1990s, their effect would be to reinforce IWRM as the dominant discursive framework.

A third network-sustaining development has been the emergence of several important professional publications (table 5.1). The IWRA began publishing *Water International* in 1975. In marked contrast to established professional publications such as *Irrigation and Drainage*, early editions stressed a wide range of themes: water law, education, and policy; global perspectives on the water cycle and human needs; technical aspects of water quality and aquatic ecosystems; and national experiences with water planning, policy, and management. Articles related to water economics and engineering began to appear regularly in the 1980s; themes of water and women, water and public health, and water-related sustainability emerged in the 1990s.

It is telling that the process of professional-conceptual networking that emerged in the 1970s and gained momentum in the 1980s did so in a context of formal institutional fragmentation. There has never been a dominant water-related entity within the institutional apparatus of the United Nations. Although the UN's Administrative Committee for Coordination (ACC) has had a Subcommittee on Water Resources since 1960, water has always been a highly fragmented intergovernmental domain. More than twenty UN-related bodies and agencies claim a freshwater mandate, including the World Health Organization (water and health), the Food and Agriculture Organization (water and agriculture, particularly irrigation), the World Meteorological Organization (hydrologic and climatologic aspects of the water cycle), the UN Education, Scientific and Cultural Organization (UNESCO; sociocultural dimensions of water, water science program), the UN Development Programme (water infrastructure development), the UN Environment Programme (freshwater ecosystems, water pollution), and several others.[22] Similarly, although many international accords signed in the 1970s and 1980s touched upon specific aspects of global water problems, such as protecting wetlands or managing transboundary rivers, there exists nothing even approaching a comprehensive framework convention on water. Instead, IWRM emerged and developed within a politically ambiguous space, bounded by several tangential intergovernmental organizations

Table 5.1
A chronology of international water network building

Period	Organizations	Events
1965–1975	1972: Founding of the International Water Resources Association (IWRA) 1972: UN creates UN Environment Programme 1975: UNESCO launches International Hydrological Program	1967: Ninth ICOLD Congress (Istanbul) 1970: Tenth ICOLD Congress (Montreal) 1972: United Nations Conference on the Human Environment (Stockholm) 1973: First World Water Congress (Chicago) 1973: Eleventh ICOLD Congress (Madrid)
1976–1980		1976: Second World Water Congress (New Delhi) 1976: Twelfth ICOLD Congress (Mexico) 1977: United Nations Water Conference (Mar del Plata) 1979: Third World Water Congress (Mexico City) 1979: Thirteenth ICOLD Congress (New Delhi)
1981–1985		1982: Fourth World Water Congress (Buenos Aires) 1982: Fourteenth ICOLD Congress (Rio de Janeiro) 1985: Fifth World Water Congress (Brussels) 1985: Fifteenth ICOLD Congress (Lausanne)
1986–1990	1990: UN General Assembly creates Water Supply and Sanitation Collaborative Council	1988: Sixth World Water Congress (Ottawa) 1988: Sixteenth ICOLD Congress (San Francisco) 1990: Global Consultation on Safe Water and Sanitation for the 1990s (New Delhi)

Programs, Projects, and Assessments	Publications	Other
1975: UNEP launches Global Environment Monitoring System	1975: IWRA launches the journal *Water International* 1976: World Health Organization and Environment Canada begin publishing *Water Quality Bulletin*	1965: Beginning of UNESCO's International Hydrological Decade
	1978: Launching of the journal *World Water*	1977: UN declares 1980–1990 the International Drinking Water Supply and Sanitation Decade
	1983: Launching of the journals *International Journal of Water Resources Development* and *Journal of Water Resources Planning and Management* 1987: Brundtland Commission releases *Our Common Future*	

Table 5.1
(continued)

Period	Organizations	Events
1991– 1995	1992: UN creates Commission on Sustainable Development 1993: Organization of American States creates Inter-American Water Resources Network 1994: International Network of Basin Organizations established with help of French government	1991: First Stockholm Water Symposium held 1991: Seventh World Water Congress (Rabat) 1991: Seventeenth ICOLD Congress (Vienna) 1992: International Conference on Water and the Environment (Dublin) 1992: UN Conference on Environment and Development (Rio de Janeiro) 1994: Interministerial Conference on Drinking Water Supply and Environmental Sanitation (Noordwijk) 1994: Eighth World Water Congress (Cairo) 1994: Eighteenth ICOLD Congress (Durban)
1996– 2000	1996: Creation of the World Water Council 1996: World Bank, UNDP, and Swedish international development agency create Global Water Partnership	1996: First international general assembly of basin organizations 1997: First World Water Forum (Marrakech) 1997: Ninth World Water Congress (Montreal) 1997: Nineteenth ICOLD Congress (Florence) 1998: International Forum on Global Water Politics (Bonn) 1998: Expert Group Meeting on Strategic Approaches to Freshwater Management (Harare) 1998: Ministerial Meeting on Water Resources and Sustainable Development (Paris)

Programs, Projects, and Assessments	Publications	Other
		1991: First "Stockholm Water Prize" awarded
1997: UN Commission on Sustainable Development releases a comprehensive assessment of the freshwater resources of the world 1999: Global Environment Facility launches Global International Waters Assessment 2000: World Commission on Dams releases *Dams and Development* 2000: WHO/UNICEF release global water supply and sanitation assessment 2000 report	1998: Launching of the journal *Water Policy*	1998: First Water Information Summit launches the WaterWeb Consortium 2000: Stockholm Water Foundation presents first annual Stockholm Industry Water Award 2000: UN proclaims 2003 the International Year of Freshwater 2000: Ministerial Declaration of The Hague on Water Security in the Twenty-First Century

Table 5.1
(continued)

Period	Organizations	Events
		2000: Second World Water Forum (The Hague) 2000: Tenth World Water Congress (Melbourne) 2000: Twentieth ICOLD Congress (Beijing)
2001– 2003		2001: International Conference on Freshwater (Bonn) 2002: World Summit on Sustainable Development (Johannesburg) 2003: Third World Water Forum (Kyoto) 2003: Eleventh World Water Congress (Madrid) 2003: Twenty-First ICOLD Congress (Montreal)

Source: Compiled by author.

and interstate accords. The absence of a coherent global water regime or global water organization seems to have created space for a broader, less state-based discursive process.[23]

By the later 1980s, IWRM was a well-established concept in some key journals and at the meetings that reunited an emerging international community of water policy professionals, but it had yet to appear as the dominant framework for discussing water issues. A telling benchmark is *Our Common Future*, the influential 1987 report of the World Commission on Environment and Development (WCED) (also known as the Brundtland Report for its chair, Norwegian Prime Minister Gro Harlem Brundtland). *Our Common Future*, which rhetorically embraced the idea of so-called sustainable development, had very little to say about water and nothing at all to say about a more holistic, IWRM-style approach

Programs, Projects, and Assessments	Publications	Other
2000: UN Administrative Committee on Coordination Subcommittee on Water Resources (UN-ACC/SCWR) launches World Water Assessment Program		
2003: International Year of Freshwater 2003: G-8 releases its "water action plan"	2003: UNESCO publishes first World Water Development Report	2000: UN Millennium Summit endorses goal of reducing world population lacking affordable access to safe water by one half by 2015 2002: World Summit on Sustainable Development focuses on water as one of five key themes

to water management. Other than passing references to problems of water supply and water quality, the discussion of water in the WCED report is limited to a few paragraphs on the need for improved water management for agricultural productivity and a brief allusion to the potential for international conflict over scarce water resources.[24] The following year, the IWRA produced a statement at its Fourth World Congress lamenting the Brundtland Report's lack of attention to water.[25]

In other words, as it shifted from networks of water professionals to the wider diplomatic and intergovernmental stage, the discussion remained more or less within the framework established at Mar del Plata a decade earlier: national action to address national water needs, expert support from intergovernmental organizations, and interstate diplomacy to manage transboundary water flows. Serious political momentum for a broader conceptual approach would come with two key developments of the 1990s: the rise of sustainability as a discursive movement and the growing density of global-conferencing opportunities to authorize and legitimize IWRM ideas and discourse.

Our Common Water Future: Sustainability, the Dublin Principles, and the 1992 Earth Summit

With the publication of *Our Common Future* in 1987, a global discourse of sustainability began to take root. What it means to put sustainability into practice has always been contested, but most who use the term would agree that doing so entails optimizing across a diverse array of ecological, economic, and social criteria so as to meet present needs without undermining the ability to meet future ones.[26] The concept validated more complex constructions of problems in the face of seemingly daunting tradeoffs.

Despite being underemphasized in the Brundtland Report, strong links between water and the concept of sustainability began to emerge in the build-up to the 1992 UN Conference on Environment and Development, which took sustainability as its mantra. The concept of sustainability resonated with the growing recognition that the twin problems of freshwater ecological stress and unmet human water needs demanded a more comprehensive conceptual framework. In preparation for UNCED, 505 participants representing 114 countries, 28 UN agencies, and 58 intergovernmental and nongovernmental organizations met in Dublin in January 1992 for the International Conference on Water and the Environment (ICWE).[27] Dublin would prove to be a seminal frame-shifting event, and the shift was unambiguously toward IWRM.

Several features of the Dublin Conference worked to maximize the influence of networks of water professionals in shaping its results.[28] The conference was defined explicitly as a gathering of water experts, "of government-appointed experts, rather than of government delegations."[29] The meeting was organized by the Intersecretariat Group for Water Resources (ISGWR) of the UN Administrative Coordination Committee. During the run-up to the conference, the rotating chair of ISGWR was held by the World Meteorological Organization, an organization emphasizing expert credentials and systems modeling, and one without strong incentives to skew the agenda toward a narrow or particular set of water resource interests. The meeting's compressed time frame—the time between conceiving and holding the conference was less than eighteen months and the agenda was set only four months in advance—enhanced the voice of readily available, off-the-shelf expertise. So did the framework for NGO participation, which was limited to international NGOs already accredited for the upcoming Earth Summit. With a few exceptions such as Greenpeace, the Worldwide Fund for Nature (WWF), and the Environmental Defense Fund (EDF), most of the thirty-five international NGOs represented at the conference were water-specific organizations with an emphasis on law, management, science, and policy.[30]

In contrast with Mar del Plata's relatively narrow focus on clean water and sanitation, or even New Delhi's emphasis on a more comprehensive approach to the same challenge, Dublin posed a set of problems of much greater complexity. The Dublin Statement on Water and Development identified multiple goals: alleviation of poverty and disease, protection against natural disasters, water conservation and reuse, sustainable urban development, agricultural production and rural water supply, protecting aquatic ecosystems, and resolving water conflicts.[31] In an effort to chart a course for attaining these goals, the conference also ratified four "Dublin Principles," which reflect elements of the larger paradigm shift:

1. Fresh water is a finite and vulnerable resource, essential to sustaining life, development, and the environment.

2. Water development and management should be based on a participatory approach, involving users, planners, and policy makers at all levels.

3. Women play a central part in the provision, management, and safeguarding of water.

4. Water has an economic value in all its competing uses and should be recognized as an economic good.[32]

The first principle, on water's finiteness and vulnerability, confronted the idea of pushing rivers around with a far more complex construction of the problem. According to the Dublin Statement:

Since water sustains life, effective management of water resources demands a holistic approach, linking social and economic development with protection of natural ecosystems. Effective management links land and water uses across the whole of a catchment area or groundwater aquifer.[33]

A similar theme had been articulated one year previously at the first Stockholm Water Symposium, which asserted that "The sectoral approaches of the past are highly ineffective and have to be replaced by new approaches."[34]

The second Dublin Principle, affirming the rights of local participation, implicitly challenged the idea of the nation-state as an inherent instrument of the public good. The same is true of the third principle emphasizing gender, which pointed to the socially differentiated character of water supply and use at scales ranging from the household to the globe. According to the summary text of the 1998 Stockholm Water Symposium,

In all water-related activities it is essential to involve women. Men and women tend to see problems quite differently, a difference that society must be able to handle. What roles women can play strongly depend on the conditions under which they live, the culture, the traditions and the education level in society.[35]

The fourth principle, on recognizing water as an economic good, was also a major departure from Mar del Plata fifteen years earlier, in that it shifted the focus away from an implicit, fundamental human right to clean water. The principle offered instead a construct in which valuation mechanisms are needed to rank order and allocate water across its many competing uses.

In addition to articulating general principles, Dublin also identified some specific ramifications for river basins and watersheds. Noteworthy here is the tension between an expanding water management paradigm and a powerful inertial tendency to reaffirm conventional stances toward authority, territoriality, and knowledge. Regarding sovereignty, the Dublin Statement wrestled with how to balance the ecologically integrated character of river basins against the divisions imposed by sovereign authority and sharply demarcated territoriality. On the one hand, Dublin asserted that "The most appropriate geographical entity for the planning and management of water resources is the river basin" and that "Ideally, the effective integrated planning and development of transboundary river or lake basins has similar institutional requirements to a basin entirely within one country."[36] However, the dominant norm for international rivers remained territorialized national sovereignty, enhanced by interstate development assistance. "The essential function of existing international basin organizations is one of *reconciling and harmonizing the interests of riparian countries,* monitoring water quantity and quality, development of concerted action programs, exchange of information, and enforcing agreements."[37] Governance of international rivers was still seen as the domain of sovereign, territorialized states: "In the coming decades, management of international watersheds will greatly increase in importance. A high priority should therefore be given to the preparation and implementation of integrated management plans, *endorsed by all affected governments and backed by international agreements.*"[38]

The value attached to stabilized knowledge was also apparent. The Dublin Statement placed a strong emphasis on national processes of generating knowledge in the service of water management, including data collection, measurement of components of the water cycle, global monitoring and data exchange, interdisciplinary research and analysis techniques, technical training, periodic national assessments of progress, and technology development. Although the general rhetoric of participation was frequently invoked and references made to the effects of cultural conditions, the envisioned flow of knowledge is clearly one-way. The only reference that extended beyond the closed club of elite managers was a call to raise public awareness.

The Earth Summit and Agenda 21: New Water in Old Bottles?

A similar tension between paradigm-shifting principles and the reinscription of sovereign, territorialized, knowledge-stabilizing institutions emerged from the treatment of water issues at the ensuing 1992 UNCED Conference. More than a decade after its occurrence, the UNCED meeting (widely referred to as the "Earth Summit") remains an ambiguous event. Most skeptics and enthusiasts alike would concur with the observation of Haas et al. that the UNCED meeting created a more complex construction of the problem, embracing "a tightly linked policy agenda that reflects the complex ecological and sociopolitical links among various human activities and between human activities and the environment."[39] Proponents point to the Summit's endorsement of links between environmental protection and development efforts; the high-level attention it received from governments, media outlets, and publics around the world; the adoption of broadly global treaties on climate and biodiversity; and the growing ties among NGOs and social movement groups around the world. Critics and skeptics point to an agenda skewed toward Northern environmental concerns about climate and biodiversity, the failure of vague conceptions of sustainability to address central issues of global production and consumption patterns, and the absence of tangible commitments at the meeting or actions in its wake.[40]

At the Earth Summit, water issues did not generate high-profile regime-building negotiations of the sort that surrounded climate, forests, and biodiversity. Instead, the UNCED's output on global water problems came in the form of Agenda 21, a voluminous "action plan" for global sustainable development. Unlike the Brundtland Report, Agenda 21 gave water issues an entire chapter, underscoring the complex problem framed in Dublin as well as the centrality of the idea of integrated water resources management. This can be seen in the chapter's subtitle—"Application of Integrated Approaches to the Development, Management and Use of Water Resources"—and in this introductory passage:

> The widespread scarcity, gradual destruction and aggravated pollution of freshwater resources in many world regions, along with the progressive encroachment of incompatible activities, demand integrated water resources planning and management. Such integration must cover all types of interrelated freshwater bodies, including both surface water and groundwater, and duly consider water quantity and quality aspects. The multisectoral nature of water resources development in the context of socio-economic development must be recognized, as well as the multi-interest utilization of water resources for water supply and sanitation, agriculture, industry, urban development, hydropower generation, inland fisheries, transportation, recreation, low and flat lands management and other activities.[41]

The Dublin Principles on participation, gender, and economic valuation were endorsed, albeit in a nonspecific way. In particular, the participatory and gender-based elements stressed in Dublin's setting of expert networks featured far less prominently in the interstate atmosphere of Agenda 21 negotiations.

Once again, however, the application of this expanded construction of the problem specifically to rivers reveals the enduring pull of sovereign territoriality, statist authority, and stabilized knowledge. Integrated water resources management is to be carried out at the level of the catchment basin, but where these extend across national boundaries, the primary task is for states to promote the "harmonization" of national strategies and action programs.[42] Moreover, in doing so, they are to use the tools of universalized, centralized knowledge: risk analysis, impact assessment, optimum allocation, research cooperation, and operational guidelines. Again, the knowledge flow is seen as unidirectional, in the form of calls for public education and the raising of awareness.

It is noteworthy that Agenda 21 remained largely silent on the highly contentious disputes surrounding the construction of large dams, canals, irrigation schemes, hydroelectric facilities, and other projects with highly destructive consequences for watersheds and local populations. Nor did it have much to say about the controversies of water pricing policies, allocation mechanisms, and privatization initiatives. These complex disputes—at once both geographically local and socially transnational—remained unacknowledged within the statist-developmentalist frame of cooperation on international rivers and sovereignty over domestic rivers.

Both the Dublin Principles and Agenda 21 showed clear movement toward a more complex construction of problems, a more holistic set of human–nature linkages, and a new ethic of stakeholder participation. Yet they also reflected the enduring force of traditional institutional forms related to the state, territory, and knowledge. Rather than reading the process of global conferencing and elite networking as merely a top-down espousal of would-be global norms, it can be understood instead as a reflection of this underlying tension, and therefore as a social space within which the struggles created by that tension have played out.

From Dublin to Bonn: Institutionalization and Fragmentation in the IWRM Paradigm

By the later 1990s, the idea of integrated water resources management had emerged as the dominant paradigm by which to view and discuss water policy issues in an international context. A professional community of water experts had crystallized around the concept, promoted it vigorously, and developed increasingly robust transnational links in doing so. These included several professional publications; well-established networks centered on the International Water Resources Association; important stock-taking exercises such as the 1997 *Comprehensive Assessment of the Freshwater Resources of the World* of the UN Commission on Sustainable Development; and an array of international symposia, congresses, working groups of experts, and global summits that had literally reached the saturation point (see table 5.1).

Much as sustainability had become the near-universal language of global environmental discussions in international settings, IWRM had achieved pride of place in global water discussions. Table 5.2 provides several illustrations of this increasingly reflexive invocation of IWRM in several key documents and global policy statements beginning in the late 1990s.

The World Water Council and the Global Water Partnership

Two ambitious efforts to give this process of institutionalization a more tangible organizational form emerged with the formation of the World Water Council and the Global Water Partnership in 1996. As indicated in chapter 1, four years later they presented a world water vision and a framework for action at the Second World Water Forum in The Hague. These organizations and the framework they presented for global water management represent the apogee of IWRM influence. They also illustrate the important ways in which IWRM has fallen short of becoming the dominant frame for global water norms, and the important fractures in the networks of experts that have championed the idea of IWRM over the past two decades.

The idea for a world water forum or council to "involve private institutions, regional and non-governmental organizations along with all interested governments in the assessment and follow-up" was broached originally at the 1992 Dublin Conference.[43] When no action was taken on this suggestion at the Earth Summit, the IWRA took up the call to create an umbrella organization to raise the profile of freshwater issues globally, provide expertise and authoritative recommendations, and undertake periodic assessments of the world water situation.[44] A resolution calling for such a body was passed at IWRA's Eighth World Water Congress in 1994. According to the WWC, "The consensus was established around the need for the creation of a common umbrella to unite the disparate, fragmented, and ineffectual efforts on global water management."[45]

Institutionally, the WWC represents a combination of water elites from national and international development agencies, the private sector, and international professional-technical associations related to the building of water infrastructure. The three founding institutions signing the original articles of incorporation were the Egyptian Ministry of Public Works and Water Resources, the Canadian International Development Agency, and the French firm, Suez-Lyonnaise des Eaux, a leading multinational corporation in the water sector (see chapter 7). These founders were backed by a set of ten supporting or "constituent organizations" drawn from intergovernmental and international professional organizations active in the water sphere.[46] The WWC's 313 member organizations are mostly private firms, government agencies, research institutes, and international organizations and associations (perhaps in part because the annual membership fee is $1,000).

Since its inception, the main activities of the WWC have been to organize three world water forums—in Marrakech (1997), The Hague (2000), and Kyoto (2003). These conferences have been attended by thousands of water professionals from around the world and have been accompanied by parallel interministerial meetings. They are intended to raise awareness of the global water challenge, disseminate knowledge about water problems and solutions, and generate political pressure on governments to respond. The definition of that challenge—and a revealing statement of the organization's understanding of its mission—are contained in the WWC's 2000 *World Water Vision*:

As the world population increased and urbanization and industrialization took hold, the demand for water kept rising while the quality continued to deteriorate. Water scarcity afflicted many more nations, and access to clean drinking water and sanitation remained poor. A decline in public health financing and a rise in transboundary water conflicts made these problems worse. But awareness of the problems was limited to a few on the "inside," in the water sector.[47]

This rhetorical position and the understanding it reflects—of a global problem reaching crisis proportions that is well understood by experts but unrecognized by politicians and the general public—pervades WWC efforts and activities.

Table 5.2
Integrated water resources management as the language of global water policy discussions

Source	Statement
UN Commission on Sustainable Development, *Comprehensive Assessment of the Freshwater Resources of the World* (1997, 45, 49)	"The findings of this report dramatize the importance of putting into practice the concept of a holistic management of fresh water as a finite and vulnerable resource, and the integration of sectoral water plans and programs within the framework of national economic and social policy.... Manage water quantity and quality together in an integrated and comprehensive manner, taking into account the upstream and downstream consequences of management actions, regional and sectoral relations and social equity."
UN Commission on Sustainable Development, Expert Group Meeting on Strategic Approaches to Freshwater Management (1998, 2)	"Integrated water resources management within a national economic framework is essential for achieving efficient and equitable allocation of water resources and thus for promoting sustainable economic development and poverty alleviation. The adoption of an integrated approach to the environmentally sustainable management of water resources is also fundamental for protecting freshwater ecosystems, water quality and human health.... There is much to be done, but an integrated approach is the way forward since it offers a means of reconciling competing demands with dwindling supplies, as well as a framework in which hard choices can be made and effective operational actions can be taken. It is valuable for all countries and at all stages of development."
World Commission on Water for the 21ˢᵗ Century, *A Water Secure World: Vision for Water, Life, and the Environment* (2000, 25, 29)	"It is essential to take a holistic approach to integrated water resources management (IWRM). Decisions must be participatory, technically and scientifically informed, and taken at the lowest appropriate level—but within a framework at the catchment, basin, and aquifer level, which are the natural units by which nature manages water.... This framework incorporates the intersection of three complex and rapidly changing systems: the environment, of which water is a vital part of all living things; the hydrological cycle, which governs the flow and regeneration of water; and the human socioeconomic system of activities."

Table 5.2
(continued)

Source	Statement
Global Water Partnership, *Towards Water Security: A Framework for Action* (2000b, 14–15)	"The philosophy underlying the translation of the Vision into action is integrated water resources management (IWRM). . . . IWRM holds that if water is managed holistically, a more equitable, efficient and sustainable regime will emerge. Instead of fragmentation and conflict, competing sectoral interests and responsibilities for the whole water domain can be resolved within a single integrated framework."
Ministerial Declaration of The Hague on Water Security in the 21st Century (2000)	"The actions advocated here are based on integrated water resources management, that includes the planning and management of water resources, both conventional and non-conventional, and land. This takes account of social and environmental factors and integrates surface water, groundwater, and the ecosystems through which they flow. . . . Integrated water resources management depends on collaboration and partnerships at all levels, from individual citizens to international organizations, based on a political commitment to, and a wider awareness of, the need for water security and the sustainable management of water resources."
International Conference on Freshwater (2001, 4)	"[Water] allocation mechanisms should balance competing demands and take into account the social, economic and environmental values of water. They should reflect the links between surface and groundwater and those between inland and coastal water, growing urbanization, land management, the need to maintain ecosystem integrity and the threats of desertification and environmental degradation. Integrated water resources management should be sustainable and optimize water security and human benefit per unit of water while protecting the integrity of ecosystems."

A second effort to give organizational form to IWRM networking is the Global Water Partnership, created in 1996 as a joint initiative of the World Bank, the UN Development Programme, and the Swedish International Development Agency. Their rationale in creating the GWP was "promoting and implementing integrated water resources management through the development of a worldwide network that could pull together financial, technical, policy and human resources to address the critical issues of sustainable water management."[48] The work program of the GWP has as its stated purpose "to help countries to apply integrated water resources management in a participatory manner as a means to provide equitable, efficient and sustainable management and use of water."[49]

Based in Stockholm, the GWP describes itself as "a working partnership among all those involved in water management: government agencies, public institutions, private companies, professional organizations, multilateral development agencies and others committed to the Dublin-Rio principles."[50] In practice, the GWP consists of a Stockholm-based secretariat with a small professional staff and a membership consisting of regionally organized networks of organizations. A steering committee elected by the membership consists primarily of water professionals from national bureaucracies, intergovernmental organizations, and water-for-development NGOs.

IWRM rhetoric, thought, and conceptualization are integral to the GWP. Along with acceptance of the Dublin-Rio Principles, involvement in IWRM activities is a criterion for GWP membership. Its associated programs, intended "to help [GWP] partners develop and implement good practices for the sustainable management of their water resources," include programs on institutional roles in IWRM, IWRM capacity building, and IWRM information systems.[51] The GWP maintains a ten-member technical committee charged with providing guidance on IWRM priorities. On its website, GWP maintains an IWRM "toolbox" containing planning tools, case studies, references, and contacts and emphasizes legal and financial issues, institutional roles, and management instruments. Its purpose is to "provide water management professionals clear examples of good and bad practices and lessons learned from real life experiences of implementing IWRM."[52]

The division of labor between the WWC and the GWP has not been entirely clear and smooth. The battery of major documents released at the Second World Water Forum (discussed later) created substantial confusion as to the central voice and message. A 2002 survey of WWC membership organizations indicated that most members saw the two organizations as having different objectives and missions: "The WWC is a think tank mostly working in the field of policy making and lobbying, whereas GWP is more active at the grass-roots level by implementing projects."[53] The survey also showed a wide diversity of views among the WWC member organizations about its most important functions. The emergence of these newer entities has also provoked discussions within IWRA about that organization's mission statement and strategic goals (discussed later).

The *World Water Vision*

The apogee of IWRM influence came in 2000 at the Second World Water Forum. Although billed as the launching of a "water movement," the meeting consisted principally of water professionals, experts, government officials, business interests, and mainstream NGOs.[54] It reflected the WWC aim of constructing a global, expert-based lobby.

The Hague event saw the launching of several major statements. The WWC had commissioned a World Water Commission for Water for the 21st Century, chaired by World Bank vice president for special programs Ismail Serageldin, to produce a forward-looking document on global water challenges. This *World Water Vision* (hereafter, *Vision*) was released at the forum, along with a companion *Framework for Action* (hereafter, *Framework*) put together by the Global Water Partnership.[55] At the meeting itself, a parallel ministerial conference involving 149 governments produced a formal ministerial declaration on water security in the twenty-first century.[56]

The WWC's *Vision* described a global water crisis—"the gloomy arithmetic of water"—driven by population growth, urbanization, and industrialization combined with declining water quality, inadequate public investment, and increasing transboundary water conflicts.[57] It projected a world in which 4 billion people will live under conditions of water stress by 2025 according to a "business as usual" scenario.[58]

The *Vision* called for a combination of research and innovation to enhance water-use efficiency; reformed management practices to enhance efficiency and accountability; "full-cost pricing" of water to promote efficiency and conservation; greatly expanded capital investment in water (coming mainly from the private sector); enhanced intergovernmental cooperation in shared river basins; and greater stakeholder involvement in decision making.

Accompanying the *Vision*, the Global Water Partnership released *Towards Water Security: A Framework for Action*, meant as a set of steps intended to make the *Vision* a reality. The report's "global water security targets" included the following goals:

· Comprehensive policies and strategies for IWRM should be in the process of being implemented in 75 percent of countries by 2005 and in all countries by 2015.

· The proportion of people not having access to hygienic sanitation facilities should be reduced by half in 2015.

· The proportion of people not having sustainable access to adequate quantities of affordable and safe water should be reduced by half by 2015.

· Water productivity for food production from rainfed and irrigated farming should be increased by 30 percent by 2015.

· The risk from floods should be reduced for 50 percent of the people living in floodplains by 2015.

· National standards to ensure the health of freshwater ecosystems should be established in all countries by 2005, and programs to improve the health of freshwater ecosystems implemented by 2015.[59]

The *Framework* identified four broad themes—making water governance effective, generating water wisdom, tackling urgent water priorities, and investing for the water future—and a series of 126 specific recommendations that largely echo the technical, financial, and managerial emphasis of the WWC's *Vision*.

The core themes of IWRM pervade both documents: multisectoral and multilevel frameworks, better technical and managerial systems, policy optimization, and enhanced participation. The *Framework* invoked

IWRM not simply as a means to the end of water security but as a measurable target in itself, calling for comprehensive policies and strategies for IWRM to be in place in all countries by 2015. The *Vision* in particular tended toward the more technocratic side of IWRM, conceiving of water policy as a set of levers to be pulled by water managers: increasing water productivity, changing the price charged for water and the value assigned to ecosystem functions, and deploying technological and administrative innovations.

Emerging Rifts: Valuation and Participation

Yet, when one shifts the focus from the documents themselves to their political context, the *Vision* and the *Framework* underscored the limitations of IWRM. The Hague meeting laid bare some important controversies that mark the limits of IWRM's political reach and governing power, as well as some important cleavages within the IWRM community itself.

Substantive controversies were evident at The Hague, including contentiousness over the construction of large dams, water pricing and privatization policies, water and gender, and cooperation on international watercourses. As indicated earlier, anti-dam protesters interrupted the opening ceremony in dramatic fashion. Among "major groups" providing formal comments on the event and its key documentary statements, support from business and scientific groups contrasted sharply with dissenting perspectives. The NGO forum rejected both the *Vision* and the *Framework*; the forum's "gender ambassadors" decried the failure to go beyond "lip service" in recognizing the gender-oriented aspects of water inequality; the international trade union confederation, Public Service International, rejected the trend toward privatization of water services.[60] Latin American and African governments issued statements dissociating themselves from the *Vision* and *Framework* and taking exception to parts of the ministerial declaration.[61] The Turkish government rejected references to international sharing of water resources; the French government expressed reservations about the emphasis on privatization.[62] The World Bank's Ismail Serageldin acknowledged in comments to the NGO forum that controversies surrounding large dams and water pricing were barriers to progress along the lines envisioned in the *Vision* and the *Framework*.

What was becoming clear at The Hague was the limited capacity of IWRM—as a set of ideas, as a policy-framing discourse, or as an expert-driven political agenda—to create a normative structure for the resolution of these conflicts. One of the central tensions underlying water-related conflict has been that of valuation. The question of whether water constitutes an economic good or a basic human right has created an increasingly problematic schism within the IWRM movement. On the one hand, getting the price of water right—for the sake of economic efficiency, as a more accurate reflection of its full social cost, and as a stimulus for more appropriate investment patterns in the water sector—has long been a central theme in IWRM reasoning and rhetoric. In this context, IWRM fits comfortably within the global trend toward so-called full-cost pricing, privatization of water service, and the overall "marketization" of water (see chapter 7). For example, the Global Water Partnership's call to increase water sector investment levels from the current $75 billion per year to $180 billion annually envisions most of the money coming from the private sector, with full-cost pricing the necessary stimulus for that investment.[63]

On the other hand, as Peter Gleick has documented, there is also growing momentum behind the idea of water as a basic human right, grounded in both water-specific considerations and the broader notion of a right to development.[64] The UN Commission on Sustainable Development's *Comprehensive Assessment of the Freshwater Resources of the World* stated that "all people require access to adequate amounts of clean water, for such basic needs as drinking, sanitation and hygiene."[65] A coalition of municipal labor unions, parliamentarians, and greens emerged in the late 1990s to push for a "social charter" for water, in which the basic water rights of all people are articulated even as the need to move toward more efficient pricing systems is acknowledged.[66] The social charter theme produced one of the liveliest and best-attended panel sessions at The Hague, although any mention of it was studiously avoided in the forum's official final report. As discussed in chapters 8 and 9, the idea of water as a public good that constitutes a human right has also been central to innovative, influential experiments with national water law reform in Brazil and South Africa.

As discussed previously, the 1992 Dublin Principles affirmed water as both a right and a commodity, stressing its life-sustaining role but also its economic value in competing uses. In the context of the times, there was a political logic to this formulation—Dublin was challenging state-allocated, state-monopolized water management practices that too often responded neither to water's growing scarcity value nor to its life-sustaining role as a basic human need. Nor is it impossible to entertain both notions. One leading figure in IWRM networks, Jerome Delli Priscoli of the U.S. Army Corps of Engineers, has described IWRM as being marked by a "dialectic between two philosophical norms; one, the rational analytic model, often called the planning norm, and two, the utilitarian or free market model, often couched in terms of privatization."[67] The long-standing presence of this "dialectic" did not inhibit the growth and institutionalization of IWRM as a set of water management norms. However, as the idea has become established that water must be managed comprehensively across its competing human, market-based, and ecosystemic uses, the debate over reconciling the tension between human need and market good has sharpened dramatically.

One example of IWRM's inability to speak to this tension is seen at the level of intergovernmental organizations, which constitute critical organizational nodes in the IWRM expert network. In the period since the Dublin Principles, the World Bank, the UNDP, and the Food and Agriculture Organization have each produced a new policy framework on fresh water, taking strikingly different positions on the question of valuation. In doing so, each organization has embraced IWRM as a fundamental policy guide and a frequently invoked rhetorical device. Yet each organization has found a markedly different basis in IWRM for approaching the valuation controversy.

In March 2002 the World Bank made public its draft "Water Resources Sector Strategy."[68] This report was prepared to assess the Bank's experience with its 1993 reform of water sector guidelines. The 1993 reforms had been based on the idea that much of the problem of poor management of water resources lay in inefficient public agencies, distorted prices, excessive centralization, and poor investment choices.[69] The 2002 report endorsed this 1993 policy framework strongly, while also calling for a repositioning of the Bank with regard to controversies surrounding water privatization and pricing reforms and water infrastructure projects.[70]

The Bank found strong conceptual support in IWRM for reducing poverty through market-oriented reforms. The report argues that "There is broad consensus on what constitutes good water resources management.... Water resources should be managed holistically and sustainably, respecting subsidiarity and ensuring participation, and treating the resource as an economic good."[71] IWRM is understood to mean creating the proper institutional framework, management instruments, and infrastructure for sector-specific water uses, while relying on price signals to allocate water to its highest-value uses within and across these sectors. Essentially, IWRM means getting the prices right within a stable, efficiency-maximizing institutional framework at the national level. The virtues of full-cost pricing, the willingness of most social actors to pay these prices, and the efficiency-enhancing value of privatization are extolled throughout the report.

The Food and Agriculture Organization has taken a very different approach toward the question of water and valuation in its water resources policy guidelines. In the wake of the Earth Summit, the FAO launched its International Action Program on Water and Sustainable Agricultural Development as a response to the water-related aspects of Agenda 21. As part of this effort, the FAO established a framework for national-level water sector policy reviews. In sharp contrast to the Bank's approach, the FAO framework stresses the special attributes of water that make a high degree of government involvement in the sector inevitable.[72] These include water's character as a basic human right, the role of nonmarket considerations such as culture in shaping water-related choices, water's high mobility but low transportability, the many externalities associated with water use, and economies of scale in collection and distribution that create natural monopolies. The FAO's bottom line on the valuation controversy is

Economic treatment of water, especially pricing, should be in balance with water as a social good, considering the basic needs of the poor and their limited ability to pay for it.... Water should be treated as an economic resource. However, a number of other criteria—which are often inter-related—come into play in planning and managing water systems, and different countries will place varying emphases on these. They include: Effectiveness, efficiency, equity and distributional effects, public health and nutrition, environmental impact, fiscal impact, political and public acceptability, sustainability, and administrative feasibility.[73]

The UN Development Programme has also taken a lead role in promoting IWRM, including its role as a co-sponsor of the Global Water Partnership. In 1998 the UNDP board of directors approved a proposal to make water resources one of the main focal points of UNDP efforts. This decision led to the development of a new strategic plan for UNDP water sector activities.[74] As with the World Bank, the UNDP's approach begins with the presumption that there is a broad consensus of experts on appropriate water management practices rooted deeply in IWRM concepts (although it stresses participation, environmental management, and building knowledge-based capacity, in contrast to the Bank's narrower emphasis on management instruments and legal and policy frameworks).[75] In terms of valuing water, the UNDP framework emphasizes the importance of pricing reforms as part of demand-management strategies. However, it invokes the comprehensive planning stressed by FAO as well as the efficiency-oriented market reforms of the Bank, and places greater emphasis on environmental protection, the status of women, and participatory reforms than either the Bank or FAO strategic plans. The UNDP framework also explicitly cautions against an overly economic approach to water valuation:

The water problem facing humanity is not simply a matter of better resource allocation in the economic sense. Even more formidable tasks are the effective and equitable distribution of water and water services to the billions of individual users, and the development of measures that can provide holistic protection of the health and viability of the entire aquatic environment. These are central precepts of sustainable water management.[76]

None of these three strategic frameworks for water management would be particularly surprising to close observers of the organizations in question. Indeed, that is the point: each organization found a reaffirmation of its predisposition toward the water valuation controversy within the malleable language of IWRM.

Of course, such gaps may be intraorganizational as well. Evidence of a split on valuation questions appeared when the World Water Council surveyed member organizations in 2002. In response to a query on WWC priorities, most of its board of governors identified "increasing investments for water" and "moving to pricing of all water services" as important priorities, whereas WWC member organizations ranked these items at the bottom of the list of ten options offered to respondents. The top priorities of the membership were those most closely aligned with a human needs and human rights valuation framework: providing safe drinking water, sanitation, and water for food security.[77]

A growing rift has also developed on the question of participation. Conceptually, enhanced participation in water-related decision making flows directly from the core IWRM theme of comprehensive management of multiple uses. Broadened participation becomes necessary, given the informational intensity and social complexity of the management task. Participation is often couched as well in terms of subsidiarity, the notion that management functions and resource decisions are generally made best when made closest to the source, or at the lowest feasible level of social aggregation.

Exactly what constitutes participation is often described in bland, universalizing, and undifferentiated terms, as in the suggestion of one working group that "The basis for a strategic approach to integrated freshwater management can be founded on a set of key elements that bring together all the relevant parties and their particular socio-economic and environmental concerns that are bound by freshwater."[78] In practice, however, IWRM's rhetorical embrace of participation leaves unresolved important tensions with its often technocratic understanding of knowledge and rationality, its emphasis on the state as the source of change, and the mounting vested interests of water experts in a global water sector that is increasingly colonized by IWRM thought.

Not surprisingly, an approach grounded in expert knowledge, scientific rationality, and increasingly bureaucratic organization has often reinforced a limited, hub-and-spoke notion of participation. Helpful information about uses, preferences, behavior, and effects flow in from society to expert centers; scientific truths as guides to social action flow out. The participatory practices surrounding the crafting of the *World Water Vision* reflected this model. The main participatory channels were a set of regional consultations organized by the Global Water Partnership and four sectoral consultations organized by "water experts and water-related interest groups" such as the International Commission on Irrigation and Drainage, the Collaborative Council on Water Supply and Sanitation, and the Consultative Group for International Agricultural Research.[79] Commenting on the *Vision* participation process, the World Resources Institute concluded that "Widespread accounts of the consultations, including accounts by the [World Water Vision] Secretariat itself, indicate that governmental and quasi-governmental water agencies did play a dominant role.... The Vision's organizers concede that, overall, the process was not as inclusive of grassroots and civil society inputs as they had hoped."[80] A coalition of NGOs was less charitable, describing the process as a "sham" and arguing "The process has been controlled from the start by a small group of aid agency and water multinational officials, mainly from the Global Water Partnership, World Water Council, World Bank and Suez-Lyonnaise des Eaux."[81]

Rather than yielding a monolithic result of water managers as technocrats, questions surrounding participation often produce fragmentation, dissension, and debate. IWRM networks can be understood as a political space in which participatory conflicts are joined, rather than as a dominant form marked by the hegemonic imposition of solutions and the negation of controversies. Rifts may form within or between nodes in expert networks, between clusters of nodes in a particular network, or across parallel or rival networks. Again, the gap between the World Water Council's board of governors and its member organizations provides an example. In the members' survey discussed previously, board members identified "governments/water agencies" and "private sector consultants" as the most underrepresented groups on the board, while member organizations identified "civil society" and "research/universities."[82]

A second source of tension related to participation is the strong tendency of the IWRM approach to define its task as pushing the state toward more rational water-management practices. This often ends up simply exporting the participation problem to the state, as can be seen in the way the *World Water Vision* understood participation:

A model for participatory basin management has developed.... A central feature is the integration of participation and the use of economic instruments. It is equally imperative that decisionmaking be informed and scientifically sound. Effective river basin management thus walks on two legs: parliaments, where users make policies and decide on the raising and spending of money, and excellent technical agencies, which provide the parliaments and users with the raw and processed information necessary for management.[83]

When parliaments and technicians do not fulfill these functions, the rational, orderly notion of participation as a knowledge guide for state action quickly breaks down, as seen in the controversies surrounding the Second World Water Forum.

There is also an ironic twist to participation controversies. As IWRM has undergone enhanced legitimization, rapid institutionalization, and growth within and among associated organizations, its main purveyors have been turned into stakeholders themselves, making it harder to maintain a detached stance of whispering in the king's (or citizen's) ear. For example, there have been ongoing organizational tensions between the IWRA as the historically established hub of IWRM networking and the WWC as a high-profile newcomer to the field. The IWRA played a key role in the formation of the WWC, with the expectation that the latter would serve as an umbrella organization for water resources policy.[84] The WWC evolved instead into a direct competitor in some important areas. It organizes a major global meeting (the World Water Forum) that competes directly with the IWRA's World Water Congress. The Second World Water Forum overlapped with the IWRA's IX World Water Congress thousands of miles away in Melbourne, complicating the lives of some jet-setting water experts. The WWC publishes the journal *Water Policy*, featuring articles from leading voices in the international water policy arena and thus competing with the IWRA's journal, *Water International*. A proposal to withdraw IWRA's membership from the WWC was voted on (but defeated) at the 1999 IWRA executive board meeting.[85]

Conclusion: Water-Expert Networks as an Institutionalized Site of Normative Struggle

Over the past few decades, the idea of integrated water resources management has emerged to offer a new paradigm for water-related decisions and practices. An integral part of that development has been the growth and extension of overlapping networks mobilizing various forms of water-related expertise. Neither the ideas nor the networks can be said to be logically or causally prior to the other. The ideas provided a crystallizing point and a powerful set of arguments for the networks; the networks carried the ideas to greater prominence, legitimacy, and influence in national and transnational policy circles. The clearest evidence of their joint success is the near-hegemony that IWRM phrases and concepts had come to enjoy by the late 1990s as the language of international water policy.

Capturing the resulting institutional configurations and orientations toward metanorms of territoriality, authority, and knowledge is more challenging in this instance than in the case of international river law. The trajectory here is far more dynamic. In the space of less than two decades a diffuse set of ideas became first the discursive frame of a specialized network of experts and eventually the dominant international language of water. At the same time, the networks tied most explicitly to these ideas have moved from the edges to the center of international water policy circles. Moreover, although networking of experts around IWRM is clearly well embedded in the sociological sense discussed in chapters 1 and 2, the institutional setting remains more diffuse and less measurable than the world of treaties, legal instruments, and global framework conventions.

Nonetheless, some clear patterns emerge. Networks of water experts have had three very different sets of effects at once. They have played a powerful role in delegitimizing historical norms of pushing rivers around, an influential role in shaping the broad outlines of a new normative structure for global governance of water; and a weak, fragmented, and ultimately ineffectual role in adapting that normative structure to the most contentious social conflicts and controversies related to water.

At the level of ideas, IWRM has undermined the notion that international water politics and policy could fit comfortably into an intersovereign, regimelike framework for discussion and action. IWRM stresses an integrated, holistic, multitask, multilevel approach. Everything is connected to everything else; everyone is a stakeholder; and all aspects must be considered. At times, the resulting framing of the problem can sound abstract and depoliticized to the point of vacuity. One of the recommendations for reform in the Global Water Partnership's *Framework* called upon "government and other agency staff to voluntarily reduce their own power and involve communities in the decision-making process from the beginning."[86]

Such statements, however, must be understood in the historical context of dismantling the practices of the era of damming, diverting, draining, and dumping. The political power of authoritative technical expertise was an important resource in that dismantling process. In this important sense, IWRM advocates have reframed water. They have moved it from the unquestioned domain of sovereign states to the realm of a more diverse array of stakeholder participants; from parsed and separable domestic and international spheres to the more fluid realm of transboundary relations and processes; and from an assumption of universalized expertise flowing out to water users to a more humble approach based on water users' knowledge and practical experience. As the roles and rules of water-expert networks have become more embedded, an institution has been born that moves outside the regime space of statist authority, bounded territoriality, and stabilized knowledge.

What IWRM and its advocates have not been able to institutionalize is an approach to managing the intense social controversies that accompany the death of a paradigm and that populate the fluid space beyond regimes. Nowhere has this limit been exposed more clearly than in the politics of rivers. As Jerome Delli Priscoli has put it:

The river basin management concept has been driven by a rational analytical model as seen in the use of the words such as "coordinated" and "comprehensive." While this model might provide an ideal, no matter what shape it takes, it does not fit reality. The reality of river basin management goes beyond notions of unified administration and rational analytic models to one of facilitated dialogue and negotiation among stake-holders in the basin.[87]

The reality is also conflict; the paradigm shifts, reframed meanings, and new policy discourses described in this chapter are intrinsic to the political struggles. To the extent that new norms regarding water management are being embraced, they are not simply the result of a technical-rational assessment or a consensual process of learning, but rather are a by-product of intense, bitter conflict about the appropriate uses of water, rivers, and watersheds. In these struggles, networks of experts have put forward norms for the technically rational management of water in a world that is not organized around metanorms of technical rationality. If the framework for international rivers illustrates the limits of a global regime based on interstate political bargaining, the IWRM framework shows the limits of one based on authoritative expert knowledge and transnational professional networking.

The limits of IWRM and the networks that sustain it were already becoming apparent in the early 1990s, with the gap between the network-defined Dublin Principles and state-defined Agenda 21. These limits could no longer be denied as the decade wore on and the often bitter disputes swirling around water, rivers, and watersheds came increasingly to a head. They were clearly on display when the German government hosted the 2001 International Conference on Freshwater in Bonn. Bonn constituted a now-familiar process. It was the next in a series of global convergence points for an increasingly well-institutionalized network of water policy experts, rubbing elbows with social movement groups, businesses, trade unionists, farmers, and government delegations. As has also become the norm, the Bonn meeting included a governments-only session that produced a ministerial declaration. Notably, however, Bonn also incorporated for the first time in global water circles a multistakeholder dialogue in which farmers, unionists, NGOs, business groups, and other nominal representatives of sectoral interests came together with government representatives to discuss key questions, such as the role of the state and the suitability of privatization.[88] The discussion of IWRM that ensued is striking in its unfocused character and the broad array of themes smuggled in under the notion of IWRM:

Integrated Water Resource Management (IWRM) was extensively discussed. **FRANCE** emphasized state water management, universal provision of drinking water and commercialization rather than privatization. **IRAQ** distinguished between water pricing and sale, stating that water sale was unacceptable. **GLOBAL WATER PARTNERSHIP** said discussion should focus on farming, which accounts for 70 percent of water use. **ADB** identified key issues for farmers as access, conservation and fair and equitable returns. **FARMERS**, the US and **MOROCCO** shared their experiences, respectively on water pricing, managing water contamination and managing riverine catchments. **UZBEKISTAN** called for donor coordination, and for donors to respect local knowledge and experience. **NGOs** stressed participatory decision making and **BRAZIL** drew attention to water quality and pricing.[89]

Table 5.3
Recommendations for action, International Conference on Freshwater (Bonn 2001)

Secure equitable access to water for all people
Ensure that water infrastructure and services deliver to poor people
Promote gender equity
Appropriately allocate water among competing demands
Share benefits
Promote participatory sharing of benefits from large projects
Improve water management
Protect water quality and ecosystems
Manage risks to cope with variability and climate change
Encourage more efficient service provision
Manage water at the lowest appropriate level
Combat corruption effectively
Ensure significant increase in all types of funding
Strengthen public funding capabilities
Improve economic efficiency to sustain operations and investment
Make water attractive for private investment
Increase development assistance to water
Focus education and training on water wisdom
Focus research and information management on problem solving
Make water institutions more effective
Share knowledge and innovative technologies

Note: The conference recommendations also included more detailed recommendations on the roles of governments, local communities, workers and trade unions, nongovernmental organizations, the private sector, and the international community.
Source: International Conference on Freshwater 2001.

The final, adopted statement emerging from this oddly personified multistakeholder dialogue was strikingly devoid of IWRM themes and imagery. It stressed instead the specific points of political controversy (on privatization, the role of business and international financial institutions, and urban and rural competition for water) and political consensus (on eliminating corruption, mobilizing financial resources, and the importance of local governments). The discussion of participation, a core IWRM theme, moved substantially beyond the notion of everyone talking to everyone else to stress specific themes, such as strengthening rights to information, creating more transparent processes, and taking action to create and enforce clear legal and regulatory frameworks.[90] Similarly, the declaration of recommendations for action adopted by the conference as a whole took as its point of departure not only such core IWRM concepts as better management, subsidiarity, and efficient allocation across competing uses, but also the very questions related to authority, privatization, valuation, and the role of the state that IWRM has proven unable to bring to closure (table 5.3).

6

The Ecology of Human Rights: Anti-Dam Activism and Watershed Democracy

Neither the dam building industry, the government officials promoting big dams, nor the World Bank can possibly feel secure about the future of large-scale dams, despite their constant refrain to the contrary. It just doesn't make sense for the 21st century, and no amount of bravado or backlash is going to change that.... In the end, the dam-building industry is a dinosaur: defiant and threatened, saving face, resting on outdated assumptions, and unable to grasp the legitimate economic, social, and environmental factors that are preventing large dams from actually getting built.

—Juliette Majot, Executive Director, International Rivers Network, *World Rivers Review* vol. 18(5)

If politics is the art of the possible, this document is a work of art.

—Kader Asmal, chair of the World Commission on Dams, in *Dams and Development: A New Framework for Decision-making*

From International River Governance to Global Watershed Politics

Over the past few decades, large dams and water infrastructure projects have become a globally linked arena of contentious politics. Indeed, the most widespread form of international water conflict in recent years has been not the interstate water wars foreseen by some prognosticators but the increasingly frequent and increasingly transnationalized episodes of social conflict between river developers and their opponents. In Guatemala, an investigation by international human rights activists revealed that in 1982 government forces killed an estimated 369 people in the village of Rio Negro who refused to be evicted from the site of the Chixoy Dam.[1] In Spain's Basque region, direct-action protests against the controversial Itoiz Dam project have provoked violent responses from state security forces.[2] The Spanish organization COAGRET (Coordinadora de

Afectadas por Grandes Embalses y Trasvases) identifies Itoiz as just one of twenty-two such conflicts across the Iberian Peninsula. In Thailand, a protest village established by local communities at the site of the Pak Mun Dam became the site of violent clashes between villagers and "raiders" with alleged ties to the state power-generating authority.[3] Dozens of other examples can be cited. The World Commission on Dams estimated that 40–80 million people have been relocated to make way for dam construction projects around the world, often with no compensation or voice in the process.[4]

These conflicts have been triggered by the enormous social and ecological dislocations associated with large water infrastructure projects, by the often highly skewed distribution of economic benefits they produce, by the tendency of river-development advocates to oversell benefits and understate costs, and by the trail of victims such projects have typically left in their wake. Because these struggles center on a development scheme for a particular stretch of river, they often occur under the radar of the international river diplomacy discussed in chapter 4. Rather than pitting sovereign states against one another, the battle lines in these disputes involve a more diverse array of actors. On one side, typically, is an array of national government organs, the national or transnational builders and funders of the project, and potential beneficiaries of the project (be they industrial or municipal users of electricity, agricultural users of irrigation water, or communities gaining flood-control benefits). On the other side, one typically finds opponents from affected local communities, supporters from sympathetic regional or national environmental or human rights organizations, and transnational advocacy groups such as Probe International, Oxfam, or International Rivers Network.

Despite crystallizing around a geographically "domestic" controversy, the resulting social conflicts are extensively—and increasingly—transnational. As discussed in chapter 3, the drive to manipulate rivers has always had a strong transnational dimension, given the role of international funding and the participation of multinational firms in the construction and operation of major projects. A more recent development has been the transnationalization of opposition, through growing links among organizations of local affected peoples and the emergence of a global advocacy network linking environmentalists, human rights activists, and indigenous peoples' groups. These links among movement groups have been aided by the communications revolution and by the expanded room for political opposition that emerged in many countries during the 1990s. As a result, many basins and watersheds around the world have become the subject of intense, conflicting transnational pressures—whether they lie within or beyond the formal reach of international law and interstate diplomacy.

As previously isolated centers of opposition have become linked across borders, so too have the socioeconomic reverberations of protest. The effects have been felt in financial markets, in development assistance and transnational investment in the water and energy sectors, and in the array of political constraints with which intergovernmental organizations, bilateral aid agencies, national water bureaucracies, and private sector multinationals must grapple. During a meeting with nongovernmental organizations at the Second World Water Forum in 2000, The World Bank's Ismail Serageldin pointed to stakeholder conflict over large dams as one of the two major obstacles to a new global blueprint for "water security" in the twenty-first century.[5] (The other obstacle cited was water privatization and pricing struggles, a set of controversies and mobilizations discussed in chapter 7).

The international regime as an institutional form is a blunt and limited instrument for responding to this type of complex, multilayered struggle, for all of the reasons discussed in chapter 2. A construct of territory as bounded, sovereign, and fixed becomes problematic because rivers are integral constituents of regional ecosystems, the global hydrologic cycle, and transnational socioeconomic relations. Under these circumstances, the neat separation of waterways into "international" or "domestic" quickly breaks down. It is difficult to make rivers sit still as domestic nature, even when they do not flow across a national boundary.

As with territory, so with authority. The presumption of state authority implicit to most regime-building diplomacy is shattered when the main axis of conflict pits the state, as an agent of "development," against some of its own people. Questions of culture, power, legitimacy, and identity quickly become central to the dispute because material conflicts between upstream and downstream interests are almost always superimposed on preexisting social divisions of class, ethnicity, gender, and access to political power. The immediate disagreement may be about how to use the water, but behind that specific frame there lurk profound disputes about what the river means, which of its potential uses are legitimate, and who has the authority to shape its flow. Consider novelist Arundhati Roy's description of the continuing struggle over India's Narmada River Valley:

In India over the last ten years the fight against the Sarovar Dam has come to represent far more than the fight for one river.... From being a fight over the fate of a river valley it began to raise doubts about an entire political system. What is at issue now is the very nature of our democracy. Who owns this land? Who owns its rivers? Its forests? Its fish? These are huge questions. They are being taken hugely seriously by the State. They are being answered in one voice by every institution at its command—the army, the police, the bureaucracy, the courts. And not just answered, but answered unambiguously, in bitter, brutal ways.[6]

Linkages between water and the legitimization of authority are not limited to anti-dam forces or political progressives. In the United States, federal officials seeking to protect endangered species of fish cut off water to farmers in the Klamath River Basin to maintain a minimum water flow in the river. When protesters forced the water gates open, a conservative Christian media outlet likened the act to the Boston Tea Party protest at the outset of the American Revolution.[7] Pro-dam forces in India have also framed the question in terms of larger forms of meaning. They invoke Nehru's description of dams as "the temples of modern India" and frame the issue as national development threatened by selfish, parochial interests backed by ignorant or ill-willed outsiders. Bargaining processes that assume fixed configurations of legitimate state authority offer no channels for the contestation and reworking of authority that is central to these disputes.

Finally, river struggles confound the type of knowledge stabilization that is critical for the legitimization of conventional international regimes. Efforts to set boundaries for the debate and establish the truth about the environmental impact of river "development" have been thwarted repeatedly by the discovery of surprising new problems and effects, such as a toll on freshwater biodiversity, ecological effects far downstream, dam-induced seismicity, impacts on floodplain ecosystems, or most recently, the discovery of potentially vast greenhouse gas emissions from dam reservoirs. Robert Goodland, an ecologist with the World Bank and a frequent intermediary between the Bank and its critics, has identified no less than seventeen separate points of knowledge-based dispute between proponents and critics, including the nature and distribution of costs and benefits, the feasibility and desirability of alternatives, the capacity of governments to regulate effectively, and the essence of "development."[8]

One reason for this conflict over fundamental knowledge is that river controversies defy neat boundaries between technical knowledge and social context. For example, traditional irrigation systems are often contrasted with modern schemes in terms of the marginal cost or efficiency of water delivery. However, concepts of efficiency, cost, price, and profit lack comparable meaning across the radically different sets of socio-cultural rules that define and legitimize land-use practices, management authorities, rights of access, or dispute resolution procedures. Far from resting on a solid foundation of stabilized knowledge, almost every important "fact" about dams and their impacts has been subject to bitter dispute. These recurring surprises, porous boundaries, and disjunctures in knowledge are symptoms of profoundly different ways of knowing, differences that are not easily resolved by the invocation of irrefutable universal truths.

Yet the chafing of global river politics against the territory-fixing, state-authorizing and knowledge-stabilizing confines of the interstate regime formula does not mean there is no international institution building. Quite the contrary. Despite continuing controversies, institutionalization around a foundational set of norms is taking place in two senses. First, as the transnational dimension of these struggles has grown, the channels in which those struggles unfold have become increasingly regularized, embedded, normalized, ritualized, and rendered more predictable to all combatants. Second, a particular set of norms—centered on what I will refer to as "watershed democracy"—have become more deeply insinuated into these increasingly ritualized interactions. In the traditional terms of reference of interstate regimes, the endurance of contentious politics is understood as an indicator of regime failure or a lack of closure on a formal institutional form. However, if we move our conception of institutions outside the box of interstate regimes, then the growing regularization and normalization of that conflict suggests the possible birth of a different sort of international institution.

The institutionalization of norms about watershed democracy has been unfolding at the intersection of several forces, including some of the parallel institution-building processes discussed in other chapters. As discussed in chapter 5, transnational networking of experts around the concept of integrated water resources management has made the idea of "participation" a staple (if somewhat abstract and rhetorical) element of the dominant water-management paradigm. As discussed in chapter 7, the neoliberal economic paradigm and the backlash against it have combined to challenge familiar practices of public finance for large water infrastructure projects. As a result, economic considerations have forced would-be dammers, diverters, and developers of rivers to come to the bargaining table with their opponents on a wide array of questions, including participation.

Without question, however, the principal motivating force for international norms of watershed democracy has been the emergence of a coherent, well-organized network linking anti-dam activists around the world.[9] Since the mid-1980s, anti-dam resistance has become more extensively transnationalized, more deeply institutionalized, and increasingly socio-ecologically integrated. Local anti-dam opposition groups around the world have been able to connect with one another and with transnationally active NGOs and movement groups, making it possible to challenge river developers in a more comprehensive manner than when they were limited to individual struggles over specific projects.[10] Also, environmentalists decrying the ecological effects of major water projects have found common cause with human rights and indigenous peoples' groups protesting the social effects of those same projects. The coalition efforts of affected peoples' groups and transnational environmental and human rights organizations have produced a new frame for viewing rivers, emphasizing the need to recognize and protect watersheds as human and natural communities. The solidification of this coalition has made it far more difficult to dismiss either ecological or social concerns around river development schemes. It has also allowed at least partial transcendence of the North–South divide that typically accompanies both environmental and human rights questions in international politics.

This chapter begins with a historical sketch of the growth and institutionalization of the anti-dam process and the growing embeddedness of contentious political engagement around large dams. Understanding the origins and effects of the transnational anti-dams coalition requires the use of several conceptual tools. Clearly, one useful framework for understanding its origins, actions, and effects is that of the social movement. Scholarship on social movements calls our attention to the context or "opportunity structures" that facilitate a movement's emergence and efficacy; to the human, financial, and symbolic resources that the movement is able to mobilize; and to the processes of framing an issue that give meaning to the movement's aims and actions, both for its adherents and for its opponents.[11]

However, characterizing anti-dam politics solely as a transnational social movement misses some of its complexity. Rather, the movement fits squarely within what Sidney Tarrow has described as the "new world of transnational contention," a world marked by international campaigns of collective action that involve a range of organizational forms, build complex coalitions, and employ a variety of tactics ranging from conventional lobbying to direct confrontation.[12] In some of its more conventional, institutionally sanctioned forms of behavior, such as lobbying or the production of knowledge-based rebuttals, one sees elements, not of a social movement, but rather of what Margaret Keck and Kathryn Sikkink refer to as a transnational advocacy network. This network-based form of politics is less purely "up from the grassroots" than a social movement, yet it is less institutionalized and more contentious than conventional processes of lobbying. "Bound together by shared values, common discourse, and dense exchanges of information and services," the actors linked in advocacy networks use their semi-insider, semi-outsider status to provide alternative sources of information and to generate frames of issues that exert moral and political pressure on powerful actors.[13] In other respects and at certain moments, it also makes sense to view the transnational network of anti-dam activists as what Khagram et al. define as a transnational coalition. Here the predominant form of political interaction is the coordination of specific campaigns.[14]

One way to sort out this conceptual complexity is to draw definitional distinctions among transnational advocacy networks (grounded in information-based and framing politics), transnational coalitions (grounded in coordinated campaigns), and transnational social movements (grounded in joint mobilization).[15] However, as the volume of activity builds and the ties among separate groups become more multifaceted over time, such distinctions increasingly lose their meaning and reduce the space for understanding more complex patterns. A single group may find itself coordinating its actions with others in a specific campaign against a specific target, jointly mobilizing in another campaign against another target, and doing information-based advocacy networking in a third sphere. Under such circumstances, it makes sense to view advocacy, campaign coordination, and joint mobilization as processes rather than as fixed organizational attributes. They reflect multiple forms of interaction that are not mutually exclusive to any single agent, dyad of cooperation within the network, or targeted entity. Viewing this complex political phenomenon as combining shifting elements of these forms of politicking—moving to a language rooted in verbs rather than nouns—allows us to more effectively capture the full range of mechanisms utilized, the interaction between institutional and extrainstitutional expressions of grievance, and the potential paths for institutionalization of norms. This perspective is consistent with the call of social movement scholars Doug McAdam, Sidney Tarrow, and Charles Tilly for a more open-ended, process-oriented perspective on contentious politics.[16]

The focus of the chapter then shifts to the evolution of norms about watershed democracy that has been part of this process of transnational dispute, with particular attention to changing understandings of authority and of what counts as relevant knowledge in watershed governance. Finally, the chapter examines the question of the institutionalization of norms, a surprisingly underdeveloped theme in the movement and advocacy-network literature. Here I pay particular attention to the World Commission on Dams, an unusual mixed-membership body that sought to forge a consensus among contending stakeholders involved in dams controversies. The work of the WCD has been subjected to many interpretations: as an informal cooperative bargaining exercise with limited binding power on states, as an example of the emerging, nonstate loci of authority in world politics, and as an example of familiar "corporatist" brokering mechanisms elevated to the global level.[17] My interpretation is concerned less with pigeonholing the essence of the WCD than with understanding its role as both a by-product of, and further catalyst for, the growing embeddedness of watershed democracy norms.

The Transnationalization of Political Struggles over Large Dams

Network Origins: Convergence of Ecological and Social Critiques

Local opposition has long accompanied the damming and diverting of rivers, but systematic, institutionalized conflict around watershed governance is a relatively new phenomenon. Until the mid-1980s, opposition to dam building around the world typically consisted of local community protests or site-specific battles by national conservation organizations, with individual struggles taking place largely in isolation from one another. Longtime anti-dam activist Patrick McCully reports that "The earliest successful anti-dam campaigns were mostly led by conservationists trying to preserve wilderness area. Resistance from those directly impacted by dams was, until recently, usually defeated."[18] Indeed, in 1984, when Edward Goldsmith and Nicholas Hildyard of the British journal *The Ecologist* published a pathbreaking report on the social and environmental impact of large dams, one of their main recommendations was to "establish links between environmental, human rights, and indigenous peoples' support groups."[19]

An important early catalyst for the transnationalization of protest and the merging of environmental and social critiques was the campaign to reform the World Bank, which began in earnest in the mid-1980s. This campaign is often described as having a predominantly environmental focus. However, as Paul Nelson points out, the Bank came under several reform-oriented pressures at once: on environment, poverty, structural adjustment, and human rights, with partially overlapping networks taking up these various themes.[20] Along with forest colonization schemes, large dam projects such as Xingu in Brazil, Three Gorges in China, and Sardar Sarovar in India came to epitomize the Bank practices being challenged by each of these strands of protest: unaccountability, a lack of transparency, a general failure to incorporate environmental and social concerns into project design and planning, and inadequate attention to alternatives.[21] The sheer scale of these projects resulted in both severe ecological consequences and the forced displacement of large numbers of local people, typically the rural poor, indigenous peoples, and ethnic minorities. Bank-funded dams offered a focal point for the convergence of environmental and human rights activism.

Along with the Bank campaigns, a second key catalyst in the transnationalization of site-specific anti-dam struggles was the emergence of the International Rivers Network. IRN was formed in Berkeley, California, in 1985 as a loose volunteer network of anti-dam activists publishing a newsletter about the toll of large dams around the world. Although its focus was global from the start, IRN was profoundly influenced by— and to a large extent an outgrowth of—anti-dam activism taking place in the western United States and of a predominantly environmental character. Nevertheless, by linking environmental considerations explicitly to questions of human rights, political participation, and social justice, IRN quickly became a critical informational and strategic node for several place-specific opposition groups around the world. IRN's description of its mission underscores this integration of social and ecological concerns:

IRN's mission is to halt and reverse the degradation of river systems; to support local communities in protecting and restoring the well-being of the people, cultures and ecosystems that depend on rivers; to promote sustainable, environmentally sound alternatives to damming and channeling rivers; to foster greater understanding, awareness and respect for rivers; to support the worldwide struggle for environmental integrity, social justice and human rights; and to ensure that our work is exemplary of responsible and effective global action on environmental issues.[22]

In June 1988, IRN hosted the first international conference of anti-dam activists. The meeting in San Francisco brought together sixty people from twenty-six countries and forged stronger ties among activist groups around the world. It produced the San Francisco Declaration, which called for impact assessment, notification and consultation of affected peoples, environmental protection efforts, and linkages to concerns for local food security.[23]

IRN's network-building efforts provided an important new bridge among local anti-dam groups. In addition to facilitating communicative links and a sense of solidarity, critical knowledge-based and symbolic resources in the struggle were created or enhanced. One such resource was independent analysis. IRN acquired sufficient technical and analytical capacity to credibly challenge and interpret claims about the costs, benefits, and effects of large dams. A second network-driven resource was the ability, for the first time, to draw a more systematic picture of the dispersed activities of organizations with global reach in the dams arena, be they the World Bank, bilateral foreign-aid agencies, or multinational corporations involved in dam construction and operation activities around the world. This made it much easier for activists struggling against a dam in a specific place to draw upon and integrate arguments, tactics, and symbolic frames being used in Brazil, Canada, Thailand, or India. Local opponents could now contrast the promises of large organizations in that locale with their performance elsewhere. As a more systematic framing of the problems with large dams emerged, it also became possible to draw a more broadly global picture of the scope and character of opposition. It became clear to local dam protesters that they were not alone.

The Role of the World Bank

By the early 1990s, dam builders found themselves in an intensifying crossfire—targeted by a growing network of anti-dam activists, challenged by the emergence of a new global water paradigm, threatened by low-cost alternatives for electricity generation, and beset by tumultuous changes in the political economy of financing for water infrastructure projects.[24] As shown in figure 6.1, these pressures converged at a time of a soft, weakening market for dam construction (which had peaked in the mid-1960s and experienced a steady decline thereafter). The net effect of these forces was to bring the proponents of traditional river

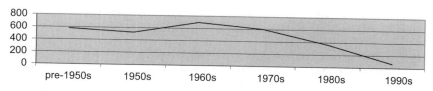

Figure 6.1
Construction of large dams over time (source: Compiled from data in Gleick 2000, 272, table 16).

development projects into increasingly sharp—but also increasingly routinized—conflict with their opponents.

A spate of major dam projects that were started or finished between the mid-1980s and the early 1990s generated some particularly strong forms of local opposition that fed transnational activist efforts. Brazil inaugurated the Tucurui Dam in the Amazon in 1984. South Africa and Lesotho signed the Lesotho Highlands Water Project Treaty in 1986 and broke ground on the project in 1989. India began construction of the Sardar Sarovar Dam, the largest of thirty planned for the Narmada River, in 1987. China's plans for the Three Gorges Dam project, which had been shelved in the face of growing domestic opposition, were resurrected in 1989 in the aftermath of the crackdown on Tiananmen protesters. Thailand built the controversial Pak Mun Dam on the largest tributary of the Mekong River in the early 1990s.

Well into the 1990s, the World Bank remained the central focal point for the trans-local activities of dam opponents. By this time the Bank had forgone or abandoned several particularly controversial projects, including both Sardar Sarovar and Three Gorges. As its increasingly defensive officials became fond of pointing out, the Bank provided only about 5 percent of total funds for large dam construction worldwide. Nevertheless, even this small slice of the total capital market for water projects made the Bank the single largest player in the global water sector. Also, water was a big part of the Bank's overall business; lending for water infrastructure projects accounted for an estimated 15 percent of cumulative Bank funding by the time of its 1993 reforms of water sector guidelines.[25] Moreover, the Bank retained influence on a far greater scale than indicated by its funding activities alone, through its intellectual leadership in establishing the "rules of the game" for dam construction and project evaluation, its power to legitimize controversial projects, and its ability to catalyze multisourced financing packages.

The Bank also remained a central target because its own efforts at incremental reform served as a useful focal point for the anti-dam movement's efforts to create an alternative knowledge frame about large dams. An important episode in this regard came with the Bank's new water sector policy guidelines, which were adopted in 1993.[26] Although billed as the result of a consensus forged at the 1992 Earth Summit, the reforms were initiated in 1990 in response to both external criticism and in-house assessments that revealed the frequently poor economic, ecological, and social performance of many Bank-funded water infrastructure projects.

The pressures on the Bank during the drafting of the new guidelines revealed a movement straddling the divide between contentious politics and lobbying. The U.S.-based nongovernmental organization, the Environmental Defense Fund, and IRN emerged as the primary coordinators of lobbying efforts to shape the guidelines and make the voice of NGOs and activist groups heard in the process.[27] The Ford Foundation provided financial support to both EDF and IRN in these lobbying efforts.[28] During the two-year period when the new guidelines were being drafted, EDF, IRN, and other involved NGOs engaged in a complex dance that mixed consultative participation and pressure tactics: agreeing to participate in consultative workshops while decrying their inadequacy for a genuine exchange of views; providing comments on interim policy drafts while demanding that the Bank move beyond its traditional practice of working with only a few elite NGOs in consultative processes; coordinating with in-house Bank sympathizers while continuing to criticize the Bank in public as a monolithic institution.

A key step in this dance was a concerted effort by the lead lobbying NGOs to broaden the base of input to the Bank to include citizens' groups from around the world. When the Bank released a summary of its working draft policy paper in March 1992, IRN and EDF forwarded it to more than 800 groups in 90 countries. The resulting comments submitted to the Bank revealed "a wide spectrum of attitudes toward the Bank: from a Prague-based ecology institute that politely invited Bank staff to a conference on watershed restoration, to an Indian action-research organization that called for a 'people's tribunal—à la Nuremberg'—to put bank officials on trial for crimes against the peasants of Rajasthan committed in the implementation of Bank-funded irrigation schemes."[29]

Meanwhile, direct action against dams was continuing to escalate in many spots around the world. In Indonesia, students and farmers mobilized in opposition to the Kedong Ombo Dam, completed in 1989. In southern Africa, the massive Lesotho Highlands Project, a cooperative venture between the apartheid government in South Africa and the military regime governing Lesotho, resulted in an escalating series of violent clashes between police, protesters, and dam workers in the wake of breaking ground on the Katse Dam in 1989. In Nepal, the Arun Dam project triggered a large-scale uprising in 1990. In the Brazilian Amazon, indigenous peoples' groups and other dam opponents organized protests against the Xingu Dam. In India, Narmada Bachao Andolan (Movement to Save the Narmada) emerged from efforts to help relocated peoples to take a more oppositional and directly confrontational position against the Sardar Sarovar project, coalescing in a series of direct-action campaigns in the Narmada River Valley.

The process of writing its new guidelines also revealed internal Bank divisions. Environment department staff proved more receptive to external criticism; policy department and country-office staff were often defensive of the Bank's record; engineers and economists within the Bank split on whether more comprehensive basin planning was to be encouraged as "the state of the art in water resources management" or to be shunned as "centralized state control of the economy"; senior staff felt pressure from borrowing countries to limit releases of information and reverse the trend of greater NGO consultation.[30]

When the new water sector guidelines were publicly released in September 1993, the preamble stressed the often poor economic performance of Bank projects as vehicles for delivering services, while acknowledging social and environmental concerns:

The investments supported by the Bank ... have often encountered implementation, operational, and social problems. Underlying these problems is a vicious cycle of poor-quality and unreliable services that result in consumers' unwillingness to pay, which, in turn, generates inadequate operating funds and a further deterioration in services. Moreover, the Bank and governments have not taken sufficient account of environmental concerns in the management of water resources.[31]

The guidelines called for "a comprehensive policy framework and the treatment of water as an economic good, combined with decentralized management and delivery structures, greater reliance on pricing, and fuller participation by stakeholders."[32] Although acknowledging critics' concerns about weak attention to environmental and social impacts, the vague language on these items stopped far short of creating the enforceable "conditionalities" demanded by the leading NGO lobbyists.[33]

The response of the anti-dam movement came in the June 1994 Manibeli Declaration, endorsed by a coalition of 326 activist groups from 44 countries. Named "in honor of the heroic resistance by the people of the village of Manibeli and others in India's Narmada Valley to the World-Bank-funded Sardar Sarovar Dam," the declaration called for an "independent comprehensive review" of the costs and benefits of Bank-funded dams.[34] It also called for reparations for dam victims; cancellation of debt related to dams whose costs were found to outweigh benefits; and stringent criteria for the construction of new dams, including the informed consent of affected local communities and comprehensive river basin management plans in which dams would be understood as a last resort rather than the sole option. Bank procedures were also targeted, via demands for public disclosure, independent monitoring of project preparation, and an end to the use of the Bank's International Development Association (IDA) on the grounds that dam projects did not meet IDA's stated purpose of channeling aid to the poorest of the poor. Manibeli also demanded a moratorium on Bank funding for dam projects until the declaration's conditions were met.

Manibeli reflected the enduring usefulness of the Bank to anti-dam activism; no other target would have produced such a broadly based opposition coalition. Recognizing that the 1993 water sector policy reforms had failed to stop the growth of criticism, the Bank's response was to undertake a review of the large dam projects that it had "assisted." The Bank's intent was to do a two-stage review, involving first an internal desk study of fifty Bank-assisted dams completed between 1960 and 1995. The second stage was to be "a broader study, involving the collection of new data and participation by other stakeholders, to evaluate the development effectiveness of large dams in terms of technical, economic, social and environmental implications for future financing by the World Bank Group, as well as other sources."[35] As discussed later, this second-stage review was never completed; it became a victim of the Bank's loss of control over the process of evaluation, review, and standards setting on large dams.

The first-stage review was completed by the Bank's Operations Evaluation Department (OED) in August 1996.[36] Only a six-page summary of the report was released publicly. The summary asserted that the projects reviewed had a "mixed record" in their treatment of displaced people and in their effects on the environment. It also asserted that "The policies the Bank has adopted on resettlement and environmental aspects of projects have improved performance 'on the ground'."[37] According to the summary, the OED found that 90 percent of the reviewed projects were acceptable under whatever Bank policies on impact mitigation and management had been in place at the time of project approval. When evaluated in terms of the stricter policies that were in place by the mid-1990s, 26 percent were judged acceptable by the newer standards, 48 percent "potentially acceptable," and 26 percent unacceptable. Also, the summary asserted that "In most of the cases reviewed, benefits have far outweighed costs, including the costs of adequate resettlement programs, environmental safeguards, and other mitigatory measures."[38] Mitigation in compliance with Bank standards reportedly would have been feasible and economically justifiable in 74 percent of the reviewed cases. The final conclusion was an endorsement of Bank involvement in large dam projects: "These results suggest that the Bank should continue supporting the development of large dams provided that they strictly comply with Bank guidelines and fully incorporate the lessons of experience."[39]

Politically, the review was a bid to reposition the Bank by distancing current practices from past problems, reframing the debate as one of compliance with the now-adequate standards, and affirming the appropriateness of existing Bank goals and policies. The Bank sought to walk two fine lines at once: to acknowledge some past mistakes while reaffirming the soundness of recently tightened policies, and to share just enough information publicly to validate its positions while preserving its knowledge-based authority and keeping standard setting and performance evaluation firmly in the Bank's hands.

The most important result, however, was to draw the Bank into deeper and more sustained dialogue with its most vocal critics. The OED review made it easier than ever before to take the debate beyond individual dam controversies and create a systemic frame around underlying Bank policies, practices, and presumptions. IRN obtained a leaked copy of the OED review and published a scathing critique, emphasizing both the quality of the report and the Bank's excessive secrecy. Among IRN's main analytical charges were that the report systematically overstated the benefits of large dams, used projected rather than actual costs and benefits, and failed to consider the full range of ecological effects of dams.[40] Far from reestablishing the Bank's knowledge-based authority, the OED internal review gave opponents a potent new focal point. As the Bank generated technical analyses to validate its position, the quality of those analyses became a rich source of ammunition for Bank critics to use in knowledge-based skirmishes.

IRN's critique of the OED review also attacked the Bank procedurally, accusing it of engaging in a process of "incremental censorship." A comparison of documents showed that negative comments about Bank performance in a background report were softened or omitted in the OED evaluation report and further softened in the four-page public summary. Accompanying the release of the IRN critique, forty-nine NGOs from twenty-one countries sent a letter to World Bank president James Wolfensohn rejecting the OED conclusions and calling instead for "a comprehensive, unbiased and authoritative review of past World Bank lending for large dams."[41]

These criticisms resonated well beyond the activist community. As discussed in chapter 7, in the wake of neoliberal structural adjustment the Bank had come to view private capital as an increasingly important funding partner for water infrastructure projects. The substantive challenge to the effectiveness and benefits of large dams stoked one of the Bank's largest concerns: the growing skittishness of private capital about the political and financial risks associated with such projects. Moreover, the procedural criticisms portraying an imperious, secretive institution provided ammunition for Bank critics on both the left and the right in key donor countries.[42] The criticism also strengthened the hand of in-house critics of Bank performance.

The cycle of contentious politics in the period surrounding the OED review revealed the now multiedged capacity of the coalitional elements of the anti-dam movement. In a sense, each side enhanced the other's opportunities. The IRN and its partners were by now able to employ substantial expertise in rebutting the technical and financial justifications offered by the Bank. The knowledge-based critique helped on-the-ground opponents of Bank projects to link their opposition to a wider frame of systematic Bank failings. At the same time, on-the-ground opposition was an important resource for the international NGOs, in that it allowed them to show the sizable gap between the Bank's practices and its newly espoused principles of local consultation.

From San Francisco to Curitiba: A Decade of Evolution in Emergent Norms of Watershed Democracy

By the second half of the 1990s, the anti-dam movement had grown well beyond its early days of rebutting project-specific World Bank claims and loosely coordinating project-specific protests. A comprehensive critique of dam-building practices—and of the transnational financial and political relationships that sustained those practices—had been developed and honed. The movement's ambitions scaled up from holding dam builders accountable to effectively putting an end to the era of large dams. Along the way, a loose consultative process centered on IRN's catalytic role had grown into a well-networked global movement and a notably stronger voice within the coalition for local affected peoples' groups.

These changes were apparent when activists gathered in Curitiba, Brazil, in March 1997 for the First International Meeting of People Affected by Dams. Curitiba illustrated the extent to which a loosely coupled network of individuals and small groups had changed over the course of a decade to become a well-linked, network-based coalition of local and international groups. The meeting, organized and hosted by the Brazilian Movement of Dam-Affected People (MAB), included thirty-eight representatives of anti-dam activist groups in twenty countries as well as sixty Brazilian activists. Financial support came from more than a dozen international and Brazilian human rights, environmental, and grassroots development organizations.[43]

As seen in table 6.1, Curitiba also illustrated the scaling up of demands over time. A decade earlier, when IRN hosted the first international gathering of anti-dam activists in San Francisco, demands had centered on comprehensive assessment; full disclosure of information; environmental protection; and local consultation. By the time of the Curitiba gathering, a more powerful, emboldened movement with a broader global reach was calling for "an end to the era of destructive dams."[44] The demands now included the implementation of "sustainable" alternatives, the restoration of damaged ecosystems, and payment of reparations to a wider array of dam-affected peoples. Two demands in particular had moved to the center of movement activism: a moratorium on construction of large dams and an independent commission to assess the performance of existing dams.

During this decade of growth and transition, some of the most fundamental elements of framing remained constant—that large dams constituted acts of violence against people and nature; that dam builders and financers were not accountable for their actions; that local communities lacked a voice in the decisions affecting them; and that corruption, inefficiency, and repression were inherent in the process of building and operating large dams. However, changes in political context, composition of the movement, and choice of strategy resulted in some important shifts at a more finely grained level of framing. As indicated in table 6.1, both the targets of anti-dam activism and the local communities with which solidarity was claimed were broadened considerably over the course of the decade. By Curitiba, activists were increasingly situating the problem in the context of an international financial system populated not only by the World Bank and its donor governments but also by private investors, multinational firms, and a range of intergovernmental organizations. In this sense, the movement was situated comfortably within the emerging "anti-globalization" discourse of the latter 1990s.[45]

Another notable trend is the broadened definition of the community with which solidarity was claimed and the larger set of community rights to be defended, a product of the growing influence of local organizations of affected peoples within the network. A decade earlier, San Francisco had stressed the problem of forcible evictions for dam construction, calling for compensation to all people losing "homes, land, or livelihood" as a result of dam construction.[46] Curitiba demanded not only compensation but reparations for affected peoples, and emphasized the impact on downstream communities as well as those forcibly displaced by a dam and its reservoir. Curitiba also emphasized a broader set of rights for local groups, including an end to violence against dam opponents and a

Table 6.1
The evolution of movement aims and frames

	San Francisco 1988	Manibeli 1994	Curitiba 1997
Demands			
Transparency and governance	Full disclosure of all information on past, present, and future dam projects Free access to project information for citizens of both lending and recipient countries	"Adequate opportunity" for review and critique by "independent experts" Independent monitoring and evaluation of World Bank activities Independent review of costs and benefits of all Bank-funded large dams	Independent commission review of all internationally financed dams
Authorization processes for dam construction	Assessment of short- and long-term effects of projects All alternatives to project goals analyzed Veto power for affected communities	"Locally approved" comprehensive basin management plan Involvement and informed consent of communities to be displaced "Last resort" after "alternatives for flood management, transportation, water supply, irrigation and power supply are exhausted"	Immediate moratorium on construction, pending reforms Informed approval by affected people

Environmental considerations	Environmental impact assessment	"No significant adverse effect" on downstream environment or protected areas Impact of industrial activities using dam electricity must be included in assessments	Environmental restoration, including dam removal
Rights and compensation for affected peoples	All affected peoples to be notified and consulted; compensation for those losing homes, lands, livelihoods	Reparations for forcibly evicted people	Reparations for people "whose livelihoods have suffered" from dams Halt violence against dam opponents
Framing			
Central rhetorical aim	"Protecting rivers and water resources"	"An immediate moratorium on all World Bank funding of large dams"	"Bring an end to the era of destructive dams"
Actors targeted	Dam funding agencies	World Bank	Multilateral and bilateral aid and credit agencies Dam construction and equipment companies Engineering and environmental consultants Energy corporations

Table 6.1
(continued)

	San Francisco 1988	Manibeli 1994	Curitiba 1997
Communities with which solidarity claimed	"Affected peoples" in the reservoir area and downstream Citizens in borrowing and lending countries	Communities experiencing forced resettlement Uncompensated victims displaced by dams Victims of forest and fishery destruction and spread of waterborne diseases, emphasizing women, minorities, indigenous peoples Demonstrators subjected to violence and arrests Debt-burdened citizens in borrowing countries	"Small farmers; rural workers; fishers; tribal, indigenous and traditional communities" Dam opponents subjected to violence "Tribal, semitribal and traditional populations"
Links to other issues	Local food security Downstream floodplain agriculture	Energy and water policies External debt	Energy and water policies Indigenous peoples' rights Land reform; community control of resources Privatization Consumption Social equity Democratic accountability

Stance toward authority and knowledge

Role of national governments	Provide access to information	Put "policies and legal frameworks" in place to assure restoration of the living standards of displaced peoples"	Independent comprehensive reviews of projects and activities of national agencies
Role of nonstate actors	Independent experts to review and critique impact assessments	Informed consent from local communities Involvement of civil society in "identification, design, implementation, and monitoring" of projects Independent monitoring and evaluation "by persons outside the Bank"	"Public participation and transparency in the development and implementation of energy and water policies" "Decentralization of political power and empowerment of local communities" Affected peoples to participate in decision making and approve dam projects Independent international commission to review performance to date of large dams
Epistemology	"Expert" assessments of environmental, social, and economic effects Burden of proof of no harm lies with dam planners and builders Economic analysis must identify range of uncertainty in costs and benefits	"New project appraisal techniques" to be grounded in actual Bank experience Cites the absence of "evidence" to demonstrate that costs are justified by the benefits	"Modern science and traditional knowledge"

Sources: Compiled from IRN 1996; Manibeli Declaration 1994; First International Meeting of People Affected by Dams 1997.

reaffirmation of the territorial rights of indigenous peoples and traditional communities.

Institutionalizing Transnational Contentious Politics: The World Commission on Dams

One useful way to interpret the growth, development, and evolution of anti-dam activism is in the language of social movement theory, with its emphasis on opportunity structures, resource mobilization, and framing processes. The period from the mid-1980s to the mid-1990s was one of increasingly favorable opportunity structures for the movement, including the growing chinks in the World Bank's armor of legitimacy, the transnational possibilities inherent in the communications revolution and emergence of the Internet, and the more substantial space for political participation during the 1990s in important dam-building countries ranging from Brazil to Thailand to South Africa. The loose network that coalesced among ongoing site-specific struggles proved able to draw upon important international political and financial resources while maintaining on-the-ground opposition in a growing number of watershed-scale struggles. One key to consolidating the movement at the international level was a potent frame that blended ecological, human rights, and grassroots development themes around the idea of defending watersheds and their people.

In order to understand the potential institutionalization of emergent norms of watershed democracy, we must complement this conventional social movement interpretation with a focus on links to more institutionalized forms of politics. One useful conceptual tool in this regard is Keck's and Sikkink's transnational advocacy network model. Like movements, advocacy networks are linked by shared values, a common political language, and particular frames for a problem. Unlike movements, advocacy networks are made possible by maintaining a semi-outsider, semi-insider status that enables them to be alternative sources of information and to generate authoritative frames that exert moral and political pressure on powerful actors. According to Tarrow, the distinction between the two forms lies in the extent to which the transnational network is rooted in domestic social networks (more so in social movements, less so in advocacy networks).[47] Keck and Sikkink also view this form of contentious politics as clearly distinct from social movements, emphasizing the network's weblike communicative structures and the importance of insider or semi-insider nodes within the network, including mainstream NGOS, foundations, media actors, and sympathetic actors within governmental and intergovernmental organizations.[48]

However, the multilayered story of transnational anti-dam activism contains both social movement and advocacy network elements. Rather than cramming this complex reality into one stylized model or the other, it is more useful to utilize elements of both to gain perspective on whether and how norms emanating from anti-dam activism gain a more permanent institutional footing. In this context, the advocacy network model is useful in at least two ways. First, by conceptualizing the network as linking like-minded individuals across a range of different institutional settings, the model calls our attention to key processes of political brokering between formal institutional and extrainstitutional realms, and on the importance of key individuals able to play that brokering role. A second useful contribution is the model's emphasis on the mobilization, interpretation, and framing of information; in short, of creating a plausible alternative to the official truths of powerful actors. This calls our attention to the social processes surrounding contestation of knowledge as a critical entry point for institutionalization of norms.

The Large Dams Workshop and the Birth of an Independent Review Process

In the wake of the OED first-stage internal review, and in response to the growing paralysis of dam-building efforts around the world, the World Bank enlisted the international quasi-NGO World Conservation Union (IUCN) to help it organize a workshop that would bring together dam proponents, dam critics, and Bank staff. The idea of holding such a workshop was presented as a way to promote "constructive" dialogue based on "objective assessments."[49] The choice of IUCN as partner was consistent with this rationale, given that organization's moderate reputation, its scientific bent, and the fact that it had not been a controversial player previously on the question of dams.[50]

In April 1997, the IUCN and the World Bank hosted the Large Dams Workshop in Gland, Switzerland. The thirty-five workshop participants included an array of dam critics, representatives of dam-building firms and agencies, and Bank staff. Notably, only a few of the participants were linked to organs of national governments. The invited participants included individuals from seven key movement groups: IRN, the Movimento dos Atingidos por Barragens (Brazil), Narmada Bachao Andolan (India), the Alliance for Energy (Nepal), the Sungi Development Foundation (Pakistan), Sobrevivencia (Paraguay), and Berne Declaration (Switzerland). This was not the first time that Bank water sector staff had engaged in direct dialogue with critics; these were some of the same groups that had injected themselves into the Bank's water sector policy reform process in the early 1990s. However, the ensuing period had seen the Bank lose substantial agenda-setting power in the large dams debate, as reflected in its turn to IUCN as an honest broker and its proactive effort to bring dam proponents and critics together for a direct dialogue.

The atmosphere at the meeting was tense. As the IUCN-World Bank summary of the proceedings pointed out, "In several cases, adversaries were meeting each other face-to-face for the first time."[51] Tensions were heightened by events leading up to the workshop, which came just a month after the Curitiba international gathering had energized protest groups. Just a few days prior to the workshop, IRN released its blistering critique of the 1996 OED internal review.[52]

Although it marked an unusual departure from past practices, the willingness of Bank officials and dam industry representatives to participate in this type of organized dialogue is not difficult to explain. They were brought to the table by the growing ability of anti-dam activists to exert sustained, meaningful pressure and by the search for more effective "political risk management," not only for the Bank itself, but also for the private investors increasingly relied upon by the Bank and dam-building governments. The willingness of activist groups to come to the table requires a bit more explanation, and seems to have been driven by a combination of considerations. First, the workshop was an opportunity to legitimize criticism by the movement. The possibility that the workshop would produce an independent review commission—a core demand of the movement since the 1994 Manibeli Declaration—made it too important an opportunity to miss. Although expressing reservations about its composition, IRN campaigns director Patrick McCully described the commission as an opportunity to create "an international forum for the voices of dam-affected people and dam critics which dam funders and builders will find difficult to ignore."[53] Second, the cost of engaging in this manner was seen to be low. Movement activists appeared to conclude that if the process were to degenerate into a smoke-screen for the Bank and the dams industry, it would not be difficult to disengage and return to more confrontational tactics. Third, as participation in decision-making processes had come to be a more central movement theme, the decision to decline an opportunity to do so came at greater cost.

Building the World Commission on Dams

Participants in the workshop were tasked with identifying "the critical advances needed in knowledge and practice" in order to assess and develop large dams, the "methodologies and approaches" needed to achieve these advances, and the appropriate process to realize these advances. The set of twenty-four items identified as "critical advances needed in knowledge and practice" ranged from better technical information (mostly related to engineering, finance, and environmental assessments) to stakeholder participation principles and an endorsement of indigenous knowledge systems.[54]

The most important result of the workshop was an agreement on the formation of a world commission on large dams. The commission was to sit for a two-year period with the following mandate:

• to assess the experience with existing, new and proposed large dam projects so as to improve (existing) practices and social and environmental conditions;

• to develop decision-making criteria and policy and regulatory frameworks for assessing alternatives for energy and water resources development;

• to develop and promote internationally acceptable standards for the planning, assessment, design, construction, operation and monitoring of large dam projects and, if the dams are built, ensure affected peoples are better off;

• to identify the implications for institutional, policy and financial arrangements so that benefits, costs and risks are equitably shared at the global, national and local levels; and

• to recommend interim modifications—where necessary—of existing policies and guidelines, and promote "best practices."[55]

The original plan was for a commission with five to eight members to be in place within six months of the workshop. A consultative group made up of workshop participants and other invitees was also to be created, to serve as a sounding board. The recommendations identified as one goal that the commission's overall process "involve stakeholders in a full and meaningful way."[56]

David McDowell, director-general of IUCN, established an interim working group of IUCN and World Bank staff to establish the commission in consultation with workshop participants. Controversy erupted as soon as the working group's list of proposed members was released. Dam opponents protested that the panel included dam industry representatives but none of the nongovernmental organizations active in the IUCN workshop and the commission-forming process. They decried also the absence of technical skill on ecological effects and dam alternatives.[57] The World Bank, IUCN, and the proposed chair of the commission, South Africa's former water minister, Kader Asmal, responded initially that the commission would proceed despite these protests. However, the threat of the activists to pull out of the process soon forced a compromise; an early 1998 meeting in Cape Town, South Africa, produced agreement on an expanded set of commissioners. The key addition was Medha Patkar, a leader in the Narmada Bachao Andolan movement against the Sardar Sarovar Dam complex in India.

In addition to Patkar, the WCD included the chief executive officer of the multinational engineering firm ABB; a past president of the International Commission on Large Dams, the international professional association for dam engineers; academics from the United States and Brazil; government organs in Australia, China, and South Africa; a retired Indian diplomat with extensive experience in intergovernmental organizations; and representatives from nongovernmental organizations active in the environment, human rights, and grassroots developments (table 6.2).

The WCD launched its operations in February 1998 and held its first meeting of commissioners in May of that year. A small secretariat and professional staff were established in Cape Town. A group of sixty-eight organizations were invited to join the WCD Forum, a loose consultative structure to be used by the WCD as a sounding board. Table 6.3 summarizes the forum's composition.

Table 6.2
WCD Commissioners

Kader Asmal (chair), Minister of Water Affairs and Forestry, South Africa
Lakshmi Chand Jain (vice-chair), High Commissioner to South Africa, India
Donald Blackmore, Murray-Darling Basin Commission, Australia
Joji Cariño, Tebtebba Foundation, Philippines
José Goldemberg, University of São Paulo, Brazil
Judy Henderson, Oxfam International, Australia
Göran Lindahl, Asea Brown Boveri, Ltd., Sweden
Deborah Moore, Environmental Defense, U.S.
Medha Patkar, Struggle to Save the Narmada River, India
Thayer Scudder, California Institute of Technology, U.S.
Shen Guoyi, Ministry of Water Resources, China (Later resigned from the WCD)
Achim Steiner (WCD Secretary General), World Conservation Union (IUCN)

Source: World Commission on Dams.

Table 6.3
Composition of the WCD Forum

Type of Organization	Percent of Total Forum Organizations
NGOs	19
Research institutes	15
Private sector firms	10
Affected peoples' groups	10
Multilateral agencies	10
Bilateral agencies and export credit guarantee agencies	8
Government agencies	8
Utilities	7
International associations	7
River basin authorities	6

Source: Dubash et al. 2001, 46.

During its two years of operation, the WCD received funding totaling $10 million from fifty-four contributing organizations, including inter-governmental organizations such as the World Bank, the Inter-American Development Bank, and the UN Environment Programme; corporate donors such as ABB, Enron, and Voith Siemens; nonprofit organizations such as the World Wildlife Fund, Berne Declaration, the Packard Foundation, and the Goldman Environmental Fund; and several national governments.[58]

The WCD generated several information products: a detailed survey of 125 dams, which collected and analyzed data on financial, technical, environmental, and social performance; eight in-depth case studies of particular dams, rivers, and watersheds; three country-level reviews focused on India, Russia, and China; and seventeen thematic reports targeted to address a list of specific social, economic, ecological, and institutional controversies. The commission also collected an extraordinarily large volume of statements and testimonials from affected groups and interested parties and conducted a series of two-day regional consultation hearings in Colombo, Sri Lanka; São Paulo, Brazil; Cairo, Egypt; and Hanoi, Vietnam. Submitted materials and interim information products leading up to the final assessment were made available on the WCD website.

Although the representation of voices and interests was far from perfectly balanced, the WCD motivated a wide range of affected groups or stakeholders to participate in its deliberative processes. In an independent assessment of WCD procedures, the World Resources Institute attributed this ability to "the WCD's efforts to cast itself as an honest broker and open listener in gathering knowledge about large dams."[59] The WRI assessment also pointed out the uneven distribution of abilities among different stakeholders to accompany the process. Not surprisingly, groups having substantially greater impact were those having access to the WCD secretariat or commissioners, a strong command of English, reliable access to communications technology, and adequate political space to operate within the constraints of their own national political context.[60]

Several other aspects of WCD operations also proved controversial. The choice of consultants to conduct the WCD's many local studies often became a battleground between different local factions. Actors on all sides of the debate criticized the quality of the country-level assessments for India and China. Finally, while the WCD won generally high marks for balance and inclusiveness in its regional consultative hearings and other outreach processes, the hearings themselves consisted largely of serial testimony rather than an interactive dialogue among contending stakeholders.[61]

Dams and Development: The WCD Report

The commission released its report in November 2000. Its findings were presented as a consensus document, with a partially dissenting opinion by Medha Patkar.[62] Among its main findings were the following:

• Large dams display a high degree of variability in delivering predicted water and electricity services—and related social benefits—with a considerable portion falling short of physical and economic targets, while others continue generating benefits after thirty to forty years.

• Large dams have demonstrated a marked tendency towards schedule delays and significant cost overruns.

• Large dams designed to deliver irrigation services have typically fallen short of physical targets, did not recover their costs and have been less profitable in economic terms than expected.

• Large hydropower dams tend to perform closer to, but still below, targets for power generation, generally meet their financial targets but demonstrate variable economic performance relative to targets, with a number of notable under- and overperformers.

• Large dams generally have a range of extensive impacts on rivers, watersheds and aquatic ecosystems—these impacts are more negative than positive and, in many cases, have led to irreversible loss of species and ecosystems.

• Efforts to date to counter the ecosystem impacts of large dams have met with limited success owing to the lack of attention to anticipating and avoiding impacts, the poor quality and uncertainty of predictions, the difficulty of coping with all impacts, and the only partial implementation and success of mitigation measures.

• Pervasive and systematic failure to assess the range of potential negative impacts and implement adequate mitigation, resettlement and development programmes for the displaced, and the failure to account for the consequences of large dams for downstream livelihoods have led to the impoverishment and suffering of millions, giving rise to growing opposition to dams by affected communities worldwide.

• Since the environmental and social costs of large dams have been poorly accounted for in economic terms, the true profitability of these schemes remains elusive.

• Perhaps of most significance is the fact that social groups bearing the social and environmental costs and risks of large dams, especially the poor, vulnerable and future generations, are often not the same groups that receive the water and electricity services, nor the social and economic benefits from these. Applying a "balance-sheet" approach to assess the costs and benefits of large dams, where large inequities exist in the distribution of these costs and benefits, is seen as unacceptable given existing commitments to human rights and sustainable development.[63]

Based on these findings, the central thrust of the commission's recommendations was twofold: to shift the focus away from dams as ends in themselves and toward comprehensive assessments of options for water and energy needs and to establish "core values" of equity, efficiency, participatory decision making, sustainability, and accountability in all decisions related to dams and their alternatives.

The report was disseminated through several channels. The WCD website made the report, summary materials, and background documents available for free downloading. The WCD secretariat distributed some 4,600 printed copies of the report and an estimated 5,000 copies of a CD-ROM version of the report with background documents. The WCD commissioners also presented the report at dissemination meetings held in some twenty-five countries. The full report was translated into Spanish and summaries were prepared in ten languages.[64]

Reactions to the WCD, Follow-up Activities, and Diffusion of the Model
In its independent assessment of the WCD, the World Resources Institute also surveyed preliminary reactions to the commission's final report. In general terms, they found that dam critics articulated more favorable initial reactions to the WCD report than did proponents.[65] Many activist groups, although dissatisfied with elements of the document, pressed for the commission's recommendations to become binding on dam builders and funders. IRN and the Swiss-based Berne Declaration issued a call to action endorsed by a coalition of 109 NGOs and movement groups from around the world, calling for intergovernmental organizations such as the World Bank to implement the WCD recommendations.[66] Grassroots

groups were slower to respond, in part because translations of the summary were not available until some six months after the report's release. The WRI assessment concluded that although many local groups were disappointed with the WCD's failure to fully grapple with questions of power, corruption, and the marginalization of affected peoples in prevailing models of development, many "found much in the WCD report to hearten them."[67]

Governments from less-developed countries were divided in their preliminary responses.[68] Some—including Brazil, Ethiopia, and Nepal—praised the framework of values underpinning the WCD recommendations, while also asserting that those values already informed their rules and procedures in decision making about development projects. India rejected the report on the grounds of national sovereignty, its failure to emphasize dam beneficiaries, and its "obsessive concern for preserving the rights of affected local peoples."[69] China also rejected the report, stating that its emphasis on bargaining and negotiation among affected groups was inferior to China's established decision-making procedures. Several governments were critical of perceived bias in the WCD's data collection methodology and procedures.

Industry provided a mixed response. According to the WRI review, industrial members of the WCD Forum were concerned primarily with the WCD's emphasis on stakeholder dialogue and revisions to national decision-making procedures, as opposed to clearer rules of engagement that could be implemented quickly in the context of existing and planned projects.[70] ICOLD, the international dam engineers association, rejected the report as flawed in its methodology and inadequate in capturing the many benefits of large dams (even though a former ICOLD president was one of the WCD commissioners).[71] Several national chapters of ICOLD, however, including those in Australia, Britain, Germany, the Netherlands, and South Africa, supported the report, in explicit disagreement with the international leadership.[72] A few important international firms, including Swedish-based Skanskaa and U.S.-based Harza Engineering, also issued positive reactions.[73]

Several donor governments, most notably Germany, Britain, and the Netherlands, indicated that they would be guided by the WCD recommendation s in making future decisions on whether to support dam projects.[74] The British and Swedish governments made financial commitments to help Southern governments seeking to implement the WCD recommendations.[75] The Norwegian government was an exception, suggesting that the WCD may have "gone too far in the direction of consensus-based decision-making systems."[76] A study of the impact of the WCD guidelines on the export credit agencies (ECAs) of donor countries, conducted by the German consulting firm Ecologic, found a mixed pattern. Few ECAs altered their environmental screening procedures for development projects to explicitly incorporate the WCD guidelines as formal rules. However,

> while there are few explicit references to the WCD Report, most environmental practitioners consider the WCD report to have had a considerable influence on the practical implementation of ECA's environmental guidelines. In this interpretation, while compliance with the WCD recommendations is not formally required, they represent a set of topics that would have to be addressed in the Impact Assessment for any large dam project.... At the same time, although the need for social and environmental standards for large dam projects is widely recognised, the WCD recommendations are frequently considered as unrealistically ambitious, and as only partly applicable to ECAs.[77]

Among intergovernmental organizations, the most positive responses came from the World Health Organization (WHO) and the UN Environment Programme. WHO indicated that the WCD report "deserves a strong endorsement by the relevant UN specialized agencies."[78] UNEP, as discussed later, launched the Dams and Development Project (DDP) as a follow-up initiative. The multilateral development banks were more equivocal. The Asian Development Bank launched a series of dissemination and consultation workshops on the report, and indicated that it would reexamine current procedures, "including our environmental and social development policies, and determine the extent to which the report's recommendations may necessitate changes in these procedures. We will also encourage our member countries to do the same."[79] The African Development Bank released a more positive response, indicating its intent to "incorporate the criteria and guidelines during the development of Bank's technical guidelines to support our recently completed policy on Integrated Water Resources Management."[80] As discussed in further detail later, the World Bank, after substantial hesitation, committed itself to the general WCD recommendations, but not to all of its specific guidelines.

In the Wake of the WCD: Nodes for the Institutionalization of Norms for Watershed Democracy

Applying the conventional terms of reference for evaluating interstate regimes, the central questions to ask about the WCD process would involve its effectiveness in codifying behavioral norms, changing actors' expectations about the behavior of others, and ensnaring individual states in compliant behavior. In this context, the WCD could be interpreted as lying somewhere between a failed attempt to catalyze formation of an interstate regime and a nonbinding, semiformal precursor to an eventual interstate regime. Evidence of failure includes the lukewarm reception—and in some cases overt hostility—that states across the global South have afforded the WCD report. The chief evidence for some progress on the road to eventual regimelike institutionalization would be the transference of the WCD initiative to the UN Environment Programme (discussed later), in a manner explicitly seeking to engage national governments. Regardless of where one falls along this interpretive spectrum, the central question becomes one of engaging and ensnaring the state through formal processes of codification and participation. The WRI assessment, for example, concluded that the effectiveness of the WCD would ultimately lie in whether follow-on activities that involved governments more centrally could build a "bridge back to formal governmental and intergovernmental processes."[81]

In the context of the conceptual framework developed in chapter 2, however, it makes sense to view the WCD not as an institution in its own right but rather as part of a broader process of institutionalization of norms of watershed democracy. This process has been occurring, in different ways and at different rates, at a half dozen nodes that bound the political space within which watershed struggles now occur. Some of these loci of normative development are direct outgrowths of the WCD process, such as UNEP's Dams and Development Project and the country-level stakeholder dialogues that the WCD sought to establish.

Others are formal organizations or informal sites of struggle that lie further afield of the WCD: the World Bank, international environmental NGOs, the networks of water experts discussed in chapter 5, the global movement opposing large dams, and site-specific dam and watershed struggles. What follows is a short discussion of developments around each of these nodes in the post-WCD period. The discussion then turns to the question of exactly what is being institutionalized, in terms of this book's conceptual emphasis on metanorms of knowledge, authority, and territoriality.

WCD Spinoffs: UNEP's Dams and Development Project and National Stakeholder Dialogues

Stakeholder participants in the WCD Forum proposed that UNEP undertake a follow-up initiative to the WCD. In response, UNEP launched the Dams and Development Project with financial support from Britain, Germany, the Netherlands, Sweden, and Switzerland. The DDP's organizational structure resembles that of the WCD, with a fourteen-member steering committee, a larger Dams and Development Stakeholder Forum, and a small professional staff. The DDP's formal objectives are to

• support country-level, regional and global dialogues on the WCD report and the issues it addresses with the aim of engaging all stakeholders with emphasis on those not currently involved;

• strengthen interaction and networking among participants in the dams debate;

• support the widespread dissemination of the WCD report and the report of the Third WCD Forum, and make available other stakeholders' responses; and

• facilitate the flow of information and advice concerning initiatives relevant to dams and development.[82]

At the first meeting of the Dams and Development Stakeholder Forum, UNEP director Klaus Toepfer stressed that a central goal was to draw governments more centrally into the process launched by the WCD, by shifting the debate to the context of an intergovernmental organization. He also stressed a broader aim of institutionalizing "core values" emanating from the WCD report:

Some may wish to reject the WCD report, others may insist that it be implemented word for word. I don't believe that these are wise reactions, and I am not alone in this view. We have seen a remarkable degree of concurrence about using the core values and strategic priorities of the report as an opportune starting point for dialogue. The DDP is committed to that aim.[83]

In this broader context of institutionalization, the DDP's ability to retain many of the key actors and stakeholder groups that coalesced around the WCD is just as significant as its explicit effort to engage states.[84] Despite the mixed reaction of many activist groups to the WCD process, the DDP steering committee includes key movement groups that were instrumental in bringing the World Bank to the table in the first place (including Narmada Bachao Andolan, IRN, and the Philippines-based Tebtebba Foundation). On the traditionally pro-dam side, the steering committee includes an important private sector firm (Harza), an influential utility owner-operator (HydroQuebec), a leading professional association (the International Hydropower Association), and the World Bank. Also enhancing continuity with the WCD are the Dams and Development Forum, which is essentially a continuation of the WCD Forum, and the appointment of Jeremy Bird of the WCD secretariat as interim DDP staff leader.

Another relatively direct extension of the WCD has been a loosely coordinated push for national-level stakeholder dialogues on dams and development. The WCD began this process, organizing some sixty meetings in dozens of countries in the period between the report's release and the transition to UNEP's DDP. Although initially these meetings tended to be report-launching publicity events, extensive dialogue among stakeholder groups at the national level emerged in several countries, including Poland, India, the Philippines, and South Africa (see chapter 9), as well as a similar discussion at the regional level around the lower Mekong River in Southeast Asia.[85] As discussed later, efforts to stimulate such dialogues have spread to international NGOs active in this arena; IUCN, for example, has helped to promote discussions along these lines in Vietnam.[86]

The World Bank's Response
The World Bank's initial response to the WCD report was cautious. In comments made at the launching ceremony, Bank president James Wolfensohn lauded the report for showing that "There is common ground

that can be found among people of good faith coming from very diverse starting points."[87] However, the Bank also rejected calls for it to adopt the WCD recommendations directly as standing policy on dam projects (something it would have been extraordinary and unprecedented for the Bank to have done, given its standard procedures for developing its project guideline rules). The WCD process and report exposed internal splits within the Bank. An early test of the report's impact came in December 2001 when the Bank adopted a new draft policy on involuntary resettlements, and in doing so rejected calls for a policy of direct negotiations with affected communities.[88] Around the same time, however, a preliminary plan for implementing WCD recommendations was rejected by a subcommittee of the Bank's governing board as too weak.[89]

A more direct test was the Bank's new water sector strategy, a draft of which was released for public comment in 2002.[90] The draft included only a passing mention of the WCD and did not address central WCD recommendations on the need for comprehensive energy and water assessments, greater transparency in the planning process, and direct consultation with affected peoples.[91] In the wake of NGO criticism, the revised final version of the strategy added a separate section on the WCD guidelines in which the Bank endorsed the WCD's "core values" and "strategic priorities" but argued that no post-WCD consensus had developed on the commission's twenty-six specific guidelines.[92] In comparing the guidelines with its own procedures, the Bank explicitly rejected the calls for giving local communities prior informed consent and direct negotiating powers as an inappropriate "veto right" and "impractical."

The new strategy did acknowledge the new climate facing the Bank, however. The main themes were the benefits of privatizing water service (see chapter 7) and questions of political risk. In the draft report, much of the focus was on the Bank's own political exposure, although this language was excised from the final report after a period of public notice and comment.[93] In the final version, the Bank announced its intention to re-engage with large and controversial infrastructure projects, but on new terms:

To be a more effective partner, *the World Bank will re-engage with high reward/ high-risk hydraulic infrastructure, using a more effective business model.* This "new business model," which will be followed by both the Bank and IFC [International Finance Corporation], puts development impact first; assesses the development impact of both engagement and non-engagement by the Bank; considers the rights and risks of those directly and indirectly affected by such projects; meets social and environmental standards; treats those projects supported by the Bank as Corporate projects from the start; rewards and supports staff who manage such projects; and aims at transparent, crisp, time-bound and predictable decisions.[94]

A Broadening Circle of Institutionalization?: International Environmental NGOs, Networks of Freshwater Experts, and the Anti-Privatization Movement

In the wake of the WCD, two important mainstream international environmental organizations, the World Conservation Union and the Worldwide Fund for Nature, began explicit dam-related campaigns. Both organizations had been extensively involved with the WCD process. IUCN was recruited by the World Bank to help organize its 1997 stakeholder workshop and is a member of the steering committee for UNEP's post-WCD dams initiative; WWF was an active member of the WCD Forum. In both cases, these new initiatives on dams were situated within ongoing programmatic activities, IUCN's Wetlands and Water Resources Program and WWF's Living Waters Program. IUCN's $15 million dams initiative emphasizes disseminating the WCD report, facilitating national-level stakeholder dialogues about energy and water planning, country-level work on environmental restoration, and "measures to mitigate or reverse the damage to downstream ecosystems and the livelihoods of local communities."[95] WWF's initiative focuses on demonstrating alternatives to dams, linking developing-country governments to Western businesses offering energy and water alternatives to dams, and pressing governments and international organizations to adopt the WCD recommendations in their aid, lending, and business decisions. Thus, while each sought to facilitate adoption of the WCD recommendations, core WCD themes of participation and the livelihoods of local communities were being joined to activities on wetlands, freshwater ecosystems, and biological conservation that traditionally fit within an integrated water resources management perspective.

Such activities raise the possibility that expert networking around the IWRM paradigm may provide more fertile ground for norms of watershed democracy than has been the case to date. As discussed in chapter 5, the idea of participation emerged as a central (if quite abstract) notion in IWRM beginning in the later 1980s. This has created substantial invocation of the idea of multistakeholder dialogues in networks of freshwater experts and in settings such as the UN Commission on Sustainable Development or the World Water Forums. As discussed previously, abstract notions of "participation" within the IWRM paradigm run the gamut, in practice, from rhetorical support for occasional consultation to calls for active participatory governance of watersheds. There is some evidence that a new and more politicized engagement with the "participation question" is beginning to emerge in IWRM circles in the wake of the WCD experience. Unlike previous meetings, such as the Second World Water Forum, the 2001 Bonn Freshwater conference—held one month after the release of the WCD report and intended as an organizing meeting for water experts leading up to the 2002 World Summit on Sustainable Development—grappled centrally with participation and governance issues.[96] According to one activist in attendance, the Bonn conference was

> an experiment in international dialogue in the sense that five major groups were identified—NGOs, Trade Unions, Local Government, Farmers and Business—as being key to the water sector debate. Unlike previous United Nations fora, these major groups were allocated equal status as the government delegates and therefore played an active role in the multi-stakeholder dialogue sessions, the three working groups and the plenary negotiations regarding the formulation of the "Recommendations for Action".... To start a conference by making space for all major stakeholder groups to say exactly what they want to say is a very empowering process.... Many of us went to Bonn quite cynically expecting that at best, lip service would be paid to participation and that at worst Bonn would just be a guise for the promotion of the private sector involvement in water delivery. We were wrong, and this was refreshing.[97]

Activist groups participating at Bonn pushed for adoption of the WCD recommendations as a central theme, along with the idea of water as a human right and a common, nontradable good.

Another preexisting network context in which to look for the spread of norms of watershed democracy is the growing struggle against the privatization and marketization of water. As discussed in chapter 7, there has been surprisingly little overlap between anti-dam and anti-privatization movements, for several reasons. One of these is the only partially overlapping set of arenas in which these struggles occur. More fundamentally, the two movements are based on substantially different orientations toward the role of the state and the importance of water-supply infrastructure, complicating convergence and coalition building. Nevertheless, the idea of an overtly political stakeholder dialogue has been growing within the movement (see chapter 7). At the 2001 Bonn Freshwater Conference, the German minister for economic cooperation and development endorsed a proposal for a WCD-like stakeholder dialogue on privatization of water, an idea originally floated by the British NGO, WaterAid.[98]

The Institutionalization of Contention: Site-Specific Dam Campaigns and the Watershed Democracy Movement

Not surprisingly, contentious political struggles around specific dams have continued in the wake of the WCD. About a year after the report's release, two particularly high-profile transnational dam controversies came to a head, with strikingly different results. The controversial Ilisu Dam project in Turkey began to unravel in November 2001 when the British-based engineering and construction firm, Balfour Beatty, and the Italian-based Imbregilo withdrew from the project, citing outstanding economic and social issues and the difficulty of meeting conditions imposed in their effort to procure a $200 million export credit guarantee from the British government. One month later, in marked contrast, the World Bank and the African Development Bank decided to forge ahead with the equally controversial $520 million Bujagali Dam project in Uganda, despite strong local and transnational NGO opposition and the earlier withdrawal from the project by bilateral funding agencies in Britain, France, Germany, Sweden, and the United States.

Both campaigns reflected what were by then well-established frames for protest. Activist groups who fought successfully against British export credit guarantees for the project, including Friends of the Earth, the Kurdish Human Rights Project, and Cornerhouse (a progressive British NGO "think tank"), framed the struggle in terms of ecological disaster, forced displacement, cultural loss, and the silencing of local voices. The Bujagali campaign also pointed to what have become well-established themes of watershed democracy. They argued that alternatives had not been considered; that social, environmental, and cultural effects had not been properly assessed; that in-house critics raising doubts related to economic analysis were ignored or suppressed; and that a secret, noncompetitive contracting process excluded meaningful local consultation with affected peoples.

The mere fact of publishing the WCD report was not a transformative event in either of these long-standing, deeply rooted struggles; both had long been infused with norms of watershed democracy. Instead, the WCD report became a newly available and authoritative referent for these norms. Shortly before Balfour Beatty withdrew from the Ilisu project, Friends of the Earth succeeded in forcing a shareholder vote on a resolution to require the firm to adhere to WCD guidelines for dam projects in which it participated.[99] The Swiss multinational, ABB, long a target of anti-hydro activists, pointed to the ongoing WCD process as part of the rationale for selling off its hydropower activities in 2000, effectively ending its involvement with Ilisu (ABB's chief executive officer had been one of the WCD commissioners).

In the case of Bujagali, IRN and the transnational coalition opposing the dam also stressed the gap between the decision process around the project and the WCD report as a best-practices framework.[100] The World Conservation Union, which has taken a more favorable perspective, also framed the project's legitimacy in terms of the WCD, with regard both to procedures and outcomes: "The dam is being redesigned in consultation with all stakeholders and displaced communities are to receive full compensation. A review showed the project to be compliant with the guidelines of the WCD."[101] The WCD has been used in similar fashion across a range of ongoing controversies, including several of the country-level examples from Brazil and South Africa discussed in chapters 8 and 9.

Territory, Authority, and Knowledge in Contentious Politics Around Dams

Neither the anti-dam movement nor the WCD process has taken a unified position toward metanorms of authority, territory, and knowledge. Nevertheless, a set of metanorms that go well beyond the standard regime model along all three dimensions can be seen in this case.

As a transnational political controversy, disputes about dams have come to have an inherently transterritorial dimension. Increasingly, controversies surrounding a specific dam will bring together opposing transnational coalitions in favor of and opposed to dams more generally, both of which assume that what they are struggling over is not simply a conflict between a state and its own people but rather a relevant matter for global rule making and governance. Dam projects, the freshwater ecosystems altered by them, and the people affected by them have refused to be governed by the state as a form of domesticated nature.

It was suggested in chapter 2 that modern norms of state sovereignty link the presumption of state authority to a spatially contiguous, mappable understanding of territory as authority's domain. In this case, the founding fiction of the modern state system—that there is a stark, essential difference between the domestic and international spheres—has grown not irrelevant, but of markedly decreased significance.

The dam controversy has been subjected to deterritorialization in two very different ways. On the one hand, the anti-dam movement has championed a conception of place that is fundamentally distinct from territory. It seeks to close the gap between the state's rights and its responsibilities, and to link place to both greatly enhanced local autonomy and stronger global standards of human rights, participation, process, and procedural safeguards. The growing marketization of the global dams industry also contributes to its deterritorialization. Large dams have often had only tenuous links to national political economies; many are part of dam–industrial enclaves constructed in remote regions to support processing of raw materials for export. What has changed is the capacity of national governments to territorialize these projects by monopolizing the bargaining with international public finance. The wooing of private funds and the emphasis on financial risk management pull dam projects in the direction of a transnationally fluid and deterritorialized form of global capitalism. (This theme is discussed in the context of water marketization in chapter 7). Caught between these two forces, national governments still routinely invoke their sovereign territorial rights in dam controversies and seek to delegitimize foreign actors on nationalist grounds, as seen in the controversy around the WCD report, but with markedly decreasing effectiveness.

The metanormative stance toward authority, which reflects the broader debate surrounding multistakeholder dialogue processes, is more complex.[102] Skeptics stress the self-appointed character of many so-called stakeholders. Marina Ottaway, for example, has characterized the WCD as a prime example of "corporatism gone global."[103] She sees direct parallels between a tripartite structure of intergovernmental organizations, businesses, and NGOs at the global level and the process by which governments, particularly in Western Europe and Latin America, have historically sought to co-opt business groups and labor unions into support and participation. This is actually two different claims about authority: that the mechanism authorizes self-appointed actors and that it retains a significantly exclusionary character. Others have suggested that the problem with multistakeholder processes of this sort is not too much authority but rather too little. Richard Falk, for example, distinguishes between governance as democratic process and governance as problem solving via rule enforcement, suggesting that instruments such as the WCD are likely to matter more for the former than the latter.[104]

Yet the specific instance of the WCD and the broader narrative presented in this chapter call for a more complex view of authority relations than either corporatism gone global or a weak bid to promote strong norms.[105] To be sure, many aspects of the process decentered state authority and radically authorized nonstate actors in its stead. States enjoyed no particular status alongside the activists, academics, technical experts, and industry representatives engaged in conflict and dialogue, or among the individuals who served as WCD commissioners. As the drama unfolded, transnational corporate interests interacted increasingly directly with transnationally networked environmental, human rights, and indigenous peoples' advocates. A politically durable balance between economic considerations and socioecological justice may or may not be attainable in practice, yet in seeking that balance, both sides in the debate transcended the traditional framework of state-provided public goods that has anchored more than half a century of water development projects around the world. The WCD recommendations—grounded in norms of human rights, watershed-scale democracy, and transnational accountability—essentially moved a set of traditional state responsibilities outside the sphere of the state.

However, states also retained some important roles in this drama. One consequence of decentering the state in the debate appears to be a countervailing reaction in which states were recentered in important ways. An explicit purpose of the call for an independent global commission was to reinject an authoritative understanding of dams back into local- and national-level conflicts (as the WCD sought to do in its support for national stakeholder dialogues).[106] In other words, one consequence of dragging state–society conflicts to a broader, global level of constructing norms has been to reinject and reinvigorate those conflicts at the domestic level. Anti-dam activists gained an important set of arguments in the process, but the state was reaffirmed as a central arena in which those struggles are to be played out.

The state in the context of the WCD also emerged with a newly enhanced role as an agent of norm legitimization. Authority for nonstate actors in the international environmental arena is typically based on some combination of knowledge and ethics, discursive forms that state actors cannot monopolize.[107] These platforms not only create enough power to occasionally herd states to the bargaining table, they also play a crucial downstream function in legitimizing or delegitimizing the protonorms that emerge from the bargaining processes in which these rounded-up states engage. In this case, however, the pattern is the opposite: a process of norm construction that takes place outside the interstate domain is dependent on the reaction of states for its validation. The embrace of the WCD recommendations by some important donor governments and its rejection by some major dam-building states has been far more important in framing the legitimization struggle around the WCD's protonorms than the pronouncements of human rights advocates, environmentalists, or dam-building professionals.

In light of these complexities surrounding state and nonstate authority, it would be a mistake to understand this process as one of simply supplanting the state with a newly authoritative "global civil society" (corporatist or otherwise). A better term is *hybridization*, in which the retention of some traditional foundations of state authority, the growth of nonstate authority grounded in a blend of expertise and moral claims, the development of new bases and realms of authority for some actors, and even elements of role reversal, coexist.

The pattern with regard to knowledge is similar in its complexity. As the World Resources Institute pointed out in its assessment of the WCD's knowledge generation process, the commission walked a middle ground between technocratic and interpretive approaches. The commission rejected an individualized, ethnographic approach to individual dams on the basis that its credibility rested on a uniform approach across case studies. At the other end of the spectrum, turning the commission process into a modeling exercise on global energy and freshwater needs was rejected as insufficiently inclusive.[108] Once the knowledge-generation process was constructed, however, knowledge stabilization in its conventional sense played a central role. The process of forming the commission had emphasized the legitimacy of its participants through their position as stakeholders rather than as authoritative technical experts, but the commission then sought to legitimize its claims primarily through the compilation of a global knowledge base about dams. The final report was framed primarily as a factually detailed accounting of the costs and benefits of large dams. Only one of the main findings emphasized uncertainty, contingency, or surprise—the profitability of large dams was said to be "elusive"—and this was attributed to a lack of careful accounting. None referred to the cultural significance of water; the contingent nature of frameworks for assessing things like costs and benefits; or the relationship between local and universal knowledge, facts, or truths.

In contrast, the anti-dam movement, employing knowledge-based frames and critiques as a tactical resource, has traded more systematically in both knowledge stabilization and its transcendence. As seen in the evolution of the movement's declarations, it has given increasing voice to notions of culturally contingent knowledge, local understandings, and different ways of knowing. As one observer described a workshop at the Second International Meeting of Dam-Affected People and their Allies, held in Thailand late in 2003:

The workshop on conducting community-based research emphasized the differences in the ways local knowledge can be presented and used. Collecting ancestral knowledge in Colombia has been invaluable for unifying the anti-dam movement. Community-based research in Thailand posed a hefty challenge to the government's promised dam benefits. Local wisdom in Senegal provided more effective and efficient solutions to health problems caused by large dams than any research produced at a university.

Just as each river's meandering path is unique, fluid, changing, so too are the struggles to keep them flowing.[109]

If this approach has made little headway with the World Bank or even the WCD, it nevertheless has been important in forging solidarity among a culturally heterogeneous group of activist organizations.

At the same time, however, activists have often used a dam's yardsticks and facts against it. IRN invariably frames its criticism as objective analysis based on careful reading of "the data," the intellectual equivalent of hoisting the Bank on its own petard. The occurrence in the space of a month of both the Curitiba meeting of dam-affected peoples and IRN's critique of the Bank's OED review reflects the range of positions toward knowledge stabilization. Activist organizations such as IRN have chosen to operate in both epistemological worlds, and have found a way to do so without fracturing the coalition or delegitimizing themselves in conventional policy circles. This has been not only a key to their success but also a central element in the broader process of institutionalization. The commitment to the WCD process as *the* factual account about dams has made it demonstrably harder to disengage from the process, despite the dissatisfaction of many activists with the failure to question the larger development model.

Conclusion: Shifting Locations of Norm Development and the Ritualization of Contentious Politics

The emergence and solidification of a transnational community of anti-dam activists transformed the international politics of large dams. The convergence of ecological and socioeconomic critiques made it harder to dismiss either form of criticism as parochial or one-sided. The growing voice and increasing ownership of local groups within the movement lessened problems of North–South paternalism, at least in the movement's internal dynamics. The combination of direct action and knowledge-based criticism simultaneously delegitimized claims about the benefits of large dams and caused investors and governments to rethink the political and economic risks involved.

None of this meant the end of contentious transnational politics around dams. Indeed, in a step backwards from the stakeholder exercises of the late 1990s, in May 2002 IRN fired this warning shot at the World Bank in commenting on its draft water sector strategy:

The World Bank's singularly negative and non-committal response to the WCD Report means that the Bank will no longer be accepted as an honest broker in any further multistakeholder dialogues. Experience since the publication of the WCD Report shows that common ground exists between civil society and forward-looking private sector and government institutions. In contrast, the World Bank's response to the WCD, its role in projects like the Bujagali dam in Uganda, and the new draft WRSS indicate that the Bank is entering a new era of intensified controversy and conflict.[110]

The Bank announced its intent to "re-engage" in the business of funding water infrastructure development rather than shirking controversies. Conflict continues between affected communities and their governments, between IRN and the World Bank, and between dam builders and dam opponents.

What is striking in this case is not the ebb and flow of intense social conflict so much as its channelization, in two senses. First, even as conflict has endured, the location of norm development has expanded. The center of normative gravity has shifted across several arenas in sequence: first within the World Bank itself and the conflictual debate among the Bank, its critics, and dam-building governments; then to the wider arena of the WCD process; and then to the multiple nodes and stakeholders grappling today with what the WCD has left in its wake. Second, and along the way, there has been a growing routinization, normalization, even ritualization of the process of contention. A socioecological controversy poorly suited to the sovereign, territorial, knowledge-stabilizing framework of an interstate regime began to take on an institutionalized form of its own.

Invisible Hand, Visible Fist: The Transnational Politics of Water Marketization

The human right to water is indispensable for leading a life in human dignity. It is a prerequisite for the realization of other human rights.... Water should be treated as a social and cultural good, and not primarily as an economic good.... Water, and water facilities and services, must be affordable for all.

—Committee on Economic, Social and Cultural Rights, United Nations Economic and Social Council, General Comment 15 in United Nations Document E/C. 12/2002/11

Free water is wasted water.

—Mohamed El-Ashry, chairman and CEO of the Global Environment Facility in Environment News Service, March 22, 2000

Water as a Market Good

Among the many panel discussions at the Second World Water Forum was a stakeholder session involving representatives of several intergovernmental organizations, citizens' groups, and professional associations. During the discussion, the World Bank's Ismail Serageldin identified two controversies standing in the way of global progress toward a sustainable water future: the polemical debate surrounding large dams (see chapter 6) and a linked set of increasingly contentious issues related to property rights, privatization, water exports, water pricing, and foreign investment and ownership in the water sector. At the heart of this debate are controversies surrounding whether, when, and how water should be treated as a market good.

I use the term *water marketization* in this chapter to refer to the process of creating the economic and policy infrastructure for treating water as a marketed commodity. Water marketization is not synonymous with water privatization, nor does it refer simply to changing the way in which water is priced. The term refers, rather, to a broader set of linked transformations related to prices, property rights, and the boundary between the public and private spheres. Observable elements of the trend toward water marketization include the following:

· the establishment of private property rights to own or use water;

· a shift toward so-called full-cost pricing of water, in the sense of pricing water to recover the operating, infrastructural, and (more controversially) full capital costs associated with its production, treatment, and delivery;

· the creation and utilization of market mechanisms for the exchange of water-related goods and services;

· the growing involvement of private sector actors in the production, delivery, and marketing of water supplies and services and the enhancement of private sector investment in water supply maintenance, upgrading, or expansion;

· policies that liberalize or facilitate bulk water transfers from one basin to another, including the international trade in water; and

· a declining role for the state in some or all of its traditional functions as service provider, regulator, and system maintainer.

Not all of these elements will be found in every place-specific or organization-specific episode along the road to water marketization. As the country-level case studies of Brazil and South Africa (chapters 8 and 9) will show, water marketization involves a complex bundle of norms and practices, not all of which have taken root to the same extent across different locales or over time.

Norms and practices of water marketization—like those of international river diplomacy, integrated water resources management, or watershed democracy—have potentially profound ramifications for the world's rivers, watersheds, and freshwater ecosystems. The world's growing demand for water is a principal source of stress on these systems. When marketization focuses on the question of how to value bulk water resources and allocate them across broad categories of social use (industry, agriculture, municipalities, in-stream uses), the link to the health of watersheds and freshwater ecosystems is direct. Even when marketization pressures focus more narrowly on a single sector, such as the provision of municipal water services according to "market" principles, the ramifications for the governance of rivers, watersheds, and freshwater ecosystems can be substantial. As the South African case study will illustrate, pressures to reform the method of supplying water for household and municipal use were a key catalyst for the decision to embark on a broad process of reform in that country's practices and institutions for managing water resources.

Some argue that the ramifications of marketization for the state of the world's watersheds, rivers, and freshwater ecosystems are positive, in that treating water as a scarce economic resource will lead to its more effective conservation and careful use, thereby reducing stress on fragile ecosystems. As seen in chapter 5, treating water as a scarce economic resource has emerged as a central (if, in practice, ambiguous) tenet of the IWRM paradigm. Others argue that the ramifications of marketization are primarily negative, in that treating water as a market commodity will inevitably undermine the in-stream, place-specific, or culturally based functions of water—functions that, it is argued, cannot be fitted adequately into market logic. As discussed later, the UN Committee on Economic, Social and Cultural Rights has argued that treating water primarily as an economic good can undermine the realization of its value as a social and cultural good. The quest for price-induced efficiency collides with fears that the price mechanism fails to guarantee that basic human and ecosystem needs will be met in a fair and affordable manner. As discussed later, recent activist initiatives to stitch together a broad global coalition on water have stressed the negative ramifications of privatization for social equity and environmental protection.

Thus, water marketization controversies reflect a central tension in the idea of sustainability, which typically revolves around a notion of efficient communities. The question that remains unresolved and highly contentious is whether the idea that price- and market-based mechanisms provide more efficient resource allocation can be reconciled with the elements of equity, voice, and participation that underpin the idea of community.

Arguments about efficiency gains, enhanced competition, shifting water to so-called higher-value uses via market mechanisms, and enhancing service by attracting private investment are by no means intellectual abstractions; they ride on powerful political and economic forces. One set of forces pushing water marketization is the broader process of structural adjustment, privatization, trade liberalization, and neoliberal economic reform that has been working its way through the world economy for more than two decades now. As a state-provided public good, water has been a prime target for restructuring. A distinct but related driver of water marketization has been the changing pattern of public and private investment in the water sector, including both the decline in public financing and the perceived need to attract private capital to fill that void. Another important pro-marketization force comes in the form of the corporate strategies of multinational firms involved in or eager to enter the water business.

The causal links among institutionalized rules, investment patterns, and corporate strategies are much debated. Are multinational firms primarily responding to the new investment and trade climate or creating it through their powerful influence on national and international policy frameworks? Without minimizing the importance of this debate, it can safely be concluded that it is the combination of neoliberal adjustment, the changing policy framework, and corporate strategies that has become a potent force for the institutionalization of water marketization over the past decade. The result of this combined force has been a notable policy shift in that direction in many important policy-making nodes, from localities to countries to intergovernmental organizations.

A growing backlash against water marketization has also emerged, carried by local opposition in various places around the world and stitched together by an increasingly linked, networked, and transnational coalition of opponents. Where proponents see efficiency gains, upgraded service, expanded supplies, more accurate price signals, and a welfare-enhancing shift to "higher-value" uses of water, opponents see commodification, a troubling increase in multinational corporate power, a loss of local control, threats to public health, and the abandonment of less profitable responsibilities such as providing service to the poor. As discussed later, opponents have won a few strongly symbolic local battles. Also, they have become sufficiently organized and networked to carry the debate into international settings ranging from global water conferences to the World Bank to international trade negotiations.

The debate around water marketization bears some striking parallels to the debate over dams and water infrastructure projects presented in chapter 6, in the sense that powerful transnational forces are being challenged by an increasingly networked and transnational opposition. Institutionally, however, this case is not as fully developed, either in terms of the rise of marketization norms or the countervailing opposition to it. Both action and reaction are at an earlier stage of development. Another important difference is the demonstration effect of the success of the anti-dam movement. Calls have been made to emulate the global stakeholder model of the World Commission on Dams to grapple with water marketization controversies. Despite these differences, the water marketization arena provides another useful opportunity to examine the processes of institutionalization of norms in the context of contentious politics, economic globalization, and transnational mobilization.

The chapter begins by tracing the emerging institutionalization of water marketization and the social, economic, and political forces driving it. The chapter then turns to a discussion of the mobilization of opposition and the key nodes and forms of contention that have emerged in this arena. It concludes with a discussion of noteworthy similarities and contrasts between this situation and that of the anti-dam movement, as well as a discussion of embedded metanorms regarding authority, territoriality, and knowledge in the emergent institutional form in this arena.

Sources of Water Marketization

As discussed in chapter 5, networks of water experts and the IWRM paradigm are one source of momentum behind the marketization of water. As part of the planning process for the 1992 Earth Summit, the Dublin-based International Conference on Water and the Environment articulated four guiding principles that have become influential benchmarks in international water policy debates. The fourth of these principles states "Water has an economic value in all its competing uses and should be recognized as an economic good." The Dublin Statement goes on to note that

Within this principle, it is vital to recognize first the basic right of all human beings to have access to clean water and sanitation at an affordable price. Past failure to recognize the economic value of water has led to wasteful and environmentally damaging uses of the resource. Managing water as an economic good is an important way of achieving efficient and equitable use, and of encouraging conservation and protection of water resources.[1]

The idea of "getting the price right" as a way to ensure water's more efficient use has long been a staple of IWRM thought. The emergence of IWRM as the language of choice in international water circles, therefore, has given impetus and greater credibility to market-based approaches.

Yet as chapter 5 underscored, expert networks have fragmented over the controversial question of how to value water in practice, undercutting their capacity to serve as an effective "epistemic community" or knowledge-brokering network in service of IWRM norms, values, and practices. Clearly, then, the rise of water marketization as rhetoric, idea, and policy frame requires a broader sociopolitical explanation, focusing on power relations and institutional developments rather than merely ideational trends or networking of experts. On the "push" side, actors promoting structural adjustment and trade liberalization have turned water into a prime battleground over the marketization and privatization of state-provided social services and public goods. On the "pull" side, actors concerned with funding the development of water infrastructure have viewed marketization as a way to attract capital to the increasingly daunting task of funding large-scale water infrastructure projects. Multinational corporate strategies have provided a bridge between these push and pull factors. Any of these trends on its own would likely have been enough to stimulate a global trend toward water marketization; working in concert, they have given it powerful impetus.

Structural Adjustment and the Washington Consensus
The most potent source of support for water marketization norms has been the broader phenomenon of neoliberal economic adjustment, grounded in a set of processes that have been working their way through the world economy since the late 1970s. A common point of demarcation is the set of dramatic policy shifts that accompanied the rise to power of Margaret Thatcher in Britain (hence the term Thatcherism) and Ronald Reagan in the United States. In the water sphere, however,

these forces have been most tangible among less-developed countries and the transitional economies of the former Soviet Union. The neoliberal paradigm referred to as the Washington Consensus, which stresses the need for "structural adjustment," has generated concrete pressures on these governments to implement two linked changes: to move the state out of its traditional role as the sole provider of water as a public good, and to implement pricing reforms that seek so-called full cost recovery.[2] As discussed later, the two changes are linked because price increases have been necessary to attract international private investors to the sector and make privatization a reality.

The International Monetary Fund (IMF) has been an aggressive proponent of privatizing water service. A review of IMF loan agreements with forty countries in the year 2000 uncovered twelve agreements that contained conditions for water privatization and/or "cost recovery" measures.[3] These included full privatization measures or other conditions to enhance private-sector participation in Benin, Guinea-Bissau, Honduras, Niger, Panama, Rwanda, Senegal, and Tanzania as well as cost-recovery pricing measures in Angola, Nicaragua, Yemen, and São Tome and Principe.

More recently, the IMF has signaled its intent to move away from microspecific conditions such as the privatization of public water services. The idea that domestic enthusiasm for the adjustment process (often referred to euphemistically as ownership or buy-in) is the key to successful adjustment has become a staple of structural adjustment thinking, in part because of the lack of success of so many recalcitrant adjustors. The IMF has also been burned by the widely perceived inequities of privatization giveaways in Russia and elsewhere, and pressed to clarify the increasingly blurry boundary between itself and the multilateral development banks (MDBs) (as the IMF has grown increasingly involved in sector-specific conditionality and the MDBs have moved increasingly into nonproject lending).

Driven by these pressures, in the fall of 2000 the IMF began a review of its conditionality policies, which may mark a turning point in the direction of more "streamlined" structural conditionality:

A central concern is that if policy conditions are excessively broad and detailed they can undermine a country's "ownership" of its policy program—a key success factor.... Conditionality should focus on those policies that are critical to the macroeconomic goals and set a clearer division of labor between the IMF and other international institutions, especially the World Bank.[4]

Some opponents of water privatization and full-cost pricing schemes have interpreted this to mean that in future the World Bank will be a more important battleground.[5]

The World Bank has also been an aggressive promoter of water privatization. Water sector lending has long been a staple of the Bank's portfolio, including loans for water-supply infrastructure, sanitation, and improvements in water service capacity. As of 2002 the Bank's portfolio of water sector loans stood at about $23 billion, or roughly 12 percent of the Bank's total lending portfolio. Of this, about $14 billion is in water supply, irrigation, and hydropower, with the remaining $9 billion constituting water resources lending (including wastewater treatment, sanitation, and flood control).[6] The water sector accounted for 8 percent of the Bank's $5.8 billion in new loan commitments for fiscal year 2002, a share exceeded by only three other sectors: transportation, public administration, and energy and mining.[7]

For much of its history, the Bank's lending for drinking water, sanitation, and wastewater treatment concentrated on infrastructural loans for public utilities. In the wake of the emphasis on structural adjustment, however, the Bank has placed much greater emphasis on privatization and full-cost recovery for water services. According to the advocacy group, Public Citizen, a review of the Bank's 2001 water and sanitation loans revealed that seven of eleven loans included full-cost recovery conditions and eight of eleven contained privatization conditions.[8] Presumably, these conditions also appear in at least some Bank structural adjustment loans, the specific terms of which are typically not disclosed. As discussed later, the Bank's new water sector strategy emphasizes that facilitating private sector financing and management is among its key "strategic options."[9] The Bank's web site contains a set of toolkits to aid municipalities in designing and implementing privatization of systems via service contracts, management contracts, leases, concessions, and other mechanisms.[10]

The Bank has also been a strong promoter of private sector involvement in water resources development. The Bank's Private Participation in Infrastructure (PPI) initiative provides combined lending, technical advice, and risk mitigation instruments to attract private firms to infrastructural investments. The Bank also maintains a Privatization Transactions Group that promotes infrastructure privatization deals through advice and technical support. With specific regard to water infrastructure, the Bank's most recent "Water Sector Strategy" (2003) notes that private sector funding of infrastructure in water has lagged behind other sectors such as transportation, energy, and telecommunications; only about 10 percent of international private investment in infrastructure in developing economies went to the water sector (including both water resources development and water services), and most of that went to a few "low-risk" economies in Latin America and East Asia. Citing projections by the Global Water Partnership of a vast public funding shortfall in water projects, the report stressed the need for the World Bank to "provide political risk insurance ... participate as an investor in priority infrastructure ... [and] provide a combination of investments, guarantees and assistance in developing legal, regulatory and institutional arrangements for sound water management."[11]

Trade Liberalization: Bulk Water Exports

Along with neoliberal adjustment pressures from international financial institutions, the changing architecture of international trade rules has given impetus to water marketization. If the main effect of privatization pressures has been to weaken the state's role in allocating water, the main effect of trade liberalization has been to create a framework of rules that promote the mobilization of water as a marketable commodity. That can be done in the direct physical sense, as in bulk exports of water from one basin (or country) to another.[12] More important, water can be traded in the virtual sense of allowing distant actors greater control over the allocation, marketing, and exchange of local water resources.

Confounding the conventional wisdom of many trade experts in the 1980s, who stressed the rise of strategic, state-managed protectionism and the so-called new mercantilism, the 1990s saw instead a resurgence of aggressive efforts to liberalize global trade.[13] The United States, capitalizing on the shifting balance of economic power in a post-Cold War, post-debt crisis world, pushed hard for both regional and global liberalization initiatives. The result was formation of the World Trade Organization and a series of ambitious liberalization initiatives: cutting so-called nontariff barriers created by governmental rules and regulations, pushing liberalization in contentious sectors such as agriculture and services, and joining trade and financial liberalization more directly through the trade-justified relaxation of investment rules and strengthened private intellectual property rights.

The push to hyperliberalize trade arrived relatively late to the water sector. Water has always been moved around in space (e.g., from one basin to another) and in time (e.g., through capture in the rainy season for use in the dry season or during episodes of drought). To date, however, such transfers generally have been economically and technically feasible only within the borders of nations or in border-spanning shared basins. Gleick and colleagues report that in addition to significant technical barriers, large-scale exports of water have been hindered by the fact that alternatives such as desalination or improvements in efficiency of use are typically more cost-efficient.[14] Another obstacle has been historical uncertainty in trade law as to whether bulk water in situ even constituted a tradable good. As a result, excluding shared international basins, there have been few international bulk transfers of water to date, mostly involving island nations or temporary responses to a supply disruption.

Despite these limitations, the prospect of bulk water exports has become an internationally controversial issue. The key source of dispute has been institutional reforms that create a legal foundation for accelerated international trading in bulk water, whether or not it is currently feasible. The North American Free Trade Agreement (NAFTA), which entered into force in 1994, defines "ordinary natural water of all kinds (other than sea water)" as a tradable good subject to NAFTA's provisions.[15] This definition, combined with NAFTA's rules on national treatment, proportional sharing, and legal standing for foreign corporations, has raised Canadian fears that U.S. firms will lay claim to Canada's rich water resources for export southward, with local communities left legally powerless to stop them.[16] Indeed, when the provincial government of British Columbia banned bulk water exports in 1998, an American company filed suit against the Canadian national government under Chapter 11 of NAFTA, seeking to hold the national government liable for profits lost as a result of the provincial government's actions.[17] In response to growing public outcry, the Canadian government renegotiated the International Boundary Waters Treaty with the United States to preclude bulk exports of boundary waters.[18] Canada has also implemented restrictions on interbasin transfers as a strategy to limit bulk water exports, applying the rule to domestic as well as international transfers as a way to avoid charges of discriminating against international trade.

The global framework of trade rules, institutionalized through the General Agreement on Tariffs and Trade and the World Trade Organization, also recognizes water as a tradable commodity. The key question is whether and how the various permissible restrictions on exports also written into global trade rules may apply to water. Gleick and colleagues argue that Article XX(g) of GATT, which defines acceptable trade restrictions for the conservation of nonrenewable resources, can be read to allow a national ban on bulk water exports "where freshwater water resources are 'nonrenewable' or exhaustible through overuse or abuse," provided that domestic measures are also in place to control production or consumption.[19] There are also provisions allowing for trade restrictions to protect human or ecosystem health.

Yet WTO rulings striking down domestic environmental regulations as illegitimate restrictions on trade, including the famous tuna–dolphin and shrimp–turtle cases, have left many environmentalists and water activists skeptical that such protections could be given real meaning. More recent decisions have suggested some space for carefully crafted restrictions, but concerns remain about the WTO's closed proceedings and the placing of the burden of proof regarding harm squarely on those who would restrict trade rather than those who would promote it.[20]

Trade Liberalization: "Trade" in Water Services
Far more important for the foreseeable future than the idea of bulk water exports, however, is the impact of trade liberalization—or, more accurately, investment liberalization—on the provision of water services, including municipal water supplies and sanitation services. Liberalizing "trade in services" has been an agenda item in the world trade talks since the Uruguay round of the 1980s. The 1994 General Agreement on Trade in Services (GATS) created a renewed commitment to liberalize trade in

services and to differentiate between legitimate and illegitimate (read: trade-restraining) regulations in the service sector.

Although nominally a trade agreement, GATS is at heart a set of investment rules. Some services can be provided directly across borders (e.g., data processing, architectural design, financial consulting); still others can be "exported" in the sense that they involve the movement of people across borders to the point of consumption (e.g., international tourism or high-end medical services). Nevertheless, the profit potential from transnationalizing the provision of service lies mainly in transnational investment that allows foreign firms to enter national markets and provide services locally to domestic consumers. One complication is that many such services are in sensitive, strategic sectors (e.g., banking and finance) or in sectors with potentially immediate ramifications for public health and well-being (e.g., water, health, education). For this reason, liberalization of trade in services has been far more complex, contentious, and slow to proceed than the historical GATT successes in liberalizing the trade in manufactured goods. Opposition from developing countries in particular has slowed progress in the wake of the 1994 GATS agreement.

While nominally modeled after the original GATT agreement, the GATS accord embraces a philosophy of gradual and partial liberalization rooted in "schedules" that define national commitments.[21] These schedules are developed through an offers-and-requests approach in which governments identify specific service sectors that they would like to see liberalized in other countries (requests) and that they are themselves willing to liberalize (offers). In 2000, a round of trade negotiations began on the specific service sectors to be the initial focus of liberalization. The November 2001 WTO meeting in Doha, Qatar, produced an agreement that governments would submit requests on specific services to be liberalized by 2002 and indicate which sectors they would offer to expose to liberalization, and to what extent, by 2003. Thus far, the majority of specific proposals have come from the more industrialized countries of the Organization for Economic Cooperation and Development (OECD).

Given the strong position of European multinationals in the water sector (including acquisition of all the major U.S. firms in the sector), much of the specific push for liberalization of water services has come from the European Union (EU). In April 2002 the draft EU position paper on liberalization of services was leaked to anti-GATS activists and made public.[22] The draft revealed that the EU was targeting water and sanitation services as a central negotiating objective, along with other traditional public utilities such as telecommunications, electricity, and postal service. The official EU requests on water services filed as part of the GATS process focused on seventy-two countries, but the leaked document revealed that liberalization pressures would be aimed in particular at several larger developing countries, including Brazil, Mexico, Argentina, India, Malaysia, and the Philippines. Commonalities among these countries include historical restrictions on the participation of private multinational firms in water services and the requisite population size and urban density to create attractive water service markets.[23]

Multinational Corporate Strategies

When it is combined with pressures on governments to privatize state assets, the liberalization of foreign investment rules creates lucrative opportunities for some of the world's largest firms to capture new markets. Thus, as Finger and Allouche point out, the rise of "public service" multinationals has been driven in part by more general processes of financial globalization, but also by the specific dynamics of neoliberal structural adjustment.[24] Twenty-six of the top 200 firms by revenue in the 2000 Global Fortune 500 list were what Finger and Allouche term "infrastructure" transnational corporations, concentrated primarily in the energy, transportation, and telecommunications sectors but also including diversified firms active in the water sector such as Suez Lyonnaise des Eaux, Vivendi, RWE and, until its scandalous collapse, Enron.[25] Although privatization has moved more slowly in water than in some other infrastructural areas, the result of these processes has been a significant global presence for several multinational firms in the water sector (table 7.1). A key element in attracting the attention of these firms to water is the sector's enormous potential for expansion, via privatization as well as growth in demand.

Finger and Allouche describe the business strategies of multinationals in the public water sector in terms of three goals:

Table 7.1
Leading multinational firms in the global water services sector (circa 2000)

Firm	Number of Countries in which Firm Has Water Sector Activities
Suez Lyonnaise des Eaux	37
Vivendi	29
Saur-Bouygues	21
Anglian Water	14
United Utilities	13
Aquas de Barcelona	9
Severn Trent	8
Yorkshire Water	6
Enron	5
RWE	2

Source: Finger and Allouche 2002, 141–142.

Vertical integration   Gaining control of multiple stages of the product chain to allow price control via intrafirm trade;

Horizontal integration   Extending into other business activities in the search for synergies; and

Collusive behavior   Building alliances and cartels to impose an oligopolistic market structure and thereby limit competitors.[26]

The largest water firms reflect these strategies. Suez Lyonnaise des Eaux, for example, was built from a merger between entities active in water, waste management, energy, and telecommunications (horizontal integration). The firm engages in water services, water engineering, water treatment engineering, water treatment chemicals, and waste collection and disposal (vertical integration). It has been an active agent in promoting concentration in the water sector, forming joint ventures or other collaborative arrangements with at least nine other water sector multinationals (collusive behavior).[27]

To this list one can add a fourth element: the socialization of risk. Guaranteed rates of return and other forms of indemnifying risk through full-cost recovery provisions are common features of the water service agreements struck between firms and local governments. They are also a central element of the strategies used by the international development banks to attract private capital to so-called public–private partnerships for development of water infrastructure.

The Pace, Scope, and Evolution of Water Marketization

The net result of structural adjustment, neoliberal ideology, changing international trade and investment rules, corporate strategies, and the wooing of private capital by public water planners has been the growing marketization of water. It is difficult to assess how quickly marketization is spreading and deepening. Comprehensive global data on the mechanisms by which water is allocated, priced, and exchanged do not exist. According to one recent estimate, private companies provide only about 5 percent of the world's water supplies, suggesting that marketization is proceeding from a low baseline.[28]

One piece of evidence for the rapid institutionalization of marketization consists of the documented activities of multilateral financial institutions. The World Bank's 2002 draft revised water sector plan reported that 40 percent of current World Bank projects for urban water services now include private participation. As indicated previously, a partial review of IMF agreements in the year 2000 revealed that a dozen contained conditions requiring some aspect of water privatization. A second piece of evidence is the number of privatization initiatives. A 1999 survey conducted by the Canadian environmental research group, Environment Probe, documented privatization initiatives in sixteen different Latin American countries, a half dozen OECD countries, and a handful of cases in Africa and Asia.[29] This pattern reflects both the high leveraging of Latin American economies via the debt crisis and the resulting power of conditionality pressures in the region's international economic relations. It is also consistent with the region's high degree of urban concentration, which makes privatization financially more attractive to potential investors.

Although privatization is the most easily measurable element of water marketization, it is hardly the only element. Water can also be marketized—in the sense of being commodified, moved, and priced according to economic criteria—by the state, without the establishment of private property rights to water or concessions that allow private actors to profit from providing it. A search of the Food and Agriculture Organization's FAOLEX database yields fifteen countries that passed framework national water legislation (or other legislation with broad ramifications for water resources management or the provision of water services) during the period 1999–2003. As indicated in table 7.2, nearly all of these contain provisions that move in a pro-marketization direction. Such cross-national comparisons mean little outside of their context. In some cases, creating a legal basis to charge for water or disconnect for nonpayment may be a strong step toward marketization, whereas in other contexts such norms are well established and may not be the central focus of legislative activity. The pattern is clear with regard to water pricing, however. Almost all the cases in table 7.2 create a basic framework for cost-based pricing; several contain provisions for pricing policies that internalize environmental externalities, send conservation-oriented signals to consumers, steer water toward "higher-value" uses, or generate a surplus for system upgrades and future investment. Non-price dimensions of marketization are less evident, although a few contain provisions such as allowing greater commercial freedom to state enterprises or enabling private concessions.

Normative Evolution

As water marketization has grown and spread, there have been notable adjustments from the early—and particularly bluntly neoliberal—variant. One change involves the delineation of public and private sector roles. The final report of the World Panel on Financing Water Infrastructure (discussed later) stated that decisions about public and private sector participation should be "pragmatic, eschewing ideology."[30] The World Bank's recently revised water sector guidelines stress that

Financing of water resources infrastructure is not cleanly separable into public and private sectors; increasingly it requires public-private partnerships, both in investment and operation. While private investment and management is playing, and must play, a growing role, this must take place within a publicly-established long-term development and legal and regulatory framework, and without crowding out community-managed infrastructure and beneficiary participation in design and management of water systems.[31]

Table 7.2
Water marketization in national water law

Country	Year	Legislation	Water Marketization Provisions
Armenia	2002	Water Code of the Republic of Armenia	National framework legislation with full-cost pricing provisions
Azerbaijan	2001	Law of the Azerbaijan Republic on Water Economy of Municipalities	Transfers authority for "water structures" to municipalities; provides for cost-based water charges to "ensure efficient water allocation" and to finance system upgrades and development of new sources
Belize	2001	Water Industry Act of 2001	No significant marketization provisions; vests rate-setting power in a public utilities commission and requires rates to be "fair and reasonable"
Burkina Faso	2001	Law No. 002/2001	Framework legislation for water resources management and water services with "polluter pays" provisions and water charges to finance water sector
Chad	1999	Law No. 16/PR/99: Water Code	Establishes cost-based tariff system; allows state to delegate public water service responsibilities to private sector
Czech Republic	2001	The Water Act	National framework legislation including water use and wastewater discharge fees
Estonia	1999	Public Water Supply and Sewerage Act	Authorizes connection charges to public water supply systems adequate to "develop the public water supply and sewerage system," "comply with environmental protection requirements," and "operate with justified profitability"
Finland	2001	Water Services Act	Requires that charges for water services "cover the investments and costs of the water supply plant in the long term," "promote the sparing use of water," and promote pollution reduction

Table 7.2
(continued)

Country	Year	Legislation	Water Marketization Provisions
Kenya	2002	The Water Act	No significant marketization provisions
Madagascar	1999	Law No. 98-029: Water Code	Establishes full-cost recovery as basis for water charges
Portugal	2002	Decree Law No. 112/2002	Decree law approving national water plan, which establishes principle of water as a scarce economic good, cost-based pricing, use of price mechanism to encourage highest-value use, and internalization of all costs
Scotland (United Kingdom)	2003	Water Environment and Water Services (Scotland) Act	Response to an EU directive that "requires member states to take account of the need to recover the costs of water services as a way of encouraging the sustainable use of water resources"
Scotland (United Kingdom)	2002	Water Industry (Scotland) Act	Replaces existing water and sewage authorities with a new entity having "a greater measure of commercial freedom"
Spain	2001	Law 46/18999: Water Law	Establishes cost-recovery basis for tariffs on water from publicly financed projects
Tajikistan	2000	Water Code	Establishes principle of fee-based water use; provides for water use fees to finance drinking water supply system; explicitly prohibits privatization of drinking water supply systems

Note: No English-language text could be found for Norway's Act No. 82 of 2000 Relative to Watercourses and Groundwater.
Source: Compiled by the author from the FAOLEX legislative database, UN Food and Agriculture Organization, http://faolex.fao.org/faolex/index.htm.

The emphasis on pragmatism, "partnerships," and walling off privatization from the provocative notion of private ownership of water is a direct response to mounting antiprivatization activism (discussed later).

Another important adaptation involves the question of risk. Structural adjustment, changing patterns of development assistance, the push for privatization, the growing emphasis on full-cost recovery, and the changing international rules for trade and investment are ushering in dramatically different scenarios for financing water projects around the world, in which water planners favoring capital-intensive projects often see little alternative to private funding. In an influential assessment, the Global Water Partnership estimated in 2000 that attaining its vision of "water security" would require a dramatic increase in capital investment in the water sector (table 7.3)—from the current rate of about $70 billion annually to approximately $180 billion. (It should be stressed that the vision behind these numbers is primarily one of expanding supply through large-scale water projects, as opposed to management improvements, enhanced efficiency, and decentralized alternatives.)

More revealing than the dollar allocations across categories of water need is the accompanying projection of where those funds could be

Table 7.3
Global Water Partnership's estimated cost of "water security" for less-developed countries

Task	Current annual expenditures (billion US$)	Estimated annual expenditures required to attain GWP's "world water vision" (billion US$)
Access to drinking water	13.0	13.0
Sanitation and hygiene	1.0	17.0
Municipal waste water	14.0	70.0
Industrial effluent	7.0	30.0
Agriculture	32.5	40.0
Environmental protection	7.5	10.0
Total	75.0	180.0

Source: Global Water Partnership 2000b, 76.

Table 7.4
Global Water Partnership's vision for funding "water security"

Source of funds	Current annual expenditures (billion US$)	Estimated annual expenditures required to attain GWP's "world water vision" (billion US$)
In-country government	48.0	50.0
In-country private sector	14.0	70.0
International private sector	4.0	48.0
International public finance	9.0	12.0
Total	75.0	180.0

Source: Global Water Partnership 2000b, 78.

found (table 7.4). According to the GWP, public sector funds—including both government spending and "international public finance" (a.k.a. development assistance or "foreign aid")—will barely keep pace with current investment levels, meaning that virtually all of the increase will have to be attracted from the private sector. From this broad planning perspective, the issue is less the theoretical benefits of private sector participation than its practical necessity. Full-cost pricing and risk guarantees for investors become simply the cost of doing business with private capital.

What has changed over time is not this assumption of a need for private investment but rather an understanding of what that requires in practice. Earlier suppositions that full-cost pricing would create attractive investment opportunities for transnational capital have given way to the recognition that attracting private international capital to the water sector on this scale is, in no small measure, a question of risk management. Consider the logic of investment decisions between hydropower and thermal options for generating electricity. As table 7.5 indicates, aspects of risk help to explain the frequent preference for the thermal option from an investor's perspective. Despite hydro's lower operating costs and its longer lifetime for an average facility, construction risks are greater, construction times are longer, and site-specific factors loom much larger.[32] A parallel problem of the profit–risk calculus for private

Table 7.5
Thermal versus hydro—Factors affecting "bankability"

Factors	Thermal	Hydro
Capital cost ($/kilowatt)	400–1,400	800–3,000
Operating cost	High	Low
Construction risk	Low	High
Construction time	2–4 years	3–6 years
Project life	15–20 years	>50 years
Site influence	Low	High
Technology	Changing	Mature

Source: Adapted from Stone 2002.

investors can be seen in water service delivery. Service areas for concessions often combine different subgroups (urban and rural users, poor and affluent users), some of which are much more attractive to and less risky for private providers. As a result, private providers will seek either to serve only the more attractive elements of the market or to receive risk-management concessions, such as full-cost recovery provisions or guaranteed rates of return. Thus, for both water resource infrastructure and water service delivery, pushing marketization beyond general pricing considerations and allocation principles to actually replace the state with private actors means creating a profit–risk balance adequate to satisfy investors who have other options.

The logic of attracting private capital through risk management was given a strong boost in *Financing Water for All*, the influential 2003 report of the World Panel on Financing Water Infrastructure.[33] The panel, which was sponsored by the World Water Council and the Global Water Partnership and chaired by former IMF managing director Michel Camdessus, presented its findings at the third World Water Forum in Kyoto. The Camdessus report carried great weight because among its twenty panelists were the presidents of the four regional multilateral development banks (African, Asian, Inter-American, and European), the managing director of the World Bank, and several senior corporate and financial sector officials.

The Camdessus panel took as its points of departure two ambitious global goals: the UN Millennium Summit target of halving the share of world population lacking sustained access to safe drinking water, and the 2003 Johannesburg Summit goal of making the same improvement in access to basic sanitation. In his comments on the panel's activities, Camdessus described the challenge as one of "giving our brothers and sisters what they need to drink" and underscored factors such as gender inequity that affect access to water.[34] However, the panel took as its central mandate the identification of the financial means to achieve these targets rather than the socioeconomic and political circumstances that made them necessary in the first place.

Along lines similar to those of the World Bank's revised water sector guidelines (discussed in chapter 6), the Camdessus panel report asserted that an emerging international consensus grounded in the Dublin Principles and integrated water resources management had been forged in the 1990s. Also, it took as its point of departure the GWP estimates of investment requirements (tables 7.3 and 7.4). The report's eighty-seven recommendations centered primarily on governments and international financial institutions and touched all of the principal themes of water marketization. Governments should provide "predictable revenue frameworks" and create "an enabling environment for the participation of the private sector." Contracts for private sector involvement should be "standardized and promoted" so that local governments could involve private participants faster and more effectively. Pricing should be based on "sustainable cost recovery" that anticipates "all future cash flow needs," with broad subsidies through public financing replaced by much more narrowly targeted "pro-poor" policies.[35]

The Camdessus panel's report is significant for its recognition—in contrast to more orthodox neoliberal conceptions—that free-market policies alone are unlikely to be sufficient to attract levels of capital adequate to the task defined by the GWP investment scenarios. The report calls for a doubling of official development assistance and more extensive subsidization from the export credit agencies of OECD countries. More important, the panel identified a class of projects, determined by a combination of project size and perceived risk, for which traditional sources of funding have not been forthcoming. Relatively risky projects that are too small for international public financing packages and too large to be funded with micro loans or development assistance have not attracted

Table 7.6
Water project financing: Typical sources of project finance as a function of project costs and investor risk

Cost of project (US$)	Level of investor risk	
	Low	High
10,000,000 to 1,000,000,000	Development project financing	Development project financing, with political insurance or guarantees
100,000–10,000,000	Corporate sector or municipal	Corporate sector, with political risk insurance
10,000–100,000	Corporate sector or municipal	"Exposed segment" (financing gap)
100–10,000	Corporate sector or municipal	Development assistance
0–100	Corporate sector or municipal	Micro loans

Source: Adapted from Winpenny (2003), figure 3.1, p. 12.

private financing unless they carried low risk ratings. Larger projects with particularly high risk ratings have attracted neither public nor private financing. This gap or "exposed segment" of the market (table 7.6) provides the rationale for several of the panel's recommendations to enhance the ability of international corporate investors to manage risk on terms favorable to them. These recommendations include the combining of public and private funds and the provision of greater "political risk coverage" by the multilateral development banks and export credit agencies. Clearly, risk is understood here as being political as well as economic in nature. As such, the growing emphasis on risk management is a concession both to the power of global capital and to the disruptive potential of anti-privatization activism.

The Rise of Transnationally Networked Opposition to Water Marketization

As water marketization has become an increasingly tangible and widespread set of practices, its normative and rule-based content has also evolved substantially, as seen in the growing emphasis on risk management and public–private partnerships. Some of this evolution can be attributed to overoptimism and subsequent learning on the part of marketization's most enthusiastic boosters in intergovernmental organizations, the private sector, and trade circles. The most important source of normative evolution, however, has been the conflictual politics surrounding water privatization specifically and water marketization more generally. Much as anti-dam protests coalesced in the 1990s into an increasingly tightly connected transnational network, anti-marketization activists have begun to find one another, come together, exchange information, coordinate activities, and build a shared set of symbolic frames about water.

Some of the most forceful opposition has taken the form of site-specific demonstrations against municipal water privatization agreements. The most famous anti-privatization protest to date occurred in the spring of 2000 in Cochabamba, Bolivia's third-largest city.[36] Late in 1999 the government entered into a $200 million contract giving control of Cochabamba's municipal water supply system to a consortium of foreign investors that included the U.S.-based Bechtel and the Italian utility Edison. The new owners promptly implemented a full-cost pricing scheme in which even families living on the minimum salary of less than $100 per month were required to pay prices reportedly rising to $20 per month or more. The result was widespread popular protest against the price hikes and, more generally, against foreign control of the water supply system. The state responded with force: shutting down or seizing local media, implementing martial law, and repelling protesters with tear gas and riot police. The protests persisted and the government eventually conceded, withdrawing from its contractual agreement with Bechtel and its partners.

Although no other single episode has attained the powerful symbolic status of Cochabamba in anti-privatization circles, similar episodes of anti-privatization protest have occurred in many places:

• In South Africa, water supply cutoffs have provoked violent uprisings among the urban poor. Between late 2000 and early 2002, South Africa suffered a severe outbreak of cholera that was traced to the use of polluted water by poor people in the face of rising water rates and service cutoffs. Although these policies have been implemented by public water utilities as well as experimental private concessions, the latter have been a particular target of protest. Suez Lyonnaise des Eaux, which has large investments in South Africa extending well beyond the water sector, had a concession cancelled in the Eastern Cape province.[37]

• The city of Buenos Aires, Argentina, granted a thirty-year water service concession to a Vivendi-Suez consortium in 1993. The concession soon came to be plagued by charges of mismanagement, cronyism, and embezzlement. Residents blocked roads to protest high connection fees. The venture turned a steady profit until its heavy reliance on foreign capital led to a default when the peso collapsed during Argentina's financial crash of 2002.[38]

• Jakarta's 1997 private concession to Thames Water and Suez became embroiled in controversy with the fall of Indonesia's authoritarian Suharto regime, with nationalist opposition and worker protests forcing a renegotiation of the terms of the concession.[39]

• Opposition by unions and dissatisfaction with costs and performance under private concessions have stalled the privatization push across Canada.

• In the United States, public opposition reversed a privatization initiative in Atlanta and stalled another in New Orleans.

• Protests in Ghana forced the government, which was facing strong privatization pressures from the IMF and World Bank, to suspend its project to negotiate a ten-year lease for urban water services to international investors.

• Protests and a boycott of water bill payments were launched in Auckland, New Zealand, after privatization led to rate increases and disconnections for nonpayment.

• Opposition in Nicaragua led the National Assembly to pass a bill, subsequently vetoed by the president, that would have banned private concessions until a national framework water law could be passed.

In many of these episodes, the catalysts have been organized coalitions of specific opponents such as trade unions. In some cases, local opposition has coalesced into national networks, as with the Council of Canadians, the Ghana Coalition against Water Privatization, the National People's Water Forum (India) and the Coalition against Water Privatization (Australia), or linked with existing national networks, as in the case of the Indonesian Forum for Environment (WALHI) or India's National

Alliance of People's Movements. Resistance to water privatization has also involved the widespread use of what James Scott refers to as "weapons of the weak," in this instance including tactics such as the sabotage of water meters or the pilfering of water via illegal taps and connections.[40] In Nelspruit, South Africa, for example, a thirty-year private concession for providing water service has been met not only with organized opposition from trade unions, progressive political parties, and anti-globalization organizations but also with "youths marching on councilors' houses in the townships, the destruction of water meters, illegal water connections and one of the highest rates of non-payment in the country."[41] As one local activist threatened, "If they come into the township to cut our water supplies or take our goods, we'll vandalize their cars and beat up their workers."[42]

Building a Transnational Anti-Privatization Movement: The Structure of Opportunities and Constraints

Despite the predominantly local character of opposition, there are important and growing transnational dimensions to the politics of opposition to water privatization. For simplicity of language, the discussion here will refer to an emerging transnational anti-privatization "movement." As with the transnational contention around dams (chapter 6), anti-privatization activism demonstrates elements of several different forms of transnational contentious politics. As transnational linkages proliferate, endure, and evolve, it should be no surprise to find the same actors and entities engaged simultaneously in efforts that look like movement-building activities, network-based advocacy, and campaign-based coalition building. Thus, in the emergence of coordinated moments of protest by local groups, we see practices suggestive of a transnational coalition. In the dogging of specific corporations and rapid exchanges of information about their performance in other locales, we see behavior suggestive of a transnational advocacy network. And in the centrality of labor-based opposition and the foundational role of existing international labor advocacy organizations we see elements of, or at least the strong potential for, a transnational social movement. Again, in this case it is more useful to focus on dynamic processes of engagement than static typologies of organizational form.

Regardless of the specific institutional form of contention, the concepts of opportunity structure, resource mobilization, and framing that are central to social movement theory can be used to understand both the growth and limitations of the transnational anti-privatization opposition, as they were used to illuminate the anti-dam struggle in chapter 6. One key element of the opportunity structure has been the availability of a series of events at which anti-privatization activists have been able to come together, exchange ideas, and forge tighter links. Several of these events have been national network-building gatherings with a strong component of transnational participation built into the mix. A conference at the University of British Columbia in July 2001 brought together an increasingly broadly based and well-networked coalition of Canadian anti-water privatization groups as well as activists from some forty other countries.[43] Italian activists protesting the marketization emphasis of the Third World Water Forum in Kyoto organized a parallel First People's World Water Forum in Florence, Italy, in March 2003, bringing together some 1,400 activists from Italy and other (predominantly European) countries.[44] The January 2004 People's World Water Forum in India played a similar role in linking Indian national activist groups to transnational actors. As discussed in chapter 6, gatherings in countries with strong domestic movements also played a critical role in the transnationalization of the anti-dam movement.

An additional element in the anti-privatization movement has been the growing institutionalization of global, multi-issue conferencing by activists, particularly through the World Social Forum (WSF). Originated in 2001 to protest the gathering of world economic elites at the World Economic Forum in Davos, Switzerland, the WSF has become an important recurring meeting for progressive activists, the anti-globalization movement in general, and opponents of water privatization in particular. At the 2002 forum, several leading organizations issued the "Porto Alegre Water Declaration," which included a commitment to form a World Coalition of Citizens Organizations against Water Privatization and Commodification. The coalition aimed to "strengthen the co-operation among founding members by all appropriate means" with particular emphasis on information, communication, coordination of activities by individual member groups, and "joint actions."[45] The 2002 forum also included a panel discussion on water that linked anti-dam and anti-privatization activists.

The 2003 People's World Water Forum included a "Dialogue on Water" workshop emphasizing the need for watershed-scale movements to plug into larger networks and operate at more aggregate levels. The January 2004 forum was timed to coincide with the 2004 World Social Forum in Delhi. In addition to network-building functions, these activist global congresses have made it possible to broaden the frame of the anti-privatization movement beyond anti-corporate, anti-WTO themes by linking with the push for water as a human right (see the later discussion on framing).

Finally, multistakeholder global conferences have also yielded opportunities to build and sustain links among movements. Although many activists spurned the Third World Water Forum in Kyoto as a pro-marketization event inspired by corporate profiteers and their intergovernmental agents, many others chose to attend and worked (successfully) for an independent civil society declaration that was highly critical of the Kyoto proceedings.[46]

A second critical element in the opportunity structure for building a global anti-privatization movement has been the ongoing negotiations over trade liberalization in services, in the context of the GATS agreement discussed earlier. In March 2001 civil society organizations and activists from some thirty countries came together in Geneva to launch a coordinated campaign against the GATS talks on service liberalization, with water used as a central example of the danger of the liberalization of services. The GATS talks have provided several important movement-building elements, including a tangible organizational target (the WTO), a powerful frame (WTO-aided multinational corporations stealing water out of greed), a series of specific goals and actions tied to the evolutionary progress of the talks, and a focal point for organizing that fills the space between the serial global gatherings sketched earlier.

However, organizing around GATS carries constraints as well as opportunities; to date the campaign has not yielded the effective combination of direct action and knowledge critique seen in the anti-dam case. The slow pace of the talks has meant that unlike the dams case, there have been few "smoking guns" to date in which GATS-based liberalization can be tied directly to privatization of specific water systems. The critique has been forced to operate at the more abstract level of looming global rules. Developments such as the leaking of the EU negotiating position are useful for media politics and as a rallying point for the movement's inner core of activists, but do not provide sustained opportunities for organized activity or direct action.

Nor has it been possible to repeat the second side of the anti-dam movement's success: a pattern of sustained, escalating delegitimization via a critique focused on knowledge. In a development reminiscent of the early stages of the anti-dam case, the WTO and movement groups have begun to exchange targeted critiques and rebuttals of one another's positions.[47] A pattern of critique and countercritique emerged after the EU negotiating position was leaked to activists in 2002.[48] However, several factors have made it harder for activists to develop the sort of knowledge power wielded in the anti-dam case. As a symbol to anti-globalization activists and a foil for media campaigns, the WTO provides an excellent target for water activists, but the small staff of the WTO, its secretive deliberations, and the multilateral and state-based character of trade negotiations have made it a far more difficult target for knowledge-based delegitimization than, say, the World Bank. Moreover, although effective deconstructions of abstract free-trade arguments are readily available, the WTO process lacks an analogue to specific development projects, which were a critical element in the anti-dam case. In principle, IMF and World Bank-inspired privatizations do afford such specific targets, but these developments thus far have been largely separated from the WTO process.[49] Moreover, the prevailing secrecy has not provided an analogous trail of project documents or official guidelines against which performance can be shown to be lacking.

Mobilization of Resources

Along with the structured context of opportunities and constraints, the available resources and the manner in which they are used are important determinants of the emergence, growth, and influence of social movements.[50] The anti-privatization and anti-dam movements have had a broadly similar array of available resources: a handful of committed organizations, the support of a few progressive foundations, several specific sites of local struggle (which constitute both specific mobilization opportunities and usable symbolic resources), the potentialities (and limitations) of the Internet as an organizing tool, and a strong potential alliance with an existing international movement, in this case, international labor rather than the human rights and environmental organizations central to the dam case. Yet these resources have been mobilized in a very different fashion.

One noteworthy difference between the anti-dam and anti-privatization campaigns is the absence in the latter case of a focal point akin to the role played by International Rivers Network. (As discussed later, the closest analogue, the Freshwater Action Network, has not performed an analogous set of catalytic functions in practice). Instead, several movement groups and nongovernmental organizations have become important nodes in a broader and more diffuse network, including the following:

• the Citizens' Network on Essential Services, an initiative opposing privatization of essential public services and funded by the progressive San Francisco-based Tides Foundation;

• the Council of Canadians, a citizens' organization founded to counter the policies of the conservative Mulroney government in the 1980s and which works as a "corporate and government watchdog" in defense of the public interest and Canadian "economic sovereignty";[51]

• Friends of the Earth International (FOE), a transnational environmental confederation that links national FOE organizations in sixty-eight countries;

• Public Citizen, the American consumer advocacy organization founded by Ralph Nader, and its "Water for All" campaign;

• Public Service International, the international trade union federation;

• the Transnational Institute, a Dutch-based international network of scholar-activists conducting research and outreach on issues related to militarism, poverty, inequality, and the environment;

• WaterAid, a British-based international charitable organization founded by the British water industry in 1981 and promoting access to water and sanitation in fifteen countries of Africa and Asia;

• the World Development Movement, a British-based organization employing a "people before profits" rubric in its campaigns on debt forgiveness, corporate responsibility, the arms trade, and international trade and investment rules.

The Internet has been a central resource for sustaining this more diffuse coalition, not simply for moving information, but also for creating some minimal sense of collective solidarity. As many observers have noted, the Internet provides a critical tool for disseminating information, forging ties, organizing events, and coordinating campaigns. For example, the GATSwatch website (www.gatswatch.org), a joint project of Corporate Europe Observatory and the Transnational Institute, allows groups to track the latest developments in the GATS talks, download key GATS documents and critical rebuttals to them, participate in coordinated letter-writing and petitioning exercises, and monitor the complex process of specific "requests and offers" exchanged by member governments in the context of trade liberalization negotiations.

As Sidney Tarrow suggests, the Internet can be understood not just as a resource to be mobilized but also as a novel form of movement organization, with its promise of

leapfrogging over the organizational deficits that plague social movement organizations, as well as the strain towards goal displacement that affects large bureaucratic organizations.... In a way, the Internet carries to its logical conclusion a trend identified since the 1960s for decentralized networks of activists to take the place of cumbersome, expensive-to-maintain bureaucratic organizations of the past.[52]

Scholars have taken a cautionary view of the Internet's effects; Bennett warns of difficulties in attaining a requisite level of "ideological definition and decision making coherence" and Tarrow hypothesizes that "Internet-based transnational movements exhibit less ideological crystallization and more centrifugal tendencies than non-Internet based movements."[53] Ideological crystallization has not been a difficult problem for the anti-privatization movement, given its specific focus, its public-versus-private delineation, and the powerful symbolism afforded by the image of greedy and corrupt multinational water corporations. (As discussed later, that challenge becomes substantially greater with the shift to a broader coalition-building effort for a global water movement.)

There are also contrasts between the anti-dam and anti-privatization movements in terms of the patterns of alliance formation with existing movements and organizations. As suggested previously, both movements have had ready alliance partners: human rights and environmental organizations in the case of the anti-dam struggle, organized labor in the case of anti-privatization efforts. These alliances have shaped both the capacity of the movements to interact with key global-level actors and steered the movements toward involvement in particular arenas. Large dams emerged as a central element of the campaign to promote environmental reform within the World Bank. As a result, the anti-dam movement's alliances with environmental NGOs enhanced its capacity to engage the Bank by creating connections to staff in sympathetic pockets of the Bank's bureaucracy, and providing familiarity with the Bank's procedures and specific vulnerabilities for knowledge-based critique. The international labor movement does not have a similar history of sustained and intense engagement with the Bank, and its particular emphasis on trade concerns has drawn the anti-privatization struggle more into the trade arena.[54]

Framing Water: From Public Good to Human Right

A critical insight of the literature on social movements and contentious politics is that the process of mobilizing resources must be understood in symbolic as well as material terms. The act of "framing" social ills and appropriate solutions exerts a strong influence on the emergence, character, and ultimate success or failure of movements. Drawing on the work of Goffman, Snow, Benford, and others, Sydney Tarrow defines frames as

cognitive understandings ... that relate to how social movements construct meaning.... Social movements are deeply involved in "naming" grievances, connecting them to other grievances, and constructing larger frames of meaning that will resonate with a population's cultural predispositions and communicate a uniform message to powerholders and others.[55]

Potent frames can help to overcome the substantial barriers to collective action that most movements face; effective "alignment" of frames with the understandings of mass publics can greatly enhance a movement's prospects for success.[56]

Much of the anti-privatization movement has been exactly that: a movement to prevent the transfer of power over water to private hands, and thus a defense of the idea of water as a public good to be controlled, decided upon, and provided by public means. Since the state has in most cases been the traditional provider of that public good, the anti-privatization movement can in this sense be seen as a defense of the status quo of monopolized state authority, public sector jobs, and subsidized water prices. An increasingly strong theme within the anti-privatization movement, however, is the idea of water not simply as a public good but also as a human right. Just as a convergent environmental and social critique—ecosystem rights and human rights, so to speak—was critical to broadening the anti-dam movement's power and appeal, the idea of water as a human right has positioned the anti-privatization movement to build bridges to a wider array of social forces.

As Peter Gleick has pointed out, there has long been a basis in international law, covenants, and declarations for recognizing a human right to water, although historically that right was understood primarily as "an implicit part of the right to food, health, human well-being and life."[57] Anti-dam activists have also linked water and human rights, as discussed in chapter 6. The existing diplomatic and activist foundations for framing water as a human right were bolstered in the late 1990s by the emergence of a third strand in the form of transnational parliamentary initiatives. These efforts have been rooted primarily in green parties and national political movements rather than issue-specific international non-governmental organizations. In 1998 a group of prominent international figures led by former Portuguese president Mario Soares issued "The Water Manifesto," which called for water to be recognized as the common property of all the Earth's inhabitants and for the recognition of water as "an inalienable individual and collective right."[58] Soares's Committee for a World Water Contract (CWWC) proposed the creation of an international network on water that would link national parliaments and negotiate a world water treaty to end the subordination of water rights to commercial instruments such as the WTO. European green parties have also become active on the issue. In June 2000 the "green group" within the European Parliament used the annual "P-7 summit" as a vehicle to call for an end to water privatization on the grounds of water as a human right. (The P-7 summit was created to bring together representatives and activists from the world's seven poorest countries as a symbolic counterpoint to the G-7 summit of the world's dominant industrial democracies).[59]

In other words, "norm entrepreneurs" have been actively building and supporting the idea of water as a human right in several circles—diplomatic, activist, and parliamentary—and for some time.[60] Finnemore and Sikkink suggest, however, that norm entrepreneurs also require an organizational platform to enhance persuasive power and legitimacy and facilitate the process by which norms become institutionalized in specific sets of international rules and organizations. If such a platform is necessary, then the human rights framework for water received an important impetus when, during its twenty-ninth session in November 2002, the UN Committee on Economic, Social and Cultural Rights adopted a General Comment declaring that access to water is "a human right and a public commodity fundamental to life and health."[61] The comment was based on an interpretation of the International Covenant on Economic, Social and Cultural Rights, which does not mention water explicitly. Adopting a key phrase already popularized by the anti-privatization movement, the comment emphasized that water should be treated as a social and cultural good, and not primarily as an economic commodity.[62]

The emergence of the human-right-to-water frame has been an important development within the anti-privatization movement. In general terms, this shift can be understood as part of the so-called anti-globalization movement's efforts to articulate a positive, people-centered vision of globalization. The frame of a human right to water has created possibilities for a broader global water coalition linking anti-dam and anti-privatization activists, transnational parliamentary initiatives, progressive environmental organizations, human rights groups, grassroots development advocates, and others. The first People's World Water Forum demonstrated the growing links among these different groups around the human-right-to-water frame; the meeting was co-organized by the Committee for a World Water Contract and several Italian social movement groups.

A Global Water Movement: Opportunities and Obstacles

There are some notable commonalities between the anti-dam and anti-privatization movements. In both cases, the focal point for opposition has been changes in the rules of access to what was widely perceived as a public good. In both cases, the specific targets are an alliance of intergovernmental organizations, private firms, and the state. In both cases, the substantive focus of protest merges with procedural grievances about the lack of popular participation in decision making. The emergence of a human rights framework within the anti-privatization movement raises the possibility of a broader global water movement, in which two largely separate struggles converge on common normative themes to create, if not a global water movement, at least more durable coalitions and more tightly connected networks.

A central element of the human rights framework is that the proper price for water and other considerations of allocative efficiency should be determined within the confines of a more fundamental commitment to social equity. The Water Manifesto of the Committee for a World Water Contract stressed that "The costs (including the negative externalities which are not taken into account by market prices) are common social costs to be borne by the collective as a whole."[63] In issuing its General Comment on water as a human right, the UN Committee on Economic, Social and Cultural Rights underscored the importance of subordinating the economic considerations surrounding water to those of social equity and nondiscrimination and noted that it "has been confronted continually with the widespread denial of the right to water in developing as well as developed countries."[64] A similar normative stance was taken in the final report of the World Commission on Dams, which argued that

The WCD Knowledge Base indicates that the poor, other vulnerable groups and future generations are likely to bear a disproportionate share of the social and environmental costs of large dam projects without gaining a commensurate share of the economic benefits. . . . These inequitable outcomes documented in the WCD Knowledge Base invalidate the prevailing "balance-sheet" approach to decision-making. The balancing of gains and losses as a way of judging the merits of a large dam project—or selecting the best option—is not acceptable where the mismatch between those who gain from the benefits and those who pay the costs is of such a serious, pervasive, and sometimes irreversible nature.[65]

Another opportunity to align frames between the two movements revolves around questions of corporate behavior and corruption. The image of greedy corporations stealing water at the expense of the public good has been a staple of the anti-privatization movement, which has generated several exposés of corporate abuse in recent years.[66] Examples of corruption and bribery in international dam construction projects have also been staple elements of the watershed democracy frame of the anti-dam movement. A related theme across the two movements has been that intergovernmental organizations and export credit agencies have provided fixed profit margins, guaranteed rates of return, full cost recovery, and other mechanisms that overinsulate private actors from any financial risk.[67]

Clearly, some activists within each movement have recognized the potential synergies. The unifying link of a panel discussion at the 2002 World Social Forum was the idea of water as "an inalienable social, economic, and human right."[68] At the Third World Water Forum in Kyoto in 2003, the NGO panel statement to the ministerial meeting raised issues related to both dam construction and privatization controversies.[69]

However, the links are still episodic and tentative. Anti-dam groups were not strongly represented among the organizing committee for the January 2004 People's World Water Forum in Delhi.[70] None of the organizing committee groups and only a few of the assembled activist groups at the Second International Meeting of Dam-Affected People and their Allies (held in Ras Salai, Thailand, in 2003) were grounded primarily in the anti-privatization struggle. Although the final declaration decried privatization and affirmed the intention to "[Strengthen] our movements by joining with others struggling against the neo-liberal development model and for global social and ecological justice," the meeting focused primarily on evaluating the performance of the anti-dam campaign in recent years and the current state of the dam-building industry rather than on developing new strategies and partnerships.[71] In general, the web sites of the principal organizations engaged in either struggle do not contain direct links to nodes in the other network. In other words, to date there appear to be under way the preliminary stages of aligning frames and invoking common themes, but not yet much in the way of concrete integration or even coordinated coalition building.

There are numerous practical obstacles to convergence of the movements, of course, and good tactical reasons for each to keep a tight focus. There are also more fundamental barriers. It would be an overstatement to suggest that the anti-privatization movement has been a knee-jerk defense of the public sector and parastatals. As Tim Kessler of the public services advocacy group, Citizens' Network on Essential Services, has argued, "In public discourse proponents of privatization vastly overstate the position of skeptics. They have set up a straw man all too easy to knock over, characterizing those who question privatization of services as unreconstructed statists."[72] Nevertheless, it remains an open question whether the state-centered model of public-goods delivery and "public-public" partnerships are themes that sit well with many of the indigenous activists and deep ecologists who make up important portions of the anti-dam movement.[73]

There is also a question as to whether the anti-privatization movement can go as far as the anti-dam movement in rejecting the larger logic of development that undergirds both large water infrastructure projects and initiatives to privatize water services. Despite their championing of the recommendations of the World Commission on Dams, anti-dam activists routinely point to its failure to question the larger development model (a theme that provided the basis for the lone dissenting opinion in the final WCD report, by Indian activist Medha Patkar). The anti-privatization movement has set itself in opposition to the specifically hyperliberalized variant of a development model that has been in place since the end of World War II, but not to some of the larger parameters of that model, such as international public financing of infrastructure for state-provided public goods.

Related to the question of the larger development model is whether the broad common ground afforded by the idea of a human right to water is taking on compatible meanings in each movement. As Balakrishnan Rajagopal has pointed out, human rights discourse in the 1990s was strongly influenced by the idea of a right to economic development, a process he refers to as the "developmentalization of human rights."[74] One ramification of this trend, according to Rajagopal, has been to reinforce a conception of the individual as the only relevant subject to realize rights and of the state as the central agent responsible for the manifestation of those rights. Aligning this conception of a right to water with the community rights framework and skepticism of the state that infuse the anti-dam movement would entail a significant challenge for both movements.

Conclusion: Institutionalizing Contention over Marketization of Water

The core precepts of water marketization are that water should be priced as a scarce economic good; that it should be recognized as a marketable commodity; that market forces should shape its allocation toward its highest-value uses; and that key aspects of the social water cycle, including investment in infrastructure and provision of service, can and should be privatized. These ideas have come to be widely embraced in important intergovernmental organizations. They are also influential in networks of water experts and are gaining a foothold in many national and local water jurisdictions.

Metanorms of authority, territoriality, and knowledge underpinning the idea of water as a market resource eschew the statist, territorial approach of prototypical interstate regimes in favor of a radically different framework. The state's authority is subsumed by the disciplining power of the market. The mobilization of water across boundaries in search of its highest-value uses vitiates notions of territorial fixity and the boundability of nature, whether it occurs through physical transfers or the virtualization of the water trade through liberalization of investment. Faith in market allocation mechanisms reflects an enduring element of high-modern rationality, to be sure. However, stabilized knowledge about the goods and bads associated with water is given over to myth and ceremony about the guiding hand of price signals and the creative destruction of market capitalism.

Such conceptual purities often get lost in the real world, where the institutionalization of water marketization has often revealed the enduring pull of statist authority, territorialization, and knowledge stabilization. Early and particularly blunt versions of neoliberalism (both water related and generally) have given way to a more sophisticated understanding of the state's role as the architect of the requisite legal, regulatory, and property rights framework.[75] The transnational fluidity of contemporary global capitalism has been tempered by enduring barriers to large-scale water trade and the slow adaptation of global rules on service sector trade and investment. Most full-cost pricing schemes rest, not on the revealed results of preference-aggregating markets, but on the behavior of administrative bureaucracies. These qualifications notwithstanding, marketization as an institutional form for governing water moves well outside the regime space conceived in chapter 2.

Despite these more fluid understandings of territory, authority, and knowledge, marketization has been unable to bound, contain, and stabilize the sociopolitical controversies around water. Quite the contrary; it has exacerbated them, often dramatically and sometimes even violently. As a result, what is actually being institutionalized is not water marketization per se but a dynamic tension between marketization and a very different framework in which water is understood as a human right and a social and cultural good. To be sure, the two sides of this dynamic tension are hardly symmetrical or equivalent in force; water marketization has made substantially more progress in becoming part of a wide array of important areas and settings of international life. Several factors—the deep commitment of powerful intergovernmental organizations to water marketization, the growing decentralization of providing water service in many national frameworks, the vast supply of local communities available to be tapped, and the liberalization of international investment rules—ensure that pressures for water marketization will endure. However, the growing normalization of water marketization is demonstrably not *everyone's* myth and ceremony; there has been ample room in this case to struggle, resist, oppose, counterframe, organize and mobilize.

At the heart of this dynamic tension is the juxtaposition of marketization norms with a countervailing normative bundle that also moves well beyond a statist, territorialized, knowledge-stabilizing framework of governance. Thus, one of the most notable features of the water marketization struggle is the extent to which both sides have transcended the statist, territorialized, knowledge-stabilizing framework of metanorms common to conventional interstate regimes. At the time of the Mar del Plata conference in the late 1970s, the right to water (such as it was) was understood to be realized through interstate cooperation, development assistance, and technical progress in developing water resources.

In other words, the inherently transterritorial, transstatist tendencies of a universal human right were tempered by the path to its realization. The early twenty-first-century variant of a human right to water frames things quite differently. States are pressed to engage in transnational stakeholder dialogues and to acknowledge the role of water in cultural practices and the livelihoods of distinct communities such as indigenous peoples, thereby ceding elements of authority to a heterogeneous array of actors.[76] The territorial construct of water within a national domain is supplanted by a sociocultural construct of water as a collective social and cultural good, on scales ranging from individuals and households to communities. Elements of knowledge stabilization remain, as seen in the widespread use of World Health Organization guidelines as the baseline standard, defined literally in gallons per person per day. The UN Committee on Economic, Social and Cultural Rights has urged the development of right-to-water indicators and benchmarks, but it also acknowledges that what constitutes "sufficient, safe, acceptable, physically accessible, and affordable water" is inherently culturally contingent.[77] These shifting understandings—not simply about water, but about authority, territory, and knowledge in the context of water—are a direct result of social activism against water privatization schemes and marketization policies.

This case is at a much earlier stage of development than the large-dam controversy. Moreover, activism in the two areas has proceeded along different trajectories, using different resources, constructing different frames, and organizing activism in different ways. Nevertheless, there are some features that are broadly similar in the institutionalization of contention in these two cases. The parameters of conflict are becoming regularized around recognizable forms and recurring sites. One can also see a normative evolution on each side of this debate, although not necessarily a convergence, which is being pulled by developments on the other side. The recently renewed focus on the principle of a human right to water—an idea that has been around since the 1970s, and which has a long-standing and well-established (if derivative) basis in international law—has occurred as a direct response to water marketization. Similarly, adaptations in the framing of marketization, stressing partnerships and risk management, are a direct response to anti-privatization activism.

There are also indications that the water marketization controversy is heading down a path of institutionalized contention that is similar to that of the large dams controversy. Taking up an idea originally proposed by the British grassroots development organization, WaterAid, the German government announced at the Bonn Freshwater Conference in December 2001 that it would assist in establishing a multistakeholder review process along the lines of that of the World Commission on Dams. From this emerged a Global Water Scoping Process Working Group, consisting of a half-dozen organizations with widely differing backgrounds and views on private sector participation, with support from the German Agency for Development Cooperation.[78] The working group included WaterAid; ASSEMAE (the Brazilian association of public sector water operators); Consumers International, an international federation of consumer organizations; the South African advocacy organization, Environmental Monitoring Group; the international labor federation's Public Services International; and RWE Thames Water, a leading water multinational. Early in 2004 the working group circulated an electronic survey among water professionals as part of a scoping study on the relative merits of launching a global multistakeholder review.

8
Brazil: Innovation through Conflict

Nobody will be surprised that we are here, proposing this National Water Agency, because this is the method by means of which we are creating a revolution in the structure of the Brazilian State.

—President Fernando Henrique Cardoso, announcing the formation of Brazil's National Water Agency

The practice of partnerships is one of the sacred aspects of Water Resources Management.

—Secretary of Water Resources Raymundo José Santos Garrido, *The World Bank and the Water Sector*

Innovative solutions encounter difficulties in being understood and accepted by juridical organs, often due to existing legal impediments but also because of traditionalism and conservatism.... Innovative solutions, implying partnerships between Public Power and society, are more achievable in basins and regions in which the conflicts are more serious and where there has been a mobilization of communities and civic entities around that theme.

—Flávio Terra Barth, founder of the Brazilian Water Resources Association, in *O Estado das Águas no Brasil 1999: Perspectivas de Gestão e Informação de Recursos Hídricos* (author's translation)

Brazil as a Test Case of the Influence of Global Water Norms

In Brazil, political change destabilized the traditional underpinnings of water law and policy, creating a window of opportunity for nonincremental adjustments. Beginning with the military's gradual withdrawal from power in the 1980s, and continuing into the postauthoritarian era of the 1990s, a combination of shifting power relations, changing attitudes, emerging social conflicts, and new institutional developments undercut the effectiveness and legitimacy of traditional practices related to water,

rivers, and watersheds. This chapter examines these changes, the normative content of the new approaches to water, and the institutionalization
of new norms and practices across a wide range of salient domains.

The chapter also examines the role that the diverse global protonorms
for watershed governance discussed in chapters 4 through 7 have played
in this process of change and assesses the extent to which they have been
inscribed in new approaches to water law, policy, or practice. Transnational influences are by no means the only causal forces at work in this
process of change; quite the contrary, as discussed later.

The forces that created the window of opportunity for change have
been many. Manipulation of water resources for hydropower, transportation, and other developmental uses has a long history in Brazil, and
was central to the industrialization drive of the military regime (1964–
1985). During this period, Brazil became a leading exemplar of the
model of pushing rivers around discussed in chapter 3. The delegitimization and eventual demise of military rule was therefore an important source of change in that it undermined the authority of that model
and allowed a broader array of voices to participate in water policy
discussions.

A related source of change was the new constitutional order that
emerged in the wake of military rule. The adoption of a new constitution
in 1988 was an important episode in Brazil's political transition. The
new constitution, which established a fundamentally new approach to
natural resource property rights, swept aside a national water code that
had been in place since the 1930s, thereby creating political space for a
new national framework law on water. The new constitution also ushered in an era of political and economic decentralization, which has redefined the terms of state–federal interaction and created opportunities
for new actors to enter national policy debates.

A third key contextual element was Brazil's 1994 "plano real"
economic reform, which ushered in a set of primarily neoliberal adjustments. These changes affected all of the critical economic variables shaping water policy, ranging from the investment climate in Brazil to the
state's budgetary resources to the regulatory philosophy underpinning
governmental actions. Also, the new economic plan enhanced the influence of the World Bank in policy reform discussions.

For all of these reasons—political democratization, a new constitutional order, reform of the state, and macroeconomic adjustment—Brazilian water politics at the turn of the twenty-first century was going to look very different from what had come before. However, the political and economic forces sweeping aside traditional water norms and institutions were largely outside the water sector itself. As such, they said little, in and of themselves, about the specific shape and normative content of new water-related practices. This makes Brazil an interesting test of the relative ability of different emerging global norms to take root institutionally once the terrain had been cleared of traditional practices.

Indeed, the Brazilian case is revealing precisely because each of the four sources of watershed protonorms discussed in earlier chapters was, in theory, well positioned to take root in national water law, policy, and practice. Two of the world's six largest international river basins, the Amazon and Paraná, lie substantially within Brazilian territory.[1] In the past three decades, Brazil has been a party to more treaties, agreements, and memoranda of understanding on international rivers than almost any other country in the world (chapter 4). This level of diplomacy creates obvious entry points through which international legal norms about water and rivers might "swim upstream" into domestic law, policy, and practice.

Global networks of water policy experts (chapter 5) are also a strong potential influence because Brazilian water managers, engineers, and policy makers are well integrated into those networks. As discussed later, a domestic network of technically skilled water professionals has long been an influential force in water policy debates. Network participants are well connected with their international counterparts. Brazil has hosted one international congress and two annual meetings of the International Commission on Large Dams. The country sent one of the largest national delegations to The Hague for the Second World Water Forum in March 2000, with its secretary of water resources as a featured speaker.

Brazil is also centrally integrated into transnational processes of activism for watershed democracy (chapter 6). As discussed later, it is home to some of the world's most active and transnationally integrated advocacy groups and social movements. Several factors, including the country's protracted struggle against military rule and its role as host of the

1992 Earth Summit, helped to galvanize a strong and outward-looking mobilization around convergent themes of environmental protection, human rights, indigenous peoples' rights, and grassroots democracy. It was no accident that the First International Meeting of People Affected by Dams was held in the southern Brazilian city of Curitiba, where struggles against large water projects had already been in operation for two decades.

Finally, Brazil has been an important battleground in struggles over neoliberal water marketization. As one of the Bank's largest water sector borrowers, Brazil became an important testing ground for some of the World Bank's marketization and policy reform initiatives. In 1999 when the Bank began to evaluate the impact of the revised water sector policy guidelines it had adopted in 1993, Brazil was chosen as the first country-level case study "because of the country's substantial progress in recent years and because the Bank has played an active role in supporting these efforts."[2]

These transnational links mean that all of the processes of the formation and diffusion of global norms discussed in chapters 4 through 7 had accessible paths and potential receptors in the Brazilian domestic sphere. This fact is important because it means that Brazil is unlikely to be a straightforward, passive recipient of a monolithic set of international influences, easily characterized in the language of "leader" or "laggard" based on its implementation of well-structured and clearly articulated international norms. Rather, the process of reworking water norms in Brazil is better understood as a complex melding of often-contradictory influences. In such a context, domestic political agendas and influences play a large part, and international norms are better understood as potential catalysts for domestic change than as something simply bought into or rejected by a monolithic Brazilian state.

The Physical, Social, and Economic Geography of Water in Brazil

Viewed in national terms, Brazil has an extraordinary endowment of water resources. According to Shiklomanov, Brazil's average annual water availability during the period 1921–1985 was over 6,000 km^3, by far the world's largest (Russia ranked second at approximately 4,000).[3] Yet the dominant feature of Brazil's hydrogeography is not abundance but variability. The world's fifth largest country in terms of land area, Brazil is slightly larger than the contiguous forty-eight states of the United States and contains the world's longest continuous north-south axis. The climate varies from superhumid in parts of Amazônia (with no dry season at all) to semiarid throughout most of the Northeast (with no significant rainfall for at least six months annually).

Acknowledging this heterogeneity, Brazil's Agência Nacional de Águas (ANA), or National Water Agency, divides the country into thirteen hydrographic regions (figure 8.1), defined primarily by the country's main river basins (figure 8.2). Chief among these are the vast Amazon River Basin, covering almost half of Brazilian national territory; the Tocantins and Araguaia Rivers, major Amazon feeders that flow north from the central highlands; the São Francisco River, which originates in the central plateau and winds through eight states of the semiarid Northeast on its way to the Atlantic Ocean; and the Paraguai, Paraná, and Uruguai Rivers, contiguous basins in southern Brazil that cover about 17 percent of the country's land area and combine to make up what is sometimes referred to as the "Prata" system.

As figure 8.1 and table 8.1 indicate, population, precipitation, and discharge rates are all distributed highly unevenly across these hydrogeographic regions. Population densities vary from more than 100 inhabitants per square kilometer in the southeast coastal region to roughly 2 in Amazônia, and regional discharge rates vary by two orders of magnitude. As a result, annual water availability varies from less than 500 m^3 per inhabitant in the semiarid and populous Northeast to more than 100,000 in the humid and sparsely populated Amazon.[4]

If the main feature of Brazil's physical hydrogeography is water variability, the dominant feature of its social hydrogeography is water inequality. The country's water riches have not translated into water security for much of Brazil's population. The United Nations Development Programme estimates that for the period 1990–1998 some 24 percent of Brazilians lacked access to safe drinking water while roughly 30 percent went without basic sanitation services.[5] An estimated 65 percent of the money spent on hospitalizations in Brazil is related to waterborne diseases, as are some 50,000 infant deaths annually.[6]

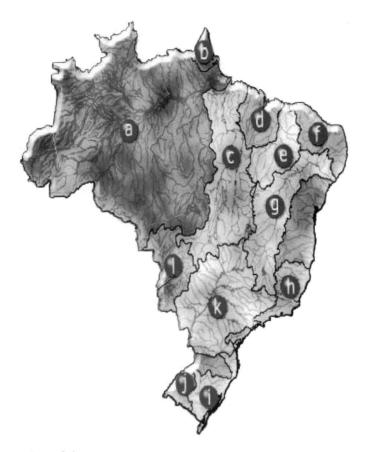

Figure 8.1
Brazil's hydrographic regions (source: Rede das Águas, n.d. http://www
.rededasaguas.org.br/apoio/bacias.htm. Reprinted with permission).

To be sure, the uneven distribution of both water resources and people
in Brazil makes it a challenge to meet basic water needs in some parts of
the country. However, widespread water insecurity also reflects the
country's more general pattern of socioeconomic inequality. Brazil's per
capita income (estimated at $7,360 in 2001) places it in the upper ranks
among less-developed countries.[7] However, the ratio of income or consumption of the richest 20 percent of Brazilians to that of the poorest
20 percent is on the order of 29:1—one of the highest disparities in the

Figure 8.2
Brazil's major rivers (source: map rendered by Ken Cousins. Reprinted with permission).

world.[8] By some measures, moreover, Brazil's water inequality is extreme even in the context of its baseline social inequality. The share of the population lacking clean drinking water is as high as the official national illiteracy rate, and the proportion without adequate sanitation exceeds illiteracy by several percentage points (table 8.2).

Table 8.3 summarizes water demand by sector in Brazil. In terms of measurable economic activities, the three dominant uses of water are irrigation, urban municipal use, and hydropower. To these can be added, of course, a wide range of nonmarket "uses" located in the ecological and cultural sphere, ranging from the subsistence-based livelihoods of river dwellers to ecosystem services to the cultural significance of rivers. As is typically the case, irrigation constitutes by far the largest economic use, although its share has been declining steadily in recent years relative to the municipal and industrial sectors. As discussed later, growing

Table 8.1
Brazil's hydrogeographic regions

Hydrographic Region	Area within Brazilian territory (km²)	Population (number of inhabitants)	Average long-term discharge rate (m³/sec)	Average precipitation (mm)	International basin?
a. Amazon	3,760,706	7,550,526	108,982	2,234	Yes
b. Northern Coastal	82,696	58,898	3,390	2,447	Yes
c. Tocantins	967,060	7,890,714	15,433	1,869	No
d. Western NE Coastal	254,100	4,742,431	2,514	1,738	No
e. Parnaíba	334,113	3,630,431	763	1,119	No
f. Eastern NE Coastal	287,348	21,606,881	813	1,132	No
g. São Francisco	638,323	12,823,013	3,037	1,036	No
h. Southeast Coastal	229,972	25,644,396	3,286	1,339	No
i. South Coastal	185,856	11,592,481	4,129	1,573	Yes
j. Uruguai	174,612	3,834,652	4,117	1,784	Yes
k. Paraná	879,860	54,639,523	10,371	1,511	Yes
l. Paraguai	363,447	1,887,401	1,833	1,398	Yes
Eastern Coastal	374,677	13,641,045	1,400	1,053	No
Brazil	8,532,770	169,542,392	160,067	1,800	

Notes: The letters key regions to the map in figure 8.1. The eastern coastal region is shown as the unlabeled southern portion of the eastern northeast coastal region (area f) in figure 8.1.

Source: Secretaria de Recursos Hídricos n.d., section 4.3, table 4.2.

Table 8.2
Measures of social inequality in Brazil

Inequality Measure	Percentage of Population
Adult illiteracy rate, 2001	13
Population living on less than $1 per day, 1990–2001	10
Population without sustainable access to an improved water source, 2000	13
Population without access to improved sanitation, 2000	24

Source: UNDP 2003, annex tables.

Table 8.3
Water demand by sector in Brazil (percent of total water use)

Sector	Water Demand
Irrigation	56
Urban	21
Industrial	12
Rural	6
Animal	5

Source: Secretaria de Recursos Hídricos n.d., section 4.3.

demand, problems with water quality, and changes in regulatory philosophy have brought these various uses of water into increasingly direct competition.

The Evolution of Brazilian Water Law and Policy

The 1934 Water Code

The first broadly significant water legislation in Brazil was the 1934 *Código de Águas* (Water Code), which would frame national water law well into the 1990s. Historically, water had been a matter of local jurisdiction. Water scarcity on the Iberian Peninsula led the Portuguese to promulgate a general framework of rules of water use in 1580, including stiff penalties for unauthorized use. Although they were nominally applicable to Portugal's Brazilian colony, given Brazil's relative water abundance, these rules were not observed or enforced.[9] Laws written in the wake of independence from Portugal gave municipal and provincial legislatures responsibility for water works (1828) and river navigation in Brazil's vast interior (1834).[10] The 1891 constitution, which marked the transition to a republican form of government, makes no mention of water, although the creation of federal authority for civil legislation enabled several specific federal water regulations to be included in the civil code of 1916.[11] Water was generally understood as a resource with limited economic value beyond its narrow and specific private uses, and therefore subject to limited public authority.

The 1934 water code established the first national framework for water policy and management. Passed as a presidential decree with the force of law, the code must be understood in the context of an era of dramatic economic and political change. Key trends of the day included the growing power of urbanizing, industrializing interests, triggered by the collapse of Brazil's agro-export markets during the Great Depression; the consolidation of a strong central state under president Getulio Vargas (1930–1945 and 1950–1954), which supplanted much of the power of the regional oligarchies; and the growing institutionalization of the military as a force in Brazil's political, economic, and technological development.[12] By defining a national interest in water development and favoring hydropower for industrial development, the 1934 water code fit squarely within the prevailing national political economy.

Brazilian legal scholars generally view the code as an advanced piece of legislation for its time.[13] Among its major provisions were a distinction between "public" and "private" waters, which replaced the traditional treatment of water as a private good, and an affirmation of both the appropriation rights of private users and the authority of states and municipalities over water falling within their dominion. The code also contained innovative provisions related to multiple uses and water quality, including a clear statement of the polluter-pays principle written several decades before the modern environmental era—but these features were never effectively implemented.[14]

The code's main impact was to catalyze state-led hydropower development. It federalized the process of allocating rights for waters used in hydroelectric generation.[15] The code also contained several provisions that anticipated the large-dam controversies of the 1980s and 1990s. Article 143 required that the exploitation of hydroelectric energy must safeguard certain "general interests," including the "health and needs" of riverbank populations, public health, irrigation, navigation, protection against flooding, the "conservation and free circulation" of fish, and water drainage.[16]

The 1934 water code survived essentially intact through several decades of turbulent political change: the military's removal of Vargas from power in 1945; Vargas's return via the ballot box in 1950 and suicide while in office in 1954; an experiment with limited democracy and competitive party politics in the late 1950s and early 1960s; the 1964 military coup, which came in the wake of growing political polarization and the emergence of a mass political left; and two subsequent decades of military rule, ending with a negotiated process of civilianization of the regime in 1985. An important refinement was added in the 1946 constitution, which distinguished between federal jurisdiction for interstate and international waters and state jurisdiction for waters falling within the states' sole dominion.[17] The adoption of four new constitutions during this tumultuous period (in 1937, 1946, 1967 and 1969) did not alter the basic framework of national water law.[18]

Institutionalized Contention: The Rise of Basin-Level Conflicts

By the time the military seized power in the 1964 coup, energy concerns had eclipsed agriculture as the main focus of water resources administration. The most important decisions related to water policy now rested with the "hydrocrats" in the energy planning sphere, specifically in the Ministry of Mines and Energy (MME). The National Department for Water and Electric Energy (DNAEE), an administrative organ linked to MME and closely tied to the federal electricity monopoly Eletrobrás, was charged with both the management of water resources and the promotion of hydroelectric generation. The predictable result was that water-related decisions became subordinated to electricity planning.[19] Powerful agricultural interests resisted the domination of the hydrocrats; the Ministry of the Interior maintained control of water management for agriculture. In 1979 the Ministry of Irrigation was formed, further fragmenting water resource policy and management decisions.[20]

With Brazil's deepening industrial development in the 1960s and 1970s came mounting water-related conflicts, particularly in the state of São Paulo, Brazil's industrial center. By the mid-1970s, several serious disputes over multiple water uses and water quality issues had emerged in some of São Paulo's more densely populated and industrially developed basins, such as the Upper Tietê, Cubatão, and Piracicaba. Within these and other basins, the convergence of several stresses—mounting levels of industrial pollution, large-scale water infrastructure projects such as canals and hydroelectric facilities, and the burgeoning water needs of explosively growing urban areas—produced escalating tensions among competing users. In the Upper Tietê, for example, the effects on river flow of damming for hydroelectricity had severe consequences for the sanitation systems of local municipalities. The 1934 water code and the balkanized structure of water resources administration were ill-equipped to address such situations.

These emerging conflicts would have several effects. One was to drag MME, a federal organ, into direct engagement with local actors, both because the ministry's development projects were significant interventions in these basins and, more generally, because the ministry itself was a stakeholder in these disputes. In the Upper Tietê case, for example, the federalization of electricity generation in the 1970s meant that MME was centrally involved in the controversy. It negotiated an agreement with the state of São Paulo to "improve sanitary conditions" in the Upper Tietê and Cubatão Basins in 1976.[21] The ministry's involvement in this and other disputes led directly to the formation of a federal Special Committee for Integrated Studies of Hydrographic Basins (CEEIBH) in 1978, involving MME, the National Department for Water and Electric Energy, the newly formed Environmental Secretariat within the Ministry of the Interior, and Eletrobrás.[22] Brazil's third national development plan (1980–1985) reflected this period of growing federal involvement in water controversies, calling for the government to "sponsor the establishment of a National Water Resources Policy."[23]

The interagency committee approach to water issues and controversies played an important role in focusing attention on the need for a more comprehensive water policy. It also produced several useful products in the form of technical assessments and basin-level studies. Ultimately, however, its impact was limited for political reasons. One limitation was its purely advisory status. A more important factor, however, was its status as a product of military rule and therefore its dubious legitimacy at a time of political transition. According to one key participant, committee-institutionalized negotiations between the federal government and the state of São Paulo fell into decline "for political reasons" once the military regime allowed a direct gubernatorial election in 1983, in favor of the more "democratic and participatory" committee that emerged at the state level.[24] One government official who had been involved in discussions during that period used the phrase *chapa branca* to describe the committee. This term, used to signify politically appointed status during the military era, was widely understood as a damning accusation during the transition.

In addition to engaging the federal government, emerging social conflicts also activated Brazil's community of water experts. The Brazilian Water Resources Association (Associação Brasileira de Recursos Hídricos, or ABRH) was formed in 1977. That year ABRH held the first of what would become a biennial national symposium on water resources; it began publishing a technical journal in 1978.[25] ABRH defines its mission as promoting the exchange of ideas and information about water resources, evaluating and proposing "the technical fundamentals of national water resources policy," and collaborating in "the elaboration of technical norms."[26]

Made up predominantly of individuals with training in civil engineering and hydrology, ABRH broadened its emphasis over time to incorporate questions of water resource economics, management, and policy. In 1987, it released the "Salvador Declaration," approved during the closing session of the Seventh Brazilian Water Resources Symposium. The declaration is striking in the extent to which it anticipated the central principles that would orient international water discussions in the 1990s (chapter 5), including the following:

- a multiple-use approach grounded in the idea of water as "an economic good of significant value, subject to conflicts among the potential users";
- decentralization and participation: "It is important to have the participation of the communities involved, in order to render the necessary actions feasible and to ensure their flexibility and continuity";
- a national water resources management system, to coordinate federal–state interaction and reconcile conflicts among users, grounded in a national water resources policy; and

• improvement of legislation, with an emphasis on the principle of integrated water resources management.[27]

Subsequent congresses produced calls for recognition of water's economic value and charges for its use (Foz do Iguaçu, 1989) and for greater attention to prevention and management of water pollution (Rio de Janeiro, 1991).[28] ABRH also organized some influential workshops during this period, and some of the leading figures in the organization would play a key intellectual role in designing water management institutions at the federal level in the 1990s.

Along with federal agencies and technical experts, basin-level disputes of this era also mobilized domestic networks of water users and affected communities. Basin-level committees formed in the southern state of Rio Grande do Sul in 1988 around the Sinos and Gravataí Rivers.[29] One senior ANA official described the context for formation of these committees as "intense mobilization." These committees were given a statutory basis by the state government.[30] In São Paulo, where by this time stakeholders in some basins had been organizing and pressing for action for well over a decade, twenty basin committees were formed in the period 1993–1997.[31]

In addition to mobilizing a wide range of political actors, basin-level conflicts spurred water-related institution building in several Brazilian states.[32] Chief among these was São Paulo, where stakeholder pressures in the Piracicaba River Basin led to the formation of a State Council of Water Resources in 1987 as a vehicle to coordinate activities across ten different state secretariats. This was followed by adoption of a state water resources policy in 1991. Around this time, the state of Espírito Santo created an intermunicipal dispute resolution body and the drought-prone northeastern state of Ceará formed a state water resources secretariat. By 1995, state-level water resource policies were in place in a half dozen states and the Federal District of Brasília.

Giving the Rivers Their Marching Orders: Military Rule, Large-Dam Construction, and the Mobilization of Protest

As the multiple-use conflicts described in the previous section were gaining steam beginning in the 1970s, more radical forms of protest and social activism also emerged, centered on a series of large dam projects.

According to Brazilian legal scholar Paulo de Bessa Antunes, the significance of the 1934 water code was the way that an increasingly interventionist state conceived of water resources as "an *essential* element for the generation of economic wealth and development, particularly as a source of electric energy."[33] Certainly the military regime that governed Brazil from 1964 to 1985 conceived of water in this way, moving aggressively to tap the country's vast hydroelectric potential. Brazil currently has some 600 large dams, with more than half dedicated to hydroelectric generation. This includes the world's largest hydroelectric dam, Itaipu (installed capacity 12,600 MW), situated on a stretch of the Paraná River that forms the border with Paraguay. An additional twenty-two hydropower stations have an installed capacity of 1,000 MW or more, including the 4,000-MW Tucuruí Dam on the Tocantins River. With 66 GW of installed hydroelectric generating capacity as of 2001, Brazil gets more than 90 percent of its electricity supply from hydro and ranks fourth in the world in installed capacity (behind the United States, China, and Canada).[34] Although the dam-building era in Brazil is by no means completed, most of the country's installed hydro capacity to date is the result of projects conceived during military rule. According to data compiled by International Rivers Network and the Brazilian Movement of Dam-Affected People, more than a million Brazilians have been displaced to make way for these dams. The area flooded by dam reservoirs, alleged by these activist groups to be at least 34,000 km², is larger than the country of Belgium.[35]

Given the scale of some of these projects and the near-total disregard for the impact on local communities, it is no surprise that they produced strong local opposition. In the eastern Amazon, the Tucuruí Dam on the Tocantins River provoked strong opposition from indigenous peoples' groups and local communities. In the northeast, the Sobradinho Dam on the São Francisco River displaced large numbers of local residents (as many as 70,000 according to anti-dam activists). On the southern border with Paraguay, the massive Itaipu Dam also displaced large numbers of people, creating resistance and helping to launch Brazil's large and aggressive movement of landless rural workers.

These struggles, although initially local and focused on compensation and fair treatment for the displaced, would converge over time to produce a national Movement of Dam-Affected People. Founded in 1991 as a "national, autonomous, popular movement," MAB's origins were tied not only to local affected communities but also to labor activism; it was formed in the aftermath of the First National Meeting of Workers Affected by Dams held in 1989.[36] The Itaipu inundation in particular was a crucial episode in the founding of Brazil's large and confrontational Landless Worker's Movement, which has sustained more than a decade of rural activism centered on the invasion and occupation of unused agricultural land.[37]

In addition to mobilizing local affected communities and linking them together in a national network, MAB became an important node in the emerging international network of anti-dam activism (chapter 6). In 1997, it hosted the First International Meeting of People Affected by Dams, held near Itaipu in the southern Brazilian city of Curitiba. The date of March 14, which the international movement has institutionalized as a global day of anti-dam activism, coincides with the Brazilian national day of action against dams, which was declared on MAB's founding.

Constitutional Reform

To this mix of growing controversy in both institutional and extrainstitutional spheres was added a new national constitution in 1988. The process of writing a new constitution came in the wake of the military's withdrawal from formal power in 1985, and was typical of the country's complex postauthoritarian transition. On the one hand, the new constitution created broadly expanded political, economic, social, and even ecological rights for the average Brazilian citizen. On the other hand, the process by which it was created (using the sitting Congress as the constituent assembly) reflected the limits of the transition and the enduring power of actors from the prior era.

With regard to water, the constitution established a new legal framework of property rights and jurisdictional authority. All of Brazil's water resources were placed squarely within the public domain, eliminating traditional private rights derived from riparian principles and land ownership. Surface waters that cross either national or state boundaries are under federal domain (Article 20, Section III); groundwater and surface waters wholly within a single state's territory fall under the domain of the states (Article 26, Section I). The federal government is authorized to promulgate legislation on water, with the states retaining the right to legislate on waters falling under their exclusive domain (Article 22, Section IV). The federal government is vested with authority over hydropower development, either directly or through private concession, authorization, or permission (Article 21, Section XII). The federal government is also charged with "instituting the national management system for water resources and defining criteria for the approval of rights for their use" (Article 21, Section XIX).

The 1988 constitution was also the first in Brazilian history to make specific reference to environmental protection. It establishes environmental protection as one of the principles of Brazil's "economic order" (Article 170, Section VI) and gives Brazilians the right to an ecologically balanced natural environment (Article 225). Legislation from the early 1980s that established Brazil's framework for environmental protection defined water as an environmental resource.[38] Unlike its clear delineation between federal and state dominion over water, however, the constitution defines environmental protection as a shared responsibility of the federal, state, and municipal governments.[39]

Politically, the new constitution had several effects in the water sphere. The definition of all water resources as public goods and the specification of national water resources management as a federal responsibility effectively invalidated almost sixty years of water law, policy, and practice in Brazil. In essence, the water sector was left in a legal vacuum. In and of itself, this hardly constituted a legislative crisis or even an unusual occurrence. The ambitious new constitution created several such lacunae across the breadth and depth of Brazilian society, and the process of creating implementing legislation for constitutional provisions continues to this day. The new constitutional order gave an additional impulse to the growing momentum for national water policy reform, but was hardly the prime motive force.

One important political ramification of the new constitution, however, was to greatly complicate the politics of state–federal interaction on water at a time when the federal government was increasingly being drawn into basin-level disputes. In principle, the constitutional distinction between federal and state bodies of water provided a clear jurisdictional delineation. In practice, however, there were numerous complexities. What, for example, was the precise jurisdictional authority for federal rivers with tributaries that fell under state jurisdiction? More generally, as pointed out in an issue brief prepared for the Chamber of Deputies (the lower house in the legislature), there were "a series of apparent incompatibilities" in "the obligation to establish a national management system for a natural resource whose possession is divided between two distinct spheres of the Federation."[40]

Institutional Change: Creating a National Water Policy Framework

By the early 1990s, the federal government's institutional apparatus for dealing with water resources was increasingly archaic in a Brazil marked by democratic opening; a resurgent civil society; mounting water conflicts; and a shifting balance of power among federal, state, and municipal governments. Speaking in the early 1990s, Federal Deputy Fábio Feldmann, an important figure in both the constitutional reforms of the 1980s and the new water politics of the 1990s, described the situation as follows:

The management of water resources remains one of the great problems of Brazilian public administration. Until now, they have been administered in a fragmented manner, with each sectoral user—electric energy generation, irrigation, human and industrial supply, sanitation and others—appropriating for itself that portion of the total resources that it requires, irregardless of the restrictions that it is causing for the other users. There is no integrated planning for the supply and use of water, based on the analysis of alternatives.[41]

This arrangement was proving inadequate for dealing with growing basin-level conflict and multiple-use disputes. Nor could it implement the sort of national water policy development envisioned in the constitutional reforms. Despite a decade of political and intellectual ferment, as of 1990 the national institutional apparatus for water management was virtually identical to that which had existed ten years earlier. In this regard the federal government was being eclipsed by policy innovation in a number of states, from São Paulo in Brazil's industrial center to rural Ceará in the semiarid Northeast. Innovative states were emphasizing a more integrated perspective, more direct stakeholder participation, and the need for mechanisms to resolve multiple-use conflicts.

Although the story to this point is primarily one of domestic activism around local-scale political conflict, international influences were present during this period. Brazil's water *técnicos* (experts) enjoyed strong international ties. Environmental NGOs built international links around the build-up to the 1992 Earth Summit. Anti-dam activists were already interacting with international compatriots and getting involved in regional initiatives across the country's southern border. The World Bank had a major funding presence in the water sector.

The 1990s were a decade of institutional reform and reorganization, with the central development being the adoption of a new framework law for national water policy in 1997. Conceptually, the new law reflected a dramatic shift from a narrow paradigm of resource exploitation to a broader perspective centered on integrated assessment, basin-level management, environmental protection, and stakeholder participation. Politically, the law reflected the declining power of the hydrocrats and the rising influence of both urban and environmental interests. Institutionally, the law reflected the continuing struggle over the character of the Brazilian state, the balance between state and federal authority, and the meaning of participation in an increasingly democratic Brazil.

Federal Law 9433: The National Water Resource Policy

In the wake of constitutional reform, legislation to create a national water policy framework was introduced in 1991. The bill emerged from the Committee for the Defense of Consumers, the Environment, and Minorities within the Chamber of Deputies. The bill's *relator* (the legislator responsible for managing the bill in legislative deliberations) was Federal Deputy Fábio Feldmann.[42] In 1997, after several years of complex and often tumultuous debate, President Fernando Henrique Cardoso signed Federal Law 9433, the National Water Resource Policy.

According to Secretary of Water Resources Raymundo Garrido, the new law established five core principles for water resource policy:

• The river basin as the territorial unit for implementation of the National Water Resources Policy.

• Management of water resources should allow for multiple uses of water.

• Water is a limited resource, which has economic value.

• The management of water resources should be decentralized and should involve participation by the Government, the users, and the community.

• When there is a shortage of water, priority is given to human consumption and watering of animals.[43]

To translate these principles into practice, the law also authorized several "management instruments":

• water resource plans, conceived as detailed basin-level planning documents to guide decision making, establish priorities, and facilitate conflict resolution among competing uses;

• a classification system for bodies of water according to their predominant use, as a means of establishing different water quality requirements;

• water permits, authorizing use rights for specific users;

• water use tariffs, intended to recover costs and send accurate price signals to users about the value of the resource; and

• a national water resource information system to collect and organize basin-level data on supply, demand, flow, quality, and related matters.[44]

To implement these principles and deploy these tools, the law creates a complex, multitiered set of institutions for managing water resources, grounded in both the state and civil society. On one level, the law creates a fairly conventional regulatory framework rooted in existing state organs and jurisdictional units. The prime administrative responsibility for water resources policy and management was assigned to the Water Resources Secretariat (Secretaria de Recursos Hídricos, SRH). Situated within the Environment Ministry (Ministério de Meio Ambiente, MMA), SRH was a new unit that had been created in 1995, in the midst of the deliberations over Federal Law 9433.

At the same time, however, the law overlays this conventional approach with newly conceived jurisdictional units and newly authorized representative organs within those units. The law states that the river basin is the proper scale for water resources management, thereby creating a domain for the exercise of authority that cuts across traditional, territorially defined jurisdictions. Following from this reasoning, the law mandates basin committees (comitês de bacias) as organs with representation from federal, state, and municipal governments; water users; and civil society groups with "a demonstrated record of action in the basin."[45] Committees are basin-level entities empowered to arbitrate disputes, approve basin management plans, and monitor the execution of those plans. Each basin committee is to have a water agency (*agência de água*) responsible for collecting funds through user fees and executing the committee's management plan for the basin.

The administrative apparatus intended to give unity and direction to these complex institutional arrangements is the National Water Resources Council (*Conselho Nacional de Recursos Hídricos*, CNRH), conceived as a mixed-membership body with representatives from the federal government, state governments, water users, and civil society.[46] CNRH is responsible for a wide array of tasks, including the arbitration of disputes among the states, monitoring implementation of the national water resources plan, and establishing criteria for assigning water use rights and setting water user fees. In keeping with the decentralizing tendencies of postauthoritarian Brazil, the federal government's representation on the council is limited to a maximum of half the seats plus one.

The Politics of 9433

As the law was being deliberated, it was well understood that blending traditional jurisdictions and conventional state organs with more innovative concepts constituted a dramatic departure. As a result, neither the core principles nor the specific provisions of the law fell into place easily. It required six years of polemical debate and intense negotiation—spanning three presidential administrations and yielding eight different drafts of the proposed legislation—before a version of the National Water Resources Policy could pass Congress and gain presidential signature. One staffer with the Water Resources Secretariat described the debate as "a fight in the dark with scythes" among powerful water interests that included agriculture, hydroelectricity, municipalities, and water-based transportation.

One key sticking point was the idea of the river basin as the appropriate unit of analysis. To some extent the controversy was a straightforward expression of state–federal tensions, which proved to be the Gordian knot of the negotiations.[47] Opponents of the river basin concept included both those favoring more traditional territorial and juridical units and those who felt that the river basin approach did not sufficiently transcend ecologically arbitrary delineations. Proponents of states' rights perceived the danger that local waters were being "federalized" and argued that the state was the proper administrative unit. At the other end of the spectrum was the argument that river basins, although not as bad as purely juridical borders, were nonetheless ecologically and hydrogeographically arbitrary units, in that they obscure important linkages to aquifers, land-use processes within the watershed, and other contextual elements. According to then-Water Resources Secretary Garrido, the resolution of this controversy involved embracing a "holistic" approach. The river basin was accepted as a practical unit for planning and management, but both traditional jurisdictional units (states and municipalities) and ecological and geographic linkages (neighboring watersheds and aquifers) would be "taken into consideration" in the process.[48]

A second source of contention was the question of social participation. Some of the early proponents of the draft legislation conceived of participation in a broader and more aggressive fashion than was reflected in the final legislation. According to the bill's first *relator*, Fábio Feldmann, water resources management should be based primarily in the basin committees, which could be formed by "any segment of society" with the right to be represented in these entities, and not requiring authorization from higher levels within the system.[49] One rationale for this was heterogeneity; the committees would observe "common principles and means" but also "locally differentiated characteristics, which reflect the physical, biotic, demographic, economic, social, and cultural diversity of Brazil's regions and hydrogeographic basins."[50] Moreover, civil society in this context was not simply a generally interested party to be represented by government, but rather a direct stakeholder, as "indirect users of these resources."[51]

Water Resources Secretary Garrido articulated a much narrower conception of participation: "Public participation does not mean that politicians and public managers will be replaced by civil society. It is expected that stakeholders influence policy formulation by means of active participation, supporting politicians and public managers to decide according to the needs of the community."[52] Bracketed by these conceptions of authority, the debate over participation is similar to the international controversies surrounding participation in the context of transnational networks of experts and integrated water resources management (chapter 5).

Predictably, resistance from the hydro-industrial complex was also a contentious issue. At the insistence of hydro interests, an article that would have allowed sector-specific legislation to preserve the special status of the hydro sector was inserted at the last minute, only to be line-vetoed by President Cardoso.[53]

The World Bank also played a role in the politics of Federal Law 9433. The Bank had long been a key player in water-related activities in Brazil; when the Bank began to review its performance under its 1993 water sector guidelines, it chose Brazil as the first country for in-depth analysis. Historically, the Bank's emphasis had been on lending for water infrastructure projects, particularly hydropower. In the 1990s the Bank began to shift its focus on water issues in Brazil, both substantively and procedurally. In substantive terms, the new emphasis centered on two themes: drought in the primarily agricultural Northeast and water quality issues in the industrial Southeast. In both cases, the Bank's diagnosis of Brazil's water problems emphasized the neoliberal reform agenda: inefficient institutional arrangements; subsidies and other distortions that shifted water away from its highest-value uses; weak property rights arrangements, which created disincentives for investment; and political intervention in water-related decisions. Procedurally, the Bank began to move away from its traditional model of large, sector-specific infrastructural loans to the federal government. The new approach emphasized lending in support of legal, regulatory, and administrative reform to tackle these problems, with the term *reform* understood to mean movement toward greater private sector participation and rationalized approaches to pricing water.

As concern for legal, regulatory, and institutional reform began to eclipse concern for building physical infrastructure, the Bank began to direct its loans to actors that it viewed as reformers, often finding them at the state level. Beginning in 1994, the Bank invested aggressively in water reform in the drought-plagued northeastern state of Ceará, with three water resource loans totaling almost $300 million.[54] Ceará's reform process stressed charges for bulk water use, along with the expansion of dam-and-pipeline infrastructure to redistribute water supplies.[55] The Ceará experience led to a $198 million loan for the northeastern region as a whole, known as Semi-Arid PROÁGUA, and with a similar

Table 8.4
World Bank water sector lending in Brazil

Purpose	Lending for Ongoing Projects as of 2000 (million US$)		Projected Lending (million US$)	
	Federal	State	Federal	State
Water supply and sanitation	430	535	335	180
Water resources	198	337	170	50
Irrigation	281	0	200	0
Total	919	872	705	330

Source: Compiled from data in World Bank 2000, 26–27, 32 and 34.

orientation. The same pattern is seen in the Bank's lending for water supply and sanitation (WS&S) in Brazil's more industrialized regions, with loans targeting a handful of key states exceeding in value loans to the federal government (table 8.4). The Bank's lending for WS&S has stressed creating incentives for reforms, chief of which are financial self-sufficiency and, when possible, privatization of local sanitation enterprises.

Despite the shift in emphasis toward innovating states, the Bank retained an interest in reform at the federal level, for several reasons. First, federal reform would be necessary if the state-level innovations in which the Bank had invested heavily were to be scaled up to the national level. Creating a more "rational" legal and regulatory framework at the national level was seen as essential to attracting private sector investment. Also, moving toward water markets would require "strong administrative systems to enforce, measure, register, and administer water rights."[56] During the debate over Federal Law 9433, the Bank organized international seminars and "technical visits" to other countries for government officials and congressional representatives.

Institutionalization Writ Large: Sites for the Embedding of Water Norms

Two central premises of the new national legal architecture are particularly noteworthy: the assumption of inevitable water-related social conflicts and the emphasis on mixed-membership bodies charged with dispute resolution as one of their central tasks. In terms of the global protonorms discussed in chapters 4 through 7, the law contains a mixed blend. Elements of integrated water resources management are seen in the law's basin-scale emphasis, its managerial orientation, its multiple-use paradigm of management, and in its reliance on planning, classification, and information systems. Elements of watershed democracy norms include the law's participatory emphasis, its basin-level unit of analysis, and its endorsement of basin committees that include civil society participants. Elements of water marketization include the law's emphasis on water as a scarce resource with market value, its use of user fees as a managerial tool, and its intent that those fees are to be returned for use in the basin where they originated. Striking and noteworthy in its absence is any reference to Brazil's rights and responsibilities as a sovereign state and a riparian on international rivers.

In order to track the resonance of Brazilian water-related practices with transnational water norms, however, it is necessary to examine not only the formal-legal structure of national policy but also the broader set of areas within Brazil where key water-related decisions are made—the contested spaces where power is exercised, purpose pursued, and water-related decisions made. A half-dozen such spaces have emerged as salient to Brazilian water politics in the past decade:

• the federal water policy bureaucracy, which underwent a major shakeup during efforts to "reform" the Brazilian state along predominantly neoliberal lines;

• the National Water Resources Council, the mixed-membership body created by the 1997 law to oversee national water policy;

• the continuing process of institutionalizing basin committees at both the state and federal level, which was given new impulse by their legitimization in the 1997 law;

• the federal government's planning process for dams and hydroelectric development, which has been substantially affected by pressures from civic activism, growing judicial oversight, and the changing political economy of dam construction;

• the Brazilian judiciary, which has played an increasingly independent and activist role in water infrastructure controversies;

• Brazil's states, which have constitutional authority over waters that lie solely within their territorial jurisdiction; and

• Brazil's dealings with its neighbors on international rivers, dealings which, despite their historical importance, are noteworthy today mainly for their isolation from the most important national water debates, disputes, and decisions.

Shifting attention from the national legal framework to these nodes brings into focus the question of precisely where and how the institutionalization of water-related practices actually occurs, or fails to occur, within a given national context of law and policy. In addition to being the places to look for evidence of the transnational protonorms described in chapters 4 through 7, these nodes are important places to look for evidence of metanormative orientations related to territoriality, authority, and knowledge as discussed in chapter 2.

Given the heterogeneity of the norms involved and the multiplicity of these politicized spaces, it should be no surprise that Brazil cannot simply be labeled a "leader" or "laggard" regarding a set of internationally articulated water norms. Rather, a more complex pattern emerges that is dominated by two processes. First, the dynamic tension between watershed democracy and neoliberal water marketization is the main norm-inscribing force across a wide array of water-related sites and domains, outstripping the role of technical-rational and legalistic influences. Second, although water-related conflicts around that dynamic tension have by no means abated, and in some ways have intensified, they have also come to be increasingly institutionalized and normalized.

Redesigning the State: The National Water Agency

In 1995, in the midst of the debate over the proposed national water policy law, a new Secretariat of Water Resources was established within the Ministry of Environment. In the wake of the 1997 framework law, SRH found itself charged with several functions: formulating the national water resources policy, integrating water resources and environmental management, and serving as executive secretary for the National Water Resources Council.

SRH failed to become the central national organ for water policy. One problem was that it became absorbed in the day-to-day aspects of water management. For example, SRH initially assumed responsibilities for water management related to irrigation (until these duties were later shifted to a Special Secretariat for Regional Development, and then to a new Ministry of National Integration). These duties were more than just a distraction; in Brazil, control of ministries and secretariats is allocated to partners in political coalitions. Several observers described SRH as "politicized" in this regard, particularly through its ties to agricultural interests in the Northeast region. SRH was also encumbered by its position within the weak Ministry of Environment. MME's portfolio required a good deal of give-and-take with states and municipalities, given their broad constitutional authority on land issues. Moreover, its basic policy framework had been laid down in the 1980s and early 1990s, prior to the era of federal water institution building. These conditions were not conducive to the task of creating a new and overarching national policy framework.

Influential water thinkers in Brazil began to conceive a different model, outside of the normal ministerial structure. According to Bruno Pagnoccheschi, a participant in federal water planning discussions since the 1980s, the rationale for a new national water agency was the need for an organ that would be "dissociated from the political agenda to which the Ministries are subjected. In other words, a highly capacitated technical structure, exempted from political influence and able to manage water resources in a professional, coherent, and permanent form and protecting a certain exemption from the political calendar at the federal level."[57]

In Brazil as in most places, however, ideals about rational management, flexibility, and institutional coherence are rarely sufficient to produce a major bureaucratic reorganization if they lack a political rationale. The idea of a cross-cutting national water agency received a powerful boost from the broader push by President Cardoso to reform the Brazilian state along neoliberal lines. As finance minister, Cardoso had been the architect of Brazil's 1994 *plano real* package of structural adjustments; emphasis on privatization, international competitiveness, and reform of the state were hallmarks of his two presidential terms (1994–2001). During Cardoso's tenure, independent agencies or "autarchies" were established in other public service sectors such as electricity and telecommunications that were being prepared for (or already in the throes of) privatization.

The creation of a water autarchy, the National Water Agency, rode this wave of neoliberal state reform. In announcing the proposal to create ANA, Cardoso asserted that it reflected "a revolution in the structure of the Brazilian state"—not to erect a "minimal" state but rather to "transform the State so that it continues to effectively be an agency that regulates the interests of the population and induces actions toward what one imagines to be the common good." Tellingly, he also identified the need for state transformation in the context of the changing public and private economics of water development (as discussed in chapter 7): "The large bureaucratic state had its functions as direct investor, it built works that were important for the population. The lack of resources for the State to be able to act directly does not allow it to continue to act as an investor—nor does it have to."[58]

The World Bank also supported the idea of creating an independent federal water agency. The concept fit several elements of the Bank's diagnosis of Brazil's principal water-related problems, including the need for a rationalized legal, bureaucratic, and regulatory framework as a condition for increased private investment; the problem of political interference in water-related decisions; and the need for a mechanism to price water efficiently across its competing uses. According to one participant in the discussions, the idea to create ANA was first conceived in a meeting among a small group of Brazilian water experts, which took place in the World Bank's offices in Brasília.

Congress passed Federal Law 9984 creating ANA in July 2000. During the congressional debate, resistance came primarily from the left, with the opposition Workers Party (PT) and its allies in Congress arguing that there were insufficient provisions for "social control." Lamenting the lack of a regulatory culture in Brazil, the PT cautioned that if water were indeed "the gold of the third millennium," care should be exercised "not to hand over the gold to the thief."[59] A PT amendment to subordinate ANA to CNRH failed, as did an amendment that would designate the Congress as the final arbiter of river disputes.

ANA was created as an "autarchy" with "administrative and financial autonomy, linked to the Ministry of Environment," with a mandate to implement the national water resources policy and "integrate" the national system of water resources management.[60] The legislation creating ANA gave it seventeen specific functions in the water sphere, ranging from technical studies and organizing a national water information system to stimulating and supporting the creation of basin committees and implementing tariffs for waters in the federal domain.

In theory, ANA would focus on implementation while SRH continued to set the course for national water policy. In practice, the flow of funds and personnel toward ANA has made it a powerful center of policy making. For example, it has taken the lead in pushing for nonincremental change that would effectively federalize sanitation policy in Brazil. ANA has also identified for itself a central role in resolving interstate river conflicts.

ANA's central thrust has been that of integrated water resources management with a neoliberal tinge: water is a scarce resource subject to multiple conflicting potential uses, demanding a more rational and integrated administrative structure to allow its efficient allocation across uses. According to the agency's official history of its own formation, one rationale was the recognition that the basin committees written into the 1997 law as management instruments would lack the capacity for complex techno-administrative tasks.[61]

For its part, SRH has adjusted to ANA's encroachment by falling back on its central role in the National Water Resources Council, and in particular that body's "normative and deliberative character."[62] As discussed previously, the SRH had not promoted a particularly broad interpretation of the stakeholder concept written into the 1997 framework law, viewing the role of society in a relatively narrow and purely advisory way. However, with the creation of ANA, SRH found itself left with CNRH as the only significant area within which it could play out its policy mandate.

Stakeholder Forums: Between Societal Legitimization and the New Corporatism

Although they define stakeholders and their roles somewhat differently, experts' constructs of integrated water resources management (chapter 5) and activist conceptions of watershed democracy (chapter 6) both envision an extensive role for stakeholders in water governance. This section examines the entry points for societal participation emerging from the 1997 framework water policy law, specifically basin committees and the National Water Resources Council. A subsequent section will examine extrainstitutional forms of participation and political mobilization, centered primarily on social movement groups coalescing around large-dam controversies.

CNRH has become an important element of Brazilian water policy and practice. As discussed previously, the creation of ANA usurped much of the Water Resource Secretariat's power, with CNRH its main remaining instrument. CNRH both formalizes a role for organized water interests and creates an entry point for more diffuse societal interests in the water sphere. The law stipulates that federal government entities are limited to one more than half of the CNRH seats. Given the large number of federal organs active on water issues, this design feature means that CNRH provides several seats for nonstate actors. Sectors represented on the council include irrigation, industrial users, hydroelectricity generation, fishing and leisure and tourism interests, municipal water treatment and sanitation services, and waterborne transportation. Beyond these direct users, CNRH also seats representatives from basin consortia and inter-municipal associations; from technical, teaching, and research organizations; and from NGOs defending "the diffuse and collective interests of society."[63] Its working groups and technical committees are organized around legal and institutional as well as technical themes, and meet in open session.

The other main entry point for societal participation is the basin committee concept. Federal Law 9433 authorizes basin committees in rivers falling under federal dominion (as discussed later, much state-level legislation also embraces this model, which originated at the state level). CNRH guidelines for the composition of federal basin committees reproduce that body's own straddle between more narrowly corporatist and broader civil-societal representation. "Civic entities" are guaranteed at least 20 percent of the voting seats, with governmental and water user group interests capped at 40 percent each.[64] It has been difficult to get working commissions into place at the federal level, in part because of state-level sovereignty concerns. As of the end of 2002, the CNRH had authorized six basin committees for federal rivers. Of these, all but one (the reconstituted committee for the São Francisco) were in the Southeast, and only two were effectively up and running (for the Paraíba do Sul and one of its main tributaries, the Muriaé Pomba). ANA has taken a strategic approach to supporting federal basin committees, concentrating on the reconstituted São Francisco committee (originally formed in 1979).

A more complex and variable pattern exists at the state level. Table 8.5 summarizes the number and location of committees in basins falling under state jurisdiction. Most are found in the industrialized southeastern and southern regions of the country (São Paulo, Rio Grande do Sul, Minas Gerais, and Santa Catarina). This is consistent with the longer history of basin-level contentious politics and water-use conflicts sketched earlier. One SRH official estimated that 80 to 85 percent of the basins in the south and southeastern regions have basin committees in place (at varying levels of functionality). As table 8.5 indicates, committee formation has been much sparser in the Northeast, despite the World Bank's emphasis on investing in reform of water resources policy in that region. In several northeastern states the emphasis has been on creating narrower water user associations rather than the more broadly participatory

Table 8.5
Formation of committees for river basins under state jurisdiction, by state

State	Number of Basin Committees
São Paulo	21
Rio Grande do Sul	13
Minas Gerais	12
Santa Catarina	9
Ceará	3
Espírito Santo	2
Pernambuco, Goiás, Rio de Janeiro, Parana	1
Alagoas, Federal District, Maranhão, Mato Grosso, Mato Grosso do Sul, Piauí, Rio Grande do Norte, Sergipe, Tocantins	Committees under study but not installed
Acre, Amapa, Amazonas, Bahia, Paraíba, Rondônia, Roraima	No committees installed or under study

Source: Moreira 2002.

basin committees. Committees are essentially nonexistent in the Amazon region.

These basin committees are a highly variable set of institutions. Some predate the innovations in federal law of the 1990s, while others are post-1997 creations. An international team of researchers working on the initiative Projeto Marca D'Água (Watermark Project), which involves comparative analysis of twenty-one basin committees, highlights this heterogeneity. In a summary of preliminary results, Rebecca Abers and Margaret Keck point out that "basins" may range in scale from encompassing a few municipalities to well over a hundred, and incorporate a diverse set of actors who "respond to different local logics, different kinds of political economies, political cultures and constellations of power, to say nothing of geophysical and ecological conditions."[65] They report that "Basin-level water management organizations vary dramatically, not only in terms of the legal contexts governing them, but also in terms of their objectives, organizational structures, practices, and ability actually to influence water management."[66] Committees differ in terms of their success in attaining authority and representing different segments of society. Yet they share the characteristic of being fundamentally deliberative organizations; there are broadly shared principles of water management, but "the different groups involved in the creation of basin organizations interpret these principles in very different ways."[67] At a general level, the effect is similar to the sociological norm-diffusion model discussed in chapter 2, in that there is convergence on a common institutional form in disparate settings. Looking inside, however, one finds great heterogeneity at the level of giving meaning to nominally similar roles and rules.

A critical issue for committees in both state and federal rivers is whether they will be able to hold on to the *cobrança*, the fees to be charged for water use. Federal Law 9433 envisions these fees being returned to the committees to fund their basin-level operations, but the two functioning federal basin committees have yet to receive them, and many of Brazil's water cognoscenti are skeptical that the Federal Treasury will ever release the funds. (As one suggested, "Money that enters the Federal Treasury for a designated purpose never comes out.") As discussed in a later section on subnational government, many states have legislation in place authorizing user fees, but the principle that these fees should be poured back into the basins from which they originate is less established in state law than in federal law.

The National Forum of Basin Committees has been meeting annually since it was formed by representatives of basin committees from thirteen different states and the Federal District in 1999.[68] Organized as a result of concerns about the impact of the formation of ANA on the state-level basin committees, the forum has sought to defend their autonomy, strengthen their role in national policy, and press for water fees to be returned to the basin level. By its fifth meeting, in 2003, more than ninety basin committees were participating in the forum.

Dam Construction: Civic Opposition and Attempted Marketization

Dam-building projects have continued into the postmilitary era. Dam building faces a much less favorable context today than in the days of military rule, when neither economic costs nor political legitimization were central considerations. In this sense Brazil is a manifestation of the changing global context described in chapters 6 and 7, marked by the twin obstacles of increasingly broad and effective opposition and the difficult new economics of financing dam construction.

As of the late 1990s, official plans for hydroelectric expansion foresaw the possibility of building up to 494 additional large dams. This figure is often seized upon by domestic and international opponents to invoke the potentially vast environmental and social effects of Brazil's current hydroelectric model.[69] Such figures are largely meaningless, however, in light of the sector's current uncertainties. Many of the 494 sites judged to be technically feasible will never make it off the drawing board as serious projects; others will not survive the more demanding process of permitting and approval in postauthoritarian Brazil. Moreover, projects surviving the planning and permitting stage must also attract funding in an economic climate increasingly shaped by private investors and an often unfavorable calculus of profit and risk.

A somewhat clearer picture of what may happen is the government's plan of expansion through 2008. The plan lists eleven major new hydroelectric dams with an installed generating capacity of 500 MW or more, as well as two major on-site expansions at existing dams.[70] Four major rivers are the targets of these projects:

• The Tocantins, a major river draining the central plateau region and feeding into the Amazon near the Atlantic Ocean, is slated for five new dams and a planned 4,125-MW expansion of the existing Tucuruí Dam.
• The Xingú, another major Amazon feeder in the eastern Amazon region, is the site of the proposed Belo Monte Dam, a generating giant of 11,000 MW.
• The Uruguai, an international river in the south of Brazil, is slated for five new dams.
• The Paraná is slated for a 1,400-MW expansion of the Itaipu Dam's generating capacity.

If completed, this wave of dam building will exploit most of the remaining attractive sites for large-scale hydro in Brazil's industrial and agricultural southern regions.[71] As a result, the locus of political struggles over dams promises to shift to the Amazon, a process that is already under way with the struggle over the highly controversial Belo Monte Dam.

As these and other projects have unfolded in the past decade, social mobilization against dams in Brazil has deepened, broadened, and become transnational. It has also begun to work through some increasingly institutionalized channels of political dialogue and judicial review, even as it retains its character of direct action and political activism. One significant development is the emergence of a truly national-scale contentious politics around dams, with MAB now having essentially a full national reach. Domestic and international media discussions of specific dam controversies in Brazil invariably include a quote from a MAB spokesperson.

Local organizing and the mobilization of protest against specific projects remain MAB's primary tools. Its mobilization strategy involves organizing base groups of five to ten families and then linking these groups across communities throughout the area affected by a particular project. The rationale for these small-scale base groups is to build a democratic and participatory movement that can disseminate information rapidly. Among their principal tasks are facilitating discussion among members, facilitating mobilizations and other MAB activities, disseminating information, and collecting ideas.[72]

Indigenous peoples' groups have also been an important source of anti-dam opposition. An important early episode was the 1989 mobilization of Kayapo resistance to a proposal for several large dams on the Xingú River. Local opposition—including such symbolically powerful acts as that of a Kayapo protester laying a machete blade against the cheek of an official from the regional electricity company, Eletronorte—reverberated through international networks to scare off World Bank funding. The 1988 constitution requires an act of Congress for any project affecting indigenous peoples. This right has become increasingly important as the locus of struggles over dams has begun to shift to the Amazon region. It was invoked in a 2001 Supreme Court decision requiring a new impact assessment for the controversial Belo Monte Dam. In June 2002, some 250 representatives of indigenous peoples' groups and others met to develop a coordinated position of opposition to Belo Monte.[73]

In clashes between protesters, dam builders, and local authorities, tensions run high and violence is common. In August 2001, Ademir Alfeu Federicci, a leading activist against the Belo Monte Dam on the Xingu River, was murdered by two men who entered his home. Local police attributed the killing to a robbery attempt, but federal police opened a broader investigation, and many activists interpreted his death as the latest in a series of acts of violence against progressive organizers in rural Brazil.[74] In October 2001, a MAB-organized protest led to the invasion and temporary takeover of the Rio de Janeiro offices of the Belgian multinational, Tractabel (builder of the Itá and Cana Brava Dams). The confrontation coincided with protests at several other dam sites. In March 2002, MAB again coordinated protests at several dam sites around Brazil. In the southern state of Rio Grande do Sul, activists blocked the worksite of the Barra Grande Dam for several days; in the western state of Mato Grosso, they took up a vigil outside the palace of the governor; in the northeastern state of Ceará, they occupied the offices of the federal irrigation agency. In Rio de Janeiro, activists occupied the offices of a subsidiary of Electricité de France. According to IRN's representative in Brazil, clashes with police left seven protesters hospitalized from injuries related to beatings and the use of rubber bullets.[75] These events coincided with the international movement's now-annual International Day of Action against Dams and for Rivers, Water, and Life.

Rather than being an alternative to pursuing remedies through accepted institutional channels, direct action has been an integral component of a multipronged strategy. MAB has never described itself as strictly "anti-dam," framing its activities in terms of justice for dam-affected peoples, a voice for local communities, and comprehensive assessment of dam impacts and alternatives. In instances where dams are clearly going forward, as in the case of the 1,450-MW Itá Dam on the Uruguai River in Brazil's industrial Southeast, MAB has worked to get a better compensation package for locally affected peoples.[76] In August 2001, it reached an agreement with the Inter-American Development Bank on the terms of a review of compensation and resettlement activities surrounding the Cana Brava Dam.[77]

Nor can a neat distinction be drawn between the movement's national and transnational strategies. To be sure, MAB has frequently sought to negotiate directly with multinational firms and multilateral development banks on behalf of local peoples, working around rather than through local government representatives. These efforts utilize international alliances in what Margaret Keck and Kathryn Sikkink have described as a "boomerang" strategy of transnational advocacy in which actors use international pressures against a state they cannot move by working solely within the domestic sphere.[78] The movement also remains squarely involved in national politics. Late in 2001, MAB joined with the labor movement and congressional actors to promote an alternative plan in response to Brazil's electricity crisis.[79] At the same time that it was coordinating government office seizures and dam-site occupations in March 2002, MAB was sitting down with federal officials to work out a formal list of dam-related social impacts and negotiating state-level agreements on dam licensing procedures in Bahia and Minas Gerais.[80] Early in 2003, in the wake of the election of a left-of-center government, the new head of Eletrobrás invited MAB to work with the company in its objective "to take greater care with environmental and social issues."[81]

MAB's involvement with the World Commission on Dams also reflects its use of both institutional engagement and popular mobilization. A

MAB representative participated in the 1997 Gland meeting among activists, international dam-industry officials, and the World Bank, in which the activist push for an independent review commission gave birth to the WCD (see chapter 6). MAB later proposed the formation of an analogous Brazilian Commission on Dams,[82] yet when the WCD held a regional hearing in São Paulo, MAB disrupted the meeting by packing it with a group of several hundred protesters.

A more institutionally oriented opposition to dam construction and large water infrastructure projects has also emerged in Brazil. IRN's Latin America campaign director, Glenn Switkes, a longtime resident of Brazil, has used a combination of technical rebuttals, human rights arguments, and network building similar to the pattern seen in IRN's global activities (chapter 6). For example, when Water Resources Secretary Garrido issued a criticism of the WCD report, stressing its "exaggerations" on resettlement issues, Switkes followed up with a point-by-point rebuttal in the influential business newspaper *Gazeta Mercantil*.[83] As discussed later, a cross-border coalition of NGOs in Brazil and several neighboring states emerged in 1994 to block international funding for the Paraguai-Paraná *hidrovia*, a major water transportation corridor.

Growing popular resistance has come at a time when Brazil's difficult fiscal situation and the reluctance of multilateral development banks to fund large and controversial water infrastructure has made the traditional model for financing dams increasingly problematic. Brazil's electricity crisis during the winter of 2001 only added to these difficulties. Privatization of much of Brazil's electricity supply system, which involved separating generation, transmission, and distribution into distinct entities, undercut long-term planning and demand management. Price distortions built into the privatization scheme also created disincentives to invest in augmented electricity supply.[84] Combined with an unusually severe drought, the result in an electricity system that is more than 90 percent dependent on hydro was catastrophic. A dramatic electricity shortfall produced rationing, brownouts, and a major controversy for the Cardoso government. Although hydro interests attempted to exploit the crisis as a rationale for more hydro, the larger effect was to raise doubts about the dominant hydro model.

nportant strategic adaptation by the state to this new climate of uncertainty has been to promote dam privatization. Dam building in Brazil has always had substantial participation from international firms, both in dam construction and as users of the resulting electricity. The prime incentive for dam building in the Amazon, for example, has been to support mineral extraction and processing activities. The new model, however, foresees a direct private ownership stake, with the state marketing attractive hydro sites to international investors. One incentive for this shift comes from the mounting difficulties of attracting support from the multilateral development banks, a consequence of the international activist pressures on those institutions and the protests surrounding controversial projects. The Inter-American Development Bank withdrew funding for a proposed water transportation corridor, the Paraguai-Paraná *hidrovia*, in 1997. In a World Bank-sponsored workshop on the Bank's water sector performance in Brazil, several "stakeholders" criticized the Bank for its new wariness in funding controversial water projects.[85]

By the end of 2001, the Secretariat for Planning and Strategic Investments within the Ministry of Planning, Budget and Management was advertising "strategic investment opportunities" in the form of concessions for the construction and operation of thirty-four hydroelectric plants totaling 23 GW of installed capacity. These include four proposed dams of 500 MW or more on the Tocantins, Uruguai, Pelotas, and Canoas Rivers, plus the massive 11,000-MW Belo Monte Dam proposal on the Xingú (table 8.6). In June 2001 Cardoso issued a presidential decree to expedite dam-licensing procedures as part of a package of responses to the electricity crisis. Dam privatization has also been an element in restructuring the electricity sector, but private capital has shown much greater enthusiasm for electricity distribution than for generation.[86]

Judicial Review: Independence, Activism, and Fragmentation of the State
As Hochstetler points out, the Brazilian legal system in the wake of democratic transition and constitutional reform provides numerous legal tools for both state and nonstate actors disputing the environmental or socioeconomic effects of water projects.[87] These include a broad

Table 8.6
Planned hydroelectric facilities in Brazil

Dam	State	Planned capacity (megawatts)	River
Aimores	Minas Gerais	396	Doce
Araçá	Piauí	120	Parnaíba
Barra Grande	Santa Catarina/ Rio Grande do Sul	690	Pelotas
Belo Monte	Pará	11,000	Xingu
Bocaina	Goiás/Minas Gerais	150	Paranaíba
Campos Novos	Santa Catarina	880	Canoas
Capim Branco I	Minas Gerais	240	Araguari
Capim Branco II	Minas Gerais	210	Araguari
Cebolão	Paraná	156	Tibagi
Couto de Magalhães	Mato Grosso/Goiás	150	Araguaia
Dona Francisca	Rio Grande do Sul	125	Jacuí
Estreito	Mato Grosso/ Tocantins	1,200	Tocantins
Funil Grande	Minas Gerais	180	Grande
Funil Ribeira	São Paulo	150	Ribeira do Iguape
Garabi	Argentina/Brazil	1,500	Uruguay
Guaporé	Mato Grosso	120	Guaporé
Irapé	Minas Gerais	360	Jequitinhonha
Itapebi	Bahia	450	Jequitinhonha
Itiquira (two facilities)	Mato Grosso	156	Itiquira
Jataizinho	Paraná	156	Tibagi
Mauá	Paraná	388	Tibagi
Peixe Angical	Tocantins	450	Tocantins
Pilar	Minas Gerais	150	Piranga
Pirajú	São Paulo	70	Paranapanema
Ponte de Pedra	Mato Grosso	176	Correntes
Sacos	Bahia	114	Formoso
Salto Pilão	Santa Catarina	181	Itajaí-Açu
São Jerônimo	Paraná	331	Tibagi
Serra do Facão	Goiás	220	São Marcos
Serra Quebrada	Tocantins/Maranhão	1,328	Tocantins
Telêmaco Borba	Paraná	112	Tibagi

Table 8.6
(continued)

Dam	State	Planned capacity (megawatts)	River
Tijuco Alto	Paraná/São Paulo	144	Ribeira do Iguape
Tupiratins	Tocantins	1,000	Tocantins

Source: Compiled from data of the Secretariat for Planning and Strategic Investments within the Ministry of Planning, Budget and Management. Downloaded from web site "Infra-Estrutura Brasil," http://www.infraestruturabrasil.gov.br/ (accessed December 24, 2001).

interpretation of the concept of legal standing, in which plaintiffs in environmental cases can invoke "diffuse" environmental interests rather than show a direct impact on themselves; broad requirements for environmental impact statements; independent attorneys general who have at times been aggressive defenders of environmental laws and procedures; and a 1998 environmental crimes law with significant penalties. The constitutional protections of indigenous peoples, discussed previously, have been another important entry point.

The controversy over the Paraguai-Paraná *hidrovia* produced a set of decisions with both legal and political importance. Originally conceived in the late 1970s, the *hidrovia* would reshape 3,400 km of the Paraná and Paraguay Rivers, linking the vast Pantanal wetlands in southwestern Brazil to the Atlantic Ocean. In part because environmental and social considerations were largely shut out of the interstate planning process, a regional NGO coalition of environmentalists, human rights groups, indigenous organizations, and labor groups opposing the project emerged in 1994; known as Rios Vivos (Living Rivers), it would eventually grow to include more than 300 organizations.[88] The group made little headway with the intergovernmental committee of ministers pushing the project forward, but was successful in pressing the Inter-American Development Bank to withdraw funding for the project in 1997.

As Hochstetler points out, this classic use of a "boomerang" strategy then turned to domestic politics.[89] In October 1999 federal judges ruled that some information critical of the project, in particular its impact on eleven local indigenous peoples' communities, had been omitted from the environmental impact assessment.[90] In 2000–2001 the courts blocked an effort to resurrect the *hidrovia* in piecemeal fashion, arguing that a comprehensive environmental impact statement must be done before further construction could be allowed. (The government had argued that the plan for the larger *hidrovia* no longer existed and that the components were separate projects.) In January 2001, a federal judge rejected the government's appeal, upholding a lower court ruling based on a suit against the project filed by a federal attorney general.

A second important series of cases involves another water transportation corridor, the proposed 2200-km Tocantins-Araguaia *hidrovia*. In October 1999, a federal judge suspended licensing for the *hidrovia*. Indigenous groups obtained the court order after evidence surfaced that the environmental impact assessment had covered up critical findings.[91] In March 2001, a federal judge suspended a state-level environmental license for the Lajeado Canal on the Tocantins River, concluding that the project was part of the Tocantins-Araguaia *hidrovia* and not an improvement to a nearby dam, as state officials had characterized it. A public procurator's office linked to the federal Ministry of Justice brought legal action, and in doing so effectively blocked another federal agency, the Ministry of Transportation.[92] Also in March 2001, a federal judge ordered the closing of two ports on the Araguaia, ruling that they functioned essentially as a *hidrovia* without the proper comprehensive impact assessment having been performed by the states of Mato Grosso and Mato Grosso do Sul.[93]

The Tocantins-Araguaia *hidrovia* controversy has also produced a battle over public hearings. A federal judge, accepting the arguments of local activist groups, suspended public hearings on the grounds that they were being conducted only in state capitals, where support for the project was strongest and where technical experts for the project were readily available. Another federal judge later overturned this ruling and reinstituted the hearings.[94]

In these and other cases, tensions abound among different government organs at both the state and federal levels. In both *hidrovia* cases, local activists and federal prosecutors have been aligned against state governments and the federal transportation ministry. Similarly, in February 2002, federal attorneys filed charges of fraud in the state-level licensing process for the Lajeado Dam on the Tocantins. A state judge had authorized filling the dam reservoir in response to Brazil's electricity crisis, despite the fact that the federal environmental agency had cited irregularities with environmental mitigation.[95]

The roles have been reversed also, with state judicial blockage of federal initiatives. In February 2001, shortly after federal environmental officials had given the go-ahead to filling the reservoir of a dam on the Paraná River, a state judge postponed the closing of the gates on the grounds that the chosen timing would interfere with fish reproduction. The dam is owned by the São Paulo state electricity company, the privatization of which has been affected by the debt and socioenvironmental controversies attached to its dams.[96]

There are some common denominators in the individual cases that mark the growing role of the courts. First, although the independence of federal attorneys general has been a critical resource for legal activism, they have taken action only in cases where a strong base of local organizing already exists. Second, federal prosecutors have been enlisted by a combination of technical and political arguments. Ecological and socioeconomic deconstruction of official project documents, particularly impact statements, has been most effective when combined with procedural grievances about voice and representation in decision making, particularly for distinct communities such as indigenous peoples.

There are also common threads in the resulting judicial rulings. One is that judicial decisions are being made largely on procedural and jurisdictional grounds—procedural in the sense of compliance with impact assessment rules, jurisdictional in the sense of sorting out whether state or federal rules apply (as suggested previously, the distinction is often ambiguous in Brazilian environmental law). A second common thread in these decisions is the willingness of the courts to treat waterways as integral units. Decisions have emphasized the need for a comprehensive assessment of the collective effects of disparate projects along the waterway. As one federal judge stated in a ruling on the Paraguai-Paraná *hidrovia*,

Can changing the name of something permit what had been prohibited? Would a book no longer be a book if we called it a pen? .... The inexistence of a project called the "hidrovia," in the view of the Transportation Ministry ... would permit construction of a port without analyzing the impact along the extension of the river, in the upper Paraguay basin, on the floodplain of the Pantanal. Everything would be carried out piecework; today a port, tomorrow another, today construction of a heavy engineering work, tomorrow another; and finally, we would have all the works for implanting the hidrovia, and the name "hidrovia" could once again be applied.[97]

The State as the States: Local Policy Innovation

Policy frameworks at the level of individual Brazilian states constitute another important set of nodes where water-related norms may become embedded. The constitutional reform of 1988 codifies the role of the states in managing waters that fall entirely within their domain (as opposed to federal dominance over interstate and international rivers). A comprehensive review of state-level water policy in Brazil's twenty-six states and the federal district of Brasília is beyond the scope of this chapter. Nevertheless, a few relevant generalizations can be made.

One pattern is that state-level institution building has paralleled the federal framework law but not the federal bureaucratic organization. All but two Brazilian states now have framework water laws in place; all but five of these were written after passage of Federal Law 9433 in 1997. A World Bank review of these laws suggested that "In all cases, this legislation incorporates the following principles: water resources management at the river basin level; state water resources management plans to guide policy and investment decision making; individual water use rights; and water pricing for both quantity and quality aspects."[98] By and large, however, the states have not produced the ANA-style "new state" model of bureaucratic organization seen at the federal level. Fifteen states and the Federal District have located their water management bureaucracies within a secretariat for environment, planning, or science and technology; five within a secretariat for water users; and only two within an independent water resources secretariat.[99]

Second, a gap is evident between the articulation of framework principles and their implementation, as illustrated in a review of state practices by SRH in December 2002.[100] Administratively, about half of the twenty-three states with water legislation in place at that time had implemented systems of water permitting and penalties. Only a handful had more systematic planning processes in place, however, and only Ceará had moved to implement bulk water fees. As suggested previously, the picture is also uneven with regard to the installation of basin committees.

Third, and despite the spotty implementation picture just presented, a few states have been important laboratories for changes in water policy that would emerge later at the federal level. São Paulo's state-level reforms in the late 1980s and early 1990s provided the basic blueprint for Federal Law 9433. Ceará's World Bank-funded innovations became the model for the federal government's regional water planning in the Northeast. More recently, the Bank has begun to invest in Bahia as it did previously in Ceará. With specific regard to the transnational protonorms discussed in chapters 4 through 7, those related to watershed democracy and marketization are most salient at the state level. Few states have developed an extensive technical expertise within their water agencies; most depend on the federal government, outside consultants, or technical experts borrowed from other organs. And the states are constrained with regard to activity on international rivers by the constitutional federalization of those waterways.

The primary entry points for watershed democracy protonorms at the state level are the basin committees, as discussed previously. With regard to marketization, a comparison of state laws indicates that the primary rationales offered for water fees are to promote environmental protection and enhance water availability. A World Bank review of thirteen state-level framework water laws passed in the 1990s found that all thirteen included protecting environmental quality and promoting water availability as the basis for charging fees (table 8.7). All thirteen also included provisions for charging fees according to type of use. Common but less universal justifications for water fees were the allocation of revenues to water management funds and/or the use of those revenues outside the watershed in which they were collected. In other words, few states have explicitly embraced one of the central marketization concepts of the 1997 federal water policy law: that of plowing water fees back into the basin in which they are collected. Also noteworthy in table 8.7 is the fact that being able to differentiate fees by type of use is one of the most com-

Table 8.7
Basis for water charges in state legislation

Basis for Charging Fees for Bulk Water Use	Number of State Laws Identifying that Basis for Charging Fees ($n = 13$)
Environmental quality	13
Water availability and features	13
Type of use	13
Application of revenue outside watershed	8
Revenue allocated to water management fund	7
Users' socioeconomic conditions	3
Change spatial occupation	2
Regional economic objectives	2
Achieve better environmental standard	2

Source: Compiled from data in Asad et al. 1999, 24.

monly shared rationales in state water law for charging water fees. This too serves as a brake on a purely marketized approach. Differential fees across sectors distort the market-based price signals meant to cause water to gravitate toward its highest-value uses.

Subnational jurisdictions have also been central to a marketization conflict related to sanitation. During the Cardoso administration legislation was proposed that would inject the national government much more strongly into sanitation policy, with an emphasis on privatization and the removal of cross-subsidies. Strong opposition under the banner of the National Front for Environmental Sanitation that included "unions, service providers, church groups, representatives, mayors and a large part of organized civil society" stalled the bill.[101]

International Water Law: The Missing Link

One notable feature of Brazilian hydrogeography is the transnational extent of the country's major basins. Drainage areas extend across national borders for six of the thirteen hydrographic regions listed in table 8.1, including two of the three largest. About one-third of the Amazon drainage basin and about half of the total drainage area of the greater Prata system (which includes the Paraná, Paraguai, and Uruguai Basins) lie outside Brazilian territory.

Brazil has been extraordinarily active diplomatically with regard to its shared rivers and lakes. Table 8.8 identifies fifteen distinct international agreements since 1933. The table includes not only ratified international treaties but also less formal instruments such as publicized exchange of notes and joint memoranda of understanding.

In many ways, the international legal framework constituted by these agreements is a legacy of the era of pushing rivers around discussed in chapter 3. This can be seen in both the timing and the content of the agreements. Almost all of them either focus explicitly on hydropower development in shared basins or were negotiated in the context of an interest in developing shared hydro resources. A significant majority (eleven of fifteen) deal with basins in Brazil's most industrially developed regions, the South and Southeast, and thus with its southern coriparians, Paraguay, Uruguay, and Argentina. Regarding timing, the most intense period of treaty formation is 1969–1984, a sixteen-year period running from the zenith to the apogee of the military dictatorship. Six of the seven accords negotiated during this period focus on hydropower. In contrast, only four minor agreements have been concluded in the post-military period since 1985. Since the 1992 Earth Summit, the only formal diplomatic product is a 1997 adjustment to an earlier agreement on the Quaraí, a small river shared with Uruguay.

A search for evidence that these agreements have played a significant role in the dynamic evolution of Brazilian water, law, policy, or practice over the past few decades turns up little or none. Returning to the analysis in chapter 4 of the normative evolution of international river agreements over the past two decades, table 8.9 presents the coded content of the six post-1980 Brazilian agreements that were included in that global analysis. Several conclusions can be drawn from these data. First, the core principles emerging from three decades of international legal development are sparsely represented in these agreements. Second, there is no evidence of convergence on these principles over time; the agreement that most closely parallels the UN framework is the oldest of the group, a 1980 accord on the Uruguai River. Third, the specific principles most reflective of a "watershed sensibility" are quite weakly represented. Avoidance of significant harm is invoked only in the 1980 Uruguai accord; environmental protection is invoked in general terms in a majority of

Table 8.8
Brazilian international river agreements

Agreement	Year	Parties
Convention regarding the determination of the legal status of the frontier between Brazil and Uruguay	1933	Brazil Uruguay
Treaty between the Federative Republic of Brazil and the Republic of Paraguay concerning the hydroelectric utilization of the water resources of the Paraná River owned in condominium by the two countries, from and including the Salto Grande de Sete Quedas or Salto del Guaira, to the mouth of the Iguaçu River	1956	Brazil Paraguay
Agreement concerning cooperation between Brazil and Paraguay in a study on the utilization of the water power of the Acaray and Monday Rivers	1956	Brazil Paraguay
Exchange of notes constituting an agreement between Brazil and Uruguay establishing a joint commission for the development of the Mirim Lagoon	1963	Brazil Uruguay
Prata Basin Treaty	1969	Argentina Bolivia Brazil Paraguay Uruguay
Treaty between the Federative Republic of Brazil and the Republic of Paraguay concerning the hydroelectric utilization of the water resources of the Paraná River owned in condominium by the two countries, from and including the alto Grande de Sete Quedas or Salto del Guaira, to the mouth of the Iguaçu River	1973	Brazil Paraguay
Treaty on cooperation for the utilization of the natural resources and the development of the Mirim Lagoon basin (Treaty of the Mirim Lagoon basin) and Protocol (Jaguarão River Protocol)	1977	Brazil Uruguay
Treaty for Amazonian cooperation	1978	Bolivia Brazil Colombia Ecuador Guyana Peru Surinam Venezuela
Agreement on Paraná River projects	1979	Argentina Brazil Paraguay

Table 8.8
(continued)

Agreement	Year	Parties
Treaty between the government of the Argentine republic and the government of the Federative Republic of Brazil for the development of the water resources contained in the border reaches of the Uruguay River and its effluent, the Pepiri-Guaçu River	1980	Argentina Brazil
Agreement concerning the Cachuela Esperanza hydroelectric plant, supplementary to the agreement on economic and technical cooperation between the government of the Federative Republic of Brazil and the government of the Republic of Bolivia	1984	Bolivia Brazil
Exchange of notes constituting an agreement for the construction of a hydroelectric plant in Cachuela Esperanza, supplementary to the agreement on economic and technical cooperation	1988	Bolivia Brazil
Agreement between the government of the Federative Republic of Brazil and the government of the Republic of Venezuela on the establishment of a non-aedificandi zone at the boundary between the two countries	1988	Brazil Venezuela
Agreement of cooperation between the government of the Eastern Republic of Uruguay and the Federative Republic of Brazil for the use of natural resources and the development of the basin of the Quaraí (Cuareim) River	1991	Brazil Uruguay
Complementary settlement to the agreement of cooperation between the government of the Eastern Republic of Uruguay and the government of the Federative Republic of Brazil for the use of natural resources and the development of the Quaraí (Cuareim) River Basin	1997	Brazil Uruguay

Source: Compiled by author.

Table 8.9
Basic content of recent Brazilian international river agreements

UN Watercourses Convention principle	Uruguai River (1980)	Cachuela Esperanza (1984)	Cachuela Esperanza (1988)	Brazil-Venezuela border (1988)	Quaraí River (1991)	Quaraí River (1997)
Participation by all watercourse states	x	x	x		x	x
Equitable-use principle	x				x	x
Obligation to avoid significant harm	x					
Sovereign equality as basis for cooperation						
Obligation to exchange information	x				x	x
Obligation for consultation				x	x	x
Obligation for prior notification						x
Environmental protection as an agreement goal	x			x	x	x
Obligation to resolve disputes peacefully	x					

the agreements, but given concrete form in only one basin (the 1991 agreement on the Quaraí River and its 1997 update).

In other words, most of Brazil's international legal commitments for shared rivers reflect the dominant domestic paradigm of the era in which they were signed: rivers as water resources to be developed, particularly for hydroelectric generation. As hydropower has become more politically controversial, both domestically and internationally, the number of such accords has fallen noticeably. Nevertheless, it cannot be said that a new era has arrived in which Brazil is actively, cooperatively managing its shared river basins, even in the limited intersovereign terms envisioned by the UN Watercourses Convention.

The case of the Paraguai-Paraná *hidrovia*, discussed previously, illustrates the limits of normative change through intersovereign channels. Although the Inter-American Development Bank withdrew funding for the project in 1997, and the Brazilian courts have greatly complicated the prospects for building the project, little else about it has changed. The institutional framework for the project remains the same interstate committee of transportation ministers and foreign ministers; a comprehensive assessment of alternatives still has not been done; no mechanism is in place for public participation or consultation; and efforts to revive the project involve "complementary" impact studies that build upon the widely criticized environmental impact assessments preceding the bank's withdrawal.[102]

This is not to suggest that international law and interstate diplomacy have played no role in shaping Brazilian watershed management. Brazil's powerful and substantially autonomous Ministry of Foreign Affairs, known as Itamaraty, can exert a strong influence on policy processes that threaten to spill over into these shared basins. Basin committees for rivers that form or cross the nation's borders must include a representative of this ministry. During a conversation with one federal water policy official, I was cautioned not to refer to the waters in Brazil's shared basins by using the term *international* or, worse, *internationalized*. The accepted concept for these rivers in Brazilian diplomatic circles is rather that they are "frontier" or "compartmentalized" waters. This can be more than a semantic difference. Itamaraty guards and exercises its authority to lead Brazilian delegations to international conferences dealing with water issues or environmental matters.

Conclusion: Institutionalizing Contention

Much about water in Brazil remains in active, contentious, even violent dispute. Protests surround and engulf dam projects and municipal water privatization schemes. Adversarial court proceedings, direct-action protests, and political intervention are understood by all participants to be important mechanisms of water allocation and control. Bureaucratic struggles and turf battles continue to divide the state. Even the constitutional status of water and water resources management remains contested.[103]

Despite these enduring conflicts—and in no small measure because of them—the governance of water, watersheds, rivers, and freshwater ecosystems in Brazil has in important ways come to be increasingly institutionalized, in the sense of being normalized, routinized, and even ritualized around shared understandings about roles and rules. Although some of this institutionalization has derived from the development of a legal and policy framework at the federal level, much of it has evolved through contentious politics across a wide range of domains, from the courtroom to the dam site to the Internet.

The development, reworking, and embedding of some of the transnational protonorms sketched in chapters 4 through 7 have been an important part of that story of institutionalization. As this chapter has suggested, transnational linkages ranging from those of activist coalitions to networks of experts to relations with the World Bank have been recurring parts of the story. These linkages have been important sources of ideas, information, funding, legitimacy, and solidarity.

It would be mistaken, however, to interpret this process as one in which Brazil is increasingly "buying into" or "implementing" the precepts of some informal, uncodified global regime for the governance of water. Debates on critical themes—valuing water, incorporating stakeholders, cutting across ill-fitting formal jurisdictions, recognizing nonconsumptive uses—were well under way in Brazil by the time they became central elements in discourses on water management at the international level. Rather than a process of policy diffusion, the Brazilian case entails a more complex story in which transnational norms have been a resource for actors struggling to shape domestic practices.

This can be seen in the recurring invocation of accepted "international practice," tied to a mythic, consensual international community, as a bid for domestic legitimacy. For example, Secretary of Water Resources Garrido, in a statement to the World Commission on Dams, suggested that

The National Water Resources Policy is a new institutional landmark in Brazil, since *it incorporates internationally accepted water management principles, norms and standards which are already practices in many other countries.* The decentralized and democratic management of water, involving various uses and different forms of sharing the resource, will bring about a true revolution not only in water resources management, but also in environmental management as a whole.[104]

On another occasion, Garrido said of the 1997 framework law that "Its text proclaims, very clearly, the basic principles practiced today in almost all countries which have advanced in water resources management."[105] Similarly, Deputy Fábio Feldmann invoked international experience to legitimize participatory approaches to water management: "Participatory, integrated management, involving all spheres of public power and the communities, principally the users of water, is consistent with successful international experience, which has come to be analyzed in our country for more than fifteen years."[106] World Bank officials offer their prescriptions as "basic, internationally accepted principles of integrated water management."[107] Activists fighting privatization schemes or dam projects use similar legitimization strategies.

The basic legal framework, as reflected in the 1997 law codifying the National Water Resource Policy, contains a mixed blend of the transnational protonorms discussed in chapters 4 through 7. Within the resulting policy framework, elements of integrated water resources management (basin-scale emphasis, managerialism, multiple-use framework, planning methodologies) coexist with elements of watershed democracy (participatory emphasis, basin-level institutions, incorporation of basin committees) and marketization (scarce-resource framework, user fees). The IWRM emphasis can be linked to a well-networked expert community (although, again, the advanced state of the debate in Brazil relative to international circles suggests a two-way rather than a one-way flow of influence). The marketization link is also direct, in the form of the World Bank's strong presence in Brazilian national policy debates. In contrast, elements of watershed democracy can be traced, not to direct links among transnational water activists—that would come later—but rather to predominantly domestic developments. These include the broad domestic mobilization of civil society around themes of environment, human rights, indigenous rights, and participatory democracy in the post-authoritarian Brazil of the 1990s, and the specific efforts of basin-level stakeholders to make their voices heard.

Moving from the legal framework to the water core of the Brazilian federal state, the institutionalization of water norms has most strongly reflected the IWRM framework. Federal bureaucratic organs staffed largely by technical experts plan, administer, and implement— embracing and turning into practice—sometimes slowly, core IWRM values of techno-managerial planning. However, as Abers and Keck have pointed out in the context of their study of basin organizations, "The various differently situated actors who adopt new ideas often understand them to mean quite different things."[108] Their discussion of the meaning of "decentralization" highlights the gap between ideas and institutionalization:

In the case of water management reform, decentralization's primary connotation for some was a reduction in the state's role, for others the increase in local state control, and for others the democratization of decision-making. For some it meant the possibility of reaching efficient solutions through negotiations among key stakeholders, and for others the possibility of reaching socially just solutions, by empowering grassroots interests hitherto neglected.[109]

A similar process is at work with regard to IWRM. As suggested in chapter 5, IWRM thought and practice lionize the themes of participation and valuation, but provide only abstract guidance on appropriate ways to realize those values. Even within the narrower confines of the federal state, this ambiguity is heightened by the diverse array of bureaucratic entities—including but not limited to ANA, SRH, and CNRH—with water-related mandates. ANA, a new organ designed to cut across bureaucratic divisions—and in the eyes of skeptics, to prepare important parts of the water sector for privatization—has used IWRM legitimization to support a pro-marketization agenda. SRH has used the same framework to reposition itself and in the process support broader participatory practice through CNRH.

The indeterminacy of the techno-rational approach on questions of valuation and participation becomes even more striking when one moves from the federal state to the wider array of water domains within Brazil, including the courts, the states, municipalities, activist campaigns, stakeholder forums, basin committees, and the hydro-industrial complex. Across these disparate spaces, social conflict has outstripped knowledge-based consensus, struggles over who has authority have decentered and fragmented the state's agency, and the tensions between water neoliberalism and watershed democracy have come to the fore. Yet even as these conflicts spill outside of the neat juridical, spatial, and cognitive confines envisioned by many architects of cooperation, they have nevertheless produced a dynamic in which elements of increasingly norm-governed, patterned behavior are readily observable.

9

South Africa: "With Water We Will Wash Away the Past"

We want the water of this country to flow out into a network—reaching every individual—saying: here is this water, for you. Take it; cherish it as affirming your human dignity; nourish your humanity. With water we will wash away the past, we will from now on ever be bounded by the blessing of water.
—South African poet Antjie Krog in *White Paper on a National Water Policy for South Africa*

If you dare to do cost recovery in the townships, it will spark a fire. It will be something you will regret forever.... If it's necessary, we'll use violence. If they come into the township to cut our water supplies or take our goods, we'll vandalize their cars and beat up their workers.... If they continue on this path, we will start with meetings and rallies and rolling mass action. Things can turn ugly. We will meet violence with violence.
—Anti-Privatization Forum activist Henry Nkuna in *The Water Barons*

South Africa as a Test Case of the Influence of Global Water Norms

Compared with the Brazilian case, South Africa presents a complex pattern of similarities and differences. In narrowly hydrogeographic terms, the two countries could not be more different. Whereas Brazil's vast resources in the Amazon and the southern basins make it the world's most water-abundant country, South Africa is a country of relative water scarcity: its estimated annual per capita water availability of 1,100 m^3 ranks 120th out of 149 countries for which data are available.[1] Exploiting perceived abundance for economic development has been the dominant historical premise of Brazilian policy toward water and rivers. The focus in South Africa has always been on water scarcity.

Hydrogeography, however, is not destiny, and there are some interesting water-related parallels between the two countries. From the rise of modern water codes in the early twentieth century until well into the 1990s, water law in each country was crafted with specific uses in mind (hydroelectricity in Brazil, irrigated agriculture in South Africa). National policy centered on a powerful national government agency that increasingly usurped local authority [the Ministry of Mines and Energy in Brazil, the Department of Water Affairs (DWA, later renamed the Department of Water Affairs and Forestry, DWAF) in South Africa]. Water has also been an important instrument of social control in both countries, whether the drought-based "political economy of hunger" in Brazil's Northeast or the hydrology of apartheid in South Africa. Finally, both countries have undergone recent episodes of dramatic, democratizing political change that created windows of opportunity for nonincremental reform in water-related law, policy, and practice.

Some of these parallels are related to broad historical and structural similarities between the two countries. In a comparative study of tax politics in the two countries, Evan Lieberman concludes that there are

enormous social, political, and economic similarities between the two countries. In terms of most development indicators, the two countries are virtually identical, with similar levels of per capita income and similar levels of industrial development. In both countries, the size of the state is relatively large when compared with other upper middle-income countries, and total central state expenditures as share of GDP is about the same. These two societies are also characterized by the most unequal distributions of income in the world ... and in both, such economic inequalities are highly correlated with racial differences. Moreover, these two countries share legacies of colonialism, European immigration, and slavery.[2]

Also, both countries underwent modernizing political-economic changes earlier in the twentieth century, driven by substantially exclusionary political systems (elite democracy punctuated by frequent military intervention in Brazil, white minority rule via the apartheid system in South Africa). In both cases, the result was rapid industrialization, semiperipheral status in the world economy, and enormous domestic inequality.

To be sure, one should not overdraw the parallels. South Africa experienced much greater political continuity from World War II through the late 1980s—the apartheid era—than did Brazil. Race-based forms of social control were far more explicit and codified. South Africa's democratic transition was much more rapid and turbulent than Brazil's slow and gradual liberalization. South Africa's fledgling democracy inherited from the struggle a well-formed political organization (the African National Congress, ANC) and a generation of high-stature leaders with credentials forged in the struggle, whereas decades of military rule and gradual liberalization in Brazil left it with a weak endowment of legitimized political resources. South Africa's first freely elected president in the new era was the remarkable Nelson Mandela; Brazil's was Fernando Collor de Mello, a little-known *caudillo* from a small and politically backward state who was soon drummed from the presidency on corruption charges.

Within the pattern of similarity and difference across the two cases, one shared feature is particularly important for the purpose at hand: South Africa, like Brazil, provides a useful test of the influence of the global protonorms discussed in previous chapters. Like Brazil, South Africa underwent a combination of political change and constitutional reform that largely invalidated the existing water policy framework. Also like Brazil, it did so at a time when all four sets of protonorms were seemingly well positioned to weave themselves into the new fabric of domestic water law, policy, and practice.

South Africa has been extremely active in international river diplomacy (chapter 4), signing several bilateral and multilateral accords, endorsing early efforts to articulate principles of international water law such as the 1966 Helsinki Rules and, more recently, joining the regional water protocol of the Southern African Development Community (SADC). As discussed later, the apartheid regime even engaged in formal water diplomacy with the allegedly autonomous black "homelands" within South Africa, invoking norms and practices of international law to bolster the fiction of the homelands' sovereign independence. At least in theory, there were ample opportunities for the norms embedded in international river diplomacy to "swim upstream" and influence domestic practices.

Networks of South African water experts are also well connected to their international counterparts (chapter 5). Growing world revulsion with apartheid plunged many facets of South African life into international isolation, but networks related to water issues felt relatively little impact. The South African National Committee on Large Dams (SANCOLD) remained an active participant in the activities of the

International Committee on Large Dams throughout the apartheid era. South Africa was chosen to host the eighteenth ICOLD congress, held in Durban in 1994. The end of apartheid saw a strong surge in transnational expert networking on water-related topics. The country's Water Research Commission, commenting on the "upsurge in international collaboration" in the wake of the 1994 political transition, identified more than twenty specific examples of international collaboration on water research in the period 1994–1996, ranging from university ties to South Africans taking leadership positions in international organizations.[3] Recently, South African water policy elites have been prominently featured participants at international networking activities such as the World Water Forums.

South Africa has also seen strong social activism around water-related issues (chapter 6). The country has a long tradition of activism and popular mobilization. Many local activist groups are well networked with transnational environmental, water, and human rights groups. For example, there are strong ties to International Rivers Network forged around the long-standing controversy of the Lesotho Highlands project, a vast damming and interbasin transfer scheme jointly mounted by the governments of Lesotho and South Africa. The country's strong and independent labor movement has spoken out forcefully on water issues, particularly with regard to the privatization of municipal water services. As indicated earlier, South Africa's former water minister, Kader Asmal, chaired the World Commission on Dams, with the WCD secretariat and staff conducting its operations out of Cape Town.

Finally, South Africa is also a strong candidate for the influence of water marketization norms (chapter 7), given its enthusiastic embrace of neoliberal structural adjustment policies. Discussions of full-cost pricing and other water marketization concepts were on the table from the start of the water law reform process of the 1990s. Beyond the influence of neoliberalism, such ideas were given currency by the widespread recognition that rich white farmers benefited enormously from the essentially free water steered their way by the apartheid-era systems of land tenure and water rights. Further marketization impetus came in the form of the government's economic adjustment policy framework of Growth, Employment and Redistribution (GEAR), which emphasizes deficit reduction, fiscal discipline, currency deregulation, tight credit, and international investment stimulus. Since GEAR's adoption in 1996, progressive critics have lambasted the ANC government for transforming itself into a poster child for the structural adjustment policies of the Washington Consensus. GEAR contains a substantial privatization effort that has targeted water and sanitation services as one of the sectors ripest for privatization.

Despite some obvious differences, there are some common elements in the two country cases. These include the limited capacity of water diplomacy to swim upstream to domestic influence, the powerful but ultimately limited impact of IWRM, and the tensions between water citizenship and water marketization as the primary engine of normative change. To develop these themes, the chapter first sketches South Africa's water geography. It then traces the historical development of water law, policy, and practice and chronicles the emergence of a new water framework in the postapartheid period. The chapter then contrasts the development of transnational water protonorms across a range of nodes and sites in South African society that are roughly comparable to those presented in the Brazilian case.

Physical, Social, and Economic Geography of Water in South Africa

The dominant features of South African hydrogeography are a predominantly semiarid climate, an uneven distribution of water in both space and time, and a poor fit between the location of water and the location of people. As Bryan Davies and Jenny Day describe it, "The task of South African water managers is frightening. Not only must they supply water to huge populations in semi-arid regions but they have also to design reservoirs large enough to contend with droughts of unpredictable magnitude at unpredictable times."[4]

Ecologically, South Africa is characterized as subtropical dry forest in the Western Cape region, temperate forest in the eastern coastal regions, and tropical shrubland and dry forest in the north.[5] Climate varies from the Mediterranean climate of the southwest coastal region to the exceedingly dry Karoo plateau in the interior, marked by hot summers and icy winters. Overall, the country's mean annual rainfall of 475 mm is well below the world average of 860 mm.[6] Rainfall exceeds evaporation only in the southwestern Cape region and a few mountain peaks around Drakensburg.[7] About one-sixth of the country has no significant surface runoff at all.[8]

Moreover, most of South Africa's water supply is not found where most of its people live. Figure 9.1 shows the country's main drainage areas and summarizes the average contribution of each to total runoff. More than half of the mean annual runoff travels a relatively short distance through the country's many eastern rivers to the Indian Ocean. In contrast, the central plateau (including the Orange and Vaal drainage regions in figure 9.1) accounts for more than half of South Africa's population, yet only about 22 percent of the mean annual runoff.[9] Eleven of the country's nineteen water management areas are currently classified

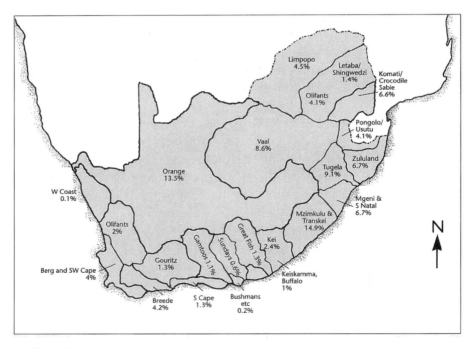

Figure 9.1
Major drainage regions of South Africa with the average percentage contribution to total runoff from each region (source: Davies and Day 1998, 40, figure 2.12. Reprinted with permission).

as being in deficit, in the sense that "requirements for water exceed its availability."[10]

In addition to this uneven spatial distribution, an important characteristic of South African hydrogeography is temporal variability, both seasonally and annually. According to Davies and Day, perhaps 40 percent of the country's 65,000 km of river channels experience natural interruptions of flow ranging from a defined dry season to a state of predominant dryness punctuated by occasional, episodic flow only during extreme rains. In addition to this seasonal variability, patterns of rainfall fluctuate widely from year to year.

The country's major river systems include a dozen rivers that drain the coastal regions to the sea (figure 9.2); the Orange and Vaal, which traverse the center of the country; and several border region rivers in the northern and eastern portions of the country, including the Crocodile, Olifants, Limpopo, Molopo, Incomati, and Maputo. These rivers and associated freshwater ecosystems have undergone dramatic human-induced changes

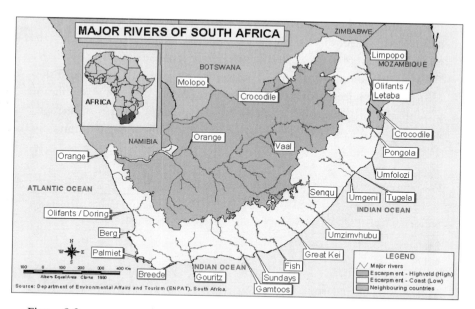

Figure 9.2
Major rivers of South Africa (source: Department of Environmental Affairs and Tourism 1999. Reprinted with permission).

in recent decades. An estimated 50 percent of the mean annual runoff is captured; there are no substantial rivers whose flow regimes remain significantly untapped or unaltered. South Africa is a significant dam builder, with an estimated 520 large dams.[11] There are also untold thousands of smaller reservoirs or "farm dams," most of which are not registered with DWAF.[12] There is no significant hydroelectricity generation in South Africa, however; the main purpose of dam building is to trap water for agricultural or municipal use. Dam building has followed the global pattern of a boom period from the 1930s through the 1970s, with a leveling off in the 1990s.[13]

The consequences of river alteration have been particularly strong for the country's many biotically rich "intermittent" rivers, which have suffered substantial impacts from engineering attempts to even out their sporadic or intermittent annual flows. So too have the rivers that are part of the country's many interbasin transfer schemes. Also, it is estimated that more than half of the country's wetlands have been destroyed or otherwise lost.[14] Floodplain impacts have been less dramatic because few of the country's major rivers are associated with extensive floodplains. (Many South African rivers cut deep channels, particularly the many short rivers in the eastern coastal region of the country.)

Table 9.1 summarizes current water use by sector. Urban and industrial uses have been growing relative to irrigation, driven by population growth and urbanization. South Africa's population, which is currently in excess of 40 million people, adds about a million people annually,

Table 9.1
Distribution of water requirements by sector, 2000

Sector	Water Requirements (percentage of total water requirements)
Irrigation	59
Urban	25
Rural (excluding irrigation)	4
Mining and bulk industrial	6
Power generation	2
Afforestation	4
Total	100

Source: DWAF 2002, 6.

with an even higher rate of urbanization. The extraordinarily difficult challenge of the HIV/AIDS crisis has introduced great demographic uncertainty, which in turn creates more than the usual level of uncertainty in forecasting water demand at the national and sectoral levels. As late as 1999, the Department of Environmental Affairs and Tourism concluded that "Water will increasingly become the limiting resource in South Africa, and supply will become a major restriction to the future socioeconomic development of the country, in terms of both the amount of water available and the quality of what is available."[15] Nevertheless, when the Department of Water Affairs and Forestry wrote a draft version of the National Water Resource Strategy in 2002, it backed away from historical projections of looming water scarcity to conclude that water supplies would be adequate over a twenty-five-year time horizon. Although not flagged explicitly in the report, projections of HIV/AIDS mortality were an important factor in this shift in perspective.

As in Brazil, water-related social inequality is severe in South Africa. Beyond the inequalities typically associated with poverty, water rights were distributed in a racially skewed fashion as part of the apartheid system. When the African National Congress came to power in 1994, it was estimated that some 12–14 million people lacked safe drinking water and that perhaps 20 million lacked adequate sanitation.[16] The impact of water-related deprivation has fallen disproportionately on black South Africans, on the rural poor, and on women and children (with women the primary providers of water at the household level and children disproportionately the victims of waterborne infectious diseases). Infant mortality rates of 20 per thousand live births among white South Africans contrast with rates of 370 per thousand in some water-deprived rural areas.[17]

The Evolution of South African Water Law and Policy

Dutch settlers in the Cape region (1652) brought with them a legacy of Roman and Dutch water law, including a well-institutionalized distinction between public and private water. Public water, which included those waters with potential community uses, fell under the dominion of the state; private water, which included small surface water supplies and all groundwater, belonged to private landowners. Beginning in the nineteenth century, British rule injected the riparian principle, in which rights to water use in a watercourse passed from the public sphere to the owners of the adjoining lands.

Legislation early in the twentieth century modified the strict riparian approach, marking a century-long trend of escalating state involvement in water allocation. The Irrigation and Conservation of Waters Act of 1912 promoted irrigation by altering the traditional riparian allocation. According to the bill's proponents, "If certain individuals along the stream are not prepared to use it we should allow others to use it who are prepared to do so."[18] The law came only two years after the formation of the South African Union (1910), in which the separate colonies of Transvaal, Cape Colony, Natal, and Orange Free State came together in the wake of the horrific Anglo-Boer War (1899–1902).[19] The Irrigation and Conservation of Waters Act brought more water into the "public" sphere by defining any water as public if it could be used in common for irrigation, regardless of whether the watercourse in question enjoyed a steady perennial flow in a defined channel (the prior definition of public water).

As A. D. Lewis explains, potential use for irrigation purposes now became the single determining factor in whether water was public or private: "Irrigation, which in the earliest days of the Common Law was somewhat nervously admitted as a common use on a public river on account of the large consumption of water, is now the use which determines the public nature of the stream."[20] The Act also freed water for irrigators' claims by distinguishing between "normal flow" (essentially, the minimum annual reliable flow) and "surplus water." Although normal flow remained subject to the traditional riparian allocation, "every riparian owner became entitled to the use of as much [surplus water] as he could use beneficially."[21] This made possible larger investments in irrigation because riparian landowners could lay claim to surplus waters well beyond what their traditional riparian allocation would provide, with the only limitation being an injunction against waste. The Act also prioritized irrigation over "mechanical and industrial" uses.[22]

The expansion of the scope of public waters, the distinction between normal flow and surplus water, and the vagueness of the concept of "beneficial" use injected the water courts much more centrally into allocation controversies. Act 40 of the Cape Colony (1899) created a system of water courts to settle disputes and apportion water among riparian users. The 1912 law gave the water courts primary responsibility for dispute resolution. It also deterritorialized and professionalized the water courts, creating permanent water judges and requiring an engineer as one of the three panel members. Legislation also authorized the water courts to grant use rights to nonriparian owners on nonriparian land, a concession to the growth of urban and industrial demand.[23] Water courts now became involved in defining normal flow, granting supply protection for water diversion projects, and granting rights for industrial uses.[24]

Not surprisingly, the main effect of the new law was to promote expansion of irrigation by making substantially more water reliably available within a water rights framework. Subsidies, introduced in the mid-1930s, also helped promote the expansion of irrigation.[25]

The Water Act of 1956

South Africa underwent rapid industrialization in the wake of the Great Depression, and in particular after World War II. Manufacturing increased from 4 percent of gross national product in 1911, the year prior to the Irrigation Act, to almost 20 percent by the early 1950s.[26] The growth of mining, industry, and urban areas, in parallel with expanded irrigation, created pressures for a new approach to water allocation, with particular attention to the needs of nonriparian users. Although the 1912 act had weakened some aspects of riparianism, emerging water-using sectors still found themselves scrambling to lock in water supplies, often with little choice but to acquire land in order to gain water rights. A Commission of Enquiry was formed in 1950 to examine the impact of existing water law on "the social and economic development of the country" and to suggest ways to "provide for the utilization of water resources in the best interest of the nation."[27] The resulting Water Act of 1956 would establish the primary legal framework for water resources for the next four decades, until the reforms of the mid-1990s. The main thrust of this voluminous law (182 sections) was twofold: to greatly expand the power of the state to allocate water, supplanting the riparian emphasis of the 1912 law; and to give industrial water users what W. J. Vos terms "a more rightful place."[28] As stated during the assembly debate, "The water of our rivers, which is severely limited, has to be utilized in the best and most beneficial way for the development of South Africa as a whole. It cannot be limited only to those who possess riparian land."[29] Although the law retained the prior distinction between public and private waters, it gave the state broad powers to declare "government water control areas" in which the state enjoyed broad water allocation authority (with some safeguards for the existing irrigation rights of riparian users). The Commission of Enquiry characterized this weakening of riparian rights as a return to the Roman-Dutch legal tradition for water, but as Uys points out, the law went beyond that tradition of the state as water "administrator in the public interest" and positioned it instead as *dominus fluminis*.[30]

The law also created a permitting system for industrial and urban users and created water boards to exercise local control over urban and industrial uses. However, the provision for declaring water control areas meant that most of the power was vested at the ministerial level, and the name of the Department of Irrigation was changed to the Department of Water Affairs "to reflect the broadened scope of its tasks more accurately."[31] Ministerial powers increased further in the post-1956 period. A 1971 water court ruling determined that private feeder streams of public watercourses were, by extension, themselves public waters,[32] and a 1972 law required the owners of private water to obtain a license before distributing private water for use beyond their land.[33]

The Hydrology of Apartheid

"Laws should be like clothes. They should be made to fit the people they are meant to serve."[34] This quote, from famed American trial attorney Clarence Darrow, graces the discussion of water law in *Management of the Water Resources of the Republic of South Africa*, an extensive analysis of South Africa's water resources prepared by the Department of Water Affairs in the mid-1980s. Although Darrow's words were no doubt cited as a general reference to the social basis of law, the quote is also an apt description of the thread that has woven together water, law, and race in modern South Africa.

Race is never very far below the surface in water policy discussions, past or present. A picture caption in the same document identifies workers building public waterworks as "poor whites." The discussion of international commitments takes great pains to reinforce the not-so-polite fiction of autonomy and independence for the so-called black homelands of the apartheid era. When the Department of Water Affairs established a public relations group in the 1980s, one of its stated goals was to raise awareness about the need to manage water among children "of all race groups."[35]

To be sure, the racial dimensions of water-related power and inequality did not originate with the formalization of the apartheid system after World War II. As Lieberman states, "White supremacy was mobilized as the basis for social and political organization almost from the day the Dutch East India Company representative Jan Van Riebeeck landed at the Cape of Good Hope in 1652."[36] In a dry land, water has historically been an intimate element of that process of social control. Thus the Irrigation and Conservation of Waters Act of 1912, which came in the wake of the newly formed South African Union, cannot be understood simply as enabling irrigation to create wealth or promote national development. It must also be interpreted in terms of the role that land played in brokering the uneasy balance between Anglo and Boer in the new union. Strengthening and extending the irrigation rights of large rural landowners helped to bind them to the new national enterprise by consolidating their control of land, and thus of people, in rural areas.

Similarly, the Water Act of 1956 must be understood in the context of a major political shakeup: the rise of the apartheid system, with its codified and pervasive racial oppression. The Nationalist government of Prime Minister D. F. Malan, which took power in June 1948, was the first purely Afrikaner regime since formation of the union. Analysis of the voting indicates that a key factor in bringing the Nationalist coalition to power was the changing political economy of black labor. Both rural white farmers and urban white workers found their interests harmed by growing migration of blacks to urban areas (the former losing a captive labor supply and the latter suffering increased competition for urban wage labor).[37] Spearheaded by Minister of Native Affairs and later Prime Minister H. F. Verwoerd, the Nationalist government delivered on its campaign promises of aggressive and white-dominated racial separation.

Racial discrimination is implicit in the 1956 water act. Under the act there were essentially two paths to obtaining water: the riparian rights that accrued to land ownership and the favorable intervention of the state, which enjoyed broad powers to reallocate water rights "in the public interest." In other words, access to water derived from the two most important institutions of the apartheid system: racially discriminatory land laws and the intervention of the racially discriminatory state.

Large users were also favored by the increasingly arcane complexity of laws and rules. The 1998 comprehensive reform of South African water law would repeal 108 separate pieces of water legislation dating back to 1914, including the entirety of the Water Act of 1956 and more than twenty subsequent amendments to it. The result was to dismantle a complex maze in which "the right to use water can be gained through Orders of the Water Court, servitudes, permits issued by the Government, or from the provisions of the [1956] Act itself."[38] DWAF's 1997 white paper on water policy portrayed water courts that published few of their opinions while catering to "specialized lawyers and technicians," and characterized DWAF itself as inaccessible to "the needs of people on the ground."[39]

Moreover, those favored by institutionalized discrimination and inaccessible processes received not just water, but water at a dramatically subsidized cost. Under apartheid, there were no charges for riparian water use outside of designated government water control areas, and the Water Act of 1956 allowed the state to subsidize up to one-third of the capital costs of approved irrigation schemes.[40] The net effect was to render agricultural water among the cheapest in the world.[41]

For South Africa's black majority, of course, the picture was quite different. Although reaping few of its benefits, blacks provided much of the labor to sustain this unequal water infrastructure. Mahlubandile Maqungo, an ANC member and political prisoner at Leeukop Maximum Prison, describes his experience with forced labor for dam construction during the 1960s:

There were 25 of us and we worked among criminals. We were handcuffed to the dam, and then made to carry sacks of mud on our backs—we were *sjambokked* while we battled to do this. We wore no shoes, but we would be made to pass through an old quarry where the stones were sharp.[42]

Water Norms and the Management of Water Scarcity in the Apartheid Era

South Africa experienced several years of severe drought in the second half of the 1960s and again in the late 1970s and early 1980s. Given the country's overwhelming dependence on surface water runoff for its water supply, both droughts prompted periods of intensive scrutiny of water resource availability and water management practices. In 1970, a Commission of Enquiry into Water Matters published a detailed report on water supplies, projected demand, and policy options for reconciling the two, which was adopted as official government policy.[43] In 1986, the Department of Water Affairs published an unprecedentedly detailed analysis of the country's water situation, which included section-by-section comments on the 1970 report and a discussion of progress and change since that period. Juxtaposing these two exercises in self-examination provides a revealing picture of the changing conceptual and normative foundations of water policy, both in general and with specific regard to the bundles of transnational protonorms discussed in chapters 4 through 7.

The diagnosis of the 1970 Commission of Enquiry was straight-forward: "Unless effective measures are applied in the planning and development of the Republic's water resources there may be serious shortages of water before the close of the century."[44] The commission forecast that strong industrial development, rapid population growth, and rising urbanization rates would produce a 7 percent annual growth in water demand for the foreseeable future. The commission's forty-five specific recommendations fit essentially into three general categories: more efficient use (including improved irrigation techniques, urban water conservation, and enhanced water reuse); improved capture and storage of available waters (including new infrastructure, more efficient storage, reduced evaporation losses, the use of vegetative cover to optimize run-off, and better flood control), and the tapping of unconventional sources (beginning with groundwater but moving eventually to desalination and atmospheric moisture).

The report acknowledged that pricing policies and conservation initiatives were tools for influencing water demand, and it was particularly critical of the "cheap agricultural water" policies of the DWA. It cited the failure to recover even operation and maintenance costs on irrigation projects and called for an effective cost-accounting system. The report's overwhelming emphasis, however, was on supply requirements in a context of structurally inevitable demand: "Galloping water demands constitute just one of those unavoidably explosive results of incorporating a compound growth rate into an economy."[45] Regional growth poles such as the Western Cape, Durban, and Port Elizabeth would require improved harvesting of available water in local catchments; for the country's main growth pole, the industrial heartland around Johannesburg known then as the Southern Transvaal, interbasin transfers would also be necessary.[46]

Although it was issued four years after the International Law Association's Helsinki Rules, with their emphasis on equitable use as the basis of international cooperation (chapter 4), the report paid almost no attention to the international legal context. The international dimension is summed up in two sentences: "Concerning use of waters from rivers in which other riparian countries have interests, it seems that international law affecting use of the waters of such rivers is very loose. The use of such waters is generally fixed by agreement."[47] The limited discussion of international considerations focused exclusively on the (largely abstract) possibilities of enhancing water supplies by "drawing substantial quantities of water from our neighbor states."[48] The idea of an interstate cooperative framework based on equitable use is only hinted at, in a passing allusion to the fact that "other factors" (read: larger political objectives) may require a "good neighbor" policy.[49] There is no recognition or discussion of the idea of shared management of internationally shared watercourses. (This is not a surprise in light of the growing sense within the regime that under apartheid South Africa confronted a hostile international legal system.[50])

In contrast, recognition of the need for something akin to integrated water resources management (chapter 5) in the domestic sphere is apparent, although the phrase itself is not yet established and is not employed here. The report stresses the need to shift from ad hoc execution of projects to systematic planning, including socioeconomic analysis of the full range of costs and benefits. There is also notable emphasis on catchment-level planning and analysis: "The planning of catchments as geographic units will be demanded.... The basic aim in formulating plans for individual catchments and their mutual coupling should be the establishment of a broad directive for the optimum use, or combination of uses, of the water resources with provision for the future needs of the region."[51] The commission also recognized the knowledge-intensive requirements of moving toward this more holistic approach, calling for creation of a water research commission (a step taken with the Water Research Act, Act 34 of 1971).

Yet the IWRM paradigm is only half formed in that it remains solidly within the context of a supply-side vision of water resource development. This is most apparent in the treatment of environmental considerations. Water quality is a concern exclusively because it affects water supply. "Reclamation of effluents" is identified as the most effective pollution control strategy, with source reduction barely mentioned.[52] The only hint at the idea of in-stream uses of water is the treatment of afforestation as an indirect use, and a problematic one at that, in that it reduces runoff otherwise available for capture and use.

With regard to marketization (chapter 7), there is a clear recognition of water as a scarce economic commodity, the consumption of which is influenced by its price.[53] The commission warned against the "artificial lowering" of water prices, called for a "realistic price policy that reflects underlying scarcities" and pointed out that irrigation schemes generally failed to cover even their operating and maintenance costs: "It is regarded as fully justifiable to gradually raise water rates at existing schemes till at least the annual operating and maintenance costs are covered, and that for all new schemes this approach be adopted from commencement."[54] Yet the report remains within the traditional framework of treating different water users as separate sectors. Although agricultural uses are clearly regarded as inefficient and therefore problematic, there is no discussion of developing market mechanisms to move water from agriculture to higher-value uses. Similarly, while there is a general acceptance of the idea that interbasin transfer schemes will be required in the future, these are framed as moving water from where it flows to where it is used, rather than as a mechanism for steering water to its most valuable uses. (The latter notion would appear as an important concept by the mid-1980s, as discussed later.)

Finally, there is no hint in the report of anything akin to a broadly participatory approach or what might be termed norms of watershed democracy (chapter 6). On questions related to the state, authority, and participation, the report places strong and monolithic emphasis on the need for the national government's commanding presence. There are several allusions to the need for economic decentralization but no hint of decentralization or devolution in the political sphere: "It is desirable for various reasons that the Republic's water resources should continue to be developed for the benefit of the country as a whole under the full control of the Central government."[55]

The report of the Commission of Enquiry became official policy in 1970 and the DWA implemented several of its recommendations. The agency embarked on a national water inventory and began more systematic efforts at long-term planning and data collection. It began to charge sliding-scale tariffs for irrigation water, calculated tariffs for industrial and municipal use on a full-cost basis, and instituted cost-benefit analysis as a more widely used planning tool. It created a new groundwater division, tightened pollution control standards, and hired a cost accountant. A Water Research Commission was established the year after the enquiry commission's report.

Beginning in 1978 and extending into the early 1980s, South Africa experienced another severe drought, triggering restrictions on water use, more aggressive demand-side management efforts, and extensive public criticism of the Department of Water Affairs. This drought and its aftermath produced the next historical snapshot of the conceptual and normative dimensions of water policy: the DWA's 1986 compendium *Management of the Water Resources of the Republic of South Africa*. The volume—known simply as "the red book" among the country's water cognoscenti—provided an unprecedentedly detailed look at the country's water resources.

The 1986 red book presents South Africa's water problems in fundamentally different terms than the 1970 Commission of Enquiry report. The problem is framed, not as one of supply chasing inexeorable growth in demand, but rather as one of economic risk management. "The DWA is … prone to finding itself walking a precarious tightrope between two extremes, both of which are of possible detriment to the consumer, namely over-capitalization and higher tariffs than necessary (in addition to placing an unnecessary burden on the limited capital market) on the one hand and inconvenience and economic risks through under-capitalization on the other."[56] Much emphasis is placed on the growing complexity of water management and policy, given the long lead times required for increasingly capital-intensive projects and the multiple conflicting claims on water for different uses.

The need to manage risk in turn produced several perceived challenges of adaptation. Some of these move in the direction of a new water paradigm, including the demand for new types of information and for better communication with user groups in society. In other ways, however, the risk management framework deepened the traditional incentive to push rivers around, in this instance, via large-scale interbasin transfers of water. The report estimates that "international or interregional" transfers of water are or will be required in "more than three quarters of the country."[57] It also underscores the role of interbasin transfers in risk management: "Greater emphasis is being placed on the need to link river systems to obtain the increased flexibility needed for the optimal management of resources."[58]

With regard to norms of interstate water law and diplomacy, the report reflects a heightened, although largely instrumental, sensitivity to international considerations. Responding to public criticism, the report repeatedly seeks to legitimize the DWA's approach by reference to international best practices: "The approach of the DWA in this publication is in line with a worldwide trend over the past few decades.... Although DWA's approach to demand and supply management has evolved locally as a result of changing needs over many years, it is nevertheless in line with international thinking."[59] The report contains a lengthy appendix documenting "world views on water management."

With specific regard to sovereign water rights and responsibilities, the report reinforced the conclusion of its 1970 counterpart, stating that "no enforceable international law exists for regulating the abstraction or use of water in international drainage basins."[60] Yet the report stresses the recommendation of a 1980 interdepartmental committee that the 1966 Helsinki Rules, which emphasize equitable sharing and cooperative bargaining, should form the basis for managing shared watercourses. In a revealing glimpse into the hydrology of apartheid, most of the discussion of the Helsinki Rules focused, not on relations with neighboring states, but on the black homelands constructed by apartheid within the borders of South Africa. The report took great pains to distinguish between the allegedly independent homelands or "TBVC states" of Transkei, Bophuthatswana, Venda, and Ciskei; the allegedly "self-governing national states" of Gazankulu, KaNgwane, KwaNdebele, KwaZulu, Lebowa, and Qwaqwa) that remained formally part of South Africa; and independent, sovereign neighboring states such as Lesotho and Botswana.[61] Most of the international discussion focused on the newly "international" character of rivers that flow between white South Africa and the black homelands. The report emphasizes the need to respect the Helsinki Rules, create interstate basin commissions, and otherwise jointly manage those rivers flowing into or out of the TBVC states, and the analogous domestic duty with regard to the allegedly autonomous "self-governing national states." In other words, rather than being seen as an embrace of interstate water norms through a logic of appropriateness, this emphasis on Helsinki is better understood as an effort to validate, or even constitute, these highly artificial and coercively constructed units. The Helsinki Rules were of interest on a more practical level as well, as a way to fend off challenges to existing uses: "A basin state may not be denied the present reasonable use of the water of an international drainage basin for the purpose of reserving such water for a future use by a co-basin state."[62]

Norms of integrated water resources management (chapter 5) are more strongly and explicitly represented than in the report of the Commission of Enquiry sixteen years earlier. The red book calls for a "holistic water management strategy"[63] and suggests that "The growing demand placed on water resources gives rise to increasingly complex problems in water management."[64] With specific regard to the environmental dimensions, the report reflects a much broader conception of environmental concerns than did the 1970 report, with emphasis on problems of salinization, eutrophication, and pollution. The paradigm remains one of contamination of water supplies, however, rather than a more holistic conception of ecosystem management or ecological uses. The idea of creating an ecological reserve, central to the reforms of the mid-1990s, does not yet appear, although research that would provide the scientific legitimization for that concept was by then well under way.

With regard to marketization norms, the red book highlights the need for full-cost pricing but stops short of embracing market-based allocation mechanisms within or across different user sectors. The idea of marginal cost pricing is endorsed in general terms, as it was in the 1970 Commission of Enquiry report. In keeping with the dominant theme of risk management, the red book also recognizes that different users will be willing to pay a different level of risk premium for guaranteed supplies. And by this point there is a clear recognition that much of South Africa's water goes to economically suboptimal uses. However, the report also cautions that water "could never move entirely into the realm of pure private goods."[65] The overarching emphasis on risk management underscores the need for sector-level planning rather than cross-sectoral price competition, with the state responsible for determining supply priorities for each user group and subsidizing strategic uses:

The principle that resources should be allocated among different users so that the marginal benefit is the same for all users, was accepted as Government policy on the recommendation of the Commission of Enquiry into Water matters in 1970. However, demand-side allocation through market forces requires an effective relationship between the supply authority and water users and implies that waterworks must be financed and operated on commercial principles aimed at the full recovery of the cost of services. Under this system, any public sector or nonmarket allocations of water that are unavoidable in the national interest require the payment of regularly reviewed subsidies to cover operating deficits. The subsidies should be paid by whatever public body, including DWA, finds justification for such arrangements.[66]

Finally, the report contains little that could be said to evoke norms of watershed democracy, which is not surprising coming from the apartheid state at the height of its repressive instincts. There is some discussion of the need to maintain effective "partnership with users," framed largely as a risk management tool.[67] The flow is clearly one-way, however, with public participation institutionalized primarily through purely advisory channels such as regional development advisory committees.

The End of Apartheid and the New Water Policy Framework
The broad outlines of South Africa's dramatic transition from apartheid to democracy are well known. External pressures against the regime mounted in the 1960s, fueled by several forces, including world condemnation of the Sharpeville massacre in 1960, the decolonization of much of sub-Saharan Africa in the early 1960s, and the emergence of an organized opposition movement spearheaded by the African National Congress and other groups. External pressures continued to build in the 1970s, when activist campaigns for sanctions and disinvestment took root in several Western countries, leading several Western governments to impose varying degrees of economic sanctions. South Africa's "trusteeship" role in South-West Africa (later Namibia) produced a costly and protracted struggle against that country's independence movement. Domestically, various forms of opposition from the black majority had been present from the start (the Sharpeville massacre, for example, was in response to a demonstration against the notorious pass laws). Opposition became increasingly well organized and effective over time, both within South Africa and from staging points in the neighboring "frontline" states.

By the late 1980s, feeling the twin pressures of international opprobrium and domestic tumult, the regime of F. W. de Klerk concluded that some form of accommodation with South Africa's black majority was necessary for Afrikaner survival. The government released longtime political prisoner Nelson Mandela in February 1990, shortly after de Klerk lifted the thirty-year ban on the African National Congress and made other concessions that would lead to direct talks with that organization. Complex, multistage negotiations ensued, producing an interim constitution in 1993, an agreed-upon set of guiding principles for the eventual drafting of a permanent constitution, the country's first multiracial democratic election in 1994 (contested by twenty-seven political parties, with a coalition "government of national unity" led by Mandela's ANC gaining a solid victory), and a new constitution (drafted in 1996 and entering into force early in 1997).

The new government enjoyed relatively broad political legitimacy, for reasons including but not limited to Mandela's presence at its head.

Economic policy would prove contentious as the government moved to embrace neoliberal principles through its 1996 Growth, Employment and Redistribution economic program. Despite a weak economy, mounting unemployment, a collapse of the rand on world currency markets, and growing opposition from the well-organized trade union movement, the ANC parlayed its political strength, fragmentation of the opposition, and the benefits of incumbency into another solid victory at the polls in June 1999. Mandela's long-time ANC compatriot Thabo Mbeki succeeded him as president, enjoying a nearly two-thirds majority in parliament and political control in seven of the country's nine provinces.[68]

The New Constitution

As in Brazil, constitutional reform played a role in driving, or at least enabling, nonincremental change in water law, policy, and practice in South Africa. In the wake of the end of the apartheid system, the country adopted a new constitution in 1996–1997.[69] The constitution speaks to water issues on several levels. First, it contains ambitious language on individual rights, social justice, and the need for national healing and reconstruction in light of apartheid's inequities. Several of these provisions speak at least indirectly to human water needs, including constitutionally created rights to equality (Section 8), life (Section 9), human dignity (Section 10), and health (in several sections).[70]

Second, the constitution contains provisions on environmental protection and land use that affect water policy and practice. All South Africans are guaranteed a constitutional right to an environment that protects human health and well-being (Section 24). Pollution control is a shared responsibility of the national and provincial levels of government. The Supreme Court of Appeal has ruled that this includes a governmental responsibility to hear public concerns before issuing permits.[71]

As with environmental protection requirements, constitutional provisions regarding land are highly relevant to water. This is so not only because of the many ways that land use affects water availability and quality, but also because of the close historical ties between access to land and access to water, as discussed previously. On the one hand, the constitution creates a state duty to "take reasonable legislative and other measures, within its available resources, to foster conditions which enable citizens to gain access to land on an equitable basis" and to create security of land tenure for historically disadvantaged groups (Section 25). At the same time, there are protections related to the expropriation or deprivation of property. The constitution also explicitly acknowledges the potential tensions between these sets of rights, stating that efforts to redress past discrimination are not violations of property rights if they are "reasonable and justifiable in an open and democratic society based on human dignity, equality and freedom" (Section 25). The Constitutional Court ruled in 1996 that property rights did not take precedence over claims for restitution and that the state must instead find an equitable balance between these rights.[72] Court rulings have also determined that the denial of water rights may constitute a form of eviction from the land.[73]

Finally, the constitution speaks directly to the water question, stating that all South Africans shall be guaranteed access to "sufficient food and water" (Section 27). As with pollution control, water supply and sanitation are shared responsibilities, with local governments responsible for delivering water supplies and sanitation services and the national government responsible for setting standards for those activities.

The various constitutional rights that relate either directly or indirectly to water must be understood in the context of South Africa's postapartheid transition. The constitution explicitly recognizes that the country's history of oppression, race-based inequality, and widespread poverty has created a particular context for the current transition toward realization of these rights. There are several explicit constitutional references to the need for affirmative action in light of past discrimination. On the other hand, the constitution also indicates that for several of these rights, the state's duty is to promote their "progressive realization," meaning that the state must be making progress within the shortest reasonable time. The progressive realization clause is a frank acknowledgment of the state's incapacity to give all guaranteed rights immediate, practical meaning. A further complication is that progressive realization applies to some constitutionally guaranteed rights (including water, housing, health care, food, and social security) but not to others (including environmental protection, basic education, and children's rights).[74]

Water Reform: Political Momentum and Conceptual Framing

By the time of the adoption of the new constitution in early 1997, the new government had already been in place for more than two years and had taken several steps on the road to reforming water law and policy. The first Minister of Water Affairs and Forestry was Dr. Kader Asmal, a professor of law and member of the ANC who spent thirty years in exile. As a leading legal scholar within the ANC, Asmal played a significant role in drafting the new constitution. He enjoyed substantial credibility within both activist and expert circles; as discussed in chapter 6, he would later chair the World Commission on Dams. His first public announcement as minister, in May 1994, called for a comprehensive revision of the country's water laws.

From the start, there was a dual emphasis in the reform agenda, including both the specific problem of water supply and sanitation for deprived South Africans and the broader question of water resource management. The political context and popular expectations were such that drinking water and sanitation concerns received priority emphasis, even before the new constitutional guarantees on water, food, and health rights were in place. By November of that first year, DWAF issued a white paper on water supply and sanitation, stressing the "problems of tackling the backlog of the past" and "dedicated to the millions of our citizens who struggle daily with the burden of not having the most basic of services."[75] It also became apparent that to make significant progress on these service questions, the broader question of reforming water resource management would have to be addressed.

Taking up the broader question of resource management, in March 1995 DWAF issued a thirty-page report titled "You and Your Water Rights: South African Law Review," which it billed as a call for public response. The document contained a detailed review of existing water law and set out the rationale for legal reform. Among the reasons offered were the inadequate protection afforded to rural peoples and the environment; the "antique systems" of water allocation currently in use; the lack of a "well-structured water pricing system, which reflects the value of water"; the need to pay greater attention to the "customs and unwritten water and land laws of rural communities"; the failure of existing law to reflect the integrated character of water resources; and the derivation of existing principles of water law from "European countries, where the climate, culture and hydrology are very different to South Africa."[76]

Just over a year later, in April 1996, DWAF released a draft list of water law principles, again emphasizing the role of public comment by publishing them as a fifteen-page pamphlet labeled as a discussion document. Later in 1996 the principles received cabinet endorsement as the "Fundamental Principles and Objectives for a New Water Law in South Africa" (table 9.2). Notable elements among these principles include the treatment of all water as a commonly held national resource under public control (principles 2 and 3) and the linked idea of the state as public trustee and custodian of water resources (principles 12 and 13). Themes of integrated water resources management feature prominently, including emphasis on the holistic character of the water cycle (principles 5 and 7), the need for integrated management (principles 15 and 18), and the importance of the catchment as a unit of water management and administration (principles 5 and 23). Also noteworthy are the explicit voiding of the riparian principle (principle 4); the idea of reserving sufficient quantities of water for basic human needs, ecological requirements, and international obligations (principles 9–11); and explicit references to the role of economic incentives (principles 16 and 24).

Also worth noting are the changes made to the principles as part of the process of public comment and cabinet approval. Some of these changes were adjustments reflecting the new constitution, the language of which was not finalized when the principles were first drafted.[77] Other differences between draft and final principles reflected ongoing policy debates or typical turf battles.[78] Yet the cabinet edits revealed as well a still-evolving normative framework and continuing controversies over the conceptualization of authority, with the cabinet-approved principles shading back toward a more traditional conception of the state's authority. The cabinet strengthened emphasis on the catchment as the basic hydrologic unit but also weakened it as the management unit, affirming that management authority should be delegated to the catchment level only where appropriate. A new principle was added on the importance of fitting water services into the broader framework of local government authority. Several explicit references were added to affirm the state's

Table 9.2
Fundamental principles and objectives for a new water law in South Africa

LEGAL ASPECTS OF WATER

1. The water law shall be subject to and consistent with the Constitution in all matters including the determination of the public interest and the rights and obligations of all parties, public and private, with regards to water. While taking cognizance of existing uses, the water law will actively promote the values enshrined in the Bill of Rights.

2. All water, wherever it occurs in the water cycle, is a resource common to all, the use of which shall be subject to national control. All water shall have a consistent status in law, irrespective of where it occurs.

3. There shall be no ownership of water but only a right (for environmental and basic human needs) or an authorization for its use. Any authorization to use water in terms of the water law shall not be in perpetuity.

4. The location of the water resource in relation to land shall not in itself confer preferential rights to usage. The riparian principle shall not apply.

THE WATER CYCLE

5. In a relatively arid country such as South Africa, it is necessary to recognize the unity of the water cycle and the interdependence of its elements, where evaporation, clouds and rainfall are linked to groundwater, rivers, lakes, wetlands and the sea, and where the basic hydrological unit is the catchment.

6. The variable, uneven and unpredictable distribution of water in the water cycle should be acknowledged.

WATER RESOURCE MANAGEMENT PRIORITIES

7. The objective of managing the quantity, quality and reliability of the Nation's water resources is to achieve optimum, long term, environmentally sustainable social and economic benefit for society from their use.

8. The water required to ensure that all people have access to sufficient water shall be reserved.

9. The quantity, quality and reliability of water required to maintain the ecological functions on which humans depend shall be reserved so that the human use of water does not individually or cumulatively compromise the long term sustainability of aquatic and associated ecosystems.

10. The water required to meet the basic human needs referred to in Principle 8 and the needs of the environment shall be identified as "The Reserve" and shall enjoy priority of use by right. The use of water for all other purposes shall be subject to authorization.

11. International water resources, specifically shared river systems, shall be managed in a manner that optimizes the benefits for all parties in a spirit of mutual co-operation. Allocations agreed for downstream countries shall be respected.

Table 9.2
(continued)

WATER RESOURCE MANAGEMENT APPROACHES

12. The national Government is the custodian of the Nation's water resources, as an indivisible national asset. Guided by its duty to promote the public trust, the National Government has ultimate responsibility for, and authority over, water resource management, the equitable allocation and usage of water and the transfer of water between catchments and international water matters.

13. As custodian of the Nation's water resources, the National Government shall ensure that the development, apportionment, management and use of those resources is carried out using the criteria of public interest, sustainability, equity and efficiency of use in a manner which reflects its public trust obligations and the value of water to society while ensuring that basic domestic needs, the requirements of the environment and international obligations are met.

14. Water resources shall be developed, apportioned and managed in such a manner as to enable all user sectors to gain equitable access to the desired quantity, quality and reliability of water. Conservation and other measures to manage demand shall be actively promoted as a preferred option to achieve these objectives.

15. Water quality and quantity are interdependent and shall be managed in an integrated manner, which is consistent with broader environmental management approaches.

16. Water quality management options shall include the use of economic incentives and penalties to reduce pollution; and the possibility of irretrievable environmental degradation as a result of pollution shall be prevented.

17. Water resource development and supply activities shall be managed in a manner which is consistent with the broader national approaches to environmental management.

18. Since many land uses have a significant impact upon the water cycle, the regulation of land use shall, where appropriate, be used as an instrument to manage water resources within the broader integrated framework of land use management.

19. Any authorization to use water shall be given in a timely fashion and in a manner which is clear, secure and predictable in respect of the assurance of availability, extent and duration of use. The purpose for which the water may be used shall not arbitrarily be restricted.

20. The conditions upon which authorization is granted to use water shall take into consideration the investment made by the user in developing infrastructure to be able to use the water.

21. The development and management of water resources shall be carried out in a manner which limits to an acceptable minimum the danger to life and property due to natural or manmade disasters.

Table 9.2
(continued)

WATER INSTITUTIONS

22. The institutional framework for water management shall as far as possible be simple, pragmatic and understandable. It shall be self-driven and minimize the necessity for State intervention. Administrative decisions shall be subject to appeal.

23. Responsibility for the development, apportionment and management of available water resources shall, where possible and appropriate, be delegated to a catchment or regional level in such a manner as to enable interested parties to participate.

24. Beneficiaries of the water management system shall contribute to the cost of its establishment and maintenance on an equitable basis.

WATER SERVICES

25. The right of all citizens to have access to basic water services (the provision of potable water supply and the removal and disposal of human excreta and waste water) necessary to afford them a healthy environment on an equitable and economically and environmentally sustainable basis shall be supported.

26. Water services shall be regulated in a manner which is consistent with and supportive of the aims and approaches of the broader local government framework.

27. While the provision of water services is an activity distinct from the development and management of water resources, water services shall be provided in a manner consistent with the goals of water resource management.

28. Where water services are provided in a monopoly situation, the interests of the individual consumer and the wider public must be protected and the broad goals of public policy promoted.

Source: DWAF 1997, 35–36.

responsibility (and by extension, its authority) to promote the public trust.

After cabinet approval of the principles, eleven technical task teams were created to translate them into a policy framework. The result was DWAF's 1997 *White Paper on a National Water Policy for South Africa*. The white paper reiterated and embraced the cabinet-approved principles and their main themes: water as an indivisible national asset, water as a common resource rather than a riparian right, the prioritization of basic needs and ecological requirements, normative commitments to equity and sustainability, the primacy of the public interest, and the state's responsibility as custodian of the public trust. The basic thrust was summarized in the new DWAF slogan "Some, For All, Forever," which refers to "access to a limited resource (some) on an equitable basis (for all) in a sustainable manner, now and in the future (for ever)."[79] The white paper also reiterated the goal articulated in the government's Reconstruction and Development (RDP) Program, that each South African should have access to a minimum quantity of 25 liters per day of clean water for basic needs.

Grounded in these goals and principles, the white paper sketched the core elements of a new policy framework: an elaborate permitting process for all water uses, a more integrated system for managing water quality and supply, enhanced efforts at water conservation, a pricing policy more reflective of the true costs of water supply and use, and more careful planning in the development of new water resources. The main instrument of policy was to be a retooled and reoriented national government serving the public interest. On the one hand, there was a clear recognition that DWAF had operated historically using a narrow model of water supply development and in the service of a narrow set of interests, and that it would require substantial retooling for its new tasks as public custodian. However, the white paper emphasized as well the legacy of apartheid in creating a lack of technical and managerial capacity in South African government and society more generally. As a result, in the short term, "a mechanical decentralization or delegation of functions is unlikely to achieve the objectives of more responsive and effective water management."[80] In other words, DWAF would continue to hold the reins.

These steps in the process of conceptualizing policy reform—the preliminary water rights report, the cabinet-approved principles, and the white paper policy framework—were exposed to what was by historical standards an unprecedented level of public discussion and comment. According to Davies and Day, "Tens of thousands of people have been involved in hundreds of consultative meetings, workshops and conferences."[81] In the process of finalizing the principles, consultative meetings were held in all nine provinces of South Africa, and bilateral meetings were held with major user groups such as industry, mining, agriculture, municipal users, and environmental organizations.[82] The impetus for reform was emanating from the new government, but the process by which reform was conceptualized involved substantially more voices from outside the state than had been the case for DWAF historically.

Legal Codification of the New Policy Framework

Armed with the two white papers, whatever legitimacy it derived from its consultative processes, and the momentum of the newly guaranteed constitutional rights, the government created two important framework laws: the Water Services Act (1997) and the National Water Act (1998). The Water Services Act focused on water supply for drinking and sanitation needs, while the National Water Act addressed the legal requirements of the new policy framework for managing water resources. This split was determined by a combination of constitutional, practical, and political considerations. Whereas the constitution placed water resources management squarely in the national government's hands, it assigned primacy for delivering water service to local governments while limiting the national government to a standard-setting role. Also, interviews with policy makers revealed that the water services framework was understood as a less complex legal task (however daunting the actual delivery of those services would prove to be). The emphasis on addressing water services prior to dealing with the broader water resources policy framework underscored as well the dominant political context: transition to majority rule and the vast unmet water needs of the black South African majority, particularly in rural areas.

The Water Services Act recognizes "the rights of access to basic water supply and basic sanitation necessary to ensure sufficient water and an environment not harmful to health or well-being."[83] The Act reiterates the constitutional right to an adequate water supply and prioritizes basic water supply and sanitation.[84] The Act gives the minister broad standard-setting power related to water service delivery, tariffs, and the quality of water delivered. Local water service authorities are tasked with appointing specific service providers; they must also develop detailed plans for delivery and development of water service.[85] The national government has monitoring responsibility and intervention powers when local water authorities fail to provide adequate service.[86]

The National Water Act, which codified the new government's policy framework for water resource management, is a substantially more complex piece of legislation. The new law repealed more than 100 prior water laws dating to 1914, including the Water Act of 1956. The law reiterates the underlying purposes of meeting basic needs, promoting equitable access, redressing historical discrimination, facilitating development, protecting the environment, and meeting international obligations, all in the context of the state as public trustee. The National Water Act creates the legal foundation for several instruments of water management and policy, including the following:

National Strategy   The Act requires the Minister of Water Affairs and Forestry to develop a national water resources strategy "as soon as reasonably practicable."[87] The purpose of the strategy is to provide "the framework for the protection, use, development, conservation, management and control of water resources for the country as a whole."[88] It also provides the framework within which water will be managed at the regional or catchment level, in defined water management areas. The strategy is binding on all actors authorized by law to perform water-related duties; local catchment-scale plans must be consistent with it.

Classification System   The Act creates a scheme for classifying specific water resources according to desired levels of environmental protection. These classifications are to inform the permitting process for acceptable water uses, local catchment management strategies, and environmental enforcement.

The Reserve   The Act identifies human and ecological needs as priorities by creating what is known as "the Reserve." This is defined as the minimum quantity and quality of water required to meet human needs for drinking water, food preparation, and hygiene (the basic human needs reserve) and to protect aquatic ecosystems (the ecological reserve). According to the Act, these needs must be given priority and an adequate amount of water to meet them set aside. The amount of water that constitutes the Reserve is to be determined for "any significant water resource."[89] Authority to determine the level of the Reserve for a given water resource is vested in the minister, with no mechanism for its calculation specified in the legislation.

Allocation Mechanism   The Act mandates a system for allocating water. Invoking the doctrine of water as a common, indivisible, national resource, the Act requires that any bulk use of water be licensed, including but not limited to taking water from a water resource, impeding or diverting the flow of a watercourse, storing water, or discharging pollutants into water.[90] Licenses are to specify the use of water, the user of water, conditions of use, and period of use (not to exceed forty years). DWAF has the authority to temporarily allow licensed water uses to be transferred to other purposes or users, but there is no provision for the market-based exchange of water-use rights. In the assignment of new licenses, the amount of water required for the Reserve, international obligations, and existing licenses and lawful uses must be considered.

Water-Use Charges   The Act allows for a system of water-use charges to finance the costs of water management and development, as well as to achieve "an equitable and efficient allocation of water."[91] Although the Act invokes the "user pays" and "polluter pays" principles throughout, charges are not mandated but merely authorized. The Act gives the minister broad powers to set fees and to differentiate them across geographic areas, categories of users, or even individual users to promote social equity.

Catchment-Level Institutions   The Act authorizes the minister to create catchment management agencies (CMAs), in order to "delegate water resource management to the regional or catchment level and to involve local communities, within the framework of the national water resource strategy."[92] CMAs are tasked with the development of catchment-level management strategies and the coordination of activities among water users. Catchment strategies must be based on public notice and comment, must take into account the requirements of the Reserve (and where applicable, international obligations), and must not be in conflict with the national water resources strategy.[93] They are to be developed in consultation with relevant government organs and "any persons, or their representative organizations (i) whose activities affect or might affect water resources within its water management area; and (ii) who have an interest in the content, effect or implementation of the catchment management strategy."[94] The membership of a CMA is determined by the water minister in conjunction with an advisory committee, "with the object of achieving a balance among the interests of water users, potential water users, local and provincial government and environmental interest groups."[95] Although CMAs are defined hydrologically, they are subordinated to the administratively defined water management area within which they are located and are required to be consistent with the national water resource strategy. The language on CMAs in the Act recognizes that their formation will be a gradual process, describing them as an ultimate aim and allowing the minister to perform the functions of a CMA or appoint an advisory committee in catchments for which a CMA is not yet established.

Water User Associations   The Act allows for the creation of water user associations, defined as "co-operative associations of individual water users who wish to undertake water related activities for their mutual benefit."[96]

Existing Lawful Uses   Recognizing that the licensing system, water resource strategy, and classification system would be a major challenge for DWAF, the Act also makes allowances for the continuation of existing lawful uses during the transition to the new system.

Politically, the law can be understood as a combination of elements, some of which constituted bold new ground (notably the Reserve, catchment-level institutions, the emphasis on demand-side management, and the break with riparian principles), some of which built on the evolutionary trend in South African water management (the IWRM framework and national planning mechanisms), and some of which were meant to mitigate impacts on the status quo (provisions regarding existing lawful uses).

Institutionalization Writ Large: Sites for the Embedding of Water Norms

As seen in the case of Brazil, South Africa's new water policy framework contains a mixed blend of the global protonorms discussed in chapters 4 through 7. As in Brazil, South Africa's National Water Act continues the trend since the 1980s of a deepening emphasis on integrated water resources management. Much like the Brazilian law, South Africa's law has a strongly managerial orientation, invokes a multiple-use paradigm for water management, and relies heavily on mechanisms of planning, classification, and information systems to shape water allocation decisions. There are also strong parallels with the Brazilian case in the normalization of the idea of water marketization, including the emphasis on water as a scarce resource with market value and the use of user fees as a managerial tool to enhance allocation "efficiency."

The South African legal framework parts company with that of Brazil in its much greater emphasis on the international dimension and its substantially lesser emphasis on civil society and direct democracy. International legal norms receive far more explicit treatment; the 1998 National Water Act identifies meeting international obligations as among its purposes. (As discussed later, the legal requirement is to incorporate whatever provisions may be contained in South Africa's specific international agreements. The law takes no particular stand on the role of emergent international norms such as equitable use, avoiding significant harm, sovereign equality, peaceful resolution of disputes, or prior notification.) The allocation of water licenses, the development of catchment management strategies, and the national water strategy are all obliged to take international obligations into account. This creates a path for the potential influence of international water law principles. South Africa is a party to the regional framework protocol on shared water resources of the Southern African Development Community, which was revised in 2000 to bring it line with the 1997 UN Watercourses Convention. (As discussed later, the effectiveness of this channel is blunted by the fact that several of South Africa's existing international agreements contain inconsistencies or omissions with regard to the UN Watercourses Principles.)

If the law creates stronger, although still indirect, channels for the influence of international legal norms, it creates a less robust platform than in the Brazilian case for emergent global norms of watershed democracy. The embrace of catchments as the unit of analysis is far more circumscribed in the South African case. Catchment-level planning remains subordinated to the national water strategy and without the promise of directly recycled water fees. Also, the South African law contains nothing equivalent to the Brazilian mixed-membership National Water Resources Council and vests substantially more power in the water minister, both with regard to water allocation and the definition of water management entities.

If the unique concept of the Brazilian law was to give standing to civil society and basin-level governance instruments, the unique concept in the South African case is the Reserve. In giving priority to basic human needs and ecological requirements, the Reserve can be read as reflecting and strengthening both watershed democracy norms (by presenting water as a human right) and IWRM norms (by requiring that environmental "uses" be factored into the process of integrated management). At the same time, the Reserve weakens marketization norms in the sense that it establishes important uses of water that are held beyond the reach of market-allocation principles.

In the Brazilian case study, the conformance of water-related practices with transnational water norms was examined not only via the formal and legal structure of national policy but also in the context of several specific domains where key water-related decisions, actions, and struggles occur. What follows is a parallel discussion of the contested spaces where power and purpose are exercised over water-related decisions in South Africa. Although the sites discussed here are sometimes analogous to those discussed in the chapter on Brazil, the focus and emphasis in the discussion reflect the specific South African context. For example, South Africa lacks some of the increasingly institutionalized sites of struggle over emergent norms of watershed democracy seen in Brazil. It does not have a large, displacement-induced anti-dam movement, a historically rooted set of active civil society committees at the basin level, or anything akin to Brazil's mixed-membership National Water Resources Council.[97] On the other hand, South Africa has a much stronger and nationally organized anti-marketization movement and a more aggressive set of recent international commitments, both of which are potentially important sites of struggle. The goal here is to create a discussion parallel to that of the Brazilian case in terms of the sites of norm inscription and normative struggle, while finding those sites wherever they may be in the specific South African context. As in the Brazilian case, the discussion begins with the water core of the state and moves outward from there.

The Custodial State: DWAF in the New Framework

In Brazil, the legal and policy dimensions of water reform proceeded in parallel with reorganization of the state apparatus for water governance: forming a water resources secretariat, cleaving off a new national water agency outside the ministerial line of authority, and sorting out constitutionally imposed distinctions between water resource management and environmental protection. This made the state apparatus itself a key site at which to examine the inscription of new water-related norms. South Africa presents a very different pattern in the sense that DWAF, a relatively powerful and autonomous ministry, survived the transition intact. It faced no significant bureaucratic challenges or turf battles with other agencies.[98] Indeed, DWAF emerged from the reforms with much stronger powers for water resources management than either Brazil's National Water Agency or Water Resources Secretariat. The water normalization of the state has been a matter of changing the historical character of a well-established, embedded institutional setting rather than building a new one from scratch.

In its first National Water Strategy, which was mandated by the National Water Act and made public in draft form in 2002, DWAF framed its purpose explicitly as that of integrated water resources management. The question is not whether the language, rhetoric, and symbolism of IWRM are invoked—as indicated in chapter 5, they virtually always are in contemporary water discussions—but rather, what specific meaning is given to the concept in practice. As discussed previously, the framing of water management as a holistic, knowledge-intensive, planning-intensive process was already well accepted by DWAF by the onset of the mid-1990s reforms; indeed, many of these themes appeared in South Africa well before they became the international conventional wisdom. The idea of the catchment as the central unit of water management has a long history in South Africa, with efforts to map the entire country at the catchment and subcatchment level already well under way by the time the language of basin-level management became fashionable at the global level. The idea of ecological requirements and "blue water" uses also appeared quite early. Work on the ecological effects of river pollution dates to the 1940s, and DWAF's first release of water from a dam for ecological purposes took place in 1970. DWAF officials

were talking about and attempting to estimate in-stream flow requirements by the 1980s; one leading DWAF official published a paper in
1983 on the environmental constraints on future water development.[99]
This early attention would evolve into the concept of the ecological
Reserve, which DWAF has always conceived of as a specifiable amount
of water.[100]

Water marketization norms have also gained a strong foothold within
DWAF during the reform process. The recent National Water Resource
Strategy stresses DWAF's mandate to promote efficient and effective
use of water, establishes pricing policies based on a rate of return on
assets approach to state-financed water resource development, establishes the opportunity cost of water as the basis for setting administratively determined water charges, and promises regulations on the
permitting of water trading.[101] On the other hand, there has been a
notable reluctance to challenge "existing lawful uses" derived from past
riparian practices, which remain the single biggest impediment to allocating water to its highest market-value uses.

DWAF has been much slower to move on the participatory dimensions of water management, reflecting many of the same debates over
the meaning of participation sketched at the international level in chapter
5. Looking back during the reform period on its apartheid-era performance, DWAF characterized its own history as that of "an inaccessible
centralized bureaucracy in which the needs of the people on the ground,
particularly the black majority, were not taken into account."[102] The
drive for water reform was rhetorically infused with the idea of the state
as the custodian of the public trust. This meant that DWAF felt pressures
not only to move from a narrower paradigm of water supply to a
broader one of water resource management, but also to shift the focus
from a narrow set of well-connected water users to a broader set of societal interests.

The pull of participatory norms can be seen clearly. DWAF officials
stress that dividing the country's water management into nineteen water
areas, each with its own catchment management agency, is in fact a compromise between the technical understanding of what constitutes a catchment and a range of administrative and political considerations. One

DWAF official described CMAs as a technical concept historically that was evolving into a social concept. There remains within DWAF great wariness, however, in turning over too much decision-making authority to the CMAs, given their unwieldy size, their sometimes poor fit with the underlying geography and ecology of water, and their potential to be dominated by a few major users. More hope is invested in the smaller-scale water user associations, which are becoming functional more quickly. These bodies are typically an offshoot of now-obsolete organs such as irrigation boards or subterranean water control boards; historically, they have been highly limited channels of participation at best. One senior DWAF official who played an important role in drafting the National Water Resource Strategy suggested that "consultation" was a better term to describe current DWAF practice. Input is welcomed and the need for dialogue is accepted, but decision making remains firmly in DWAF's grasp. The National Water Resources Strategy reflects this orientation, stressing that the Minister of Water Affairs and Forestry promotes the "empowerment" of the various mixed-membership water management institutions by "delegating and assigning powers and duties to them."[103]

Also uneven has been the incorporation in DWAF practice of some of the core norms of interstate water diplomacy. As discussed later, since the early 1990s South Africa has been entering into an ambitiously expanding set of international water commitments. DWAF's activities in giving meaning at the agency level to emergent norms of interstate water diplomacy can be described as rhetorically correct but institutionally superficial. Its international directorate has only twenty-three staff members, despite being the designated organ for managing the vast Lesotho Highlands project (discussed later) and South Africa's other international water commitments. Formally, the directorate's purpose is to promote joint projects and foster DWAF's external relations (it is also charged with promoting dam safety). In practice, the directorate describes its purpose in international settings such as the Komati Basin Water Authority as "protect[ing] South Africa's interests."[104] The thirty-five-page draft summary of the proposed National Water Resources Strategy limited its discussion of DWAF's international activities and responsibilities to a bulleted listing of South Africa's participation in shared-basin management institutions and a few cursory paragraphs on SADC and international technical exchanges. This bureaucratic underemphasis contrasts with the great emphasis that senior-level officials such as Minister Asmal, his successor Ronnie Kasrils, and Director-General Mike Muller have given to South Africa's international relations, primarily via less narrowly intersovereign channels such as the World Commission on Dams and the World Water Forum meetings.

Judicial Review: The Framing of Water Rights

Prior to the end of apartheid, the principal role of the South African courts in the water sphere was to validate the expansion of the state's power to allocate water. That expansion left the water courts with what the 1986 red book described as "only a minor role in the administration of the [Republic of South Africa's] water resources."[105] The transition to the new constitution led to several court rulings that framed the meaning of new water-related rights in more specific terms. As discussed previously, these include rulings strengthening public participation in the state's permitting processes, balancing claims for restitution and the defense of property rights, and opening the door to treating the denial of water rights as an illegal form of eviction from the land.

To date, the main area of impact of court decisions has been in framing the rights of the poor to a minimum adequate water supply. In a ruling that emphasized "substantive" as opposed to merely "formal" equality, the Constitutional Court determined in *City Council of Pretoria v. Walker* that different systems of charging for water did not constitute unfair discrimination, in light of the historically inferior service afforded to blacks and the temporary nature of the difference as equal service levels were being phased in.[106] In *Grootboom v. Oostenberg Municipality and Others*, the Cape Supreme Court ruled that a group of evicted squatters had certain rights to temporary shelter (under the children's rights provisions of the constitution), including a regular supply of water.[107] According to Johann Mettler and colleagues, a consistent theme running through these rulings is that of human dignity and basic human needs:

The Court consistently places human dignity at the centre of the test [sic] whether or not state action is reasonable: "human beings are required to be treated as human beings." The deprivation of a basic supply of water removes the inherent dignity of people: it strips an individual of the possibility to live a dignified life and poses serious health risks.[108]

The courts have not always been clear as to the specifics, however. In *Residents of Bon Vista Mansions v. Southern Metropolitan Local Council*, the high court ruled that disconnection could be construed as "a prima facie breach of the State's duty to respect the right of access to water."[109] But in *Manquele v. Durban Transitional Metropolitan Council*, the high court allowed the disconnection of a user who had exceeded the basic, free-of-charge water allotment.[110] Moreover, the Constitutional Court has emphasized the constitution's clauses on "progressive realization" and "within available resources" as qualifications of the absolute nature of the socioeconomic rights in Sections 26 and 27. According to the court,

What is apparent from these provisions is that the obligations imposed on the State by [sections] 26 and 27 in regard to access to housing, health care, food, water and social security are dependent upon the resources available for such purposes, and that the corresponding rights themselves are limited by reason of the lack of resources.[111]

And

The State is not obliged to go beyond available resources or to realize these rights immediately.[112]

As a result, the central struggles are to define how slowly is too slowly (that is, the rate at which progressive improvement must be realized) and how little is too little (that is, the amount of water adequate for basic human needs).

The courts have also been less than clear on the balance of responsibilities among federal, provincial, and local governments. As Mettler and colleagues observe, "The Constitution contains an intricate 'division of responsibilities' over the three spheres of government. . . . In *Grootboom*, the Court stayed away from delineating the responsibilities. Instead, it placed the emphasis on co-operative government."[113]

With the move toward privatization of water service, the imposition of enforceable obligations on private actors is emerging as an important area of judicial decision making. As Danwood Chirwa observes,

Although still rudimentary, international law, certain municipal legal systems and the South African Constitution suggest that the obligations of non-state actors for socio-economic rights have both negative and positive aspects. In principle, there is no socio-economic right that can be said to bind the state only. All private actors are enjoined, at the very minimum, to respect socio-economic rights. The difficulty, however, lies in distinguishing the levels of positive obligations among private actors considering that these actors are of different character and nature.[114]

Municipalities: Front Lines of the Marketization Struggle

Water supply and sanitation services are the responsibilities of local government. They are financed by a combination of annual grants from the national government to municipalities for basic services, user fees, local resources, and international aid. The quality of service and the range of coverage vary dramatically. Affluent communities enjoy high-quality household water service, while millions of South Africans still lack adequate drinking water and sanitation services.[115] Underserved communities are found primarily, but not exclusively, in rural areas, with the burden of the disparity falling disproportionately on women and children. Women often find themselves responsible for providing water within the household political economy; children suffer devastatingly high mortality rates in water-deprived areas.

Municipal water service has been an ongoing controversy on several levels, all of them an outgrowth of the enormous apartheid-era social deficit inherited by the new government in 1994. Critics have challenged the government's commitment and rate of progress in adding basic water service connections as well as the adequacy of the legal standard defining a connection: a community water tap within 200 m of a dwelling. DWAF estimated in the late 1990s that the Finance Ministry's austerity budget plan as part of the structural adjustment program would seriously hamper the Department's progress in expanding water supply and sanitation services. DWAF estimated that it would require an additional 1 percent of total federal budget expenditures over a seven-year period to meet the service delivery targets.[116]

The linked issues of water for the poor and privatization have been the main focal points of contention, conflict, and social activism around water services. Controversy over the price of water is an outgrowth of the tension between the constitutional right to water and the policy of full-cost pricing. The 1994 white paper on water supply and sanitation (not to be confused with the 1997 white paper on water policy) set the benchmark for fulfilling the basic right to water at the level of 25 liters per person per day, at a cartage distance no greater than 200 m. In February 1996, the cabinet decided that major users of water should pay the full cost of providing it.[117]

A 2002 national survey by the Municipal Services Project estimated that 10 million South Africans had experienced a water service cutoff at least once since 1994.[118] Water cutoffs have led to violent uprisings, as in Tafelsig in September 2001 when several hundred homes were forcibly disconnected.[119] A major outbreak of cholera was traced back to the installation of prepaid meters in Kwazulu, which left thousands unable to pay for water. (The meters require the use of purchased water cards and shut off when the card's funds are exhausted. Several of the meters also malfunctioned.) Local residents turned to polluted river water, which resulted in a cholera outbreak that ultimately affected 120,000 people and produced 265 deaths.

In the wake of the rising controversy, in 2000 DWAF adopted a new policy that allowed 6,000 liters per month of free water for poor households (the equivalent of 25 liters per person per day for a family of eight, or 50 liters for a family of four). The controversy has continued, focusing on the adequacy of the monthly threshold. The installation of prepaid meters has also been highly contentious and the meters are frequent targets for destruction.[120] Johannesburg Water's decision to begin installing prepaid meters in Soweto led to the formation of a coalition linking a local residents' committee, anti-privatization groups, environmental justice activists, the landless peoples' movement, and Jubilee South Africa.

Although full-cost recovery, prepaid meters, price increases, and other instruments of water marketization can be implemented by either public or private water service providers, privatization has emerged as a particular focal point of controversy. The Water Services Act makes local governments the default water service provider, but gives them the power to subcontract that responsibility. There are currently five private concessions or contracts for delivering water service in South Africa:

• The British multinational, Biwater, won a thirty-year concession in Nelspruit in 1999.

• Dolphin Coast, a community north of Durban in Kwazulu-Natal Province, signed a thirty-year concession in 1999 with the local affiliate of the French firm, Saur.

• Two Eastern Cape municipalities have long-term contracts with Water Services South Africa (WSSA), a Suez-Lyonnaise subsidiary. A third WSSA contract, in Nkonkobe, was nullified by the courts at the municipality's request in 2001. The context was a dispute over the level of fees, but the court ruling was based on illegalities in the contract's secretive negotiation process.

• In 2001 South Africa's largest city, Johannesburg, formed a private company (Johannesburg Water) in which the city is sole shareholder, and entered into a partnership with Suez to provide water service.

Opposition to privatization of water service has been part of the broader anti-privatization movement in South Africa. The South African Municipal Workers Union (SAMWU) has taken a strong stand against privatization of municipal services such as water and electricity. SAMWU charges that privatization initiatives in Johannesburg, Nelspruit, and the Dolphin Coast violate both the Water Services Act (which SAMWU interprets to define private service providers as a last resort), and a 1998 agreement between trade unions and local governments, which identified the public sector as the provider of first choice.[121] In addition to its opposition to privatization, SAMWU supports an expansion of the free basic water allocation from 25 to 75–100 liters per person per day and opposes prepaid meters.[122] SAMWU is an affiliate of Public Services International (PSI), a key node in the transnational anti-privatization network discussed in chapter 7.

The Congress of South African Trade Unions (COSATU), of which SAMWU is an affiliate, has also taken a strongly anti-marketization approach on water. COSATU supported the principle of cross-subsidization in pricing policy and opposed tradable water rights during the debate over the National Water Act.[123] During debate on the Water Services Act, COSATU opposed the "seeming reliance on the private sector's role in water delivery."[124] COSATU and SAMWU mobilized demonstrators to protest the signing of the Dolphin Coast concession, which they felt violated both the "public first" agreement they had with the government and the specific details of labor guarantees they had negotiated.[125]

In the context of great social pressure to expand water services and the financial constraints of the neoliberal austerity program, the legally codified "partnership" between national and local authorities has also been a source of dispute. DWAF has been critical of the capacity and actions of many local jurisdictions. For their part, local jurisdictions have complained that they have been assigned a function without adequate resources and capacity to perform it. In a review of progress toward the realization of economic and social rights, the South African Human Rights Commission found in 1998 that

> There is clearly an urgent need for on-going measures to build the resources and institutional capacity of local government to fulfill their critical role in water service delivery.... Moreover, it is essential that synergy is created between national goals and strategies to achieve the right to water and those existing at provincial and local levels.[126]

The cabinet approved a new strategic framework for water services in 2003, which devolved full responsibility onto municipalities, with the DWAF's role defined as one of policy, support, and regulation rather than direct provision of service.[127]

Marketization is also altering the status and function of South Africa's fifteen water boards, which serve as purifiers of "raw" water and providers of bulk water to industrial users and domestic distributors (such as municipalities or their subcontractors). The water boards are nominally nonprofit entities, but in the new South African water framework, they operate according to an increasingly commercialized logic. They are forced to be largely self-funding through water fees for both operations and capital improvements. Industry observers view private providers as potential direct competitors, particularly to the smaller water boards.

Dam Construction and Interbasin Transfer Schemes: Indirect Channels

South Africa's peculiar water needs have moved it along a path of water engineering and technological development very different from that in Brazil. South Africa has built more than 500 large dams as well as thousands of smaller "farm dams." As Davies and Day point out, most South African dams are designed for the single, simple purpose of trapping and holding water until it is needed for agricultural or municipal use. The authors report that as of the late 1990s not one large dam in South Africa had been built with multilevel offtake points; most have no means of releasing water downstream other than flooding; and prior to 1992, only two had fish passes or ladders for migratory fish species.[128] On the other hand, the poor fit between water flows and the location of major population and industrial centers has made South Africa "one of the world leaders in the field of [interbasin water transfer] technology."[129]

Dam construction and water engineering projects within South Africa have displaced far fewer people than they have in Brazil. The main activity within the country's borders has been to develop projects that move water to people, rather than moving people away from water development projects. Despite protests tied to specific dam projects, there is nothing in South Africa comparable to Brazil's large, aggressive, and nationally linked displaced-peoples' movement.[130] As Sidney Tarrow and other social movement theorists have pointed out, the emergence of effective transnational social movements requires integration into existing domestic social networks.[131] As Sanjeev Khagram concludes, "Outcomes are most likely to be altered when domestic communities and social movements capable of generating sustained mass mobilization and linked to transnational advocacy efforts contest these projects."[132] The absence of such broadly based mobilization in South Africa would lead one to expect that anti-dam protest would be a less robust channel for the transmission and inscription of norms in this case.

Moreover, state borders retain some relevance in shaping the pattern of social mobilization. One reason for limited anti-dam mobilization is that South Africa's most controversial dam-building scheme has taken place outside its borders. The Lesotho Highlands scheme delivers water to South Africa from neighboring Lesotho, a tiny mountainous country surrounded entirely by South Africa. In 1986 the two governments signed the Lesotho Highlands Water Project Treaty, committing them to complete the first two of the envisioned four phases. The agreement came shortly after a military coup d'etat against the sitting Lesotho government, which was rumored to have been instigated by South Africa; South

Africa insisted on linking the deal to a security pact.[133] The project envisioned five large dams to trap water in Lesotho and more than 100 km of mountain tunnels to deliver 70 m^3 of water per second to South Africa's greater Johannesburg region (Gauteng Province).

The centerpiece of phase IA is the 185-m Katse Dam on the Malibamatso River, as well as more than 80 km of transfer tunnels to deliver water to South Africa's Ash River. The gates of the Katse Dam closed in 1995; the project began delivering water in 1998 and hydropower in 1999. Phase IB, which includes the 145-m Mohale Dam and an additional 32 km of tunnels to link the two dam reservoirs, is under way. The remaining phases of the project have been cast into doubt by the ecological, financial, and sociopolitical controversies surrounding the project and by South Africa's decreased projections for water demand.[134] Cost estimates, which are sensitive to projected completion dates, typically run from $5 to 10 billion.[135] The high price tag means high prices for water that is not needed nearly as soon as had been projected, even in the absence of available demand management practices. Also, from its start the project has been dogged by charges of poor planning, corruption, and incompetence. Environmental impact and in-stream flow assessments were not conducted before the project began. (A quickly done and shoddy environmental impact statement was commissioned only after construction had begun.)[136] In June 2002, a Lesotho court convicted the chief executive of the project of fraud and bribe-taking from several international firms; in August 2003, a judgment was reached against the first of several international firms to be indicted, Acres International of Canada.

The project has become one of the highest-profile campaigns of the international anti-dam movement, with the South African government drawn into the international human rights and ecological controversies because it is the chief financier and water beneficiary. Nevertheless, while there have been some attempts to promote cross-border solidarity with project opponents in Lesotho, domestic opposition within South Africa has centered mainly on the project's impact on water costs. In Lesotho, in contrast, the project has stimulated strong local opposition. International Rivers Network alleges that the first phases of the project have displaced more than 30,000 rural people from their homes, farms, lands, and livelihoods.[137] Matlosa estimates that phase IA alone affected 3,000 households or 18,000 people, with only a small fraction resettled.[138] Widespread grievances among affected people have forced revisions to the resettlement package without resolving the issues involved; late in 2001 more than 2,000 protesters assembled at the project sites to demand fair compensation and the delivery of promised development benefits.[139] Striking workers at the project sites have clashed violently with security forces, leaving several dead or wounded after one episode in 1996. Violence triggered by charges of electoral fraud in 1998 led to a SADC-sanctioned military intervention by forces from South Africa and Botswana, at the request of the country's besieged government. One of the first acts of the 600-person force was to secure the Katse Dam.

A more robust channel for normative exchange around dams has been the World Commission on Dams (chapter 6). The WCD's emphasis on stakeholder participation and public comment made South Africa a hub for regional activities related to the commission and produced a vigorous domestic debate about dams and democracy.

A South African multistakeholder initiative on the WCD report was established before the release of the report. The forum for the initiative, which includes a wide array of stakeholders, has met regularly following the report's release, and soon began a scoping process to take "the WCD guidelines further in the South African context."[140] The coordinating committee includes environmental and human rights organizations, private sector firms, the Development Bank of Southern Africa, DWAF, Rand Water (the bulk water supplier to the greater Johannesburg area), and the Water Research Commission. The coordinating committee's final scoping report, released one year after the WCD report, concluded that "The key message from the WCD is that *public acceptance of key decisions is essential for equitable and sustainable water and energy resources development.*"[141]

One striking result of the scoping process is the emphasis on procedural and normative controversies rather than substantive ones. Forum participants identified controversies over participation in the process and the weighting of key values as the key debating points, rather than the substantive controversies of how to finance dams, how to set the ecological reserve, whether to implement a construction moratorium, or how to share the development benefits of dams (table 9.3).

Table 9.3
Key debating points of the South African Multistakeholder Forum on the WCD Report

Debating point	Number of forum participants ranking that point among top five key debating points
Are social and environmental issues given equal weight when assessing water development options? How should this be improved?	42
What does stakeholder involvement mean in South Africa? How should the rights-and-risks method of identifying stakeholders be used?	39
When can it be said that public acceptance is demonstrated?	38
How should the WCD priorities and principles be carried forward into the New Partnership for Africa's Development (NEPAD)?	26
How widely should the benefits be shared for a dam development?	25
Are specific legally binding agreements needed for project-specific technical, social, and environmental commitments? How should compliance be monitored?	25
How are strategic issues balanced against local needs during comprehensive assessment of options?	24
What is the optimal process for setting the Reserve so that it incorporates WCD principles?	24
Should a moratorium be placed on dam construction? Until what conditions are met? Or should we ensure that committed steps are adhered to?	22
Will the establishment of an independent regulator promote or detract from compliance?	22
How should the parameters of the process to audit existing dams be defined?	20
What needs to be done to address the distortions in financing mechanisms favoring large dams over other options?	19
Who pays for the ecological reserve?	17

Source: South African Multi-stakeholder Initiative on the World Commission on Dams 2002, 49.

The organizational presence of the WCD in Cape Town also stimulated initiatives by South African environmental and human rights NGOs, as well as regional ties. In 1999 Southern African NGOs and IRN organized hearings for communities affected by large dams in Cape Town. The two-day meeting, attended by WCD staff and several prominent South African officials, included testimonials from representatives of the Tonga, Zulu, Basotho, Himba, Swazi, Xhosa, and Tswana peoples.[142]

The WCD report and associated processes have not ended dam-related conflict in South Africa, but they have channeled it in the sense that the WCD guidelines have become an important symbolic benchmark of legitimacy. The debate over the planned Skuifraam Dam on the Berg River, which is meant to enhance Cape Town's municipal water supply, illustrates this process. DWAF has extolled the project's planning and approval process as a model of participatory practice that "broadly complied with the WCD guidelines," even as it has criticized those guidelines for their rigidity, complexity, overlap, and insensitivity to local conditions.[143] The debate between DWAF and opponents of the dam has centered on whether the WCD guidelines have been effectively implemented in the process of conceiving and approving the dam.[144]

South Africa, International Water Law and Regional Diplomacy: A Two-Way Flow of Norms

South Africa shares four major river systems with neighboring states (figure 9.2). The Orange River enters South Africa from the mountain kingdom of Lesotho (where it is known as the Senqu) and in its lower reaches forms part of South Africa's border with Namibia. South Africa is an upstream riparian in the other three shared basins. The Limpopo forms part of the border with Botswana and Zimbabwe with Mozambique as the downstream riparian state, and the Inkomati and Maputo systems are both shared with Swaziland and Mozambique.

Table 9.4 summarizes South Africa's international river agreements with neighboring states prior to the end of apartheid. A few of the accords involve the establishment of permanent technical commissions; most are tied to specific damming or diversion projects. Several bilateral river agreements were reached with colonial Portugal. In terms of

Table 9.4
South African international river agreements: apartheid and preapartheid period

Agreement	Year	Parties
Agreement between South Africa and Portugal regulating the use of the water of the Cunene River	1926	Portugal, South Africa
Exchange of notes ... respecting the boundary between the mandated territory of South Africa and Angola	1931	Portugal, South Africa
Agreement between the government of the Republic of South Africa and the government of Portugal in regard to rivers of mutual interest and the Cunene Scheme	1964	Portugal, South Africa (Swaziland acceded 1967)
Agreement between South Africa and Portugal related to hydropower development on the Zambesi River	1967	Portugal, South Africa
Agreement between the government of the Republic of South Africa and the government of Portugal in regard to the first phase of development of the water resources of the Kunene River Basin, Lisbon, January 21, 1969	1969	Portugal, South Africa
Agreement between the government of the Republic of South Africa, the government of the Kingdom of Swaziland and the government of the People's Republic of Mozambique relative to the establishment of a tripartite permanent technical committee. Signed at Pretoria, February 17, 1983	1983	South Africa, Swaziland, Mozambique
Agreement between the governments of the Republic of Portugal, the People's Republic of Mozambique, and the Republic of South Africa relative to the Cahora Bassa project at Cape Town, May 2, 1984	1984	Portugal, Mozambique, Swaziland
Treaty on the Lesotho Highlands water project between the government of the kingdom of Lesotho and the government of the Republic of South Africa signed at Maseru, October 24, 1986	1986	Lesotho, South Africa
Agreement on the Inkomati River Basin joint study signed at the tripartite meeting of ministers responsible for water affairs ("Piggs Peak" agreement)	1991	South Africa, Mozambique, Swaziland

Table 9.4
(continued)

Agreement	Year	Parties
Treaty on the establishment and functioning of the joint water commission between the government of the Kingdom of Swaziland and the government of the Republic of South Africa	1992	South Africa, Swaziland
Treaty on development and utilization of the water resources of the Komati River Basin between the Kingdom of Swaziland and the government of the Republic of South Africa	1992	South Africa, Swaziland
Agreement between the government of the Republic of Namibia and the government of the Republic of South Africa on the establishment of a permanent water commission signed at Noordoewer, September 14, 1992	1992	Namibia, South Africa

Source: Compiled by author.

watershed impact, the most consequential agreement is the 1986 Lesotho Highlands accord, given the massive scope of that project.

In addition to the agreements listed in table 9.4, an unusual potential entry point for international norms emerged at the height of apartheid, with the effort to legitimize the apartheid-era "homelands" intended for South Africa's black majority. The Department of Water Affairs began to describe rivers that flowed between nominally white South Africa and the homelands as international watercourses. As stated in the 1986 red book:

In parts of the [Republic of South Africa] that lie within international drainage basins or watercourse systems, the use of water is also subject to requirements relating to the international uses of water. With the attainment over the past decade of self-government by the national states and independence by the TBVC states [Transkei, Bophuthatswana, Venda, and Ciskei] within the borders of what was formerly the RSA, the number of international drainage basins has increased greatly. Water resource development and management will be more demanding in future because of the additional legal and political considerations.[145]

In theory, these attempts to formalize the geography of apartheid created two potential entry points for international water principles: the embrace of the 1966 Helsinki Rules as the relevant body of soft international law, and the creation of formal basin commissions joining the parties in these artificially "international" basins. In practice, however, the basin commissions had little meaning for water management, which continued to be governed by the logic of apartheid. They were swept away with the end of apartheid and the water law reform of the 1990s. Nor did the formal embrace of the Helsinki Rules have a tangible impact; the principal interpretation was that they created no meaningful constraints and allowed wide latitude for bargaining among the parties to determine the use of shared watercourses.

The 1990s saw a dramatic upsurge in South Africa's international river diplomacy (table 9.5), with the focus shifting to the creation of joint water commissions with neighboring states that included Swaziland (1992), Namibia (1992), Mozambique (1996), and the Orange-Senqu riparian states Namibia, Lesotho, and Botswana (2000). This spike in diplomacy predates the rise of the ANC to power in 1994 but was accelerated by that transition. The ANC came to power intent on repairing the heavy damage to regional relations during the apartheid era, and with a specific eye on shared water resources as one element of broader regional cooperation. There was also a clear sense at that time that South Africa would require substantial water from beyond its borders in the future, necessitating stable rules for shared governance of rivers.[146]

The process of regional reconnection via water diplomacy has not always been easy. The tripartite Inkomaputo accord with Mozambique and Swaziland announced at the 2002 World Summit on Sustainable Development took four years to negotiate rather than the anticipated one year. What was envisioned as a two-year study on the Komati in the early 1990s ended up requiring a decade.

The most direct potential entry point for international norms surrounding shared river basins came with South Africa's entry into the Southern African Development Community in 1994. SADC originated in 1980 as the Southern African Development Coordination Conference (SADCC), essentially an alliance of the "frontline" states seeking to reduce their economic dependence on apartheid South Africa. The 1992 Windhoek Treaty transformed SADCC into the Southern African Development Community, with an emphasis on trade, development, cooperation, and economic integration as a response to global economic change,

Table 9.5
Recent South African international river agreements

Agreement	Year	Parties
Limpopo River Basin Commission	2003	South Africa, Botswana, Zimbabwe, Mozambique
Tripartite interim agreement between the Republic of Mozambique and the Republic of South Africa and the Kingdom of Swaziland for cooperation on the protection and sustainable utilization of the water resources of the Incomati and Maputo watercourses	2002	Mozambique, Swaziland, South Africa
Orange-Senqu River Commission	2000	Botswana, Lesotho, Namibia, South Africa
Revised protocol on shared watercourse systems in the Southern African Development Community	2000	Angola, Botswana, Democratic Republic Of Congo, Lesotho, Malawi, Mozambique, Namibia, South Africa, Swaziland, Tanzania, Zambia, Zimbabwe
Joint Water Commission Terms of Reference	1996	Mozambique, South Africa
Protocol on shared watercourse systems in the Southern African Development Community region signed at Johannesburg August 28, 1995	1995	Angola, Botswana, Lesotho, Malawi, Mozambique, Namibia, South Africa, Swaziland, Tanzania, Zambia, Zimbabwe
Treaty on Walvis Bay	1994	Namibia, South Africa

Source: Compiled by author.

and the Mandela government quickly brought South Africa into the new institution.[147] South Africa's early forays within SADC were both cautiously extended and cautiously received, with all parties sensitive to the country's regional economic power and hegemonic potential. There have been tensions around SADC institutional arrangements and South African economic power.[148]

Water—more specifically, the region's many shared river basins—has been a central theme of SADC cooperative initiatives. Larry Swatuk attributes this to an emerging regional vision of sustainable economic development that blends elements of coordinated resource management, ecotourism, and external neoliberal pressures.[149] The SADC Protocol on Shared Watercourse Systems seeks to "foster closer cooperation for judicious, sustainable and co-ordinated management, protection and utilisation of shared watercourses and advance the SADC agenda of regional integration and poverty alleviation."[150] The protocol was signed in 1995, entered into force in 1998, and was amended in 2000 to address several concerns of member states. The 2000 amendments also reconciled several inconsistencies with the 1997 UN Watercourses Convention (chapter 4). According to Phera Ramoeli, SADC's water sector coordinator, the accord's main principles include respect for member states' sovereignty, equitable use, a "proper balance" between environment and development, joint projects, information sharing, and prior notification.[151]

Conflicting national interests and institutional inconsistencies complicate the challenge of reconciling the existing patchwork of international arrangements with the comprehensive vision of the SADC protocol. For example, the four countries of the Limpopo River Basin have articulated different priorities for the Limpopo Basin Permanent Technical Committee (LBPTC), formed in a 1986 agreement among the basin states. According to a 2002 SADC appraisal of the basin, "Botswana is interested in water use control in order to ensure water use efficiency; South Africa is interested in the upliftment of its marginalised people; Zimbabwe is interested in developing irrigation and agriculture; and Mozambique is interested in flood control."[152] The report further indicates that

The LBPTC does not yet have a permanent secretariat, a consolidated budget and regular meetings. And it is not clear how the LBPTC will work towards achieving the objectives of the Protocol on Shared Watercourses, which should provide a framework upon which institutions such as the LBPTC are built. Plans to turn the committee into a commission with a full time secretariat, an operational budget and with the mandate to manage, coordinate and monitor social, ecological and economic activities of the Limpopo basin are plausible. The objectives and mandate of the LBPTC need to be realigned so that they are supportive of the SADC Protocol on Shared Watercourses.

Moreover, it is not clear how the LBPTC feeds into the institutional mechanisms responsible for the implementation of the Protocol.... Efforts to operationalize the LBPTC while commendable, have not received the zeal and urgency expected from member countries to address key issues afflicting the basin, especially in so far as they seek to address [integrated water resources management].[153]

Table 9.6 presents the content of several South African international basin agreements using the analyses described in chapter 4. As the table indicates, in the period prior to the 1997 UN Watercourses Convention and the 1995 SADC Protocol, consultation and peaceful resolution of disputes are the only principles invoked explicitly in a majority of the agreements.

More recently, South Africa has reached two new international agreements; formation of the Orange-Senqu River Commission with Botswana, Lesotho, and Namibia (2000) and the so-called Incomaputo accord (on the Inkomati and Maputo Rivers) with Swaziland and Mozambique in 2002.[154] The South African water minister touted the Orange-Senqu agreement's significance as the first accord since the revised SADC Protocol and described it as conforming to "the best international practice regarding the joint management of shared rivers."[155] The Incomaputo accord invokes the 1997 UN Watercourses Convention and explicitly articulates its core principles. Article 3 states general principles of sustainable, equitable, and reasonable use, prevention, and cooperation. Article 4 commits the parties to preventing, reducing, and controlling pollution; preventing, eliminating, mitigating, and controlling transboundary impacts; coordinating management plans and planned measures; establishing comparable monitoring systems; and exchanging information on water quality, quantity, and uses. Article 13 on transboundary impacts requires prior notification and consultation before undertaking actions with significant transboundary impacts. There are also provisions for peaceful resolution of disputes via consultation and

Table 9.6
Content of selected South African river agreements

Agreements	Komati tripartite committee agreement (1983)	Lesotho Highlands Treaty (1986)	Permanent water commission agreement (1992)	Komati permanent water commission agreement (1992)	Komati development and utilization agreement (1992)	Treaty on Walvis Bay (1994)
Parties	Mozambique, Swaziland, South Africa	Lesotho, South Africa	Namibia, South Africa	Swaziland, South Africa	Swaziland, South Africa	Namibia, South Africa
Participation by all watercourse states	x					x
Equitable use principle		x		x		
Obligation to avoid significant harm						
Sovereign equality as basis for cooperation				x		
Obligation to exchange information		x	x	x		
Obligation for consultation		x	x	x	x	x
Obligation for prior notification		x			x	
Environmental protection as an agreement goal		x	x	x		
Obligation to resolve disputes peacefully	x	x	x	x	x	

negotiations (Article 15) and an annex listing the intended development projects of each party for the period of the agreement. Sovereignty is not mentioned explicitly.

How will the recent trend of formalizing shared-basin principles translate into practice? The recent accords will be a strong test because the new water law gives international commitments priority and because there is a riparian state downstream of South Africa on every international river. The Orange-Senqu Commission (ORASECOM), for example, was formed largely at the behest of Namibia, the downstream riparian state. Turton describes ORASECOM as "probably the most complex [river basin organization] in Southern Africa, because it involves so many riparians, and existing, often highly elaborate bilateral schemes, without necessarily taking over jurisdiction of those schemes."[156] The unresolved question, of course, is the impact of the commission on development projects along the river, most notably the Lesotho Highlands project. Piet Heyns suggests that there is growing interest among South African water planners in tapping some of the country's eastern coastal rivers via interbasin water transfer schemes as an alternative to the currently stalled remaining phases of the Lesotho Highlands project.[157] It may be that the main path by which international norms will "swim upstream" into domestic practice is by blocking transnational water-tapping schemes in favor of purely domestic ones, particularly in light of the relatively weak social activism within South Africa against interbasin transfers, as discussed previously.

At the same time that international law may be emerging as a path to the South African domestic sphere, the reverse is also true, in the sense that the agreements represent a way for the changing character of South African water law, policy, and practice to reach outward via the country's water relations with neighboring states. DWAF's 1997 white paper stressed the goal of projecting emerging domestic water principles into regional water relations: "The objective in relation to our neighbors is the same as it is within South Africa's borders, to ensure that we adjust to the pressures and demands of the future through co-operation, not conflict, in harmony with the needs of our common developmental goals and the protection of our environment."[158]

The IWRM-grounded character of the reforms can be seen in the path to international agreement. In the case of the Incomaputo accord, South Africa and Swaziland had previously reached agreements related to development projects (the Driekoppies and Maguga Dams). Mozambique, the downstream riparian, depends on international rivers for more than half of its surface water supplies. Mozambique joined the basin management regime when the other parties agreed in 1999 to conduct a study on current water uses and water availability in the Incomati.[159] According to Turton and Quinn, another force spurring cooperation was success in cooperative transboundary research in Kruger and Limpopo National Parks on the South Africa-Mozambique border, which led the Swedish government to fund trilateral cooperative research and analysis on the Incomati.[160] More generally, South Africa's international cooperative initiatives bear a strong paradigmatic stamp of IWRM. The draft National Water Resource Strategy foresees a diplomatic route in which joint basin studies lead to comprehensive agreements and management plans for the Orange, Limpopo, Incomati, and Maputo in the period 2003–2010.[161]

Conclusion: The Struggle for Social Citizenship

South African water law, policy, and practice in the postapartheid period reveal the presence of a somewhat different mix of global protonorms than seen in the Brazilian case. Norms of integrated water resources management have exerted a strong influence in both countries, at least when one is in close proximity to the water apparatus of the state. However, South Africa's version of integrated water resources management is somewhat more technocratic and less participatory than in Brazil. Norms of interstate diplomacy have also translated differently: being a good water neighbor, or at least a better one than was historically the case, has played a more tangible role in shaping water governance in South Africa than in Brazil. The sources of contentious environmental politics are also different. Water marketization and its problems have created a greater level of controversy and resistance in South Africa than in Brazil; water infrastructure projects, a lesser level.

To some extent, these differences lie in the mix of the transnational channels available for normative influence. The World Bank has played an extensive role intellectually in South Africa, but is less engaged financially there than in Brazil. Despite the close links to the World Commission on Dams, the less ambitious scale of dam construction projects than in Brazil (as well as the exporting of the most dramatic controversies to Lesotho) has made South Africa less fertile ground for the development of norms of watershed democracy. South Africa's active regional water diplomacy and the stronger investment presence of water multinationals have enhanced the significance of those particular channels.

More fundamentally, even if normative influences were able to flow through the same transnational channels, they would encounter very different domestic contexts. South Africa emerged from its political transition with a more intact water bureaucracy, a less robust network of organized civil society groups, a stronger trade union movement, and a governing regime with substantially greater popular legitimacy than in Brazil.

Despite these differences, the South African case reflects many of the patterns seen in Brazil. IWRM norms are strong within the national bureaucratic organs of the state (in this case, DWAF), but fade rapidly in salience as one moves from the state to the half dozen key sites of the institutionalization of water norms in society. There are substantial limits to the capacity of diplomatically channeled norms to "swim upstream" and exert domestic influences. A nonincremental change in policy yielded a framework national water law that incorporated norms legitimized in international policy circles, but scratching below the surface, one finds that the precursors of those norms sometimes have their own history of domestic development that predates their arrival at the international level.

The South African case also matches the Brazilian case in shedding light on how norms are institutionalized. As in Brazil, there are at least a half-dozen important sites where various forms of water "normalization" are taking place. In some of these settings, such as shared river basins or transnational stakeholder dialogues, transnational agents and influences are directly present and immediately felt. In others, such as the South African legal system, a predominantly domestic logic of appropriateness prevails, but that logic is being forced to respond to a set of increasingly transnational processes (in the case of the courts, the tension between human rights advocacy and neoliberal constraints on access to resources). Speaking of South Africa or Brazil as a leader or laggard in norm implementation has little meaning without reference to this complex, multidimensional geography of normative change.

Perhaps most important, in South Africa as in Brazil we see that controversies over how to value water and who may participate in its governance have emerged as the prime forces for creating new water-related practices and relationships. As Jacklyn Cock and others have pointed out, perhaps the most consequential form of social activism in South Africa today is the struggle of the poor majority for "social citizenship" in the realms of clean water, electricity, public health, and other survival and livelihood considerations in the face of the state's neoliberal inclinations and policy orientations.[162] Compared with Brazil, the struggle between water citizenship and water marketization is centered on a different arena (community water supplies rather than river basins) and involves controversies for which the normalization of transnational contention is at a less advanced stage (privatization of water service rather than water infrastructure projects). Nonetheless, that struggle remains the principal force for the development of a new normative framework for water.

10

Institution Building as the Social Embedding of Political Struggle

Men's evil manners live in brass; their virtues we write in water.
—Shakespeare, *King Henry VIII*

I believe in getting into hot water; it keeps you clean.
—G. K. Chesterton

The Limits of Conventional Institutions and the Emergence of Transnational Contentious Water Politics

Policies, laws, and practices related to water, rivers, watersheds, and freshwater ecosystems have been pushed and pulled simultaneously by several incongruous, even contradictory, forces: the international law of shared watercourses, marked by a sovereign rights and responsibilities approach; neoliberal structural adjustment, with its attendant values of privatization, marketization, and commoditization; elite networking among water policy experts, who seek to elevate techno-rational norms of integrated water resources management; and increasingly transnational activism for the rights of local communities, with attendant norms of human rights, grassroots democracy, and the preservation of local cultures and ecosystems.

These diverse influences on the governance of water share some important features. First, each has been thoroughly transnationalized. Second, each is sufficiently well embedded in important spaces of international life to constitute a set of protonorms bidding to govern, shape, influence, and "normalize" water practices around the world. They share a third feature as well; none has generated a dominant normative frame governing watershed practices. To the extent that watershed governance is being normalized across national boundaries, that process is taking place at the intersection of these forces.

As Martha Finnemore and Kathryn Sikkink have pointed out, new norms do not emerge in a vacuum; rather, they replace existing ones.[1] Certainly that has been the case with water. Each of the trajectories of normative development and institutionalization sketched in this book is in one way or another a response to a fading era of pushing rivers around, with its understanding of water as a gift from nature that is problematic only when it is tapped at less than the maximum extent allowed by human ingenuity.

Water continues to be a source of normative tumult in world politics. Activists opposing the construction of large dams continue to press the World Bank, donor governments, and dam-building firms. Water privatization remained a contentious question within the negotiations on trade in services and was a prominent theme at the 2004 World Social Forum in Mumbai, India. Diplomacy and expertise also continue to press forward in the search for water governance frameworks. In 2003, UNESCO's World Water Assessment Programme released the first *World Water Development Report*, which proclaimed a world water crisis rooted in ineffective water management.[2] Diplomats continued with the difficult and protracted multilateral negotiations to create a framework of interstate governance for the Nile River Basin. Protonorms of diplomacy, expertise, activism, and neoliberal adjustment—and their advocates—were all on prominent display at the 2003 World Water Forum in Kyoto.

The development of new water norms has not followed the familiar pattern of formation of an international regime, in which a dominant normative construct comes to the fore via some combination of interstate diplomacy, the moral pressure of advocacy groups, and the epistemological triumphs of the wielders of knowledge power in the service of a particular framing of the problem. Instead, we have seen several parallel, distinct trajectories of normative development, rooted in diplomacy, technical and administrative expertise, neoliberal economic adjustment, and social activism. If we understand governance as the performance of governing functions—including the mobilization of resources, the authorization of official knowledge, the framing of policy, and the setting of standards—then all four of the normative trajectories around water discussed in this book are at least nascent governing institutions. As a result, those who govern water, rivers, watersheds, and freshwater ecosystems find themselves at the intersection of several different and frequently contradictory normative pulls and pressures.

These multiple, parallel processes of norm formation epitomize the contrasting paradigms of global environmental governance sketched in chapter 1. If we view the problem as one of water spilling outside of established national borders, the focal points of institution building have been interstate bargaining at the global-framework and river-basin levels. Within this conventional construction of a problem, the foundational norms remain sovereign territoriality, statist authority, and stabilized knowledge.

The interstate regime approach has not effectively institutionalized a response to the cumulative toll on the world's rivers. Diplomacy has produced a stalled global framework convention that skirts the central political conflicts around shared rivers and a modest set of basin-level accords that are demonstrably not converging on a global normative framework. Moreover, these weak forays into institution building do not speak to most of the world's watersheds and freshwater ecosystems, which lie either in international basins not covered by any agreement, or outside the main channels of international basins entirely. There is some evidence of normative institutional development in the diplomatic sphere, as in the principle of preventing significant harm to other riparian states and the growing practice of creating international river basin commissions. However, for the most part, damming, diverting, draining, and dumping have resisted the controlling efforts of interstate bargaining.

Water expertise, based on a fundamentally different normative orientation than water diplomacy, has also fostered international institution building. The primary engine for this has been the emergence and growing influence of an interlinked set of transnational networks of water experts. Beyond the confines of formal diplomacy, these networks exercise and channel power through knowledge-based advocacy. Grounded in a technically expert, rationalist understanding of the problem of water, expert networks have put into play a rhetorically powerful, all-encompassing concept of integrated water resources management.

IWRM and its network advocates move beyond the conventional meta-normative position of the regime paradigm, promoting a more transterritorial understanding of water as a global problem and legitimizing participatory systems that begin to devolve authority away from states.

As a cognitive and rhetorical force, water expertise has surpassed water diplomacy as a driver of institution building. Networks of experts have redefined the conceptual map for thinking about and acting on water in an international context. IWRM has become a far-reaching cognitive construct and rhetorical device, penetrating important water governance nodes such as the World Bank and creating its own home in settings such as the Global Water Partnership. Yet the water governance paradigm advanced by these developments has also proven brittle and easily fractured when it is confronted with highly contentious questions of valuation and participation. The tensions between water as a human right and water as a marketized good have refused to sit still for knowledge stabilization in the service of normative convergence. Efforts to operationalize or even define suitable participatory mechanisms for making IWRM real have met a similar fate.

As a result, the most important institutional mechanisms for networking of experts—which include global water conferences, authoritative blueprint documents, and elite global commissions—have become, not the de facto elements of techno-rational governance, but important battlegrounds in the continued airing of these controversies. These mechanisms have become increasingly institutionalized, but as focal points for dissent and controversy rather than of knowledge closure to achieve cooperation. When delegates converged on Kyoto for the Third World Water Forum in 2003, they encountered a pattern of protest, disruptiveness, and contention strikingly similar to that which marked the preceding forum in The Hague in 2000, as described in chapter 1.[3]

Moving beyond a diplomatic understanding of rivers as border-spanning water channels or an expert's view of water as a multidimensional resource to be managed, one finds the contentious politics of socioecological water controversies. The most common form of water conflict today is not the interstate water wars foreseen by so many international relations prognosticators, but rather the societally based conflicts between the proponents and opponents of controversial ways of manipulating water or the rules controlling it. One cluster of controversy involves the long, slow, and still incomplete death of the era of pushing rivers around, centered on large, centralized water infrastructure schemes. A second cluster of controversy surrounds the neoliberal bid to define a new water era, in which marketized water resources flow to their highest-value use. These conflicts are rooted in the fact that water has become three things at once: a critical ecosystem, a central element of local livelihoods and communities, and a marketable commodity. The resulting controversies have enormous financial, social, and ecological stakes. And although they focus primarily on specific places, these conflicts are extensively and increasingly linked transnationally as the alliances on both sides of the dispute drive it to the level of a global controversy.

Science and the state have provided inadequate frameworks for the development of robust governing norms for this sort of physically local but socially transnational controversy. As anthropologist Luther Gerlach has stressed, "Managing interactions sounds less manipulative than managing people, but ultimately it is people who are managed.... Resource management is a euphemism for managing how people use resources, which means managing people."[4] In this context, universalized high-modern knowledge and unreconstructed states are decidedly not everyone's myth and ceremony. Important anti-social (in the sense of nonsocialized) elements have been introduced into global water politics.

Territoriality, Authority, and Knowledge in Transnational Contentious Water Politics

It was suggested in chapter 1 that the restrictive metanormative orientation of regimes as institutions—the state as authority, nature as territory, knowledge as stabilized truth—helped to explain the failure to create robust, effective, and enduring regimes around water. The institutional forms being born out of contentious water politics take a different position; they move away substantially from the origin in the three-dimensional regime space conceptualized along the axes of territoriality, authority, and knowledge.

An increasingly deterritorial understanding of water pervades both the dams and marketization arenas. Marketization forces, which are at the core of the privatization controversy and are increasingly present in the debate over dams, deterritorialize by pulling the world's water places into a transnationally fluid and deterritorialized form of global capitalism. The mobilization of water across social boundaries in search of its highest-value uses or the linking of large dams to production of goods for global markets obliterates notions of territorial fixity and the boundability of nature. Activists also deterritorialize water, although in a different way and for a different purpose. They seek to frame specific water places both subterritorially and supraterritorially. They link water places to greatly enhanced local autonomy, but also to stronger global standards of human rights, participation, and procedural safeguards. This understanding of place both fragments the construction of national territory and links the resulting fragments to a broader global framework.

In both the anti-dam and marketization controversies, nominally domestic conflicts between a "developmental" state and a portion of its citizenry have been dragged into important transnational arenas via the alliances forged on both sides of the dispute. As a result, a territorial construct of water as a national resource is replaced by an understanding of water as a very different sort of good, on scales that encompass individuals, households, and distinct communities, but which are linked to global frameworks of allocation mechanisms and rights.

Metanorms about knowledge in transnational contentious water politics also move beyond a conventional regime orientation. To be sure, actors on all sides of these disputes seek to stabilize knowledge in configurations favorable to their positions. As suggested in chapter 6, although the World Commission on Dams was by no means reducible to a global modeling process, it did seek to authorize a global knowledge base as a way to validate or reject competing claims about dams. Anti-dam activists have also played the knowledge stabilization game, turning the World Bank's own methods against it and using knowledge-based frames and critiques as a tactical resource. Something similar seems to be appearing in the water marketization struggle, with activists framing the claims about the benefits of privatized water services as inflated and rebutting those claims with data about prices, service interruptions, shutoffs, and the like. In both cases, these maneuvers may destabilize specific knowledge claims, but they also reinscribe the larger optimism that a stabilized knowledge about water lies just around the corner.

In the dams struggle, however, the most important effect of these battles over knowledge has been to legitimize much greater attention to local contingencies and differences. The claim that knowledge about dams is contingent on local circumstances pervades the knowledge-based delegitimization of large dams. As Jasanoff has suggested, "If expert knowledge (both scientific and technical) is even partly contingent on local circumstances, then one would expect differences in the institutionalization of expertise within governments and in the larger political culture to lead to important cross-national differences in policy implementation."[5] In the specific context of dams, the inability of centralized technical and financial institutions to incorporate or even see these local circumstances has led to the highly variable performance documented by the World Commission on Dams and to some of the spectacular failures fueling the anti-dam movement's momentum.

Although the marketization struggle is at a much earlier stage of institutional development, one can see elements of a similar path beginning to appear. In what social and cultural contexts is the daily minimum supply of water recommended by the World Health Organization an adequate amount? Why has experience with communally shared piped water systems been so highly variable? Under what circumstances is 200 m a reasonable distance to expect someone to haul water? Who is doing the hauling and why? As actors seek clearer answers to questions such as these, recognizing them as political resources, the resulting knowledge trajectory creates a broader space for multiple ways of knowing, even if regime-style knowledge stabilization is not fully transcended.

As with knowledge, so with authority. On the one hand, state authority is inherently challenged in these struggles. The successful transnationalization of state–society conflicts means that the dispute can no longer be credibly framed as nobody's business outside the state. The multiplicity of relevant knowledge systems also undercuts a traditional foundation of state authority. However, not all aspects of state authority are eroded at a similar pace or to a similar extent. And there are ways in which the emerging institutionalization of contention reinscribes state authority. As a result, states in contentious transnational water politics are neither the authoritative bargainers often depicted in the literature on international regimes nor the irrelevant distractions often depicted in the literature on global civil society.

Neoliberal marketization also has complex ramifications for state authority. Just as the failures of particularly blunt forms of neoliberalism led the World Bank and others to rediscover the role of the state, so too has water marketization stepped back from its ultraliberal variant to focus on public–private partnerships and the state's role in managing political risk. These shifts can be understood not simply as a shifting in the balance of power between state and market but also as part of an emerging new regime of global regulation to accompany the economic restructuring of a new mode of global accumulation.[6]

However, neoliberalism has not carried the day easily in the water sphere, within either the dams or privatization struggle. As suggested in chapters 6 and 7, what is actually being institutionalized is a set of practices that result from the growing embeddedness of conflict and controversy. In the process, the more institutionally developed large-dams controversy converged on a multistakeholder dialogue as a particular mechanism of interaction; the more recently unfolding marketization controversy is showing signs of doing the same.

As suggested in chapter 6, the emerging pattern of authority relations in transnational contentious water politics cannot be reduced either to a state-centric corporatism gone global or a weak bid by nonstate actors to promote strong norms for states. States are clearly decentered in the increasingly institutionalized transnational dialogues among corporate interests, activists, and intergovernmental organizations. Yet states retain important powers to influence those dialogues. They also play a crucial, although hardly monopolistic, "downstream" function in legitimizing (or delegitimizing) the protonorms that emerge from those bargaining processes. Elsewhere I have referred to this combined set of effects that decenter and recenter the state as the hybridization of authority in global environmental politics.[7] The central elements of this hybridization are the retention of some traditional foundations of state authority, the growth of nonstate authority grounded in a blend of expertise and moral claims, the development of new bases and realms of authority for some nonstate actors, and even elements of role reversal between the state and the nonstate.

Governance, Norms, and the State

Are these metanormative orientations actually being institutionalized as a result of transnational contentious water politics? What does it mean to be institutionalized? At what point do they cease to become proto-norms offered by a particular community and begin to exert significant and tangible effects on the governance of water?

There are no simple answers to these questions because, as the cases in this book reveal, there is no single "governor" of water at any level of social aggregation. One way to understand governance is as a set of governing acts. Austin Ranney, writing in 1958, identified dozens of such acts, ranging from law making to tax collection to the establishment of property rights, performed typically, but hardly exclusively, by governments.[8] Many scholars of international relations equate the idea of governance, not with functional acts, but with an authoritative adoption of norms as rules that impose constraints on behavior. Ronnie Lipschutz defines governance in terms of the answers to a set of questions about those rules: "Who rules? Whose rules? What rules? What kind of rules? At what level? In what form? Who decides? On what basis?"[9]

According to either an act-based or rule-based understanding of governance, the Brazilian and South African cases discussed in this book make it clear that governance of water occurs at several nodes and sites of political life, few of which reside fully within the administrative apparatus of the state. The country cases can therefore be read in two ways: first, as the creation and adaptation over time of national-level frameworks of law and policy; second, as aggregations of these multiple water-governing sites, linked by those national frameworks but also by the actors (domestic or otherwise) who move across them and the normative orientations they bring with them.

The cases also reveal that across many of those water-governing sites, ranging from those within the state to those most peripheral to it, there is a substantially transnational character to governance of water. Critical resources are created and deployed across borders, including money, skilled people, information, ideas, technology, and persuasive imagery and rhetoric. Agendas are established, legitimized, and actively changed over time. Authoritative knowledge is created and wielded to shape national policies. Management practices and objectives begin to be drawn toward convergence as standards and techniques come to be universalized and externally legitimized. Governance as the inscription of rules snakes across borders, along with the governing acts.

Under these circumstances, it makes little sense to speak of Brazil or South Africa as a leader or laggard in the embrace of a set of water-governing norms or the implementation of water-governing rules. The proliferation of both sites and rule sets requires us instead to visualize a process of struggle among competing and often conflicting norms that are marked by more complex spatial distributions across multiple sites (which are of course social and thus not exclusively geographic). Viewed in those terms, the case studies suggest that those protonormative frameworks rooted in contentious politics and socioecological controversy are outstripping their diplomatic and techno-rational counterparts as sources of normative force for changing water practices in both South Africa and Brazil. This process is not driven in some simple or monolithic fashion by the playing out of the dams and privatization controversies at the global level, but has certainly been facilitated and speeded by it.

This is not to suggest that diplomatic or techno-rational norms exert no effect on law, policy, and behavior at the domestic level. The country-level case studies reveal that diplomacy has been a tangible, if secondary, aspect of changing water practices in postapartheid South Africa and a conservative force not to be ignored in Brazil. As with diplomacy, so with expertise; both country cases show the influence of IWRM thought on state-based institutions. However, the larger message of both cases is the same as that of the institution-building pattern at the global level: There are severe limits to both diplomatic and techno-rational approaches in the presence of strong social forces pressing beyond the confines of fixed territoriality, state-based authority, and stabilized high-modern knowledge.

Implications for Global Environmental Governance

More than a decade after the 1992 Earth Summit, it has become clear that the momentum for interstate environmental diplomacy has ebbed dramatically, if it was ever really there in the first place. Serious diplo-

macy on the world's forests has gone nowhere since the failure to negotiate a forests regime in Rio de Janeiro. Despite entry into force of the
Kyoto accord, climate diplomacy has run aground on American intransi-
gence, unworkable emissions trading schemes, and the inability to con-
front either the North's visceral dedication to high-throughput lifestyles
or the South's unsustainable trajectory of "development." Several years
of difficult diplomacy culminated in a 2001 agreement to control twelve
persistent organic pollutants—twelve chemicals, that is, from among the
tens of thousands of human-fabricated chemicals in regular use, despite
a paucity of knowledge about the ecological or health effects of almost
all of them. Much less than concluding an agreement, it is difficult to
imagine even launching negotiations today for something like the Convention on International Trade in Endangered Species or the Basel Convention on the toxic waste trade, considering that those instruments use
the now-taboo concept of trade restrictions as a central instrument of
policy.

Yet, at the same time, environmental governance is indeed growing
increasingly transnational—for water, forests, biological conservation,
toxics management, coastal zone protection, agroecological practices,
and other socioecological domains. The impetus for the development of
the instrumentalities of governance in these cases is less that of formal
interstate bargaining and more the clash of local and nonlocal meanings
in these areas: marketable commodity, local livelihood, critical ecosystem. Nevertheless, it makes just as much sense to think of the increasingly routinized, reconciled, and embedded practices emanating from
the ensuing controversies as the institutionalization of global environmental governance as it does to view formal treaty structures and codified interstate commitments in that light.

This observation raises a crucial question: How do we proceed? How
are institutions to be built when we decenter the foundational elements
of state as authority, nature as territory, and knowledge as stabilized
truth? In other words, the metanormative content of regimes is closely
linked to the process by which they are created. Throughout this book I
have repeatedly used a language stressing embeddedness, routinization,
and normalization to describe institutional development beyond the
metanormative space of regimes. This suggests that we should think of

those institutions not as something to be designed but rather as something to be nurtured.

What would be the elements of such nurturing? One critical starting point is the frank acknowledgment of social conflict, as opposed to the more common practice of trying to deny or paper over differences. This approach stands in marked contrast to, say, the climate talks, where genuine, fundamental social conflicts came to be buried beneath a gentlemen's agreement on arbitrary emissions caps and a set of so-called flexible mechanisms and emissions trading schemes meant largely to evade those caps.

A second key element lies in the kind of institutions we seek to build. Scholarship on the effective sustained management of common-property resources has shown the importance of institutions as second-order public goods that help to provide the underprovided good of social cooperation. One obvious area in which such second-order public goods would facilitate the nurturing of institutions is resolution of environmental disputes. A call for an international mechanism for resolving environmental disputes was made in "The Jo-Burg Memo," a statement issued by a group of prominent environmental activists and scientists prior to the 2002 World Summit on Sustainable Development in Johannesburg, South Africa. According to "The Jo'Burg Memo,"

Global society, not unlike national societies, is pervaded by conflicts. As nations and corporations, communities and individuals bring extraordinarily diverse experiences, interests and worldviews to bear on the global stage, conflict cannot be dreamed away; on the contrary, conflicts generate the upheavals, alliances, and ideologies of that amalgam called global society. There is no universal way of seeing; there are only context-bound viewpoints that offer particular perspectives. Any architecture of global governance is therefore well-advised to start with the assumption that conflicts bubbling up from society are neither avoidable nor finally resolvable. In the best case, they can be identified before turning violent, peacefully settled, and redirected into a productive tension.[10]

The memo's authors pointed specifically to the Permanent Court of Arbitration (PCA) in The Hague, created in 1899, as "the most advanced mechanism currently available for settling international environmental and/or natural resources disputes."[11] The PCA supports a range of dispute-resolution techniques, including arbitration, conciliation, mediation, fact-finding, and assisted negotiation.

Although "The Jo'Burg Memo" pointed to the court primarily as a means of resolving trade–environment disputes in a more balanced setting than the World Trade Organization, there is no reason to limit a dispute-resolution process to such a narrow field. The PCA has recently completed the prepartion of draft rules specifically for the settlement of environmental disputes. The rules "seek to address the principal lacunae in environmental dispute resolution.... Presently there is no unified forum to which States, intergovernmental organizations, non-governmental organizations, multinational corporations, and private parties can have recourse when they have agreed to seek resolution of controversies concerning environmental protection, and conservation of natural resources."[12] The principal limitation of the PCA as it is currently constituted to play this broader role is its relatively narrow formal-legal epistemology, in which claims and evidence presented by disputants are viewed predominantly in the context of existing international law, expert testimony, and legalistic procedural rules. In process terms, however, the PCA has begun to broaden its approach; its design principles in the area of environmental dispute resolution include mechanisms for resolution of multiparty disputes, accommodating commercial and non-governmental actors as direct participants, along with states.

The dispute-resolution approach could also be linked to growing interest in the idea of environmental peacemaking. Scholarship on opportunities for environmental peacemaking has suggested that processes such as cooperative knowledge ventures and the emergence of regional-scale identifies might help to transform situations of conflict and insecurity using environmental relationships as catalysts, with non-state channels as important venues.[13] The nascent activities of the United Nations Environment Programme in conflict resolution and conflict transformation could be strengthened and enhanced substantially, as well as encouraged to move beyond the technical experts framework common to UNEP activities.

Along with the frank acknowledgment of conflict and the development of process-oriented channels for dispute resolution, another approach to nurturing productive institutionalization in transnational contentious environmental politics is to pay more attention to what Lipschutz describes as the narrative aspects of governance. He stresses the importance of the politics of "the (re)construction of place and meanings" as a form of resistance in a world where "capital seems to be in charge."[14] Beyond resistance, the challenge is to nurture "a governance system that privileges local choice and, at the same time, takes into account … global complexities and connections."[15] In such a system "rules … take the place of explicit rule; governance replaces government; informal networks of coordination replace formal structures of command."[16] Although he is not specific about what such systems of governance might look like, Lipschutz suggests that they are marked by a complexity rooted in overlapping authorities and the fact that they extend across multiple levels of social aggregation. In the context of such complexity, politics becomes centrally about "negotiating over the terms of the story that will prove most compelling."[17] The water controversies described in chapters 6 and 7 can be understood as such processes of negotiation, although they are played out on fields that are far from level.

This brings us to processes of multistakeholder dialogues such as those of the World Commission on Dams. Do they level the playing field in the effort to find the most compelling stories? Doubts have been raised by those who note the self-appointed character of many so-called stakeholders. Marina Ottaway has characterized the WCD, for example, as a prime example of a phenomenon she refers to as corporatism gone global.[18] She suggests that "it is doubtful that close cooperation between essentially unrepresentative organizations—international organizations, unaccountable NGOs and large transnational corporations—will do much to ensure better protection for, and better representation of, the interests of populations affected by global policies."[19]

The Third World Network has voiced a broadly similar concern:

An underlying concern that has emerged is that the [multistakeholder dialogue] approach, be it national or global, may sideline other forms of participation. While it can be useful, it is inherently restrictive, especially in relation to the diversity of civil society organizations. Where local communities are concerned, the situation is more problematic, as can be seen from the inadequate participation of farmers, non-organized workers and other marginalized groups in our societies.[20]

Others have suggested that the problem is not too much authority for stakeholders but rather too little. Richard Falk has drawn a useful distinction between governance as democratic process and governance as problem solving via rule enforcement, suggesting that the World Commission on Dams is likely to be of lasting significance more for the former than the latter.[21] The independent assessment of the WCD conducted by the World Resources Institute, Lokayan, and the Lawyers' Environmental Action Team provided a sobering account of some of the problems related to "buy-in" and the challenge of extending the consensus beyond the commission itself.[22]

Both of these cautions seem well founded, but the cases documented here suggest a substantially more complex process than corporatism gone global or a weak bid to promote strong norms.[23] Both the international and country-level cases suggest that institutionalization of contention has occurred across several different sites and nodes. In this multiarena process of institutional development, multistakeholder processes provide important channels for incorporation of the "anti-social" elements, again, using this term to refer to actors who reject prevailing metanormative arrangements as part of their acts of contention. Moreover, as the dams case makes clear, such arrangements are not quasi-legislative bodies of formal representation of interests. They are better understood as key elements in a broader process of the institutionalization of contention and the resulting adoption of norms. As Minu Hemmati describes it, they are as much about "decision finding" as they are about decision making.[24] The more they come to reflect Ottaway's feared global iron triangle—and there is a significant danger of this, particularly in the way the concept has emerged within the UN system—the less effectively they will perform this crucial function.

More to the point, in a world where governments have manifestly failed to come together effectively on a wide array of physically local but globally cumulative socioecological controversies, more flexible and hybridized approaches to authority in institutional arrangements would seem to be the only alternative. The debates over dams and privatization show that it will not be possible to ignore dissenting voices on these matters. For better or for worse, processes of economic and sociocultural globalization are dragging these otherwise local controversies into the global arena. The ability of the international community to foster effective stakeholder dialogue around such controversies will therefore be a critical variable shaping the future of the global environment.

Implications for Understanding World Politics

Finally, there is the question of ramifications for how we think conceptually about world politics. According to social movement theorists Doug McAdam, Sydney Tarrow and Charles Tilly, "The study of politics has too long reified the boundary between official, prescribed politics and politics by other means. As an unfortunate consequence, analysts have neglected or misunderstood both the parallels and the interactions between the two."[25] In the study of international relations, this divide between the formal and the informal has produced a repeating cycle of language shifts—whether it be in terms of international regimes, global governance, transnationalism, global civil society, or globalization—that reflects an underlying struggle against premature closure. In each instance, a term emerges to help scholars interpret a seemingly important but poorly understood phenomenon rooted in the increasingly trans-state character of social and political life. A definitional struggle soon follows, and a narrow and specific definition asserts its supremacy. The narrower definition lends itself to testing and measurement, but crowds out the complex, the informal, and the unmeasurable. Soon thereafter, a newly broadened concept is sought by those who reject the resulting constraints.

The image of authoritative states trying to respond collectively to a tragedy of the commons dominates in the study of international environmental regimes, and regime scholarship dominates in the study of global environmental governance. There are good reasons to define international regimes narrowly if one seeks to understand the willingness of governments to codify norms of international cooperation, or to assess the effects of codified norms upon nature, society, or the state. However, we should not forget that the set of international institutions captured by such a definition is a small and skewed subset of the range of potential institutional forms through which environmental or other problems that have a transnational reach can be governed.

A close companion of the trap of premature closure is the trap of limited imagination. It is not clear whether the scholarly choice to focus overwhelmingly on codified, intentional, state-based institutional forms shapes the institutional design choices of practitioners or merely reflects them. However, one thing is clear: The now-routine practice in the scholarly literature of equating institutions with regimes is mirrored in the world of environmental diplomacy, where a particular type of treaty negotiation is the now-reflexive response to emerging environmental problems. Pragmatism may be offered as a justification; as scholars of institutional development have noted, "it takes only a little entrepreneurial energy" to reproduce a familiar and widely legitimized institutional form.[26] However, it is hardly pragmatic to try to cram a heterogeneous array of environmental problems, and the contested social relations surrounding them, into a single type of institutional mold.

In the effort to protect the planet's places, struggles over authority, the destabilization of fixed territoriality, and limits to knowledge stabilization are the political facts of life. As such, they demand new institutional responses. Realizing the promise of and possibilities for such arrangements entails challenges for scholars. We must allow ourselves to conceive of institutions that construct more complex, diverse, or fluid spaces for fair and effective responses to a growing class of socioecological controversies. And we must be ready to see those institutions emerging in the world around us.

Notes

Chapter 1

1. For the origins and membership of the World Water Council, see Gleick 1998, 172–176.

2. World Water Commission 2000.

3. GWP 2000b.

4. This definition follows Finnemore and Sikkink (1998), who define a norm as "a standard of appropriate behavior for actors with a given identity" (p. 891).

5. GWP 2000b, 78.

6. Sharma 2000.

7. The concept of global governance remains contested. As Lawrence Finkelstein (1995) has pointed out, although the idea of governance "turns up often in scholarly discourse about how states relate to each other in the international system, little attention has been given to what it means" (367).

8. World Commission on Environment and Development 1987, 27.

9. This problem is sometimes framed in terms of the challenge of managing common-pool resources. See Keohane and Ostrom 1995 and Barkin and Shambaugh 1999.

10. For examples of the range of specific and general rules embedded in several important international environmental regimes, see Weiss 1998.

11. Krasner (1982) defines international regimes as "sets of implicit or explicit principles, norms, rules and decision-making procedures around which actors' expectations converge in a given area of international relations" (p. 2). Rittberger (1993) defines international regimes as "rules of the game agreed upon by actors in the international arena (usually nation states) and delimiting, for these actors, the range of legitimate or admissible behaviour in a specified context of activity" (p. xii). I discuss these and other definitions in greater detail in chapter 2.

12. See in particular Young et al. 1999a. Chayes and Chayes 1995 develop a theory of compliance with international rules based on efficiency considerations, the impact of institutions on interests, and the power of norms.

13. This point is made in Kutting 2000.

14. D. Thomas and Middleton 1997.

15. Mulligan 1999 and Raustiala and Victor 1996.

16. FAO 1997. For criticisms of the FAO data, see WRI 1998, 185.

17. WRI 1998, 156–157.

18. Oldeman 1998, 4.

19. World Conservation Union 1996; WRI 1998, 190–191; Oud and Muir 1997; Abramovitz 1996.

20. United Nations Secretariat of the Convention to Combat Desertification n.d.

21. WRI 1998, 193.

22. UNEP 2002a, xx.

23. Turner 1990.

24. Lovelock 1987.

25. WRI 1998, 180–181. A metric ton is equal to 1.1 U.S. ton.

26. As Paul Wapner (1996a, 252) describes it,

The new challenge to environmentalism, captured in the word globalization, is the recognition that it is no longer simply the transnationalization of ecological processes that needs addressing but also, and perhaps more fundamentally, the transnationalization of social, cultural, political, and especially economic phenomena.... Globalization ... poses new challenges to environmentalists because it represents processes that zip around the globe with increasingly less resistance with significant ramifications for global environmental well-being. (p. 252)

27. Costanza et al. 1997.

28. See Blaikie 1985.

29. Crosson 1994 and WRI 1998, 157.

30. Berry 1990, 200; emphasis in original.

31. For Basel and the WTO, see Krueger 1999.

32. The Montreal Protocol prohibits trade in regulated chemicals with non-parties to the agreement. It is not clear whether this trade ban violates GATT requirements for most-favored-nation and national-treatment requirements or falls under an exception for health and safety considerations. See Weiss 1998 and Brack 1996.

33. This idea is discussed in Conca 1993.

34. World Commission on Environment and Development 1987, annex 1.

35. P. Haas 1989, 1990, and 1992a. For the concept of epistemic communities, see also the Winter 1992 special edition of *International Organization*.

36. Litfin 1994 and 1995.

37. Keck and Sikkink 1998, 2.

38. Wapner 1995 and 1996b.

39. See, for example, Price 2003; Kaldor 2003; Batliwala 2002; Khagram et al. 2002; Smith 2002; Klotz 2002; Smith et al. 1997; Lipschutz with Mayer 1996; Princen and Finger 1994; Taylor 1995.

40. This theme is stressed in particular in Wapner 1995.

41. See Dawson 1996.

42. See Comor 2001; Ford 2003; Amoore and Langley 2004; Baker 2001.

43. On this point see Finnemore 1996.

44. For the debate over the continuing salience of the state in global environmental politics, see Barry and Eckersley 2005.

Chapter 2

1. The Montreal Protocol followed from the 1985 Vienna Convention for the Protection of the Ozone Layer. In its provisions, the Montreal document called for parties (other than developing countries) to freeze CFC production and consumption at 1986 levels and to implement deeper cuts by 1999. The 1990 London Amendments to the Vienna Convention created a funding mechanism to aid developing countries in the transition to CFC substitutes. The 1994 Copenhagen Amendments solidified the regime's implementation procedures and brought additional chemicals under control. The parties have also used the original treaty's built-in adjustment process to tighten restrictions and accelerate timetables without formally amending the agreement; this was the means used in 1990 to adopt the dramatic plan to ban CFCs by 2000. See Weiss 1998, 136.

2. See Benedick 1998; Roan 1989; Parson 2003.

3. Benedick 1998, 332.

4. The decision to ban the waste trade from OECD to non-OECD states was taken at the second Conference of the Parties to the Basel agreement in 1994. However, the United States and other opposing states argued that the ban must be adopted as a formal amendment to the original agreement rather than a decision of the parties present at the conference. The ban was adopted as a formal amendment to the 1989 agreement at the third Conference of the Parties in 1995; it takes effect when ratified by three-fourths of the eighty-two parties present, or sixty-two countries. As of late 2004, forty-eight countries and the European Union had ratified the ban amendment. For Basel and the WTO, see Kreuger 1999.

5. For an example of framing the problem as toxic colonialism, see Center for Investigative Reporting and Moyers 1989 and the website of the Basel Action Network, http://www.ban.org.

6. Clapp 2001.

7. For the role of Greenpeace, see Clapp 2001. For a critical account stressing Greenpeace's use of toxic symbolism, see Kellow 1999.

8. Tolba 1987.

9. On the idea of Montreal as a model for climate change, see Benedick 1998 and Meadows et al. 1992. For a skeptic's view, see Rowlands 1991.

10. One such critic is Kellow (1999), who argues that Basel "seems to have succeeded in combining nearly all the pitfalls of international environmental policy."

11. POPs are carbon-based chemicals that resist breakdown and therefore accumulate and endure in the environment for long periods of time. They include pesticides such as DDT, chlordane, or toxaphene; industrial chemicals such as polychlorinated biphenyls (PCBs); and by-products of industrial processes such as dioxins.

12. For the effects of persistent organic pollutants, see WRI 1996. See also Colborn et al. 1987.

13. See UNEP 1997. The twelve priority POPs targeted for action include eight pesticides (aldin, chlordane, DDT, dieldrin, endrin, heptachor, mirex, and toxaphene), two industrial chemicals (hexachlorobenzene and PCBs), and two "unintended" by products (dioxins and furans).

14. For the UNEP/FAO system, see Victor 1998a. Under the current division of labor, UNEP handles industrial chemicals and FAO handles pesticides. The UNEP/FAO system is weaker than current proposals for a persistent organic pollutants regime because it allows exports with the prior informed consent of the importing nation and because the relative handful of chemicals it covers does not include all of the major persistent organic pollutants of concern.

15. Rittberger 1993, xii.

16. Victor 1998b and Greene 1998.

17. One seeming exception to this observation is the use of ad hoc working groups of technical and legal experts, a question to which I return later.

18. See Litfin 1997.

19. Young and Levy 1999, 14 (emphasis added).

20. According to Young et al. (1999a), "Regimes sometimes operate at the constitutive level, shaping the identities (and therefore the interests) of actors and, in the process, influencing the way actors behave as occupants of the roles to which they have been assigned" (p. 25).

21. The Montreal Protocol exempted developing countries from complying with restrictions on the use of chlorofluorocarbons and other ozone-depleting chemicals, and the 1990 London amendments created an interim fund to help developing countries adjust to the regime's restrictions. Basel exempted the "North-North" trade in hazardous waste from both the original informed-consent procedures and the subsequent ban on the waste trade. An appendix to the agreement specifies which countries are not banned from receiving waste (essentially the OECD states) and which countries are (the bulk of the global South).

22. See, for example, Victor et al. 1998; P. Haas et al. 1993; Weiss and Jacobson 1998; Bernauer 1995.

23. For a discussion of these foundations of nonstate influence in the context of changing norms of sovereignty, see Litfin 1997.

24. Chayes and Chayes 1995, x.

25. See UNEP 1999.

26. Lapidoth 1992.

27. See Lipschutz and Mayer 1993.

28. Cleary 1993, 344.

29. This theme is discussed in Conca 1995.

30. See Ribot 1999. See also Raju and Ragu 1996.

31. Mason 1999, 104.

32. Montes 1996.

33. United Nations 1973, 5.

34. Wapner 1998, 279.

35. A report of the United Nations Environment Programme (UNEP 2001) identifies "at least 502 international treaties and other agreements related to the environment, of which 323 are regional. Nearly 60 per cent, or 302, date from the period since 1972, the year of the Stockholm Conference" (p. 3).

36. P. Haas and Sundgren 1993.

37. The authors chose 1973 as the watershed year rather than 1972 because it marked the beginning of operations for the UN Environment Programme. They describe the six treaties signed in 1973 as largely consistent with the pre-Stockholm pattern, with the trends of the post-Stockholm period showing up "later in the decade" of the 1970s. See Haas with Sundgren 1993, 404.

38. Conca 2000.

39. For a discussion of the ecology-sovereignty debate, see Litfin 1997 and 1998 and Conca 1995.

40. Kuehls 1996, 71–72.

41. See Sachs et al. 1998; Rees et al. 1995; MacNeill et al. 1991.

42. Commenting on the idea of full-cost pricing of commodity production and use to account for environmental externalities, Wapner (1998) suggests that "The internationalization of such a system would work against the parceling of the Earth's environment into separate, seemingly autonomous jurisdictions and could help to inculcate a sense of global responsibility as people understood and took actions to respect the geographical range of their resource use" (p. 292).

43. Ostrom 1990. See also Keohane and Ostrom 1995 and Dolšak and Ostrom 2003.

44. Levy et al. 1993, 410–411.

45. My use of the term *knowledge stabilization* is similar to that of Jasanoff (1998), who refers to a knowledge-stabilization effect brought about through international technical standards.

46. As Jasanoff (1998) suggests, "The picture that has emerged ... from a growing body of recent research shows science as a deeply social institution whose claims are situated within, rather than outside, politics and culture" (p. 65). See also Wynne 1987; Litfin 1994; Bijker et al. 1987; Nelkin 1992.

47. Young 1998, ch. 1.

48. Young 1998, 13.

49. My point is not that technical-rational standards form the only metric of regime legitimacy, merely that they are one important yardstick. Kellow (1999) points out that "The presence of a chemical has little meaning unless we assign some subjective value to it.... As Mary Douglas noted, pollution is a moral category and risk is a social construct.... Ironically, it is this moral dimension in environmental issues which combines with scientific reductionism to help generate the consensus necessary for international action" (p. 8).

50. Levy et al. 1993, 410–414. Key elements of open-ended creation of knowledge identified by the authors include gathering and disseminating information, catalyzing policy-relevant development of knowledge, and focusing the regime's rules on environmental harm rather than more narrowly on specific pollutants.

51. Jasanoff 1998, 86.

52. Litfin 1994.

53. As Greene (1998) describes it, "No substantial review of the quality of submitted data (versus completeness of data) has developed.... The [Implementation Committee] has avoided highly politicized issues and has established itself gradually and cautiously. It has tried to gain confidence among the parties in its procedures and operations and to promote compliance in a nonconfrontational, nonjudicial, and transparent way" (pp. 94–95).

54. See, for example, Kellow 1999, ch. 5.

55. Clapp 1994, 25.

56. See Wynne 1987 and Kellow 1999, 128.

57. Goodland 1997.

58. See Philip 1985, 70.

59. On the concept of knowledge brokers, see Litfin 1994 and 1995. On epistemic communities, see P. Haas 1989, 1990, and 1992b.

60. Feyerabend 1979.

61. Krasner 1982, 2.

62. For a discussion of other early definitions of the concept, see Krasner 1982, 2.

63. See Krasner 1982, particularly the chapters by Ruggie, Cohen, Jervis, and Puchala and Hopkins.

64. For the debate between broad and narrow interpretations, see Haggard and Simmons 1987; see also Keohane 1993.

65. Meyer and Rowan 1977. See also Finnemore 1996.

66. Meyer and Rowan 1977, 345.

67. Meyer and Rowan 1977, 345.

68. For a discussion of the application of this perspective to world politics, see Finnemore 1996.

69. Meyer et al. 1992, 2.

70. Finnemore 1996, 327; emphasis in original.

71. Thomas et al. 1987 and Finnemore 1996.

72. Meyer et al. 1997, 623.

73. Meyer et al. 1997, 645.

74. Meyer and colleagues (1997, 645–646) posit two possibilities in this latter case. Where state interests and responsibilities are strong, the institutional pattern will be dominated by conventional interstate relations (as in the case of security affairs). Where state interests and responsibilities are weak, there will be little world-level mobilization or structuration.

75. Finnemore 1996, 343.

76. This argument is foreshadowed in Conca 1993.

77. Keck and Sikkink 1998.

78. See Rosenau 1990; Smith et al. 1997; Keck and Sikkink 1998; Khagram et al. 2002.

Chapter 3

1. WRI et al. 2000, 9.

2. Covich 1993, 40–55.

3. Hecht and Cockburn 1990.

4. IRN 1997b, 77.

5. Swatuk 2002a, 125.

6. Revenga et al. 1998. See also WRI et al. 2000, 102.

7. UNEP 1995.

8. UNCSD 1997, paras. 55–57.

9. WRI et al. 2000, 105. The watersheds included in this estimate are the Amazon, Congo, Mississippi, Nile, Ob, Parana, Yenisey, Lake Chad, Lena, and Niger. "Largest" in this context refers to the land area of the watershed.

10. WRI et al. 2000, 103.

11. According to Oud and Muir 1997, the International Commission on Large Dams defines a large dam as a dam at least 15 m high, or a dam of 10–15 m in height if it has a crest length of over 500 m, a spillway discharge of 2000 m^2, or a reservoir volume of more than 1 million m^3. Within this category of large dams, "major dam projects" are defined as those meeting one or more of the

following criteria: dam height of more than 150 m, dam volume of more than 15 million m^3, reservoir volume of more than 25 billion m^2, or installed electric generating capacity of more than 1000 MW.

12. According to the assessment, "'Strongly affected' systems include those with less than one-quarter of their main channel left without dams, as well as rivers whose annual discharge has decreased substantially. 'Unaffected rivers' are those without dams in the main channel and, if tributaries have been dammed, river discharge has declined by no more than 2 percent" (WRI et al. 2000, 106).

13. WRI et al. 2000, 106.

14. Chao 1995.

15. WCD 2000c, 6.

16. UNCSD 1997, para. 44.

17. UNCSD 1997, para. 44.

18. Postel 1993; Seckler et al. 1998. See also UNCSD 1997, para. 40.

19. Revenga et al. 1998, 19.

20. Revenga et al. 1998, 16.

21. Dugan and Jones, 1993.

22. Garbvrecht 1997.

23. Gleick 1998, 69.

24. Schnitter 1994, chs. 2–4.

25. Worster 1985.

26. Gleick 1998, ch. 6, appendix A. See also Hatemi and Gleick 1992.

27. Schnitter 1994, 102–103.

28. Ostrom 1990. See also Feeny et al. 1990 and Birkes 1989.

29. Worster 1985, 266.

30. Gleick 1998, 69.

31. Worster 1985. See also Reisner 1986.

32. McCully 1996, 237 and 240.

33. Barlow 1999, 9. For the history of the Aral disaster, see Weinthal 2002.

34. McCully 1996.

35. Gleick 1998, 70.

36. Compiled from data in Gleick 1998, 281–287. The nineteen dams include six begun during the military era but completed after Brazil elected a civilian president in 1989.

37. Worster 1985.

38. Moore and Sklar 1998. See also Sklar and McCully 1994 and World Bank 1993.

39. World Bank 1996.

40. ICOLD n.d.

41. ICOLD n.d.

42. ICID n.d.

43. McCully 1996, 49.

44. The only exceptions among the nations and firms listed by McCully are Japanese equipment manufacturers (5) and American, British, and Swiss engineering and environmental consulting firms (4, 3, and 3, respectively).

45. WRI 1998, 190.

46. Gleick 1998, 6. See also UNCSD 1997.

47. Of total global runoff of about 40,700 km^3/yr, an estimated 20,400 constitutes uncaptured floodwater and an additional 7,800 involves flow in remote river basins (the Amazon, the Zaire-Congo, and remote northern rivers). The remaining 12,500 constitutes the "accessible runoff," with an estimated 54 percent already subject to human appropriation. See Jackson et al. 2001. See also UNCSD 1997, introduction.

48. World Water Commission 2000, 14.

49. WRI 1998, 190–191.

50. WRI 1998, 190.

51. Gleick 1998, 76.

52. Myers 1997. See also Finlayson and Davidson 1999.

53. WCD 2000c, 16.

54. Citing statistics from the UN Food and Agriculture Organization (FAO 1999a and FAO 1999b), the PAGE assessment reports that freshwater aquaculture production was 17.7 million tons in 1997 compared with 7.7 million metric tons from wild stocks (1 metric ton = 1.1 American ton). FAO estimates, however, that the harvest from inland fisheries is greatly underreported, "perhaps by a factor of two or three." See WRI et al. 2000, 113.

55. WRI et al. 2000, 107.

56. WRI et al. 2000, 118. Other ecosystems examined in the PAGE assessment were agroecosystems, coastal systems, forests, and grasslands.

57. UNCSD 1997, para. 60.

58. UNCSD 1997, para. 63.

59. WRI et al. 2000, 107. The 2025 scenario uses the UN's low-end scenario for population growth and assumes no change in current water consumption patterns. Using different assumptions, the UN Commission on Sustainable Development concluded in 1997 that "as much as two thirds of the world population in 2025 may be subject to moderate-to-high water stress, and almost half the world could have clear difficulties in coping owing to inadequate financial resources" (UNCSD 1997, para. 84).

60. UNCSD 1997, paras. 81-b and 89.

Chapter 4

1. Wolf et al. 1999. The survey on which this article was based put the new figure at 261; a 2002 update adjusted it to 263. See Transboundary Freshwater Dispute Database (n.d. b), table 4 (International River Basin Register).

2. The increase in international waterways compared with the 1978 estimate is due partly to improved remote sensing techniques (identifying new border-crossing waterways) and partly to changing political boundaries with the breakup of several states in the post-Cold War era (turning previously domestic waterways into border-crossing ones).

3. Wolf 1999, 2.

4. Metcalfe 2000, 47.

5. *Economist* 2000, 78.

6. See, for example, Homer-Dixon 1991 and 1994.

7. Schnitter 1994.

8. Hamner and Wolf 1997.

9. United Nations 1997. See also McCaffrey 2001.

10. A rivers regime is also conceivable on a subglobal or regional scale, of course, in the form of framework principles meant to shape the governance of a specific set of internationally shared basins. The 1995 Protocol on Shared Water-course Systems in the Southern African Development Community (SADC) is a regional-scale example of such a would-be regime.

11. The International Law Commission consists of thirty-four international legal experts elected by the UN General Assembly. Commission members serve as individuals rather than representatives of their respective countries, with the commission's areas of focus defined by the member states of the General Assembly. See Sinclair 1987 and McCaffrey 1993.

12. McCaffrey and Sinjela 1998, 97.

13. United Nations 1997, Articles 20, 21, and 23; emphasis added.

14. McCaffrey and Sinjela 1998, 104.

15. McCaffrey and Sinjela 1998, 103–104.

16. See Gleick 1998, 210; Wolf 1999; and McCaffrey and Sinjela 1998.

17. McCaffrey 1993, 98; emphasis in original.

18. Annuaire de l'Institute de Droit International 1961. See also McCaffrey 1993.

19. Annuaire de l'Institute de Droit International 1961, See also McCaffrey 1993.

20. McCaffrey 1993, 98.

21. McCaffrey 1993, 99.

22. According to McCaffrey and Sinjela (1998, 101), the primacy of avoiding significant harm was stated more clearly in the ILC's commentrary than in the draft articles themselves.

23. The third opponent, Burundi, is a riparian state in the upper Nile Basin but is not a central figure in Nile politics.

24. In comparison, the Law of the Sea Convention requires sixty national ratifications; the UN Framework Convention on Climate Change, fifty; the Convention on Biological Diversity, thirty; the Vienna Convention for Protection of the Ozone Layer, twenty; the Basel Convention on the Control of Transboundary Movements of Hazardous Wastes and their Disposal, twenty; and the Convention on International Trade in Endangered Species of Wild Fauna and Flora (CITES Convention), ten.

25. Although it failed to be ratified by a sufficient number of states to enter into force, the convention remains open indefinitely for states to ratify, accept, approve, or accede to it. As of August 2002, the convention had collected sixteen signatures and four accessions, and only seven states had ratified or accepted it. Ratifying states are Jordan, Namibia, Norway, South Africa, and the Syrian Arab Republic. States that have accepted the agreement (Finland and the Netherlands) are signatories and are bound to it in the same manner as ratifying states, but have not ratified the agreement. States that have acceded to the agreement (Iraq, Lebanon, Qatar, and Sweden) are bound to it in the same manner as ratifying states, but are nonsignatories.

26. FAO n.d.

27. Rittberger 1993, xii.

28. McCaffrey and Sinjela 1998, 106.

29. They point in particular to the Southern African Development Community's 1995 Protocol on Shared Watercourse Systems, the 1991 Argentine-Chilean Protocol on Common Water Resources, and the 1995 Agreement on Cooperation for the Sustainable Development of the Mekong River Basin. See McCaffrey and Sinjela 1998, 106.

30. Wolf 1999, 4.

31. Hamner and Wolf 1997.

32. Wolf 1999, p. 5.

33. Wolf et al. 1999.

34. Compiled from the Transboundary Freshwater Disputes Database n.d. a. For 1967–1976, the treaties involving newly independent states are those for the Mekong, Senegal, and Sepik/Fly Basins. For 1957–1966, they include the Senegal and Zambezi river basins and Lake Chad.

35. The Transboundary Freshwater Dispute Database has since been expanded substantially to include less formal agreements.

36. Agreements were excluded if they fell into one or more of three categories: (1) agreements dealing with narrow or isolated aspects such as fishing rights,

navigation, or border demarcation; (2) more general cooperative agreements in which water played only a tangential role; and (3) agreements unrelated to specific basins, such as agreements on water sector technical cooperation between noncontiguous countries.

37. For a detailed account of data assembly and coding procedures, see Conca et al. 2003.

38. For a more detailed presentation of findings, see Conca et al. 2003.

39. The deepening indicator developed for the principle of prior notification failed the test of intercoder consistency and was removed from the analysis. Additional indicators for sovereign rights and information exchange also failed and were removed.

40. An example is the 1994 Lake Victoria agreement among Kenya, Uganda, and Tanzania, Article xvi: "Nothing in this convention shall be interpreted as affecting the existing territorial limits of the contracting parties, or of their sovereignty in respect of the portions of Lake Victoria falling within their respective boundaries."

41. Deudney 1990 and Levy 1995.

42. Stockholm Water Symposium 1997.

Chapter 5

1. Gleick 1998, p. 9.

2. On the evolution of IWRM, see White 1998.

3. Cosgrove and Rijsberman 2000b, 1.

4. Global Water Partnership n.d. d, 5. See also Global Water Partnership 2000a.

5. Vandeveer 1997.

6. Litfin 1994; Haas 1990 and 1992a, b; Social Learning Group 2001.

7. World Water Commission 2000.

8. This distinction is similar to Kuehls's (1996) distinction between "smooth" and "striated" spaces in international environmental politics.

9. For the Stockholm Conference, see McCormick 1989 and Caldwell 1996. Water issues were first discussed within the UN framework at the 1949 Conference on the Conservation and Utilization of Resources. See United Nations 1951.

10. United Nations 1977b, 554–555.

11. United Nations 1977b, 555.

12. United Nations 1977a.

13. United Nations 1977b, 556.

14. Resolution X denounced the water policies of colonizing powers in occupied territories, singling out the territories of Palestine, Zimbabwe, Namibia, and

Azania (South Africa). The resolution passed by a vote of 52 to 17, with 22 abstentions (United Nations 1977b, 557–558).

15. See, for example, early editions of the journal, *Water International*, launched in 1975.

16. Preliminary UN estimates of the effects of the International Drinking Water Supply and Sanitation Decade suggested that significant progress had been made during the 1990s. The number of people with access to clean, adequate water supplies reportedly jumped by 1.3 billion from 1980 to 1990, while those with adequate sanitation jumped by an estimated 750 million, leaving some 1.2 billion without safe drinking water and 1.7 billion without sanitation services. However, the World Health Organization, pointing to problems of underreporting and overly optimistic notions of access, revised these 1990 estimates upward in 1996, to 1.3 billion lacking safe drinking water and 2.6 billion lacking sanitation services. See Gleick 1998, 40.

17. UNCSD 2000. See also WHO and UNICEF 2001.

18. WSSCC 1990.

19. UNDP 1998, ch. 4.

20. WSSCC 1990.

21. IWRA n.d.

22. Björklund n.d.

23. The notion that fragmentation and ambiguity play a role in promoting paradigm shift is suggestive of Ernst Haas's (1991) ideas about the institutional context of learning in international relations.

24. See WCED 1987, 134 and 293.

25. IWRA 1988.

26. Although the concept of sustainability has deeper historical roots, most observers agree that the key catalyst behind its rise to prominence was *Our Common Future*, the influential 1987 report of the World Commission on Environment and Development chaired by Gro Brundtland.

27. Young et al. 1994. These attendance figures differ slightly from those in the Dublin Statement itself.

28. On these and related aspects of planning for the Dublin Conference, see Young et al. 1994, ch. 1.

29. Young et al. 1994, 33.

30. For a list of NGOs represented at the conference, see Young et al. 1994, 180 (annex 3).

31. International Conference on Water and the Environment 1992.

32. International Conference on Water and the Environment 1992.

33. International Conference on Water and the Environment 1992.

34. Stockholm Water Symposium 1991.

35. Stockholm Water Symposium 1998. On water and gender, see also International Conference on Freshwater 2001; World Water Council 2000a; Gender Plenary Session 2001, and van Wijk et al. 1998.

36. International Conference on Water and the Environment 1992.

37. International Conference on Water and the Environment 1992; emphasis added.

38. International Conference on Water and the Environment 1992; emphasis added.

39. P. Haas et al. 1992, 32.

40. For a range of viewpoints on the significance of UNCED, see Conca and Dabelko 1998. For a critical view, see Chatterjee and Finger 1994.

41. UN Conference on Environment and Development (1992), ch. 18, para. 18.3.

42. UN Conference on Environment and Development (1992), ch. 18, section 18.12.o.c. Grover and Biswas (1993) concluded that "Agenda 21 ... reflects no substantive inputs from the Dublin Conference" (p. 81).

43. International Conference on Water and the Environment 1992.

44. Grover and Biswas 1993.

45. World Water Council n.d. a.

46. The ten constituent organizations are the Canadian International Development Agency (CIDA); the International Water Resources Association; the International Commission on Irrigation and Drainage (ICID); the World Bank; the International Water Association (IWA); the United Nations Development Program; the United Nations Educational, Scientific and Cultural Organization (UNESCO); the World Conservation Union (IUCN); the Water Supply and Sanitation Collaborative Council (WSSCC); and CIHEAM—Bari (Istituo Agronomico Mediterraneo). See World Water Council n.d. b.

47. Cosgrove and Rijsberman 2000b, iv.

48. GWP n.d. e.

49. GWP 2001, 6.

50. GWP n.d. b.

51. Other associated programs include gender mainstreaming and awareness, water resources assessment, flood management, groundwater management, water management and ecosystems, water supply and sanitation, and water conservation in agriculture. See GWP n.d. c.

52. GWP n.d. a.

53. World Water Council 2002, 3.

54. World Water Council 2000b, 5. According to the conference's final report, the event's 5,700 participants included 400 "nontraditional" participants from the global South sponsored by the conference organizers (p. 6).

55. For the latter, see GWP 2000b. For the *World Water Vision*, see World Water Commission 2000 and Cosgrove and Rijsberman 2000b.

56. Ministerial Declaration of The Hague 2000.

57. World Water Commission 2000, 15. See also Cosgrove and Rijsberman 2000b, chs. 2 and 3.

58. Cosgrove and Rijsberman 2000b, 25.

59. GWP 2000b, 13.

60. World Water Council 2000b, 79–92.

61. The delegations of Brazil, Costa Rica, Paraguay, and Uruguay took the unusual step of issuing a formal joint statement dissociating their governments from the *Vision* and *Framework* documents and reiterating Agenda 21 as the "sole document" for future UN initiatives. The regional meeting of ministers of the Americas issued a statement underscoring the "nonbinding" character of the ministerial declaration, citing its inappropriate use of the term *water security* and its underemphasis on stakeholder participation in decision-making processes. The report from the regional session on Africa (involving ministers and other heads of delegation) called for the documents to be noted rather than adopted and rejected language that "welcomed" the statements from the major groups. See World Water Council 2000b, 58, 78, and 153.

62. See World Water Council 2000b, 107–110 and 146–148.

63. GWP 2000b, 78.

64. Gleick 1999, 8.

65. UNCSD 1997, 3; see also Gleick 1999.

66. See, for example, Académie de l'Eau 1999.

67. Delli Priscoli 1996, 30.

68. World Bank 2002.

69. World Bank 1993.

70. The report's main conclusions—that the Bank should stress public–private partnerships for water service delivery and manage more effectively the political risk associated with large infrastructure projects—and the larger question of the Bank's roles in global water governance are discussed in chapters 6 and 7.

71. World Bank 2002, 28. The report finds the basis for this consensus in the 1992 Dublin Principles, although these principles are characterized in a very different fashion than in the original Dublin Statement.

72. FAO 1995.

73. FAO 1995, ch. 3.

74. UNDP 1998.

75. UNDP n.d.

76. UNDP 1998, ch. 3, section 1.

77. See World Water Council 2002, 3. The survey question on council priorities listed ten options: meeting basic needs/helping to provide access to drinking water and sanitation facilities in emergency situations; meeting basic needs/ helping to provide access to drinking water and sanitation facilities in the long term; promoting peaceful cooperation in international river basins; promoting better management of water services; moving toward pricing of all water services; increasing investments in water; helping to improve agricultural water management to enhance food security and sovereignty; protecting aquatic ecosystems; managing risks associated with water, including those related to climate change; and avoiding transboundary water-related conflicts.

78. UNCSD 1998, para. 11, p. 2.

79. Cosgrove and Rijsberman 2000a, 5.

80. Dubash et al. 2001, 77.

81. Dubash et al. 2001, 77.

82. See World Water Council 2002, 6. The survey question on board representation listed eleven options: civil society, women, media, trade unions, governments or water authorities, water supply companies, private-sector consultants, other private sector, research and universities, international organizations, and banks and financial institutions.

83. World Water Commission 2000, 29.

84. For a discussion of IWRA–WWC tensions, see IWRA 1998.

85. See IWRA 1999.

86. GWP, n.d. d, 6; GWP 2000b, 27.

87. Delli Priscoli 1996, 33. The author attributes these ideas to Allee 1989.

88. Stakeholder models are discussed in chapter 7.

89. IISD 2001; emphasis in original.

90. International Conference on Freshwater 2001.

Chapter 6

1. Stewart et al. 1996.

2. COAGRET n.d.

3. Bangkok *Post* 2000.

4. WCD 2000b.

5. Serageldin 2000.

6. Roy 1999.

7. *Discerning the Times* 2001; Liberty Matters News Service 2001.

8. Goodland (1997, 73) also identified ten main issues underlying the "dam controversy," which he labeled (1) transparency and participation; (2) demand-side

management, efficiency, and conservation; (3) balance between hydro and other renewables; (4) rural versus urban supply balance; medium versus big projects; (6) sectoral least-cost ranking; social and environmental criteria; (7) storage dams versus run of the river: area lost to flooding; (8) involuntary resettlement; (9) project-specific mitigation versus tradeoffs; (10) costs of damage from greenhouse gas emissions.

9. Many activists are careful to stress that they are not ideologically anti-dam, but rather believe "that dams (and other development projects) should only be built after all relevant project information has been made public, the claims of project promoters of the economic, environmental and social benefits and costs of projects are verified by independent experts, and when affected people agree that the project should be built" (McCully 1997b, 73). I use the phrases anti-dams network and anti-dam activists in part to stress the conflictual side of the controversy over large dams, and in part because applying the social, economic, and ecological screens demanded by the movement's mainstream would radically reduce the number of large dams being constructed.

10. For a discussion of the history of the anti-dam movement, with particular attention to the Narmada controversy, see Khagram 2004.

11. Tarrow 1998.

12. Tarrow 2002.

13. Keck and Sikkink 1998, 2.

14. Khagram et al. 2002.

15. Khagram et al. 2002.

16. McAdam et al. 2001.

17. See, for example, Ottaway 2001; Khagram 2004; Conca 2002.

18. McCully 1996, 281.

19. Goldsmith and Hildyard 1984, 13.

20. Nelson 1995.

21. For the campaign against the Bank, see Nelson 1995 and Rich 1994.

22. IRN n.d. a.

23. IRN 1996.

24. The changing economics of hydropower during this period are discussed in Churchill 1997b.

25. World Bank 1993.

26. World Bank 1993.

27. Moore and Sklar 1998.

28. Moore and Sklar 1998, 357.

29. Moore and Sklar 1998, 361–362.

30. Moore and Sklar 1998, esp. pp. 365–369.

31. World Bank 1993, executive summary p. 1.

32. World Bank 1993, executive summary p. 1.

33. Moore and Sklar 1998, 373.

34. McCully 1996, 316.

35. World Conservation Union and World Bank 1997, 8–9.

36. Lieberthal et al. 1996.

37. World Bank 1996, 1.

38. World Bank 1996, 1.

39. World Bank 1996, 1.

40. McCully 1997a.

41. IRN 1997c.

42. Rich 1994.

43. Identified funders included Swedish Society for Nature Conservation, Misereor, Bilance, Christian Aid, Bread for the World, Novib, Development and Peace, Bischufliches Hilfs, Socio-Environmental Institute of Paraná State, Euronatur, DUH, European Rivers Network, International Rivers Network, and CPT of Paraná (see IRN 1997b, 9).

44. See "Declaration of Curitiba Affirming the Right to Life and Livelihood of People Affected by Dams" in IRN 1997b.

45. See Broad 2002.

46. IRN 1996.

47. Tarrow 1998, ch. 11.

48. Keck and Sikkink 1998, ch. 1.

49. World Conservation Union and World Bank 1997, ii.

50. The IUCN and the World Bank had signed an agreement in 1994 as part of an IUCN initiative to "seek strategic partnerships with key international agencies so that they might work to resolve controversial issues and meet joint interests" (World Conservation Union and World Bank 1997, 5).

51. World Conservation Union and World Bank 1997, 9.

52. IRN 1997c.

53. IRN 1998.

54. World Conservation Union and World Bank 1997, 12 (box 5).

55. World Conservation Union and World Bank 1997, 9–10.

56. On the original plan for the commission, see the recommendations coming out of the IUCN–World Bank workshop (World Conservation Union and World Bank 1997, 9–12).

57. An initial press release from the IRN (IRN 1997a) charged that "NGOs also believe that the World Bank and IUCN have reneged on commitments to a

consensus process by selecting the Commission members on their own and by disregarding suggested changes from others involved in the process". As the controversy dragged on, a subsequent IRN press release (IRN 1998) stated that "NGO concerns on the composition of the WCD include the underrepresentation of technical experience on ecological issues and alternatives to large dams, the exclusion of critics of large dams with an engineering background, and the lack of any Latin American who is trusted by NGOs and affected people's groups in the region".

58. For details on the commission's composition, funding, and procedures, see Dubash et al. 2001.

59. Dubash et al. 2001, 70.

60. Dubash et al. 2001, 70.

61. Dubash et al. 2001, chs. 5 and 6.

62. Patkar's dissent stressed the WCD's failure to examine the larger logic of "development" driving water infrastructure decisions.

63. WCD 2000b, xxxi.

64. McCully 2001.

65. For an overview of immediate reactions to the report, see Dubash et al. 2001, ch. 8.

66. IRN and Berne Declaration 2000. See also Dubash et al. 2001, 103.

67. Dubash et al. 2001, 102–103.

68. Dubash et al. 2001, 110–112.

69. Dubash et al. 2001, 111. See also Sekhar 2001.

70. Dubash et al. 2001, 107.

71. See Varma 2001.

72. McCully 2001.

73. Skanska 2000 and McCully 2001.

74. For the German position, see Deutsche Gesellschaft fur Technische Zusammenarbeit 2002. For the British position, see Mullin 2001.

75. McCully 2001.

76. Quoted in Dubash et al. 2001, 112.

77. Knigge et al. 2003, 3–4.

78. WHO n.d.

79. See Asian Development Bank 2001 and Chinao 2000.

80. Aw 2001.

81. Dubash et al. 2001, 127.

82. UNEP 2002c.

83. Toepfer 2002.

84. For an overview of the DDP's formation, structure, goals, and work plan, see WCD 2002.

85. WCD 2002, 5 and appendix 1.

86. World Conservation Union 2002.

87. McCully 2001, 15.

88. McCully 2001. See also World Bank 2001a and 2001b.

89. McCully 2001.

90. World Bank 2002.

91. McCully 2002b.

92. World Bank 2003.

93. See, for example, the statement on the need for "enhanced corporate risk management," (World Bank 2002, 35).

94. World Bank 2003, vii–viii; emphasis in original.

95. World Conservation Union n.d.

96. The Bonn conference is discussed in chapter 5.

97. Greeff 2002. Greeff is the Water Justice Programme manager for the South Africa-based Environmental Monitoring Group.

98. See closing address by Heidemarie Wieczorek-Zeul in Federal Ministry for the Environment and Federal Ministry for Economic Co-operation and Development n.d. See also McCully 2002a.

99. Brown 2001.

100. IRN 2001c.

101. World Conservation Union 2001.

102. Hemmati 2002a.

103. Ottaway 2001.

104. Falk 2001.

105. The following argument is made in Conca 2005.

106. I am grateful to Navroz Dubash for this observation.

107. Litfin 1997.

108. See Dubash et al. 2001, 55–56.

109. Wesely 2003.

110. McCully 2002b, 39.

Chapter 7

1. International Conference on Water and the Environment 1992.

2. For a discussion of structural adjustment and the Washington Consensus, see Williamson 1990; Krueger 1993; Broad and Cavanagh 1999.

3. Citizen's Network on Essential Services 2001, 23–25 (table 9).

4. IMF 2002, 40.

5. Citizen's Network on Essential Services 2001, 23.

6. World Bank 2002.

7. World Bank 2002, figure 4.2.

8. Public Citizen 2002, 7.

9. World Bank 2003.

10. See World Bank (n.d.).

11. World Bank 2003, 47–48.

12. "Bulk" in this context refers to high-volume sales of unprocessed water, as opposed to the export of small units of processed water such as bottled water.

13. For the new mercantilism, see Gilpin 1987.

14. Gleick et al. 2002, 11–14.

15. Barlow 2001.

16. Barlow 2001.

17. Chalecki 2000, 12–13.

18. Department of Foreign Affairs and International Trade 2002.

19. Gleick et al. 2002, iii.

20. Conca 2000 and Esty 2000.

21. On differences between GATS and GATT, see WTO 1999.

22. World Development Movement 2002.

23. Joy 2000, 11–12.

24. Finger and Allouche 2002, ch. 4.

25. Finger and Allouche 2002, 16 (table 1.1).

26. Finger and Allouche 2002, 143–148.

27. Finger and Allouche 2002, 114–121, 144 and 146.

28. Public Citizen 2002.

29. Orwin 1999.

30. Winpenny 2003, 49.

31. World Bank 2003, 10.

32. See Churchill 1997b.

33. Winpenny 2003.

34. Camdessus 2003, vi.

35. Winpenny 2003, 47–48.

36. Schultz 2000.

37. Pauw 2003.

38. Santoro 2003.

39. Harsono 2003.

40. Scott 1985.

41. Pauw 2003.

42. Pauw 2003.

43. Dunn 2002.

44. Walker-Leigh 2003.

45. Porto Alegre Water Declaration 2002.

46. Civil Society World Water Vision for Action n.d.

47. See, for example, WTO 2001, which was released in response to a 2001 gathering of anti-GATS activists, and the subsequent reply in GATSWatch 2001.

48. In response to the leaked documents and subsequent press coverage, the European Commission issued a reaction, prompting a reply from World Development Movement, Corporate Europe Observatory, and Friends of the Earth Europe. See GATSWatch n.d.; and Corporate Europe Observatory et al. 2002.

49. For an example of a movement-based critique of World Bank privatization arguments, see Kessler 2002.

50. For resource mobilization, see Zald and McCarthy 1987. For a critical perspective, see McAdam et al. 2001, 15 and 44.

51. Quoted from Council of Canadians n.d.

52. Tarrow 2002, 15. See also Rosenthal and Schwartz 1989.

53. W. Bennett 2002, 2 and Tarrow 2002, 18.

54. In recent years there have been mounting efforts by international labor to pressure the international financial institutions, as in the initiatives of the International Confederation of Free Trade Unions on globalization, worker rights, and trade liberalization.

55. Tarrow 1994, 122. See also Goffman 1974 and Snow and Benford 1992.

56. For frames as vehicles for collective action, see Tarrow 1998. For frame alignment, see also Snow et al. 1986.

57. Gleick 1999, 490.

58. Global Committee for the Water Contract 1998.

59. Reuters 2000.

60. The term *norm entrepreneur* is from Finnemore and Sikkink 1998.

61. South-North Development Monitor 2002.

62. South-North Development Monitor 2002.

63. Global Committee for the Water Contract 1998, 4.

64. UN Committee on Economic, Social and Cultural Rights 2000, 1.

65. WCD 2000b, 130.

66. See, for example, Corner House 2000; Friends of the Earth UK 2001; Public Citizen 2002; Finger and Allouche 2002.

67. In a background paper for the World Bank/IUCN 1997 workshop, longtime hydro consultant Anthony Churchill (1997a) offered this scathing indictment of the "sorry state of affairs" in the international hydropower industry: "The industry is currently composed of diverse and specialized firms that compete for contracts in which all of the risk is undertaken by government. As such, it is not well-suited to a [sic] environment in which private capital is playing an increasingly central role.... The industry's record of overruns is an embarrassment.... Poorly defined products, lack of discipline and political, rather than economic, decision-making have combined to turn the industry into another fat sow elbowing its way to the public trough." Churchill concluded that "only through a restructuring of the industry will firms emerge with the ability to compete in the international power market" (pp. 112–113).

68. World Social Forum 2002.

69. Freshwater Action Network 2003.

70. Partner organizations for the event were Bread for the World (Germany), Council of Canadians (Canada), Cry of Water (Brazil), DWD (India), Funsolon (Bolivia), Ibon Foundation (Philippines), Navdanya (India), Polaris Institute (Canada), Public Citizen (U.S.), RFSTE (India), Sweet Water Alliances (U.S.), Water Workers Alliances (India) and Water Stewards Network (USA).

71. Second International Meeting of Dam-Affected People and their Allies 2003.

72. Kessler 2002, 3.

73. See Watson and Calaguas 2000 and Gutierrez et al. 2003.

74. Rajagopal 2003.

75. See World Bank 1997.

76. UN Committee on Economic, Social and Cultural Rights 2002, 3–4.

77. UN Committee on Economic, Social and Cultural Rights 2002, 2.

78. Global Water Scoping Process Working Group 2004.

Chapter 8

1. Measured in terms of drainage area, the world's six largest international river basins are, in descending order, the Amazon, Congo, Nile, Ob, Mississippi, and Paraná. See Revenga et al. 1998.

2. World Bank 1999, 2.

3. Shiklomanov 1998; see also Gleick 2000, 23.

4. ANA 2002, 47.

5. UNDP 2000, 169 (annex table 4).

6. Garrido 2000, 30.

7. This income estimate is adjusted for purchasing power parity and is from UNDP 2003, 238 (annex table 1).

8. UNDP 2003, 283 (annex table 13).

9. Consultoria Legal n.d.

10. Antunes 1999, 341.

11. Antunes 1999, 342.

12. Skidmore 1967; Wirth 1970; Conca 1997.

13. See, for example, Granziera 2001, 15.

14. ANA 2002, 12; Consultoria Legal n.d., 2.

15. Código de Águas, Decree no. 24.643, July 10, 1934, in Ministério das Minas e Energia 1980.

16. Código de Águas, Decreto no. 24.643, July 10, 1934, in Ministério das Minas e Energia 1980.

17. Antunes 1999, 343.

18. Antunes 1999, 343–345.

19. Pagnoccheschi n.d. a.

20. Pagnoccheschi n.d. a, 5.

21. ANA 2002, 13 and Barth 1999, 28.

22. Cabral 2000.

23. ANA 2002, 13.

24. Barth 1999, 29; my translation. See also Pagnoccheschi n.d. b; Abers and Keck 2003.

25. The journal's title since 1996 has been *Revista Brasileira de Recursos Hídricos*. It was originally titled *Revista Brasileira de Hidrologia e Recursos Hídricos* and later *Revista Brasileira de Engenharia: Caderno De Recursos Hídricos*.

26. ABRH n.d.

27. ABRH 1987.

28. Barth 1999, 28.

29. ANA 2002, 20.

30. Barth 1999, 30.

31. ANA 2002, 22.

32. ANA 2002, 19–20.

33. Antunes 1999, 343; emphasis in original.

34. As of 2001 the world's leaders in installed hydro capacity were the United States (98.9 GW), China (79.4), Canada (67.2), Brazil (61.9), Russia (43.4), Norway (27.7), India (25.1), Japan (22.0), and France (21.1). See U.S. Department of Energy n.d.

35. IRN n.d. c.

36. MAB n.d.

37. Wright and Wolford 2003.

38. Granziera 2001, 97–99.

39. Consultoria Legal n.d., p. 7.

40. Consultoria Legal n.d., p. 6.

41. Feldmann 1994, 13.

42. Feldmann left the Congress in 1995 to become the Secretary of Environment for São Paulo state, at which time Deputy Aroldo Cedraz took over as the bill's *relator*.

43. Garrido n.d., 1.

44. Federative Republic of Brazil 1997. For an English-language description of the law, see Secretaria de Recursos Hídricos 1999b.

45. Federative Republic of Brazil 1997, Title II, Chapter II, Article 39, Sections I–V.

46. CNRH members include "Representatives of the Presidential Ministries and Departments concerned with the management or use of water resources; representatives designated by the State Councils on Water Resources; representatives of users of water resources; and representatives of civil organizations concerned with water resources." Federative Republic of Brazil 1997, Title II, Chapter II, Article 34, Sections I–IV.

47. Consultoria Legal n.d.

48. Garrido n.d., 2.

49. Feldmann 1994, 16.

50. Feldmann 1994, 16.

51. Feldmann 1994, 15.

52. Garrido n.d., 3.

53. Consultoria Legal n.d., 12. The Brazilian constitution gives the president broad authority to veto specific line items in congressional legislation.

54. World Bank 1999, 26.

55. See Simpson and Ringskog 1997, 44–45.

56. Simpson and Ringskog 1997, 43–44.

57. Pagnoccheschi n.d. a, 5; my translation.

58. ANA 2002, 29.

59. *Jornal do Senado* 2000, 3.

60. Federative Republic of Brazil 2000, Section 1, Article 1.

61. ANA 2002, 27.

62. I am grateful to Rebecca Abers for this observation. The quote is from Kettelhut 2003.

63. Kettelhut 2003.
64. CNRH 2000, Article 8, Sections I–III.
65. Abers and Keck 2003, 3.
66. Abers and Keck 2003, 4.
67. Abers and Keck 2003, 7.
68. On the National Forum, see Rede das Águas n.d.
69. See, for example, *Multinational Monitor* 1997 and Brown and McCully 1997.
70. See Poole n.d.
71. Poole n.d.
72. MAB n.d.
73. See Aldeia 2002.
74. Switkes 2001b.
75. Switkes 2002.
76. Barros 2001.
77. IRN 2001b.
78. Keck and Sikkink 1998.
79. MAB 2001.
80. Switkes 2002.
81. Switkes 2003a.
82. WCD 2000a.
83. See Garrido 2001 and Switkes 2001d.
84. Relatório da Comissão de Análise 2001.
85. World Bank 1999.
86. Switkes 2001c.
87. Hochstetler 2002, 51.
88. Fundaçao Centro Brasileiro de Referência e Apoio Cultural and Instituto Centro de Vida 1994; see also Hochstetler 2002.
89. Hochstetler 2002, 52.
90. Rios Vivos n.d.
91. IRN 1999.
92. Weber 2001.
93. Diário de Cuiabá 2001a, b.
94. Almeida n.d.
95. IRN 2002.
96. IRN 2001a.
97. Federal Judge Tourinho Neto, as quoted in Switkes 2001a, 6.

98. Asad et al. 1999, 22.

99. Moreira 2002.

100. Moreira 2002.

101. Wartchow 2002, 2.

102. Switkes 2003b.

103. A transitional provision of the 1988 constitution allowed for a revision, after five years from the date of adoption of the constitution, by a majority vote of the National Congress meeting in unicameral session. In the 1994 constitutional revision process, proposals were put forward to define water resource management as a shared responsibility of the federal union, the states, and the municipalities; to replace exclusively federal legislative competence with shared state and federal legislative competence; and to eliminate all specific constitutional references to hydroelectric energy, thereby giving hydro uses common treatment with all other water uses. See Feldmann 1994, 17–18.

104. Garrido n.d., 11; emphasis added.

105. Secretaria de Recursos Hídricos 1999, 7.

106. Feldmann 1994, 13.

107. World Bank 2000, 10.

108. Abers and Keck 2003, 9.

109. Abers and Keck 2003, 9.

Chapter 9

1. World Resources Institute et al. 2000, 276–267 (table FW.1).

2. Lieberman 2001, 516–517.

3. Water Research Commission 1996, 54–56.

4. Davies and Day 1998, 33.

5. FAO 2000, chapter 12.

6. Davies and Day 1998, 315.

7. Davies and Day 1998, 30.

8. Davies and Day 1998, 315.

9. Davies and Day 1998, 39.

10. DWAF 2002, 1.

11. Davies and Day 1998, 252.

12. Davies and Day 1998, 47.

13. Davies and Day 1998, 265.

14. Davies and Day 1998, 136.

15. Department of Environmental Affairs and Tourism 1999.

16. DWAF 1997, 9.

17. Liebenberg and Pillay 2000, 292.

18. Lewis 1932, 71.

19. Laws in the Cape Colony (1906) and Transvaal (1908) anticipated several features of the new nation's first major water legislation. For South African water law during this period, see Lewis 1932; Hall 1939; Vos 1978.

20. Lewis 1932, 73.

21. DWA 1986, 8.7.

22. Lewis 1932, 74. The act created an absolute preference for animal uses (primary) over irrigation (secondary), and for irrigation over industrial (tertiary).

23. DWA 1986, 8.7.

24. Hall 1939, 84.

25. DWA 1986, 1.10.

26. DWA 1986, 1.12 (table 1.2.1).

27. Uys n.d., 284.

28. Vos 1978, 6–7; see also Uys n.d., 283.

29. See the assembly debates of June 5, 1956 as cited in Uys n.d., 283.

30. Uys n.d., 287.

31. DWA 1986, 8.8.

32. See the case *Du Toit v. Krige* as cited in Vos 1978, 9.

33. Vos 1978, 10.

34. DWA 1986, 8.2.

35. DWA 1986, 9.20.

36. Lieberman 2001, 529.

37. Legassick 1974 and O'Meara 1996. See also Davenport and Saunders 2000, 372.

38. DWAF 1995, 12.

39. DWAF 1995, 28 and 30.

40. DWAF 1995, 16.

41. DWAF 1995, 26.

42. Quoted in Bennett 2001. A sjambok is a small whip, similar to a riding crop or cattle prod, used by the South African police.

43. Commission of Enquiry on Water Matters 1970.

44. Commission of Enquiry on Water Matters 1970, 1.38.

45. Commission of Enquiry on Water Matters 1970, 1.14.

46. Commission of Enquiry on Water Matters 1970, 1.17–18.

47. Commission of Enquiry on Water Matters 1970, 1.37.

48. Commission of Enquiry on Water Matters 1970, 1.38.

49. Commission of Enquiry on Water Matters 1970, 1.38.

50. I am grateful to Larry Swatuk for this observation.

51. Commission of Enquiry on Water Matters 1970, 1.30.

52. Commission of Enquiry on Water Matters 1970, 1.25.

53. "Neither demand nor supply can ... be regarded as fixed quantities but rather as quantities that can be influenced by price and administrative policies" (Commission of Enquiry on Water Matters 1970, 1.17).

54. Commission of Enquiry on Water Matters 1970, 1.29.

55. Commission of Enquiry on Water Matters 1970, 1.35.

56. DWA 1986, xx.

57. DWA 1986, xvii.

58. DWA 1986, xxv.

59. DWA 1986, xxi.

60. DWA 1986, 8.3.

61. DWA 1986, xxii.

62. Quoted in DWA 1986, 8.4.

63. DWA 1986, xxv.

64. DWA 1986, xviii.

65. DWA 1986, xx.

66. DWA 1986, xx.

67. DWA 1986, xvii–xviii.

68. Davenport and Saunders 2000, 588–592.

69. The National Assembly served as a constitutional assembly for the drafting of the new constitution, completing its work in May 1996. President Mandela signed the text in December. The legislature affirmed the new constitution in February 1997, at which time it entered into force.

70. Health rights include the right to bodily and psychological integrity (Section 12), a safe environment (Section 24), access to health care services and emergency medical treatment (Section 27), basic health care services (28), and adequate medical treatment at state expense (Section 35). See Liebenberg and Pillay 2000.

71. See *The Director, Mineral Development Gauteng Region and Sasol Mining (Pty) Ltd. v. Save the Vaal Environment and Others, 1999*, as summarized in Liebenberg and Pillay 2000, 139.

72. See *Transvaal Agricultural Union v. The Minister of Land Affairs, 1996*, as summarized in Liebenberg and Pillay 2000, 165–166.

73. See *Ndhladhla and others v. Erasmus, 1998* and *Van der Walt and others v. Lang and others, 1999* as summarized in Liebenberg and Pillay 2000, 296.

74. On the progressive realization clause, see Liebenberg and Pillay 2000, 31–32.

75. DWAF 1994. White papers are policy documents for drafting new laws, as opposed to a "green paper" crafted at an earlier stage of the policy process.

76. DWAF 1995, 4.

77. Such changes include emphasis on promoting the values enshrined in the Bill of Rights and the sharpening of the definition of water rights to specify environmental and basic human needs, with all other water uses referred to as authorizations rather than rights.

78. Stronger language was added on the need for water conservation and the importance of environmental sustainability. Language on the need to protect "lawful existing water rights" and pay compensation for lost rights was removed, and a reference to the right of appeal "to an independent tribunal" was replaced with the right to appeal to an unspecified body. The need to manage land use with an eye toward water-related impacts was qualified by the need to conform to the broader framework of land use management. The idea that beneficiaries of water services should contribute to the cost of establishing and maintaining water systems was qualified with the added language "on an equitable basis."

79. DWAF 1997, 5.

80. DWAF 1997, 29.

81. Davies and Day 1998, 364.

82. DWAF 1997, 6.

83. Republic of South Africa 1997, preamble.

84. Republic of South Africa 1997, Chapter 1, Sections 3 and 5.

85. Republic of South Africa 1997, Chapter 3, Sections 12–14.

86. Republic of South Africa 1997, Chapter 8, Sections 62–63.

87. Republic of South Africa 1998, Chapter 2, Part 1, Section 5.

88. Republic of South Africa 1998, Chapter 2, Part 1, Preamble.

89. Republic of South Africa 1998, Chapter 2, Part 3.

90. Under the Act, a license is required for any of the following uses of water: taking water from a water resource; storing water; impeding or diverting the flow of water in a watercourse; engaging in a stream flow reduction activity contemplated in Section 36; engaging in a controlled activity identified as such in Section 37(1) or declared under Section 38(1); discharging waste or water containing waste into a water resource through a pipe, canal, sewer, sea outfall or other conduit; disposing of waste in a manner which may detrimentally impact on a water resource; disposing in any manner of water which contains waste from, or which has been heated in, any industrial or power generation process; altering the bed, banks, course, or characteristics of a watercourse; removing, discharging, or disposing of water found underground if it is necessary for the

efficient continuation of an activity or for the safety of people; and using water for recreational purposes.

91. Republic of South Africa 1998, Chapter 5, Part 1.

92. Republic of South Africa 1998, Chapter 7, introduction.

93. Republic of South Africa 1998, Chapter 2, Part 2.

94. Republic of South Africa 1998, Chapter 2, Part 2, para. 10, subsection c.

95. Republic of South Africa 1998, Chapter 7, Part 2, para. 81, subsection 1.

96. Republic of South Africa 1998, Chapter 8, Preamble.

97. On the challenges of implementing catchment management agencies in South Africa, see Schreiner and van Koppen 2002.

98. South Africa is no exception to the chronic problem of coordination between water resources management and environmental protection when those tasks are separated bureaucratically. However, the DWAF's legal authority over water quality issues has to some extent reduced those obstacles.

99. Roberts 1983. See also Davies and Day 1998, 284–285.

100. The importance of seeing the Reserve as a science-based, measurable amount of water was stressed repeatedly in conversations with DWAF officials.

101. DWAF 2002, 18–19.

102. DWAF 1995, 28 and 30.

103. DWAF 2002, 23.

104. DWAF n.d.

105. DWA 1986, 8.17.

106. *City Council of Pretoria v. Walker* 1998 (3) BCLR 257 (CC) as cited in Liebenberg 2000.

107. *Grootboom v. Oostenberg Municipality and Others* 2000 (3) BCLR 277(C) as cited in Pillay and Liebenberg 2000.

108. Mettler et al. 2002.

109. de Visser et al. 2002, 19.

110. de Visser et al. 2002, 19.

111. Chirwa 2002.

112. Chirwa 2002.

113. Mettler et al. 2002.

114. Chirwa 2002.

115. Exactly how many persons lack water services is a subject of dispute. DWAF claims to have reduced the number of unserved from roughly 13 million to 6 million, a figure disputed by critics.

116. South African Human Rights Commission 1998, 33.

117. DWAF 1997, 22.

118. Pauw 2003.

119. Bond et al. 2001.

120. Pauw 2003.

121. Ronnie 2001.

122. South African Municipal Workers Union 2003.

123. Congress of South African Trade Unions 1998.

124. Congress of South African Trade Unions 1997.

125. Hemson and Batidzirai 2002.

126. South African Human Rights Commission 1998, 34.

127. DWAF 2003.

128. Davies and Day 1998, 288.

129. Davies and Day 1998, 49.

130. On the limits of anti-dam mobilization in South Africa, see Khagram 2004, 165–170.

131. Tarrow 1998.

132. Khagram 2004, 3.

133. Matlosa 2000, 178.

134. South Africa has invoked its treaty rights to postpone phase II, which was originally slated to deliver water in 2008. See National Assembly 2003.

135. The scheme is jointly financed, with South Africa responsible for the water transfer costs and Lesotho the costs related to hydropower development. South Africa has raised its funds primarily in private capital markets, Lesotho via international loans. The World Bank, European Investment Bank, and Development Bank of South Africa have also provided funds. The project envisions recovering costs for each phase over a twenty-year period dating from completion of that phase. Revenues from the sale of water and other project-related fees account for more than one-quarter of the Lesotho government's budget.

136. According to Davis and Day (1998), the project "has been the subject of many years of international negotiations and technical investigations but, although some might argue otherwise, we believe that no true environmental impact assessment has yet been undertaken" (299).

137. IRN n.d. b.

138. Matlosa 2000, 181. The IRN alleged that as of the end of 2001, only 2,000 of 27,000 persons displaced by the first three dams had been resettled. See Hoover 2001.

139. Hoover 2001, 1.

140. UNEP 2002b.

141. South African Multi-stakeholder Initiative on the World Commission on Dams 2002, 11; emphasis in original.

142. See Environmental Monitoring Group 1999.

143. See Luger and van Niekerk 2001, 1. See also Shand et al. 2000.

144. See Wildlife and Environment Society of South Africa n.d.

145. DWA 1986, 8.3.

146. One interview subject within DWAF pointed to fears of future water short-falls, domestic water planning needs, and South Africa's postapartheid emphasis on regional cooperation as the key forces behind renewed international river diplomacy in the 1990s.

147. On the political origins of SADCC and its transformation into SADC, see Schoeman 2002.

148. Swatuk 2000.

149. Swatuk 2002b. See also Swatuk 2002a.

150. SADC 2000.

151. Ramoeli 2002.

152. SADC 2002, 105.

153. SADC 2002, 106.

154. Tripartite Interim Agreement 2002.

155. DWAF 2000.

156. Turton n.d.

157. Heyns 2002.

158. DWAF 1997, 5.

159. Africa News Service 1999.

160. Turton and Quinn n.d.

161. DWAF 2002.

162. Cock 2003.

Chapter 10

1. Finnemore and Sikkink 1998.

2. World Water Assessment Programme 2003.

3. For an account of the protests, see Caplan 2003.

4. Gerlach 1993, 188.

5. Jasanoff 1998, 66.

6. Castells 2000 and Hoogvelt 2001.

7. See Conca 2005.

8. Ranney 1958.

9. Lipschutz with Mayer 1996, 237.

10. Sachs 2002, 67.
11. Sachs 2002, 68.
12. Permanent Court of Arbitration n.d.
13. Conca and Dabelko 2002.
14. Lipschutz with Mayer 1996, 237.
15. Lipschutz with Mayer 1996, 248.
16. Lipschutz with Mayer 1996, 252.
17. Lipschutz with Mayer 1996, 251.
18. Ottaway 2001.
19. Ottaway 2001, 266.
20. UNCSD 2002, para. 35.
21. Falk 2001.
22. Dubash et al. 2001.
23. This argument is developed in more detail in Conca 2005.
24. Hemmati 2002b, 63.
25. McAdam et al. 2001, 6.
26. Meyer and Rowan 1977, 345.

References

Acronyms used in citations:

ANA:	Agência Nacional de Águas (Brazil)
ABRH:	Associação Brasileira de Recursos Hídricos
CNRH:	Conselho Nacional de Recursos Hídricos (Brazil)
DWAF:	Department of Water Affairs and Forestry (South Africa)
FAO:	Food and Agriculture Organization
GWP:	Global Water Partnership
ICID:	International Commission on Irrigation and Drainage
ICOLD:	International Commission on Large Dams
IISD:	International Institute for Sustainable Development
IRN:	International Rivers Network
IWRA:	International Water Resources Association
MAB:	Movimento dos Atingidos pôr Barragens (Brazil)
SRH:	Secretaria de Recursos Hídricos (Brazil)
SADC:	Southern African Development Community
UNCSD:	United Nations Commission on Sustainable Development
UNDP:	United Nations Development Programme
UNEP:	United Nations Environment Programme
UNICEF:	United Nations Children's Fund
WCD:	World Commission on Dams
WCED:	World Commission on Environment and Development
WHO:	World Health Organization
WRI:	World Resources Institute
WSSCC:	Water Supply and Sanitation Collaborative Council

Abers, Rebecca and Margaret E. Keck (2003). "Networks, Relations, and Practices: Reflections on Watershed Management Organization in Brazil." Paper presented at the XXIV International Congress of the Latin American Studies Association, Dallas, Texas, March 27–29.

Abramovitz, Janet (1996). "Imperiled Waters, Impoverished Future: The Decline of Freshwater Ecosystems." Worldwatch Paper No. 128 (Washington, D.C.: Worldwatch Institute).

Académie de l'Eau (1999). "La Charte Sociale de L'Eau: Une Nouvelle Approche de la Gestion de l'Eau au 21e Siecle" (Paris: Académie de l'Eau).

Africa News Service (1999). "Three Nations Sign Incomati Basin Agreement." http://www.swazinews.co.sz/stories/3aug99.htm (accessed June 1, 2003).

Agência Nacional de Águas (Brazil) (2002). *A Evolução da Gestão dos Recursos Hídricos no Brasil* (Brasília: ANA).

Aldeia, Paquiçamba (2002). "Final Document of the First Meeting of the Indigenous Peoples of the Volta Grande Region of the Xingu River," June 10.

Allee, David (1989). "River Basin Management." Position paper for *The Assessment of the Social Science of Water Planning and Management*, Southern Illinois University, Carbondale, Illinois.

Almeida, Rogério (n.d.). "Hidrovia do Araguaia: Organizações populares de cinco estados se organizam para barrar projeto." Manuscript.

Amoore, Louise and Paul Langley (2004). "Ambiguities of Global Civil Society," *Review of International Studies* 30: 89–110.

Annuaire de l'Institute de Droit International (1961). 49-II, Salzburg Session, September, Basel, pp. 381–384. Cited in Stephen C. McCaffrey, "Water, Politics, and International Law," in Peter H. Gleick, ed., *Water in Crisis: A Guide to the World's Fresh Water Resources* (New York: Oxford University Press, 1993), p. 98.

Antunes, Paulo de Bessa (1999). *Direito Ambiental* (Rio de Janeiro: Lumen Juris). 3rd ed.

Asad, Musa, Luiz Gabriel Azevedo, Karin E. Kemper, and Larry D. Simpson (1999). *Management of Water Resources: Bulk Water Pricing in Brazil* (Washington, D.C.: World Bank). World Bank Technical Paper no. 432.

Asian Development Bank (2001). "ADB Planned Responses to Report of the World Commission on Dams: Strategic Priorities, Good Practices, and Institutional Responses." Draft report, August 2001. www.adb.org/ngos/adb_responses.asp (accessed October 30, 2002).

Associação Brasileira de Recursos Hídricos (1987). "Salvador Declaration," November 13, 1987.

——— (n.d.). "Statute of the Brazilian Water Resources Association." http://www.abrh.org.br/ (March 24, 2003).

Aw, Oumar (2001). Letter from the African Development Bank to Kader Asmal of the World Commission on Dams, January 26, 2001.

Baker, Gideon (2001). "Problems in the Theorization of Global Civil Society," *Political Studies* 50: 928–943.

Bangkok *Post* (2000). "Gangsters beat up protest villagers." November 21. http://www.probeinternational.org/pi/Mekong/index.cfm?DSP=content&ContentID=3836 (accessed September 13, 2002).

Barkin, J. Samuel and George E. Shambaugh, eds. (1999). *Anarchy and the Environment* (Albany: State University of New York Press).

Barlow, Maude (2001). "Water Privatization and the Threat to the World's Most Precious Resource: Is Water a Commodity or a Human Right?" *IFG Bulletin*, summer 2001. (San Francisco: International Forum on Globalization).

Barros, Selma (2001). "IDB-Financed Cana Brava Dam Causes Controversy in Brazil," *World Rivers Review* 16 no. 4 (August): 7.

Barry, John and Robyn Eckersley, eds. (2005). *The State and the Global Ecological Crisis* (Cambridge, MA: MIT Press).

Barth, Flávio Terra (1999). "Evolução nos Aspectos Institucionais e no Gerenciamento de Recursos Hídricos no Brasil," in Agência Nacional de Energia Elétrica, Ministério de Minas e Energia, Ministério do Meio Ambiente, World Meteorological Organization, and United Nations Development Programme, *O Estado das Águas no Brasil 1999: Perspectivas de Gestão e Informação de Recursos Hídricos* (Brasília: ANEEL).

Batliwala, Srilatha (2002). "Grassroots Movements as Transnational Actors: Implications for Global Civil Society," *Voluntas: International Journal of Voluntary and Nonprofit Organizations* 13 no. 4 (December): 393–409.

Benedick, Richard Elliot (1998). *Ozone Diplomacy: New Directions in Safeguarding the Planet* (Cambridge, Mass.: Harvard University Press). Rev. ed.

Bennett, Janette (2001). "The dove trail." *Sunday Times* (South Africa), November 18, travel section.

Bennett, W. Lance (2002). "Communicating Global Activism: Some Strengths and Vulnerabilities of Networked Politics." Paper presented at the Pacific Sociological Association meeting, Vancouver. Cited in Sidney Tarrow, "The New Transnational Contention: Organizations, Coalitions, Mechanisms." Paper presented at the 98th annual meeting of the American Political Science Association, Chicago, September 1, p. 17.

Bernauer, Thomas (1995). "The Effect of International Environmental Institutions: How We Might Learn More," *International Organization* 49 (Spring): 351–377.

Berry, Wendell (1990). "Word and Flesh," in Wendell Berry, *What Are People For?* (San Francisco: North Point Press).

Bijker, W. E., Thomas P. Hughes, and Trevor Pinch (1987). *The Social Construction of Technological Systems* (Cambridge, Mass.: MIT Press).

Birkes, Fikret, ed. (1989). *Common Property Resources: Ecology and Community-Based Sustainable Development* (New York: Columbia University Press).

Björklund, Gunilla (n.d.). "UN and Freshwater Issues, a Brief Survey of Facts and Links." A report commissioned by the Global Water Partnership. www.gwpforum.org/unsynposis.htm (accessed October 28, 1999).

Blaikie, Piers (1985). *The Political Economy of Soil Erosion in Developing Countries* (London: Longman).

Bond, Patrick, David McDonald, Greg Ruiters, and Liane Greeff (2001). "Water Privatization in South Africa." Report of the Environmental Monitoring Group, Cape Town, December.

Brack, Duncan (1996). *International Trade and the Montreal Protocol* (London: Royal Institute of International Affairs).

Broad, Robin, ed. (2002). *Global Backlash: Citizen Initiatives for a Just World Economy* (Lanham, Md.: Rowman & Littlefield).

Broad, Robin and John Cavanagh (1999). "The Death of the Washington Consensus?" *World Policy Journal* XVI no. 3 (Fall): 79–88.

Brown, Aleta and Patrick McCully (1997). "Coalition Call for International Moratorium on Large Dams," *World Rivers Review* 12 no. 2 (April).

Brown, Kevin (2001). "Balfour Beatty faces dam clash." *Financial Times*, May 2.

Cabral, Bernardo (2000). *Recursos Hídricos e o Desenvolvimento Sustentavel III* (Brasília: Senado Federal).

Caldwell, Lynton (1996). *International Environmental Policy* (Durham, N.C.: Duke University Press). 3rd ed.

Camdessus, Michel (2003). "Foreword," in James Winpenny, *Financing Water for All: Report of the World Panel on Financing Water Infrastructure*, Marseilles: World Water Council.

Caplan, Ruth (2003). "World Water Warriors." A report of the Alliance for Democracy from the Third World Water Forum in Kyoto, March 16–22. www.thealliancefordemocracy.org/html/eng/2049-AA.shtml (accessed December 15, 2003).

Castells, Manuel (2000). *Rise of the Network Society* (Oxford: Blackwell). Rev. ed.

Center for Investigative Reporting and Bill Moyers (1989). *Global Dumping Ground: The International Traffic in Hazardous Waste* (Washington, D.C.: Seven Locks Press).

Chalecki, Elizabeth (2000). "Bulk Water Exports and Free Trade," *Pacific Institute Report*, Fall 2000, pp. 12–13.

Chao, B. F. (1995). "Anthropological Impact on Global Geodynamics due to Water Impoundment in Major Reservoirs," *Geophysical Research Letters* 22 (1995): 3533–3536. Cited in Peter H. Gleick, *The World's Water 1998–1999: The Biennial Report on Freshwater Resources* (Washington, D.C.: Island Press, 1998), p. 70.

Chatterjee, Pratap and Matthias Finger (1994). *The Earth Brokers* (London: Routledge).

Chayes. Abram and Antonio Handler Chayes (1995). *The New Sovereignty* (Cambridge, Mass.: Harvard University Press).

Chinao, Tadao (2000). Letter from the president of the Asian Development Bank to Kader Asmal, chair of the World Commission on Dams, December 22, 2000.

Chirwa, Danwood Mzikenge (2002). "Obligations of Non-state Actors in Relation to Economic, Social and Cultural Rights under the South African Constitution." Socio-Economic Rights Project, Community Law Centre, University of the Western Cape, Bellville, South Africa.

Churchill, Anthony (1997a). "Hydropower: A New Business or an Obsolete Industry?" in World Conservation Union and World Bank, *Large Dams: Learning from the Past Looking at the Future.* Workshop proceedings, Gland Switzerland, April 11–12, 1997 (Washington, D.C.: IUCN), pp. 111–118.

——— (1997b). "Meeting Hydro's Financing and Development Challenges," in World Conservation and World Bank, *Large Dams: Learning from the Past Looking at the Future.* Workshop proceedings, Gland Switzerland, April 11–12, 1997 (Washington, D.C.: IUCN), pp. 103–110.

Citizen's Network on Essential Services (2001). "IMF and World Bank Push Water Privatization and Full Cost Recovery on Poor Countries," *News and Notices* 2 no. 4 (Spring). http://www.challengeglobalization.org/html/news _archive.shtml#26 (accessed December 15, 2003).

Civil Society World Water Vision for Action (n.d.). "Water Is Life: A Civil Society World Water Vision for Action." http://www.blueplanetproject.net/cms _publications/12.pdf (accessed January 10, 2004).

Clapp, Jennifer (1994). "Africa, NGOs, and the International Toxic Waste Trade," *Journal of Environment and Development* 3 no. 2 (1994): 17–46.

——— (2001). *Toxic Exports: The Transfer of Hazardous Wastes From Rich to Poor Countries* (Ithaca, N.Y.: Cornell University Press).

Cleary, David (1993). "After the Frontier: Problems with Political Economy in the Modern Brazilian Amazon," *Journal of Latin American Studies* 25: 331–349.

COAGRET (n.d.). "Water conflicts in the Iberian peninsula." http://www .geocities.com/RainForest/Jungle/1839/index.htm (accessed December 13, 2002).

Cock, Jacklyn (2003). "The World Social Forum and South Africa: The Local and the Global," Research Report No. 5. Centre for Civil Society, Durban, South Africa.

Colborn, Theo, Dianne Dumanoski, and John Peterson Myers (1987). *Our Stolen Future* (New York: Plume/Penguin).

Commission of Enquiry on Water Matters (South Africa) (1970). *Findings and Recommendations of the Commission of Enquiry on Water Matters.* Reprinted in Department of Water Affairs, *Management of the Water Resources of the Republic of South Africa* (Pretoria: DWAF, 1986), section 1.3, pp. 1.13–1.61.

Comor, Edward (2001). "The Role of Communication in Global Civil Society: Forces, Processes, Prospects," *International Studies Quarterly* 45: 389–408.

Conca, Ken (1993). "Environmental Change and the Deep Structure of World Politics," in Ronnie D. Lipschutz and Ken Conca, eds., *The State and Social Power in Global Environmental Politics* (New York: Columbia University Press).

—— (1995). "Rethinking the Ecology-Sovereignty Debate," *Millennium: Journal of International Studies* 23 no. 3 (January): 701–711.

—— (1997). *Manufacturing Insecurity: The Rise and Fall of Brazil's Military-Industrial Complex* (Boulder, Col.: Lynne Rienner Publishers).

—— (2000). "The WTO and the Undermining of Global Environmental Governance," *Review of International Political Economy* 7 no. 3 (Autumn): 484–494.

—— (2002). "The World Commission on Dams and Trends in Global Environmental Governance," *Politics and the Life Sciences* 21 no. 1 (March): 67–70.

—— (2005). "Old States in New Bottles? The Hybridization of Authority in Global Environmental Governance," in John Barry and Robyn Eckersley, eds., *The State and the Global Ecological Crisis* (Cambridge, Mass.: MIT Press).

Conca, Ken and Geoffrey D. Dabelko (1998). "The Earth Summit: Reflections on an Ambiguous Event," in Ken Conca and Geoffrey D. Dabelko, eds., *Green Planet Blues: Environmental Politics from Stockholm to Kyoto* (Boulder, Col.: Westview Press). 2nd ed.

Conca, Ken and Geoffrey D. Dabelko, eds. (2002). *Environmental Peacemaking* (Washington, D.C. and Baltimore, Md.: Woodrow Wilson Center Press and Johns Hopkins University Press).

Conca, Ken, Fengshi Wu, and Joanne Neukirchen (2003). "Is There a Global Rivers Regime? Trends in the Principled Content of International River Agreements." A research report of the Harrison Program on the Future Global Agenda, University of Maryland, September 2003. www.bsos.umd.edu/harrison.

Congress of South African Trade Unions (1997). *Submission on the Water Services Bill (B65–97).* Presented to the Portfolio Committee on Agriculture, Water Affairs and Forestry, September 10, 1997.

Congress of South African Trade Unions (1998). *Parliamentary Submission on the National Water Bill.* Presented to the Portfolio Committee on Agriculture, Water Affairs and Forestry, March 17, 1998.

Conselho Nacional de Recursos Hídricos (2000). CNRH Resolution no. 5, April 10, 2000.

Consultoria Legal, Câmara dos Deputados (Brazil) (n.d.). "Evolução da Gestão dos Recursos Hídricos no Brasil." Manuscript.

Corner House (2000). "Exporting Corruption: Privatisation, Multinationals and Bribery." CornerHouse Briefing, June 19, 2000.

Corporate Europe Observatory, World Development Movement, and Friends of the Earth Europe (2002). "Urgent need for EU transparency in trade talks on services: What the EC needs to understand." http://www.wdm.org.uk/cambriefs/EUtransp.pdf (accessed October 1, 2004).

Cosgrove, William J. and Frank R. Rijsberman (2000a). "The Making of the World Water Vision." March 2000. Cited in Navroz K. Dubash, Mairi Dupar, Smitu Kothari, and Tundu Lissu, *A Watershed in Global Governance? An Independent Assessment of the World Commission on Dams* (Washington, D.C.: World Resources Institute, 2002), p. 77.

———— (2000b). *World Water Vision: Making Water Everybody's Business* (London: Earthscan).

Costanza, Robert, Ralph d'Agre, Rudolf de Groot, Stephen Farber, Monica Grasso, Bruce Hannon, Karin Limburg, Shahid Naeem, Robert V. O'Neill, Jose Paruelo, Robert G. Raskin, Paul Sutton, and Marjan van den Belt (1997). "The Value of the World's Ecosystem Services and Natural Capital," *Nature* 387 no. 15 (15 May): 253–259.

Council of Canadians (n.d.). "Our History." www.canadians.org (January 6, 2004).

Covich, Alan P. (1993). "Water and Ecosystems," in Peter H. Gleick, ed., *Water in Crisis: A Guide to the World's Fresh Water Resources* (New York: Oxford University Press), pp. 40–55.

Crosson, Pierre (1994). "Degradation of Resources as a Threat to Sustainable Agriculture." Paper presented at the first World Congress of Professionals in Agronomy, Santiago, Chile, Sept. 5–8, 1994. Cited in World Resources Institute, *World Resources 1998–99* (Washington, D.C.: WRI, 1998), p. 157.

Davenport, Rodney and Christopher Saunders (2000). *South Africa: A Modern History* (New York: St. Martin's Press). 5th ed.

Davies, Bryan and Jenny Day (1998). *Vanishing Waters* (Cape Town: University of Cape Town Press).

Dawson, Jane (1996). *Econationalism: Anti-nuclear Activism and National Identity in Russia, Lithuania, and Ukraine* (Durham, N.C.: Duke University Press).

Delli Priscoli, Jerome (1996). "The Development of Transnational Regimes for Water Resources Management," in Mahmoud A. Abu-Zeid and Asit K. Biswas, eds., *River Basin Planning and Management* (Calcutta: Oxford University Press, 1996).

Department of Environmental Affairs and Tourism (South Africa) (1999). *State of the Environment South Africa: The National State of the Environment Report.* http://www.ngo.grida.no/soesa/nsoer/issues/water/index.htm (accessed July 9, 2003).

Department of Foreign Affairs and Trade (Canada) (2002). "Canada Announces Coming into Force of Amendments to International Boundary Waters Treaty Act." Press release, December 10.

Department of Water Affairs (South Africa) (1986). *Management of the Water Resources of the Republic of South Africa* (Pretoria: DWAF).

Department of Water Affairs and Forestry (South Africa) (1994). *Water Supply and Sanitation Policy White Paper* (Pretoria: DWAF).

———— (1995). *You and Your Water Rights* (Pretoria: DWAF).

———— (1997). *White Paper on a National Water Policy* (Pretoria: DWAF).

———— (2000). "Agreement on the Establishment of the Orange-Senqu River Commission." Press release, November 1.

———— (2002). *National Water Resource Strategy: Summary* (proposed first edition). (Pretoria: DWAF).

———— (2003). "New Strategic Framework for Water Services Approved by Cabinet." Press release, September 19.

———— (n.d.). "Chief Directorate: International Projects." http://dwaf-www .pwv.gov.za/Dir_IntProj/ (accessed July 16, 2002).

Deudney, Daniel (1990). "The Case Against Linking Environmental Degradation and National Security," *Millennium: Journal of International Studies* 19 (Winter): 461–476.

Deutsche Gesellschaft fur Technische Zusammenarbeit (2002). "Umsetzung der Empfehlungen der World Commission on Dams (Dissemination of the Recommendations of the World Commission on Dams)." http://www.gtz.de/themen/ ebene3.asp?Thema=110&ProjectId=313&Reihenfolge=&spr=2 (accessed October 30, 2002).

de Visser, Jaap, Edward Cottle, and Johann Mettler (2002). "The Free Basic Water Supply: How Effective Is It in Realizing the Right?" *ESR Review* 3 no. 1 (July): 18–19.

Diário de Cuiabá (2001a). "Juiz determina suspensão de cargas." March 17.

———— (2001b). "Para Taques governo quer 'empurrar projeto no grito.'" March 21.

Discerning the Times (2001). "Klamath River: 21st Century Boston Tea Party?" *Discerning the Times* 3 issue 7–8, July–August 2001. http://www .discerningtoday.org/members/Digest/2001digest/jul-aug/klamath_river--boston _tea_party.htm (accessed August 8, 2002).

Dolšak, Nives and Elinor Ostrom (2003). *The Commons in the New Millennium: Challenges and Adaptation* (Cambridge, Mass.: MIT Press).

Dubash, Navroz K., Mairi Dupar, Smitu Kothari, and Tundu Lissu (2001). *A Watershed in Global Governance? An Independent Assessment of the World Commission on Dams* (Washington, D.C.: World Resources Institute).

Dugan, P. J. and T. Jones (1993). "Ecological Change in Wetlands: A Global Overview," in M. Moser, R. C. Prentice, and J. van Vessem, eds., *Waterfowl and Wetland Conservation in the 1990s: A Global Perspective* (Slimbridge, UK: The International Waterfowl and Wetlands Research Bureau, pp. 34–38). Cited in Carmen Revenga, Jake Brunner, Norbert Henninger, Ken Kassem, and Richard Payne, *Pilot Analysis of Global Ecosystems: Freshwater Ecosystems* (Washington, D.C.: World Resources Institute, 2000), p. 21.

Dunn, Jamie (2002). "International Conference Mirrors Local Struggles Against Water Profiters," *Defend the Global Commons* 1 no. 1 (February): 17–18.

Economist (2000). "Water Fights," in *The World in 2000* (London: The Economist Group), p. 78.

Environmental Monitoring Group (1999). "Southern African Hearings for Communities Affected by Large Dams." http://www.emg.org.za/frame/frameset.htm (accessed January 15, 2004).

Esty, Daniel (2000). "Environment and the Trading System: Picking up the Post-Seattle Pieces," in Jeffery J. Schott, ed., *The WTO after Seattle* (Washington, D.C.: Institute for International Economics), pp. 243–252.

Falk, Richard (2001). Remarks at the World Resources Institute, November 21.

Federal Ministry for the Environment, Nature Conservation and Nuclear Safety, and Federal Ministry for Economic Co-operation and Development (Germany) (n.d.). *International Freshwater Conference Bonn 2001: Conference Report.* http://www.water-2001.de/ConferenceReport.pdf (accessed June 1, 2003).

Federative Republic of Brazil (1997). Federal Law 9433, Política Nacional de Recursos Hídricos, January 8.

——— (2000). Federal Law 9984, Agência Nacional de Águas, July 17, 2000.

Feeny, David, Fikret Berkes, Bonnie J. McCay, and James M. Acheson (1990). "The Tragedy of the Commons: Twenty-Two Years Later," *Human Ecology* 18 no. 1 (1990).

Feldmann, Fábio (1994). "Revisão Constitucional e Recursos Hídricos," in Ministério de Integração Regional, SEPLAN, World Bank, and Instituto Interamericano de Cooperação para a Agricultura, *O Gerenciamento dos Recursos Hídricos e o Mercado de Águas* (Brasília: MIR).

Feyerabend, Paul K. (1979). *Science in a Free Society* (London: Routledge).

Finger, Matthias and Jeremy Allouche (2002). *Water Privatisation: Trans-National Corporations and the Re-Regulation of the Water Industry* (London: Spon Press).

Finkelstein, Lawrence S. (1995). "What Is Global Governance?" *Global Governance* 1 no. 3 (September–December): 367–372.

Finlayson, C. M. and N. C. Davidson (1999). *Global Review of Wetland Resources and Priorities for Wetland Inventory. Summary Report* (Australia: Wetlands International and the Environmental Research Institute of the Supervising Scientists). Cited in World Resources Institute, United Nations Development Programme, United Nations Environment Programme, and World Bank, *World Resources 2000–2001: People and Ecosystems: The Fraying Web of Life* (Washington, D.C.: World Resources Institute, 2000), p. 106.

Finnemore, Martha (1996). "Norms, Culture, and World Politics: Insights from Sociology's Institutionalism," *International Organization* 50 no. 2 (Spring): 325–347.

Finnemore, Martha and Kathryn Sikkink (1998). "International Norm Dynamics and Political Change," *International Organization* 52 no. 4 (Autumn): 887–917.

First International Meeting of People Affected by Dams (1997). "Declaration of Curitiba Affirming the Right to Life and Livelihood of People Affected by Dams," in *Proceedings of the First International Meeting of People Affected by Dams*, Curitiba, Brazil, March 11–14. www.irn.org/programs/curitiba.html (accessed October 13, 1999).

Food and Agriculture Organization (1995). *Reforming Water Resources Policy: A Guide to Methods, Processes and Practices* (Rome, Food and Agriculture Organization).

———— (1997). *State of the World's Forests 1997* (Rome: FAO).

———— (1999a). *Review of the State of World Fishery Resources: Inland Fisheries* (Rome: FAO). Fisheries Circular No. 942.

———— (1999b). *The State of World Fisheries and Aquaculture, 1998* (Rome: FAO).

———— (2000). *Global Forest Resources Assessment 2000* (Rome, FAO).

———— (n.d.). FAOLEX database. http://faolex.fao.org/faolex/

Ford, Lucy H. (2003). "Challenging Global Environmental Governance: Social Movement Agency and Global Civil Society," *Global Environmental Politics* 3 no. 2 (May): 120–134.

Freshwater Action Network (2003). "NGO Panel Debate Outcome Presentation to the 3rd World Water Forum and Ministerial Conference, Kyoto, Japan 22 March 2003." http://www.freshwateraction.net/conferences/kyoto/fanAtKyoto .asp (accessed January 6, 2004).

Friends of the Earth UK (2001). "Dirty Water: The Environmental and Social Records of Four Multinational Water Companies." Briefing, December.

Fundaçao Centro Brasileiro de Referência e Apoio Cultural and Instituto Centro de Vida (1994). *Hidrovia Paraguai-Paraná: Quem Paga a Conta? Análise da Viabilidade Econômico-Financeira do Projeto da Hidrovia Paraguai-Paraná* (Brasília: CEBRAC).

Garbvrecht, G. (1997). "Sadd-el-Kafra, the World's Oldest Large Dam," in Donald C. Jackson, ed., *Dams* (Aldershot, UK: Ashgate).

Garrido, Raymundo (2000). "Proposals for a Brazilian Vision on Water Management for 2025" (Brasília: Ministério de Meio Ambiente).

———— (2001). "Exaggerations of the Commission on Large Dams." *Gazeta Mercantil*, March 27.

———— (n.d.). "Water Resources National Policy in Brazil." Contributing paper prepared for Thematic Review V.3: River-basin institutional frameworks and management options, World Commission on Dams.

GATSWatch (2001). "GATS: What Is Fact and What Is Fiction? A Civil Society Response to the WTO's Publication 'GATS: Fact and Fiction.'" http://www .gatswatch.org/docs/rebuttal.html (accessed June 1, 2003).

———— (n.d.). "GATS 2000 Negotiations: Reactions to Leaked EC Documents." http://www.gatswatch.org/ECleaknews.html (accessed October 1, 2004).

Gender Plenary Session, International Conference on Freshwater (2001). "Integrating Gender Perspectives: Realizing New Options for Improved Water Management." Report of the Gender Plenary Session, Bonn, Germany, December 2001.

Gerlach, Luther (1993). "Negotiating Ecological Interdependence through Societal Debate: The Minnesota Drought," in Ronnie D. Lipschutz and Ken Conca, eds., *The State and Social Power in Global Environmental Politics* (New York: Columbia University Press).

Gilpin, Robert (1987). *The Political Economy of International Relations* (Princeton, N.J.: Princeton University Press).

Gleick, Peter H. (1998). *The World's Water 1998–99: The Biennial Report on Freshwater Resources* (Washington, D.C.: Island Press).

——— (1999). "The Human Right to Water," *Water Policy* 1 no. 5: 487–503.

——— (2000). *The World's Water 2000–2001: The Biennial Report on Freshwater Resources* (Washington, D.C.: Island Press).

Gleick, Peter H., Gary Wolff, Elizabeth L. Chalecki, and Rachel Reyes (2002). *The New Economy of Water: The Risks and Benefits of Globalization and Privatization of Fresh Water* (Oakland, Calif.: Pacific Institute).

Global Committee for the Water Contract (1998). *The Water Manifesto: The Right to Life* (Lisbon: Global Committee for the Water Contract).

Global Water Partnership (2000a). "Integrated Water Resources Management." Technical Advisory Committee, Background paper no. 4, Stockholm.

——— (2000b). *Towards Water Security: A Framework for Action* (Stockholm, Global Water Partnership). Report prepared for presentation at the Second World Water Forum, The Hague, Netherlands, March 17–22, 2000.

——— (2001). "Comprehensive work programme and follow up to the Framework for Action" (Stockholm: Global Water Partnership).

——— (n.d. a). "About the Toolbox." http://www.gwpforum.org/servlet/PSP?iNodeID=2379 (accessed June 4, 2002).

——— (n.d. b). "About Us." http://www.gwpforum.org/servlet/PSP?chStartupName=_about (accessed June 2, 2002).

——— (n.d. c). "Associates at Work." http://www.gwpforum.org/servlet/PSP?chStartupName=_associates (accessed June 4, 2002).

——— (n.d. d). "IWRM at a Glance" (Stockholm: Global Water Partnership).

——— (n.d. e). "Mission statement." www.gwpforum.org (accessed June 2, 2002).

Global Water Scoping Process Working Group (2004). "Is There a Case for a Global Multistakeholder Review of Private Sector Participation In Water And Sanitation? Survey Questionnaire." January. Electronic mail from the Global Water Scoping Process Working Group.

Goffman, Erving (1974). *Frame Analysis: An Essay on the Organization of Experience* (Cambridge, Mass.: Harvard University Press).

Goldsmith, Edward and Nicholas Hildyard (1984). *The Social and Environmental Effects of Large Dams* (Cornwall, UK: Wadebridge Ecological Center). Volume 2.

Goodland, Robert (1997). "Environmental Sustainability in the Hydro Industry," in World Conservation Union and World Bank, *Large Dams: Learning from the Past Looking at the Future.* Workshop Proceedings, Gland Switzerland, April 11–12, 1997 (Washington, D.C.: IUCN), pp. 69–102.

Granziera, Maria Luiza Machado (2001). *Direito de Águas: Disciplina Jurídica das Águas Doces* (São Paulo: Editora Atlas S.A.).

Greeff, Liane (2002). "International Conference on Freshwater Bonn and the Multistakeholder Process: Lessons for the WSSD." http://www .worldsummit2002.org/index.htm?   http://www.worldsummit2002.org/issues/ waterconfviews.htm (November 18, 2002).

Greene, Owen (1998). "The System for Implementation Review in the Ozone Regime," in David G. Victor, Kal Raustiala, and Eugene B. Skolnikoff, eds., *The Implementation and Effectiveness of International Environmental Commitments: Theory and Practice* (Cambridge, Mass.: MIT Press).

Grover, Brian and Asit K. Biswas (1993). "It's Time for a World Water Council," *Water International* 18 (1993): 81–83.

Gutierrez, Eric, Belinda Calaguas, Joanne Green, and Virginia Roaf (2003). *New Rules, New Roles: Does PSP Benefit the Poor?* Synthesis report, WaterAid and Tearfund.

Haas, Ernst B. (1991). *When Knowledge Is Power* (Berkeley and Los Angeles, Calif.: University of California Press).

Haas, Peter M. (1989). "Do Regimes Matter? Epistemic Communities and Mediterranean Pollution Control," *International Organization* 43 no. 3 (Summer): 377–403.

——— (1990). *Saving the Mediterranean: The Politics of International Environmental Cooperation* (New York: Columbia University Press).

——— (1992a). "Epistemic Communities and International Policy Coordination," *International Organization* 46 no. 1 (Winter): 1–35.

——— (1992b). "Banning Chlorofluorocarbons: Epistemic Community Efforts to Protect Stratospheric Ozone," *International Organization* v. 46 no. 1 (Winter): 187–224.

Haas, Peter M. with Jan Sundgren (1993). "Evolving International Environmental Law: Changing Practices of National Sovereignty," in Nazli Choucri, ed., *Global Accord: Environmental Challenges and International Responses* (Cambridge, Mass.: MIT Press).

Haas, Peter M., Robert O. Keohane, and Marc A. Levy, eds. (1993). *Institutions for the Earth: Sources of Effective International Environmental Protection* (Cambridge, Mass.: MIT Press).

Haas, Peter M., Marc A. Levy, and Edward A. Parson (1992). "Appraising the Earth Summit: How Should We Judge UNCED's Success?" *Environment* 34 no. 8 (October): 7–11 and 26–32.

Haggard, Stephan and Beth Simmons (1987). "Theories of International Regimes," *International Organization* 41: 491–517.

Hall, C. G. (1939). *The Origin and Development of Water Rights in South Africa* (Oxford: Oxford University Press).

Hamner, Jesse and Aaron Wolf (1997). "Patterns in International Water Resource Treaties: The Transboundary Freshwater Dispute Database," *Colorado Journal of International Environmental Law and Policy*. 1997 Yearbook.

Harsono, Andreas (2003). "Water and Politics in the Fall of Suharto," in International Consortium of Investigative Journalists, *The Water Barons* (Washington, D.C.: Center for Public Integrity).

Hatemi, Haleh and Peter H. Gleick (1992). "Chronology of Conflict Over Water in the Legends, Myths, and History of the Ancient Middle East." Report of the Pacific Institute for Studies in Development, Environment, and Security, Oakland, Calif.

Hecht, Susanna and Alexander Cockburn (1990). *The Fate of the Forest: Developers, Destroyers, and Defenders of the Amazon* (New York: HarperCollins, 1990).

Hemmati, Minu (2002a). *Multi-Stakeholder Processes for Governance and Sustainability: Beyond Deadlock and Conflict* (London: Earthscan).

——— (2002b). "The World Commission on Dams as a Multi-Stakeholder Process: Some Future Challenges," *Politics and the Life Sciences* 21 no. 1 (March): 63–66.

Hemson, David and Herbert Batidzirai (2002). "Public Private Partnerships and the Poor: Dolphin Coast Water Concession." Monograph, Water, Engineering and Development Centre, Loughborough University, UK.

Heyns, Piet (2002). "Interbasin Transfer of Water between SADC Countries: A Development Challenge for the Future," in Anthony Turton and Roland Henwood, eds., *Hydropolitics in the Developing World: A Southern African Perspective* (Pretoria: African Water Issues Research Unit).

Hochstetler, Kathryn (2002). "After the Boomerang: Environmental Movements and Politics in the La Plata River Basin," *Global Environmental Politics* 2 no. 4 (November): 35–57.

Homer-Dixon, Thomas F. (1991). "On the Threshold: Environmental Changes As Causes of Acute Conflict," *International Security* 16 no. 2 (Fall): 76–116.

——— (1994). "Environmental Scarcities and Violent Conflict: Evidence from Cases," *International Security* 19 no. 1 (Summer): 5–40.

Hoogvelt, Ankie (2001). *Globalization and the Postcolonial World: The New Political Economy of Development* (Baltimore, Md.: Johns Hopkins University Press). 2nd ed.

Hoover, Ryan (2001). "Demonstrators Protest Large Dams' Impacts in Lesotho," *World Rivers Review* 16 no. 6 (December): 1.

International Commission on Irrigation and Drainage (n.d.). "Objects and Activities." http://www.icid.org/index_e.html (accessed July 11, 2001).

International Commission on Large Dams (n.d.). "About ICOLD." http://www.icid.org/index_e.html (accessed July 11, 2001).

International Conference on Freshwater (2001). "Conclusions of the Multi-Stakeholder Dialogues Facilitated by David Hales." http://www.water-2001.de/outcome/msd/msd-en.asp (accessed June 11, 2002).

International Conference on Water and the Environment (1992). "Dublin Statement on Water and Sustainable Development." www.wmo.ch/web/homs/icwedece.html (accessed July 30, 2000).

International Institute for Sustainable Development (2001). "Highlights from the International Freshwater Conference," *Sustainable Developments*, December 4, 2001. http://www.iisd.ca/linkages/sd/water/sdh20/index.html (accessed June 13, 2002).

International Monetary Fund (2002). *Annual Report 2002* (Washington, D.C.: IMF).

International Rivers Network (1996). "The San Francisco Declaration: The Position of Citizens Organizations on Large Dams and Water Resource Management," *World Rivers Review* 11 no. 4 (September).

——— (1997a). "NGOs Condemn World Bank/IUCN Dam-Building Commission." Press release, November 25.

——— (1997b). *Proceedings, First International Meeting of People Affected by Dams, Curitiba, Brazil, March 11–14, 1997* (Berkeley, Calif.: International Rivers Network).

——— (1997c). "World Bank Dam Evaluation Seriously Deficient." Press release, Monday, April 7.

——— (1998). "World Commission on Dams Launched: NGOs Call for Moratorium on Dam-Building." Press release, February 16.

——— (1999). "Judge Suspends Hidrovia." Press release, October 26.

——— (2001a). "Privatization of Porto Primavera Dam Still on Hold," *World Rivers Review* 16 no. 1 (February): 6.

——— (2001b). "MAB, IDB Agree on Review of Cana Brava Dam Compensation." Press release, August 14.

——— (2001c). "WB Approves Bujagali Dam Despite Major Economic Risks." Press release, December 18.

——— (2002). "Updates: Brazil," *World Rivers Review* 17 no. 1 (February): 12.

——— (2003). "Dam Industry's Dream World," *World Rivers Review* 18 no. 5 (October): 2.

———— (n.d. a). "About International Rivers Network." www.irn.org/basics/whoweare.html (accessed October 21, 1999).

———— (n.d. b). "Lesotho Highlands Water Project, Senqu River, Lesotho." http://www.irn.org/wcd/lhwp.shtml (accessed October 11, 2003).

———— (n.d. c). "Brazil's Movement of Dam-Affected People (MAB)." http://www.irn.org/wcd/mab.shtml (accessed October 1, 2004).

International Rivers Network and Berne Declaration (2000). "A Call to Action." Statement released November 16, 2000.

International Water Resources Association (1988). "Sustainable Development and Water: Statement on the WCED Report *Our Common Future.*" Reproduced in Robin Clarke, *Water: The International Crisis* (Cambridge, Mass.: MIT Press, 1993), appendix II.

———— (1998). Meeting minutes for the June 6, 1998 meeting of the executive board of the International Water Resources Association, Paris. http://www.iwra.siu.edu/board/index.html (accessed June 6, 2002).

———— (1999). Draft minutes of the August 11–12, 1999 executive board meeting, Stockholm, Sweden. http://www.iwra.siu.edu/board/index.html (accessed June 6, 2002).

———— (n.d.). "The IWRA Vision." http://www.iwra.siu.edu/membership/brochure.html (accessed April 22, 2002).

Jackson, Robert B., Stephen R. Carpenter, Clifford N. Dahm, Diane M. McKnight, Robert J. Naiman, Sandra L. Postel, and Steven W. Running (2001). "Water in a Changing World," *Issues in Ecology* no. 9. Ecological Society of America. http://esa.sdsc.edu/issues9.htm

Jasanoff, Sheila (1998). "Contingent Knowledge: Implications for Implementation and Compliance," in Edith Brown Weiss and Harold K. Jacobson, eds., *Engaging Countries: Strengthening Compliance with International Environmental Accords* (Cambridge, Mass.: MIT Press).

Jornal do Senado (Brazil) (2000). "Para relator, novo orgão trará gestão moderna ao setor," *Jornal do Senado* 21 (July), p. 3.

Joy, Clare (2000). "The General Agreement on Trade in Services: Impacts on Water Delivery and the Need for a Civil Society Response," in Cathy Watson and Belinda Calaguas, eds., *Making Waves: Civil Society Advocacy on International Water Policy.* Report of the seminar held at NCVO, All Saints Street, London, December 14–15, 2000, pp. 11–12.

Kaldor, Mary (2003). "The Idea of Global Civil Society," *International Affairs* 79 no. 3: 583–593.

Keck, Margaret and Kathryn Sikkink (1998). *Activists Beyond Borders: Advocacy Networks in International Politics* (Ithaca, N.Y.: Cornell University Press).

Kellow, Aynsley (1999). *International Toxic Risk Management: Ideals, Interest and Implementation* (Cambridge: Cambridge University Press).

Keohane, Robert O. (1993). "The Analysis of International Regimes: Toward a European-American Research Programme," in Volker Rittberger, ed., *Regime Theory and International Relations* (Oxford: Clarendon Press).

Keohane, Robert O. and Elinor Ostrom, eds. (1995). *Local Commons and Global Interdependence: Heterogeneity and Cooperation in Two Domains* (London: Sage).

Kessler, Tim (2002). "Services for All? Analyzing Public Utility Reform in Developing Countries." Citizens' Network on Essential Services, Policy Analysis Series, Paper no. 1, September.

Kettelhut, Julio Thadeu Silva (2003). "Breve Histórico do Conselho Nacional de Recursos Hídricos." http://www.cnrh-srh.gov.br/ (accessed May 29, 2003).

Khagram, Sanjeev (2004). *Dams and Development: Transnational Struggles for Water and Power* (Ithaca, N.Y.: Cornell University Press).

Khagram, Sanjeev, James Riker, and Kathryn Sikkink, eds. (2002). *Restructuring World Politics: Transnational Social Movements, Networks, and Norms* (Minneapolis: University of Minnesota Press).

Klotz, Audie (2002). "Transnational Activism and Global Transformations: The Anti-Apartheid and Abolitionist Experiences," *European Journal of International Relations* 8 no. 1: 49–76.

Knigge, Markus, Benjamin Görlach, Ana-Mari Hamada, Caroline Nuffort, and R. Andreas Kraemer (2003). "The Use of Environmental and Social Criteria in Export Credit Agencies' Practices: A Study of Export Credit Agencies' Environmental Guidelines with Reference to the World Commission on Dams. A report to Deutsche Gesellschaft für Technische Zusammenarbeit." http://www.ecologic.de/download/projekte/1800-1849/1809/1809wcd_ecas_en.pdf (accessed October 1, 2004).

Krasner, Stephen D. (1982). "Structural Causes and Regime Consequences: Regimes as Intervening Variables," in Stephen D. Krasner, ed., *International Regimes* (Ithaca, N.Y.: Cornell University Press).

Kreuger, Jonathan (1999). *International Trade and the Basel Convention* (London: Earthscan).

Krueger, Anne O. (1993). *Political Economy of Policy Reform in Developing Countries* (Cambridge, Mass.: MIT Press).

Kuehls, Thom (1996). *Beyond Sovereign Territory: The Space of Ecopolitics* (Minneapolis: University of Minnesota Press).

Kutting, Gabriela (2000). *Environment, Society and International Relations: Towards More Effective International Environmental Agreements* (London: Routledge).

Lapidoth, Ruth (1992). "Sovereignty in Transition," *Journal of International Affairs* 45 no. 2 (Winter): 325–346.

Legassick, M. (1974). "Legislation, ideology and economy in post-1948 South Africa," *Journal of Southern African Studies* 1: 5–35. Cited in Rodney Davenport and Christopher Saunders, *South Africa: A Modern History* (New York: St. Martin's Press, 5th ed. 2000), p. 372.

Levy, Marc A. (1995). "Is the Environment a Security Issue?" *International Security* 20 no. 2 (Fall): 35–62.

Levy, Marc A., Robert O. Keohane, and Peter M. Haas (1993). "Improving the Effectiveness of International Environmental Institutions," in Peter M. Haas, Robert O. Keohane, and Marc A. Levy, eds., *Institutions for the Earth: Sources of Effective International Environmental Protection* (Cambridge, Mass.: MIT Press).

Lewis, A. D. (1932). *Water Law. Its Development in the Union of South Africa* (Cape Town and Joahnnesburg: Juta & Co.).

Liberty Matters News Service (2001). "Farmers versus Fish in Fight for Water Rights." May 7. http://www.libertymatters.org/5.8.01farmervfish.htm (accessed August 8, 2002).

Liebenberg, Sandra and Karrisha Pillay, eds. (2000). *Socio-Economic Rights in South Africa: A Resource Book*. Socio-Economic Rights Project, Community Law Centre, University of the Western Cape, Bellville, South Africa.

Lieberman, Evan S. (2001). "National Political Community and the Politics of Income Taxation in Brazil and South Africa in the Twentieth Century," *Politics & Society* 29 no. 4 (December): 515–555.

Lieberthal, Andres et al. (1996). "The World Bank's Experience with Large Dams: An Overview of Impacts." Unpublished report, Operations Evaluation Department, World Bank, August.

Lipschutz, Ronnie D. and Judith Mayer (1993). "Property Rights, Constitutive Rules, and the Renegotiation of Resource Management Regimes," in Ronnie D. Lipschutz and Ken Conca, eds., *The State and Social Power in Global Environmental Politics* (New York: Columbia University Press).

Lipschutz, Ronnie D. with Judith Mayer (1996). *Global Civil Society and Global Environmental Governance: The Politics of Nature from Place to Planet* (Albany: SUNY Press).

Litfin, Karen T. (1994). *Ozone Discourses* (New York: Columbia University Press).

——— (1995). "Framing Science: Precautionary Discourse and the Ozone Treaties," *Millennium: Journal of International Studies* 24 no. 2: 251–277.

——— (1997). "Sovereignty in World Ecopolitics," *Mershon International Studies Review* 41 no. 2 (November): 167–204.

Litfin, Karen T., ed. (1998). *The Greening of Sovereignty in World Politics* (Cambridge, Mass.: MIT Press).

Lovelock, J. E. (1987). *GAIA: A New Look at Life on Earth* (New York: Oxford University Press).

Luger, Mike and Peter van Niekerk (2001). "Experiences in Applying The World Commission on Dams' Guidelines to the Proposed Skuifraam Dam, Near Cape

Town." Paper presented at the SANCOLD symposium on the World Commission on Dams report, Midrand, July 23–24, 2001.

MacNeill, Jim, Pieter Winsemius, and Taizo Yakushiji (1991). *Beyond Interdependence: The Meshing of the World's Economy and the Earth's Ecology* (New York: Oxford University Press).

Manibeli Declaration Calling for a Moratorium on World Bank Funding of Large Dams (1994). www.irn.org/basics/ard/index.asp?id=manibeli.html (accessed July 1, 2003).

Mason, Michael (1999). *Environmental Democracy* (New York: St. Martin's Press).

Matlosa, Khabele (2000). "The Lesotho Highlands Water Project: Socio-Economic Impacts," in Daniel Tevera and Sam Moyo, eds., *Environmental Security in Southern Africa* (Harare: Southern Africa Regional Institute for Policy Studies).

McAdam, Doug, Sidney Tarrow, and Charles Tilly (2001). *Dynamics of Contention* (Cambridge: Cambridge University Press).

McCaffrey, Stephen C. (2001). *The Law of International Watercourses: Non-Navigational Uses* (Cambridge: Oxford University Press).

———— (1993). "Water, Politics, and International Law," in Peter H. Gleick, ed., *Water in Crisis: A Guide to the World's Fresh Water Resources* (New York: Oxford University Press).

McCaffrey, Stephen C. and Mpazi Sinjela (1998). "Current Developments: The 1997 United Nations Convention on International Watercourses," *American Journal of International Law* 92: 97–107.

McCormick, John (1989). *Reclaiming Paradise: The Global Environmental Movement* (Bloomington: Indiana University Press).

McCully, Patrick (1996). *Silenced Rivers: The Ecology and Politics of Large Dams* (London: Zed Books).

———— (1997a). "A Critique of 'The World Bank's Experience with Large Dams: A Preliminary Review of Impacts'." International Rivers Network, April 11, 1997.

———— (1997b). "Questions and Answers on the International Movement Against Large Dams," in International Rivers Network, *Proceedings, First International Meeting of People Affected by Dams, Curitiba, Brazil, March 11–14, 1997* (Berkeley, Calif.: International Rivers Network, 1997).

———— (2001). "One Year After the World Commission on Dams: Reflections on the Diverse Reactions to Groundbreaking Report," *World Rivers Review* 16 no. 6 (December): 8–9 and 15.

———— (2002a). "NGOs Making Waves in the International Water Establishment," *World Rivers Review* 17 no. 1 (Feb. 2002): 6.

———— (2002b). "Avoiding Solutions, Worsening Problems: A Critique of 'World Bank Water Resources Sector Strategy: Strategic Directions for World

Bank Engagement Draft for Discussion of March 25, 2002'." International Rivers Network, May 27, 2002.

Meadows, Donella H., Dennis L. Meadows, and Jørgen Randers (1992). *Beyond the Limits: Confronting Global Collapse, Envisioning a Sustainable Future* (Post Mills, Vt.: Chelsea Green Published).

Metcalfe, Ed (2000). "Nor Any Drop to Drink," *Ecologist* 30 no. 5 (July/ August): 46–50.

Mettler, Johann, Jaap de Visser and Edward Cottle (2002). "Realizing the Right of Access to Water: Pipe-dream or Watershed?" Executive summary of a paper presented at a colloquium of the Socio-Economic Rights Project, CLC, University of the Western Cape, 17–19 March.

Meyer, John W. and Brian Rowan (1977). "Institutionalized Organizations: Formal Structure as Myth and Ceremony," *American Journal of Sociology* 83: 340–363.

Meyer, John W., David H. Kamens, and Aaron Benavot with Yun-Kyung Cha and Suk-Ying Wong (1992). *School Knowledge for the Masses: World Models and National Primary Curricular Categories in the Twentieth Century* (Washington, D.C.: Falmer Press).

Meyer, John W., David John Frank, Ann Hironaka, Evan Schofer, and Nancy Brandon Tuma (1997). "The Structuring of a World Environmental Regime, 1870–1990," *International Organization* 51 no. 4 (Autumn): 623–651.

Ministerial Declaration of The Hague on Water Security in the 21st Century (2000). The Hague, the Netherlands.

Ministério das Minas e Energia, Departamento Nacional de Águas e Energia Elétrica (1980). *Código de Águas 1* (Brasília: Republica Federativa do Brasil).

Montes, Margarita Pacheco (1996). "Colombia's Independent Recyclers' Union: A Model for Urban Waste Management," in Helen Collinson, ed., *Green Guerrillas: Environmental Conflicts and Initiatives in Latin America and the Caribbean* (London: Latin America Bureau).

Moore, Deborah and Leonard Sklar (1998). "Reforming the World Bank's Lending for Water: The Process and Outcome of Developing a Water Resources Management Policy," in Jonathan A. Fox and L. David Brown, *The Struggle for Accountability: The World Bank, NGOs, and Grassroots Movements* (Cambridge, Mass.: MIT Press).

Moreira, Maria Manuela Martins Alves (2002). "Quadro Atual de Implantação da Política de Recursos Hídricos no Pais." Presentation of the Secretária de Recursos Hídrocos, Ministério de Meio Ambiente, April 17. www.mma.gov.br/ port/sh/acervo/palest/palest02.html (accessed June 2, 2003).

Movimento dos Atingidos pôr Barragens (2001). "Um Novo Modelo do Setor Elétrico é Possível ... e Necessário." http://www.mabnacional.org.br/site/ index.html (accessed June 2, 2003).

———— (n.d.). "A Organização do Movimento dos Atingidos pôr Barragens." http://www.mabnacional.org.br/site/index.html (accessed May 20, 2003).

Mulligan, Shane P. (1999). "For Whose Benefit? Limits to Sharing in the Bioprospecting Regime," *Environmental Politics* 8 no. 4 (Winter): 35–65.

Mullin, Chris (2001). Address of the Parliamentary Under-Secretary of State for International Development to the British Dams Society, February 1, 2001.

Multinational Monitor (1997). "Uniting to Block the Dams," *Multinational Monitor* 18 no. 5 (May).

Myers, Norman (1997). "The Rich Diversity of Biodiversity Issues," in M. L. Reaka-Kudla, D. E. Wilson, and E. O. Wilson, eds., *Biodiversity II: Understanding and Protecting Our Biological Resources* (Washington, D.C.: Joseph Henry Press), pp. 125–138. Cited in World Resources Institute, United Nations Development Programme, United Nations Environment Programme, and World Bank, *World Resources 2000–2001: People and Ecosystems: The Fraying Web of Life* (Washington, D.C.: World Resources Institute, 2000), p. 107.

National Assembly (South Africa) (2003). Reply of Department of Water Affairs and Forestry to question no. 153 of Mr. R. Jankielsohn, June 11, 2003.

Nelkin, Dorothy ed. (1992). *Controversy* (Newbury Park, Calif.: Sage).

Nelson, Paul J. (1995). *The World Bank and Non-Governmental Organizations: The Limits of Apolitical Development* (New York: St. Martin's Press).

O'Meara, D. (1996). *Forty Lost Years: The Apartheid State and the Politics of the National Party, 1948–1994* (Johannesburg: Ravan Press). Cited in Rodney Davenport and Christopher Saunders, *South Africa: A Modern History* (New York: St. Martin's Press, 5th ed. 2000), p. 372.

Oldeman, L. R. (1998). "Soil Degradation: A Threat to Security?" International Soil Reference Information Centre. Cited in United Nations Development Programme, United Nations Environment Programme, World Bank, and World Resources Institute, *World Resources 2000–2001* (Washington, D.C.: World Resources Institute, 2000).

Orwin, Alexander (1999). "The Privatization of Water and Wastewater Utilities: An International Survey." Environment Probe, August 1999. http://www.environmentprobe.org/enviroprobe/pubs/ev542.html (accessed December 15, 2003).

Ostrom, Elinor (1990). *Governing the Commons: The Evolution of Institutions for Collective Action* (Cambridge: Cambridge University Press).

Ottaway, Marina (2001). "Corporatism Goes Global," *Global Governance* 7 no. 3 (July–September): 265–292.

Oud, Engelbertus and Terence C. Muir (1997). "Engineering and Economic Aspects of Planning, Design, Construction and Operation of Large Dam Projects," in World Conservation Union and World Bank, *Large Dams: Learning from the Past Looking at the Future*. Workshop proceedings, Gland Switzerland, April 11–12, 1997 (Washington, D.C.: IUCN), pp. 17–40.

Pagnoccheschi, Bruno (n.d. a). "Água: Gestão, Acesso e Qualidade." Deposition for the project "O Ambientalismo no Brasil: Balanço e Perspectivas." ISER, Rio de Janeiro.

—— (n.d. b). "Política Nacional de Recursos Hídricos." Manuscript.

Parson, Edward A. (2003). *Protecting the Ozone Layer: Science and Strategy* (Oxford: Oxford University Press).

Pauw, Jacques (2003). "Metered to Death: How a Water Experiment Caused Riots and a Cholera Epidemic," in International Consortium of Investigative Journalists, *The Water Barons* (Washington, D.C.: Center for Public Integrity).

Permanent Court of Arbitration (n.d.). "Background pertaining to draft rules for resolution of disputes relating to natural resources and the environment." http://www.pca-cpa.org/ENGLISH/EDR/ (accessed February 18, 2004).

Philip, Mark (1985). "Michel Foucault," in Quentin Skinner, ed., *The Return of Grand Theory in the Human Sciences* (Cambridge: Cambridge University Press).

Pillay, Karrisha and Sandra Liebenberg (2000). "Grootboom v. Oostenberg Municipality and Others," *ESR Review* 2 no. 3 (September).

Poole, Alan (n.d.). "The Challenge and Limits of Large Dams in Brazil." Submission to the World Commission on Dams. http://www.dams.org/kbase/submissions/showsub.php?rec=ins074 (accessed May 23, 2003).

Porto Alegre Water Declaration (2002). Revised version February 4, 2002.

Postel, Sandra (1993). "Water and Agriculture," in Peter H. Gleick, ed., *Water in Crisis: A Guide to the World's Fresh Water Resources* (New York: Oxford University Press).

Price, Richard (2003). "Transnational Civil Society and Advocacy in World Politics," *World Politics* 55 (July): 579–606.

Princen, Thomas and Matthias Finger, eds. (1994). *Environmental NGOs in World Politics: Linking the Local and the Global* (London: Routledge).

Public Citizen (2002). *Profit Streams: The World Bank and Greedy Global Water Companies*. A special report by Public Citizen's Water for All Program.

Rajagopal, Balakrishnan (2003). *International Law from Below: Development, Social Movements and Third World Resistance* (Cambridge: Cambridge University Press).

Raju, G. and Manju S. Ragu (1996). "The Owl and the Panther: The Case of People's Institutions in Joint Forest Management in India." Paper presented at the Conference of the International Association for the Study of Common Property, Berkeley, California, June 1996.

Ramoeli, Phera (2002). "The SADC Protocol on Shared Watercourses: Its Origins and Current Status," in Anthony Turton and Roland Henwood, eds., *Hydropolitics in the Developing World: A Southern African Perspective* (Pretoria: African Water Issues Research Unit).

Ranney, Austin (1958). *The Governing of Men* (New York: Holt).

Raustiala, Kal and David G. Victor (1996). "Biodiversity Since Rio: The Future of the Convention on Biological Diversity," *Environment* 38 no. 4 (May): 16–20 and 37–45.

Rede das Águas (n.d.). "Rede das Águas." http://www.rededasaguas.org.br/ Fundaçao Mata Atlântica (accessed September 28, 2004).

Rees, William E., Phil Testemale, and Mathis Wackernagle (1995). *Our Ecological Footprint: Reducing Human Impact on the Earth* (Gabriola Island, British Columbia: New Society Publishers).

Reisner, Marc (1986). *Cadillac Desert: The American West and its Disappearing Water* (N.Y.: Viking).

Relatório da Comissão de Análise do Sistema Hidrotérmico de Energia Elétrica (2001). Brasília, July 21.

Republic of South Africa (1997). *Water Services Act No. 108 of 1997.*

——— (1998). *National Water Act No. 36 of 1998.*

Reuters (2000). "End to Privatization of Global Water Resources Sought." June 12.

Revenga, Carmen, Siobhan Murray, Janet Abramovitz, and Allen Hammond (1998). *Watersheds of the World: Ecological Value and Vulnerability* (Washington, D.C.: World Resources Institute).

Revenga, Carmen, Jake Brunner, Norbert Henninger, Ken Kassem, and Richard Payne (2000). *Pilot Assessment of Global Ecosystems: Freshwater Systems* (Washington: World Resources Institute).

Ribot, Jesse C. (1999). "Integral Local Development: Authority, Accountability and Entrustment in Natural Resource Management." Working Paper prepared for the Regional Program for the Traditional Energy Sector (RPTES) in the Africa Technical Group (AFTG1—Energy) of the World Bank.

Rich, Bruce (1994). *Mortgaging the Earth: The World Bank, Environmental Impoverishment, and the Crisis of Development* (Boston: Beacon Press).

Rios Vivos (n.d.). "Acusações de Fraude na América Sujam as Águas da Hidrovia." Press release.

Rittberger, Volker (1993). "Editor's Introduction," in Volker Rittberger, ed., *Regime Theory and International Relations* (Oxford: Clarendon Press).

Roan, Sharon (1989). *Ozone Crisis: The 15-year Evolution of a Sudden Global Emergency* (New York: Wiley).

Roberts, C. P. R. (1983). "Environmental Constraints on Water Resources Development," in *Proceedings of the Seventh Quinquennial Convention of the South African Institution of Civil Engineers*, pp. 16–23.

Ronnie, Roger (2001). "The Folly of Water Privatization in South Africa," *Sowetan*, August 15.

Rosenau, James N. (1990). *Turbulence in World Politics: A Theory of Change and Continuity* (Princeton, N.J.: Princeton University Press).

Rosenthal, Naomi B. and Michael Schwartz (1989). "Spontaneity and Democracy in Social Movements," in Bert Klandermans, ed., *Organizing for Change: Social Movement Organizations in Europe and the United States* (Greenwich, Conn.: JAI).

Rowlands, Ian H. (1991). "Ozone Layer Depletion and Global Warming: New Sources for Environmental Disputes," *Peace and Change* 16 no. 3 (July): 260–284.

Roy, Arundhati (1999). "The Greater Common Good." Friends of the River Narmada. www.narmada.org/gcg/gcg.html (accessed November 2, 1999).

Sachs, Wolfgang, ed. (2002). *The Jo'Burg Memo: Fairness in a Fragile World* (Berlin: Heinrich Böll Foundation).

Sachs, Wolfgang, Reinhard Loske, and Manfred Linz (1998). *Greening the North: A Post-industrial Blueprint for Ecology and Equity* (London: Zed Books).

Santoro, Daniel (2003). "The 'Aguas' Tango: Cashing in on Buenos Aires' Privatization," in International Consortium of Investigative Journalists, *The Water Barons* (Washington, D.C.: Center for Public Integrity).

Schnitter, Nicholas J. (1994). *A History of Dams: The Useful Pyramids* (Rotterdam, Netherlands: A.A. Balkema).

Schoeman, Maxi (2002). "From SADCC to SADC and Beyond: The Politics of Economic Integration." Paper presented at the XIII International Economic History Congress, Buenos Aires, July 16–22, 2002. http://www.eh.net/XIIICongress/Papers/Schoeman.pdf (accessed September 5, 2003).

Schreiner, Olive and Barbara van Koppen (2002). "Catchment Management Agencies for Poverty Eradication in South Africa," *Physics and Chemistry of the Earth* 27: 969–976.

Schultz, Jim (2000). "Bolivia's Water War Victory," *Earth Island Journal* 15 no. 3 (Autumn): 28–29.

Scott, James C. (1985). *Weapons of the Weak: Everyday Forms of Peasant Resistance* (New Haven: Yale University Press).

Seckler, D. U. Amarasinghe, D. Molden, R. de Silva, and R. Barker (1998). *World Water Demand and Supply, 1990 to 2025: Scenarios and Issues.* Research Report 19. Colombo, Sri Lanka: International Water Management Institute, Cited in Carmen Revenga, Jake Brunner, Norbert Henninger, Ken Kassem, and Richard Payne, *Pilot Analysis of Global Ecosystems: Freshwater Ecosystems* (Washington, D.C.: World Resources Institute, 2000), p. 26.

Second International Meeting of Dam-Affected People and their Allies (2003). "Rivers for Life! The Rasi Salai Declaration." Statement endorsed at the Second International Meeting of Dam-Affected People and their Allies, Rasi Salai, Thailand, November 28–December 4.

Secretaria de Recursos Hídricos (Brazil) (1999). *Federal Law 9,433 January 8 1997: National Water Resource Policy* (Brasília: Ministério de Meio Ambiente).

—— (n.d.). *Plano Nacional de Recursos Hídricos.* http://www.mma.gov.br/port/srh/pnrh/capa/index.html (accessed March 10, 2003).

Sekhar, A. (2001). Letter from the Ministry of Water Resources, Government of India, to Achim Steiner, Secretary General, World Commission on Dams, February 2, 2001.

Serageldin, Ismail (2000). Comments to the NGO Forum, Second World Water Forum, The Hague, March 17–22, 2000.

Shand, M. J., P. R. Little, and P. H. van Niekerk (2000). "A South African Experience of the Approval Process for a Large Dam," in International Committee on Large Dams, *20th Congress on Large Dams, Beijing, China, 19–22 September 2000*, vol. 2 (Paris: ICOLD), pp. 393–401.

Sharma, Kalpana (2000). "Hecklers Disrupt World Water Meet," *Hindu*, March 18.

Shiklomanov, I. A. (1998). Archive of world water resources and world water use, State Hydrological Institute, St. Petersburg, Russia. Cited in Peter H. Gleick, *The World's Water 2000–2001: The Biennial Report on Freshwater Resources* (Washington, D.C.: Island Press, 2000), p. 23, figure 2.1.

Simpson, Larry and Klas Ringskog (1997). *Water Markets in the Americas* (Washington, D.C.: World Bank).

Sinclair, Ian (1987). *The International Law Commission* (Cambridge: Grotius Press). Cited in Stephen C. McCaffrey, "Water, Politics, and International Law," in Peter H. Gleick, ed. (1993), *Water in Crisis: A Guide to the World's Fresh Water Resources* (New York: Oxford University Press), p. 104, note 122.

Skanska (2000). "Skanska supports the World Commission on Dams Recommendations for Long-Term Sustainable Hydropower Projects." Press release, November 16. http://thehub.skanska.com/700_External/70002_Pressrelease.asp?EntryID=3789&LangID=1 (accessed October 30, 2002).

Skidmore, Thomas (1967). *Politics in Brazil 1930–1964: An Experiment in Democracy* (New York: Oxford University Press).

Sklar, Leonard and Patrick McCully (1994). *Damming the River: The World Bank's Lending for Large Dams*. Working Paper no. 5, International Rivers Network, Berkeley, Calif.

Smith, Jackie (2002). "Bridging Global Divides? Strategic Framing and Solidarity in Transnational Social Movement Organizations," *International Sociology* 17 no. 4 (December): 505–528.

Smith, Jackie, Charles Chatfield, and Ron Pagnucco, eds. (1997). *Transnational Social Movements and Global Politics: Solidarity Beyond the State* (Syracuse, N.Y.: Syracuse University Press).

Snow, David E. and Robert Benford (1992). "Master Frames and Cycles of Protest," in Aldon Morris and Carol McClurg Mueller, eds., *Frontiers in Social Movement Theory* (New Haven, Conn.: Yale University Press).

Snow, David E., E. Burke Rochford, Steven K. Worden, and Robert D. Benford (1986). "Frame Alignment Processes, Micromobilization, and Movement Participation," *American Sociological Review* 51: 464–481.

Social Learning Group (2001). *Learning to Manage Global Environmental Risks* (Cambridge, Mass.: MIT Press).

South African Human Rights Commission (1998). *Economic & Social Rights Report: Researcher's Evaluation of Government Responses*. volume IV, 1997–98 (Houghton: South African Human Rights Commission). http://www.sahrc.org.za/volume_iv.PDF (accessed July 16, 2002).

South African Multi-stakeholder Initiative on the World Commission on Dams (2002). *Scoping Report*, October 22.

South African Municipal Workers Union (2003). "Closing Declaration," SAMWU Seventh National Congress, Pretoria, August 2003.

Southern African Development Community (2000). *Revised Protocol on Shared Watercourses in the Southern African Development Community*, Windhoek, Namibia.

—— (2002). *Rapid Environmental Appraisal of the Limpopo River Basin*. Technical report prepared for the SADC Water Sector by the Southern African Research and Documentation Centre, Musokotwane Environment Resource Centre for Southern Africa, and ZERO Regional Environment Organisation.

South-North Development Monitor, "United Nations: Access to Water Enshrined as a Human Right." SUNS no. 5245, November 29, 2002.

Stewart, Julie, Kevin O'Connell, Marian Ciborski, and Matthew Pacenza (1996). *A People Dammed: The Impact of the World Bank Chixoy Hydroelectric Project in Guatemala* (Washington, D.C.: Witness for Peace).

Stone, Debby (2002). Untapped Resources. US Hydropower, Council for International Development. www.us-hydropower.org/Documents/Untapped _Resources.htm (accessed May 1, 2002).

Stockholm Water Symposium (1991). *Water Resources in the Next Century*. The 1991 Stockholm Water Symposium. www.siwi.org/sws/sws.html (accessed July 30, 2000).

—— (1997). *With Rivers to the Sea: Interaction of Land Activities, Fresh Water and Enclosed Coastal Seas*. The 1997 Stockholm Water Symposium. www.siwi.org/sws/sws.html (accessed July 30, 2002).

—— (1998). *Water: The Key to Socio-Economic Development and Quality of Life*. The 1998 Stockholm Water Symposium. www.siwi.org/sws/sws.html (accessed July 30, 2000).

Swatuk, Larry A. (2000). "South Africa in the Region: 'Botha Would be Proud'," *Southern Africa Report* 15 no. 3 (May): 12–30.

—— (2002a). "Environmental Cooperation for Regional Peace and Security in Southern Africa," in Ken Conca and Geoffrey D. Dabelko, eds., *Environmental*

Peacemaking (Washington, D.C. and Baltimore, Md.: Woodrow Wilson Center Press and Johns Hopkins University Press).

————— (2002b). "The New Water Architecture in Southern Africa: Reflections on Current Trends in the Light of 'Rio+10'," *International Affairs* 78 issue 3 (July): 507–530.

Switkes, Glenn (2001a). "Brazilian Judge Forbids 'De-Construction' of the Pantanal Channelization Scheme," *World Rivers Review* 16 no. 1 (February): 6.

————— (2001b). "Leader of Movement to Stop Amazon Dams Murdered," *World Rivers Review* 16 no. 5 (October): 13.

————— (2001c). "New Crisis, Old Tune: Brazil's Energy Woes Accelerate Plans for New Dams," *World Rivers Review* 16 no. 4 (August): 6, 11.

————— (2001d). Reply to "Exaggerations of the Commission on Large Dams," *Gazeta Mercantil*, April 9.

————— (2002). "Brazil's Day of Action Mobilizes Thousands to Protest Destructive River Schemes," *World Rivers Review* 17 no. 2 (April): 1.

————— (2003a). "Will Brazil's Rivers Get a Break in 2003?" *World Rivers Review* 18 no. 1 (February): 7.

————— (2003b). "New Studies, Same Old Problems for Latin America Industrial Waterway," *World Rivers Review* 18 no. 2 (April): 10.

Tarrow, Sidney (1994). *Power in Movement: Social Movements and Contentious Politics* (Cambridge: Cambridge University Press).

————— (1998). *Power in Movement: Social Movements, Collective Action and Politics* (Cambridge: Cambridge University Press). 2nd ed.

————— (2002). "The New Transnational Contention: Organizations, Coalitions, Mechanisms." Paper presented at the 98th annual meeting of the American Political Science Association, Chicago, September 1, 2002.

Taylor, Bron, ed. (1995). *Ecological Resistance Movements: The Global Emergence of Radical and Popular Environmentalism* (Albany: State University of New York Press).

Thomas, David S. G. and Nicholas J. Middleton, eds. (1997). *World Atlas of Desertification* (London: Edward Arnold).

Thomas, George W., John W. Meyer, Francisco O. Ramirez, and John Boli, eds. (1987). *Institutional Structure: Constituting State, Society, and the Individual* (Newbury Park, Calif.: Sage).

Toepfer, Klaus (2002). Opening address to the First Dams and Development Forum, July 8–9, 2002, Nairobi, Kenya.

Tolba, Mostafa K. (1987). "The Ozone Agreement—and Beyond," *Environmental Conservation* 14 no. 4: 290, as quoted in Richard Elliot Benedick, *Ozone Diplomacy: New Directions in Safeguarding the Planet* (Cambridge, Mass.: Harvard University Press, rev. ed. 1998), p. 330.

Transboundary Freshwater Disputes Database (n.d. a). http://www.terra.geo.orst.edu/

―――― (n.d. b). "International River Basins of the World." http://www.transboundarywaters.orst.edu/publications/register/tables/IRB_table_4.html

Tripartite Interim Agreement Between The Republic of Mozambique and The Republic of South Africa and the Kingdom of Swaziland for Co-operation on the Protection and Sustainable Utilization of the Water Resources of the Incomati and Maputo Watercourses. Johannesburg, August 29, 2002.

Turner, B. L., II, Roger E. Kasperson, William B. Meyer, Kirstin M. Dow, Dominic Golding, Jeanne X. Kasperson, Robert C. Mitchell, and Samuel J. Ratick (1990). "Two Types of Global Environmental Change: Definitional and Spatial-Scale Issues in their Human Dimensions," *Global Environmental Change* 1 no. 1 (December): 14–22.

Turton, Anthony (n.d.). "The Hydropolitical Dynamics of Cooperation in Southern Africa: A Strategic Perspective on Institutional Development in International River Basins." Monograph, African Water Issues Research Unit.

Turton, Anthony R. and Nevil Quinn (n.d.). "The Shared River Initiative on the Incomati." Paper presented to the Portfolio Committee for Environmental Affairs and Tourism in the National Assembly during the GLOBE Southern Africa "Partnership for Sustainability II" Conference, Cape Town, South Africa.

United Nations (1951). *Proceedings of the United Nations Scientific Conference on the Conservation and Utilization of Resources* (New York: United Nations). Cited in Faye Anderson, "The Internationalizing World of Water Management," *Water Resources Impact* 3 no. 2 (March 2001): 3–8.

―――― (1973). *Report of the United Nations Conference on the Human Environment.* United Nations document A/Conf.48/14/Rev.1, 1973.

―――― (1977a). "Report of the United Nations Water Conference, Mar del Plata, March 14–25, 1977." (New York: United Nations). United Nations Document E.77.II.A.12, 1977.

―――― (1977b). *Yearbook of the United Nations 1977* (New York: United Nations).

―――― (1997). *Convention on the Law of the Non-Navigational Uses of International Watercourses.* United Nations General Assembly document A/51/869, April 11, 1997.

United Nations Commission on Sustainable Development (1997). *Comprehensive Assessment of the Freshwater Resources of the World.* Report of the Secretary-General, fifth session, April 7–25, 1997. United Nations document E/CN.17/1997/9, February 4, 1997.

―――― (1998). "Strategic Approaches to Freshwater Management: Report of the Expert Group Meeting on Strategic Approaches to Freshwater Management." Sixth session, April 20–May 1, 1998. United Nations document E/CN.17/1998/2/Add.1, February 10, 1998.

—— (2000). "Progress Made in Providing Safe Water Supply and Sanitation for All during the 1990s." United Nations document E/CN.17/2000/13, April 2000.

—— (2002). "Secretary-General's Note for the Multi-Stake Holder Dialogue Segment of the Second Preparatory Committee. Addendum No. 4: Dialogue Paper by Non-governmental Organizations." United Nations document E/CN .17/2002/PC/2.Add.4, January 28, 2002.

UN Committee on Economic, Social and Cultural Rights (2002). "Substantive Issues Arising in the Implementation of the International Covenant on Economic, Social and Cultural Rights: The Right to Water." General Comment No. 15. United Nations document E/C.12/2002/11, November 26, 2002.

UN Conference on Environment and Development (1992). *Agenda 21*. Adopted by the UN Conference on Environment and Development, June 14, 1992. http:// www.un.org/esa/sustdev/documents/agenda21/index.htm

United Nations Development Programme (1998). *Capacity Building for Sustainable Management of Water Resources and the Aquatic Environment* (New York: UNDP).

—— (2000). *Human Development Report 2000* (New York: Oxford University Press).

—— (2003). *Human Development Report 2003* (New York: Oxford University Press).

—— (n.d.). "Sustainable Management of Water Resources and the Aquatic Environment: UNDP's Role To Date and Strategy Framework." http://www .undp.org/seed/water/ (accessed June 7, 2002).

United Nations Environment Programme (1995). *Water Quality of World River Basins* (Nairobi: UNEP). UNEP Environment Library No. 14.

—— (1997). Decision 19/13C of the Governing Council of the United Nations Environment Programme, Nineteenth Session, 1997. http://www.irptc.unep.ch/ pops/gcpops_e.html (November 15, 1999).

—— (1999). "Report of the Nineteenth Meeting of the Open-ended Working Group of the Parties to the Montreal Protocol." United Nations document UNEP/OzL.Pro/WG.1/19/7, June 18, 1999.

—— (2001). "Multilateral Environmental Agreements: A Summary." Background paper for the First Meeting of the Open-Ended Intergovernmental Group of Ministers or Their Representatives on International Environmental Governance, New York, April 18, 2001. United Nations Document UNEP/IGM/1/ INF/1, March 30, 2001.

—— (2002a). *Global Environment Outlook 3* (London: Earthscan).

—— (2002b). "Promoting Dialogue: South African Multi-stakeholder Initiative on the World Commission on Dams (WCD) Report." Dams and Development Project, Information Sheet no. 1.

——— (2002c). "What Are Our Objectives?" Dams and Development Project. http://www.unep-dams.org/document.php?doc_id=131 (accessed November 8, 2002).

United Nations Secretariat of the Convention to Combat Desertification (n.d.). "Fact sheet 2: Causes of desertification." www.unccd.ch/publicinfo/fssub.htm (accessed December 8, 1999).

United States Department of Energy (n.d.). "International Electricity Installed Capacity Data." Energy Information Administration. www.eia.doe.gov/emeu/international/electric.html#IntlCapacity (accessed December 15, 2003).

Uys, Maritza (n.d.). *A Structural Analysis of the Water Allocation Mechanism of the Water Act 54 of 1956 in the Light of the Requirements of Competing Water User Sectors.* Water Research Commission Report no. 406/1/96.

van Wijk, C., E. de Lange, and D. Saunders (1998). "Gender Aspects in the Management of Water Resources," *Natural Resources Forum* 20 no. 2: 91–103.

Vandeveer, Stacy (1997). "Normative Force: The State, Transnational Norms, and International Environmental Regimes." PhD dissertation, Department of Government and Politics, University of Maryland, College Park.

Varma, C. V. J. (2001). "ICOLD's final position about the WCD report 'Dams and Development'." http://www.icold-cigb.org/anglais.html (accessed December 16, 2002).

Victor, David G. (1998a). "'Learning by Doing' in the Nonbinding International Regime to Manage Trade in Hazardous Chemicals and Pesticides," in David G. Victor, Kal Raustiala, and Eugene B. Skolnikoff, eds., *The Implementation and Effectiveness of International Environmental Commitments: Theory and Practice* (Cambridge, Mass.: MIT Press).

——— (1998b). "The Operation and Effectiveness of the Montreal Protocol's Non-Compliance Mechanism," in David G. Victor, Kal Raustiala, and Eugene B. Skolnikoff, eds., *The Implementation and Effectiveness of International Environmental Commitments: Theory and Practice* (Cambridge, Mass.: MIT Press).

Victor, David G., Kal Raustiala, and Eugene B. Skolnikoff, eds. (1998). *The Implementation and Effectiveness of International Environmental Commitments: Theory and Practice* (Cambridge, Mass.: MIT Press).

Vos, W. J. (1978). *Principles of South African Water Law* (Cape Town: Jut & Co.).

Walker-Leigh, Vanya (2003). "Alternative Water Future Outlined." *BBC News,* Monday, March 24, 2003, 17:50 GMT.

Wapner, Paul (1995). "Politics Beyond the State: Environmental Activism and World Civic Politics," *World Politics* 47 (April): 311–340.

——— (1996a). "Globalization and the Future of Environmental Activism," *The Brown Journal of World Affairs,* III no. 2 (Summer/Fall): 249–255.

——— (1996b). *Environmental Activism and World Civic Politics* (Albany: State University of New York Press).

—— (1998). "Reorienting State Sovereignty: Rights and Responsibilities in the Environmental Age," in Karen T. Litfin, ed., *The Greening of Sovereignty in World Politics* (Cambridge, Mass.: MIT Press).

Wartchow, Dieter (2002). "Don't Squander Intelligence: Save the Waters," *Defend the Global Commons* 1 no. 1 (February): 1–4.

Water Research Commission (South Africa) (1996). "Water Research Commission: Twenty-Five Years." Special edition of *SA Waterbulletin*.

Water Supply and Sanitation Collaborative Council (1990). "New Delhi Statement: 'Some for all rather than more for some'." http://www.wsscc.org/resources/briefings/ndelhi.html (accessed April 23, 2002).

Watson, Cathy and Belinda Calaguas, eds. (2000). *Making Waves: Civil Society Advocacy on International Water Policy*. Report of the Seminar held at NCVO, All Saints Street, London, December 14–15, 2000.

Weber, Demétrio (2001). "Justiça suspende licença ambiental de eclusa em TO," *Estado de São Paulo*, March 2.

Weinthal, Erika (2002). *State Making and Environmental Cooperation: Linking Domestic and International Politics in Central Asia* (Cambridge, Mass.: MIT Press).

Weiss, Edith Brown (1998). "The Five International Treaties: A Living History," in Edith Brown Weiss and Harold K. Jacobson, eds., *Engaging Countries: Strengthening Compliance with International Environmental Accords* (Cambridge, Mass.: MIT Press).

Weiss, Edith Brown and Harold Jacobson, eds. (1998). *Engaging Countries: Strengthening Compliance with International Environmental Accords* (Cambridge, Mass.: MIT Press).

Wesely, Tara (2003). "Rivers for Life Meeting," *Grist*, Thursday, December 4.

White, G. F. (1998). "Reflections on the 50-year International Search for Integrated Water Management," *Water Policy* 1 no. 1 (1998): 21–27.

Wildlife and Environment Society of South Africa, Western Cape Region (n.d.). "Skuifraam Dam." http://www.wcape.school.za/wessa/SWFskuifraam.htm (accessed January 17, 2004).

Williamson, John (1990). *The Progress of Policy Reform in Latin America* (Washington, D.C.: Institute for International Economics).

Winpenny, James (2003). Financing Water for All: Report of the World Panel on Financing Water Infrastructure, March.

Wirth, John D. (1970). *The Politics of Brazilian Development 1930–1954* (Stanford, Calif.: Stanford University Press).

Wolf, Aaron T. (1999). "Water and Human Security," *Aviso* no. 3 (June). Global Environmental Change and Human Security Project, University of Victoria, British Columbia.

Wolf, Aaron T., Jeffrey A. Natharius, Jeffrey J. Danielson, Brian S. Ward, and Jan K. Pender (1999). "International River Basins of the World," *International Journal of Water Resources Development* 15 no. 4 (December).

World Bank (1993). *Water Resources Management: A World Bank Policy Paper* (Washington, D.C.: World Bank).

——— (1996). "World Bank Lending for Large Dams: A Preliminary Review of Impacts." Operations Evaluation Department. OED Précis No. 125, September 1996.

——— (1997). *World Development Report: The State in a Changing World* (New York: Oxford University Press).

——— (1999). "Roundtable on Brazil's Water Policy Reforms and the Role of the World Bank." Operations Evaluation Department, May 1999.

——— (2000). *The World Bank and the Water Sector* (Brasília: World Bank). Brazil Country Management Unit.

——— (2001a). Operational Manual, OP 4.12, "Operational Policies: Involuntary Resettlement."

——— (2001b). Operational Manual, BP 4.12, "Bank Procedures: Involuntary Resettlement."

——— (2002). "Water Resources Sector Strategy: Strategic Directions for World Bank Engagement." Draft report, March 25.

——— (2003). "Water Resources Sector Strategy: Strategic Directions for World Bank Engagement." Final report, February.

——— (n.d.). "Toolkits for Private Participation in Water and Sanitation." http://www.worldbank.org/html/fpd/water/wstoolkits/ (accessed October 1, 2004).

World Commission on Dams (2000a). "Brazil: A National Commission?" *Dams: The WCD Newsletter* no. 7 (August).

——— (2000b). *Dams and Development: A New Framework for Decision-Making. The Report of the World Commission on Dams* (London: Earthscan).

——— (2000c). *Dams and Development: A New Framework for Decision-Making. The Report of the World Commission on Dams: An Overview* (Cape Town: World Commission on Dams).

——— (2002). "From World Commission on Dams to UNEP Dams and Development Project: Report on the Transition Period May–November 2001." April.

World Commission on Environment and Development (1987). *Our Common Future* (New York: Oxford University Press).

World Commission on Water for the 21st Century (2000). *A Water Secure World: Vision for Water, Life, and the Environment* (Paris: World Water Commission).

World Conservation Union (1996). *1996 IUCN Red List of Threatened Animals* (Gland, Switzerland: World Conservation Union).

———— (2001). "IUCN Launches New Strategy: Global Action to Improve Dams." Press release, November 5.

———— (2002). "A Flood of Words: Dams Discussions Progress in Vietnam." http://www.iucn.org/themes/wetlands/vietnamdamsoct2002.html (November 8, 2002). IUCN Wetlands and Water Resources Programme.

———— (n.d.). "Dams in the IUCN Programme." http://www.iucn.org/themes/wetlands/IUCNDamsStrategy.PDF (accessed November 4, 2002).

World Conservation Union and World Bank (1997). *Large Dams: Learning from the Past Looking at the Future*. Workshop Proceedings, Gland Switzerland, April 11–12, 1997 (Washington, D.C.: IUCN).

World Development Movement (2002). "Leaked European Negotiating Documents Confirm WDM's Fears about the GATS." GATS Campaign Update, May.

World Health Organization (n.d.). "The World Commission on Dams Launches its Report." http://www.who.int/water_sanitation_health/vector/dams2.htm (accessed October 30, 2002).

World Health Organization and United Nations Children's Fund (2001). *Global Water Supply and Sanitation Assessment 2000 Report* (New York, WHO/UNICEF). http://www.who.int/water_sanitation_health/Globassessment/GlobalTOC.htm

World Resources Institute (1996). *Pesticides and the Immune System: The Public Health Risks* (Washington, D.C.: World Resources Institute).

———— (1998). *World Resources 1998–99* (New York: Oxford University Press).

World Resources Institute, United Nations Development Programme, United Nations Environment Programme, and World Bank (2000). *World Resources 2000–2001: People and Ecosystems: The Fraying Web of Life* (Washington, D.C.: World Resources Institute).

World Social Forum (2002). "Water: Our Common Heritage." Panel discussion, Porto Alegre, Brazil, February 2.

World Trade Organization (1999). "An Introduction to the GATS." www.wto.org/english/tratop_e/serve_e/serv_e.htm (accessed June 4, 2002).

———— (2001). "GATS: Fact and Fiction." www.wto.org/english/tratop_e/serv_e/gats_factfiction_e.htm (accessed June 4, 2002).

World Water Assessment Programme (2003). *Water for People and Life: The United Nations World Water Development Report* (Paris: UNESCO Publishing).

World Water Council (2000a). "Statement of the Gender Ambassadors to the Ministerial Conference," *Second World Water Forum and Ministerial Conference: Final Report*, July.

———— (2000b). *Second World Water Forum and Ministerial Conference: Final Report*, July.

———— (2002). "Results from the questionnaire." http://www.worldwatercouncil.org/download/Results_questionnaire.pdf (accessed June 4, 2002).

———— (n.d. a). "About WWC: Background." http://www.worldwatercouncil .org/background.shtml (accessed June 4, 2002).

———— (n.d. b). "Membership." http://www.worldwatercouncil.org/membership .shtml (accessed June 2, 2002).

Worster, Donald (1985). *Rivers of Empire: Water, Aridity, and the Growth of the American West* (New York: Oxford University Press).

Wright, Angus and Wendy Wolford (2003). *To Inherit the Earth: The Landless Movement and the Struggle for a New Brazil* (Oakland, Calif.: Institute for Food and Development Policy).

Wynne, Brian (1987). *Risk Management and Hazardous Waste: Implementation and the Dialectics of Credibility* (Berlin: Springer Verlag).

Young, Gordon J., James C. I. Dooge, and John C. Rodda (1994). *Global Water Resource Issues* (Cambridge: Cambridge University Press).

Young, Oran R. (1998). *Creating Regimes: Arctic Accords and International Governance* (Ithaca, N.Y.: Cornell University Press).

Young, Oran R. and Mark A. Levy with Gail Osherenko (1999a). "The Effectiveness of International Environmental Regimes," in Oran R. Young, ed., *The Effectiveness of International Environmental Regimes: Causal Connections and Behavioral Mechanisms* (Cambridge, Mass.: MIT Press).

Young, Oran R. with contributions from Arun Agrawal, Leslie A. King, Peter H. Sand, Arild Underdal, and Merrilyn Wasson (1999b). *IDGEC Science Plan.* IHDP Report No. 9, Institutional Dimensions of Global Environmental Change Scientific Planning Committee of the International Human Dimensions Program on Global Environmental Change.

Zald, Mayer and John D. McCarthy (1987). *Social Movements in an Organizational Society* (New Brunswick, N.J.: Transaction Books).

Index

Global Environmental Accord: Strategies for Sustainability and Institutional Innovation